The
environmental
brief

The architectural brief is the most crucial part of the design process but the focus is typically on achieving high quality buildings rather than environmental design strategies. The built environment is responsible for an estimated forty-five per cent of all greenhouse gas emissions and it is during the briefing stage that decisions which have the greatest impact on the atmosphere can be made.

This important new book considers the use of an environmental brief to drive building design towards goals where high environmental performance is paramount. Enhancing the briefing process to include environmental standards, objectives and design strategies offers a significant opportunity for realising environmentally sensitive buildings.

The book is divided into three parts: 'Context', in which theoretical issues of environmental briefing are discussed, 'Pathways', which looks at the briefing method and process and 'Case studies' which are international in scope. It cuts through the plethora of information to provide concise feedback on the ways in which leading building professionals are adapting their approach to address environmental principles.

Richard Hyde is an Associate Professor and Director of the Centre for Sustainable Design at the University of Queensland, Australia. He is a practising architect and teaches interdisciplinary courses in the field of sustainable design.

Steve Watson is an ESD Architect working for the TVS Partnership Architects in Brisbane, Australia. He has a PhD in Architecture which focused on the process of Environmental Design.

Wendy Cheshire is a Director of Hamilton Hayes Henderson Architects, Gold Coast, Australia. Wendy is an architect registered with the RAIA and has a professional practice focus on ecologically sustainable design.

Mark Thomson is Director of TVS Partnership, Brisbane, and is an active board member of the Centre for Sustainable Design, The University of Queensland, Australia.

The
environmental
brief
Pathways for green design

Richard Hyde, Steve Watson,
Wendy Cheshire and Mark Thomson

Taylor & Francis
Taylor & Francis Group

First published 2007 by Taylor & Francis
2 Park Square, Milton Park, Abingdon, Oxon, OX14 4RN

Simultaneously published in the USA and Canada
by Taylor & Francis
270 Madison Avenue, New York, NY10016

Taylor & Francis is an imprint of the Taylor & Francis Group, an informa business

© 2007 Richard Hyde, Steve Watson, Wendy Cheshire and Mark Thomson

Designed and typeset in Optima by Alex Lazarou, Surbiton, Surrey
Printed and bound in Great Britain by The Cromwell Press, Trowbridge, Wiltshire

British Library Cataloguing in Publication Data
A catalogue record for this book is available from the British Library

Library of Congress Cataloging in Publication Data
The environmental brief: pathways to green design/Richard Hyde ... [*et al.*].
     p. cm.
  Includes bibliographical references.
  ISBN 0-415-29044-9 (hardback: alk. paper) – ISBN 0-415-29045-7 (pbk.: alk. paper) 1. Sustainable
architecture. 2. Architecture – Environmental aspects. 3. Sustainable development. I. Hyde, Richard, 1949–
  NA2542.36.E58 2006
  720'.47–dc22

                                                                              2006007956

ISBN10 0-415-29044-9 (hbk)
ISBN10 0-415-29045-7 (pbk)

ISBN13 978-0-415-29044-9 (hbk)
ISBN13 978-0-415-29045-6 (pbk)
ISBN13 978-0-203-96681-5 (ebk)

Contents

Foreword

That so many ecological low-energy projects have been built is impressive, considering all the things that can go wrong after good intentions have been declared at the first discussions between client and architect. Thereafter, compromises start to occur: during preliminary planning to assure functionality; with the production of plans and specification to keep the budget in line; and during construction, as unforeseen issues crop up. To increase the likelihood that the goals initially discussed will continue to guide this process, and to retain key attributes without compromise, it is essential to have a design brief that has been well thought through.

The importance of the success of this process cannot be overstated. A building has to be conceptualized to be serviceable – not only in today's energy and economic environment, but under the circumstances of tomorrow. In the not-so-distant future, such conditions can be expected to change dramatically.

To help the building's clients and designers articulate their wishes and visions into concrete statements of a design brief, various tools and techniques have proved successful. They start with the writing down of the goals and continue all the way through to quality assessment during construction. Examples are presented in four chapters here, including briefing, benchmarking, blueprinting and rating schemes. Their applications are illustrated in case studies.

In the case studies, it is interesting to observe how very different buildings, responding to very different climates and client needs, nonetheless all have to cope with similar problems, which can be minimized by using an orderly design process. Regardless of which process is chosen, the examples illustrate various needs and the success that can result from applying a systematic, disciplined process from beginning to end.

Robert Hastings
Leader, International Energy Agency, SHC Task 28
Department of Building and Environment
Danube University Krems
Dr. Karl Dorrek Street 30
AT 3500 Krems
Austria

Acknowledgements

We would like to thank a number of groups and individuals who have provided invaluable expertise and assistance with this project. In particular:

Caroline Mallinder from Taylor & Francis for providing the vision to help communicate the ideas in this project;
Professor Terry De Lacy, CEO, Collaborative Research Centre for Sustainable Tourism, Australia;
Professor Deo Prasad and Ms Shailja Chandri, University of New South Wales, Australia;
Melinda Watt, General Manger Earth Check Pty Ltd;
Cathy Parson, Green Globe;
Ross Meakin, Property and Facilities, The University of Queensland;
Alan Yates and David Crowhurst, Building Research Establishment, UK;
Nigel Howard, US Green Building Council, LEED, USA:
Huston Eubank, Rocky Mountain Institute:
Ann Bodkin, Bennetts Associates;
Emily Turk, US Green Building Council:
Chris Klehm, Clearview Project Services Company;
Jerry Cardinale, Pt Wisata Bahagia Indonesia.

Dr Veronica Soebarto, Senior Lecturer, School of Architecture, Landscape Architecture, and Urban Design, University of Adelaide, South Australia;
Ms Pene Mitchell, Environmental Scientist, CSIRO Manufacturing and Infrastructure Technology, Sustainable Built Environment. CSIRO;
Dominique Hes, Manager Sustainable Building Program, Centre for Design, RMIT University;
Joyce Law, Research Assistant and BArch graduate, Centre for Sustainable Design.

Additional acknowledgements

The following persons and groups who have refereed this project:

Per Heiselberg (DK) and Conny Rolén (S), International Energy Agency;
Professor Roger Fay, School of Architecture, University of Tasmania. Australia;

Editing and images

Geoff Foster, Hal Dobbins, Judith Matthews, Luke Watson, Rhys Williams, Sara Bridges.
Psychometric and weather data: D. A. Sketch Pad, University of Tasmania.
Cover image: Lin Martin.

Financial support for the research

The Australian Research Council, Discovery Grant.
Sustainable Tourism Cooperative Research Centre.

Contributors

Associate Professor Richard Hyde. Director, Centre for
Sustainable Design, The University of Queensland.
Dr Steve Watson, Environmental Consultant, TVS Partnership,
Brisbane, Research Scholar, Centre for Sustainable Design,
The University of Queensland.
Mark Thomson, Director, TVS Partnership, Brisbane, Centre
for Sustainable Design, The University of Queensland.
Wendy Cheshire, Director, Hamilton Hayes Henderson
Architects, Southport, Queensland.
David Clark, Director, Cundall Johnston & Partners Pty Ltd.
Dr Dominique Hes, Lecturer, Sustainable Architecture,
University of Melbourne.
Fiona Martin, PhD scholar, Sustainable Building Programme,
Centre for Design, RMIT University.

Preface

The concept for *The Environmental Brief* came primarily from research work carried out into using the project brief and the briefing process as a way of furthering green design. The creation of the environmental briefing system has since been tested and developed in practice. Experience in practice has taught us that front-loading the design process, clarifying the environmental objective at the outset, is essential to delivering high-quality green buildings. This means that green design is not an add-on but an assurance that the design team will always consider environmental criteria.

In parallel to this research work, there has been a general increase in information, tools, methods and legislation concerning green design and its integration within ecological sustainable development (ESD). Such a plethora of systems is complex and some people would say confusing. This has made it necessary to develop a cognitive overview of the progress towards ESD and the role these tools play. Attempts to compare tools was found to be fraught with difficulty; some are used in the design phase, some post construction, some for different building types. It becomes clear that designers will need to use whatever tool is favoured by the particular industry sector or build type for which it was developed. Fortunately, while there are differences in environmental criteria and scoring systems, the underlying principles remain the same.

Finally, there is a lack of well-documented case studies that use post occupancy evaluation of green buildings. The studies presented here provide data on the assessment criteria used and strategies and solution sets used to meet the criteria. We have found that blueprinting is a crucial part of design research that helps to transform industry. It demonstrates what can be achieved and how this can be done.

We hope that sharing this overview will provide a basis for further discussion on how better to achieve ESD and help reshape green design.

1 Serendib Hotel, Sri Lanka, 1967–70. Architect: Geoffrey Bawa. Evidence of the use of ecological factors in the design helps creates a sense of delight for the guests.

Defining the environmental brief

The increasing pressures of human population growth, technical change and consumption on the ecological systems of the planet demand immediate review of the form and character of development in general, and of the built environment in particular. This need for change, which has been called the environmental imperative, has resulted in new development goals that embrace economic, social and environmental issues in a collective way. Termed ecological sustainable development (ESD), this new focus for the built environment offers an *environmental brief* for building design professionals.

The aim of this Introduction is to provide an overview of the key arguments for the environmental brief, while subsequent chapters will provide further reference material. First, it examines the context for green design and argues the need to advance it by incorporating appropriate *form* and *substance* in green buildings. Arguments can be advanced for both of these: with regard to *form*, the focus is on creating meaningful architectural expression of the ecological principles underlying the building, while *substance* deals with improved environmental performance. In these ways green buildings can address the disturbances to ecosystems that are at the heart of the environmental imperative.

Second, the nature of green design is a core debate of the environmental brief, and this Introduction is essentially a mapping exercise aimed at identifying the main issues and examining why green design is needed, what principles and initiatives have been developed to support it, and finally how green design can transform industry.

Third, opportunities for advancing green design in the design phase are discussed, with a particular focus on the tools and systems that are currently available. If these opportunities are taken up by building design professionals, they have the power to transform design and procurement. Those projects that have responded to the environmental brief realize, as main outcomes, case studies from which important lessons can be learnt.

The context

One way of defining the environmental brief would be to draw a conceptual boundary around the environmental design of buildings and consider those activities that are within and outside the designer's sphere of responsibility. The environmental context can be regarded as the 'commons', over which many have influence but for which few have responsibility, including such areas as maintenance and upkeep.

The predominant practice of unsustainable development, based on theories of unlimited growth, is being challenged by a shift to sustainable development and reduced environmental impact through green building design. Green design and building procurement practices are gaining favour with building designers, builders and clients as the benefits become better understood and the processes to achieve them better known.

The environmental imperative

There is a growing body of scientific knowledge to support the need for sustainable development. This body of knowledge, called the 'pressure–state–response model' (PSR), is well doc-

2 Serendib Hotel. Circulation, light and form are timeless elements in the architecture that require very little maintenance. The limewash walls and polished terracotta tiles only need minimal attention.

umented and demonstrates the scale of human impacts on the planet's ecosystems.[1]

Pressure–state–response model

This model has given rise to the 'environmental imperative', a term used by Victor Papanek in his book of that name, which sets an agenda for the design profession's response to the PSR model.[2] The imperative is a form of natural justice that has come to underlie the design thinking process. It can provide a set of necessary considerations for addressing sustainable development in the future.

The sustainable development debate

At present there is little measurable evidence of anything constituting sustainable development. At best there is debate around the nature of sustainable development and an assortment of principles and initiatives to assist designers.[3]

Contextual barriers

Furthermore, there are contextual barriers to sustainable development, which means that micro-economic reform is needed to establish a serious agenda for change. The dilemma that this creates for designers is that, while many may favour an environmental approach, the political, social and economic environment is unfavourable.

Local action model: ecological sustainable design

A way of addressing this dilemma is to adopt the so-called local area model. This proceeds by drawing boundaries around areas of development and examining the environmental impact of each of the areas. This model makes little or no reference to sustainability, but deals more with the strategies that can be used to reduce environmental impact that is tangible and measurable.

Boundary definition is necessary for three reasons. The first is that we need to address the scale of our policy responses to environmental factors. For example, in Australia, while there may be no national policy on subscribing to the Kyoto Protocol, nor an agenda to address such a policy, there are local councils and states that are addressing Agenda 21 issues. Similarly, without adequate boundaries, assessment using green design tools is less likely to be effective.

Tools like life cycle assessment have clear boundary definitions, as do Building Environmental Assessment (BEA) tools, but ways of linking them together into a comprehensive framework for sustainable development are still missing. For example, Green Globe, an international benchmarking system for tourism (see Chapter 5), is developing a suite of tools and standards for the tourism industry that operate for a range of scales of development, from buildings through precincts and ultimately to cities. The approach covers both the design and operational phases; at its core is the adoption of a local action model, breaking the development process into areas and seeking to effect meaningful change in each area. This approach is viewed as being highly effective; research on the city of Melbourne has shown that 10 per cent of the city is in process of refurbishment and renewal each year.

A simplistic argument suggests that the application of green design to local areas of refurbishment could rapidly increase the move to reduced environmental impact. Chapter 1 describes the components of the environmental imperative in more detail.

Principles, initiatives and responses

Responses to the environmental imperative led to a set of principles for sustainable development. They have been taken further and will be discussed in Chapter 2.

Principles

For responding to the environmental imperative, as a useful modus operandi in the context of green design, research has identified the following principles:

- the polluter pays;
- pollution is dealt with at source;
- the quality of life is improved; and
- the triple bottom line is balanced.

Push and pull initiatives

The application of these principles to reduce environmental impacts has evolved by means of two main types of measure: push (legislative measures) and pull (voluntary measures). Three examples are used, from Australia, UK and USA, to describe the way in which change has been initiated in these countries.

Perhaps the most integrated approach to regulating the building development and construction industry is found in the UK, with a combination of pull and push measures. In Australia there has been a significant push approach to greenhouse abatement, while in the USA the pull approach has evolved, thanks to trans-professional organizations, as a shift in design and procurement.

Responses by building design professionals

The responses by building design professionals and trans-professional groups has been to increase the use of green design through various strategies:

- plugging the knowledge gap;
- articulating the benefits of green building;
- addressing the first-cost barrier;
- establishing a 'road map' to green design from policy to realization;
- introduction of life cycle thinking;
- developing environmental standards;
- certification of green buildings;
- identification of leverage points for checking environmental standards in the development process; and
- promoting the needs of the user in terms of environmental quality.

This list of responses to the environmental imperative identifies important steps in improving the environmental performance of buildings. More steps are possible by transforming the building design and procurement industry through changes to the legislative and economic frameworks. While this remains a matter for social and political concern, additional steps can be taken within existing structures simply by transforming them to reduce environmental impact. The next section identifies some of these steps.

Opportunities in the design phase: some pathways

Advancing green design

Defining green design

Green design and green architecture are inextricably linked. Wines argues that green architecture has emerged as a response to the new Age of Information and Ecology of the twentieth century. He argues that this new Age presents the most complex and problematic issues that have faced humanity.[4] Building design professionals face these issues and at present there are concerns about the way they are being addressed.

Wines (2000) argues that there are problems with the form of architecture. The main thrust of his criticism is that, conceptually, the present view of 'sustainable architecture' is that the form of the buildings lacks meaning.[5] He observes that sustainable architecture is about the use of technology, such as photovoltaic systems or passive systems, and essentially that

THE SERENDIB HOTEL

The project was conceived as a low-cost guesthouse, with the use of 'low-tech', low-energy, low-impact, low-maintenance systems. Sri Lanka is approximately eight hours from Europe by plane and the beaches on the south-east coast provide an excellent location for tourism centres.

SITE AND CLIMATE

The site follows the coastal plain, creating a rectangle with its main axis north–south. The eastern boundary provides access to the beach, and the western boundary access from the coast road and the railway.

The building was created in two stages, the first being constructed in 1967, on the northern boundary of the site. The second stage, completed in 1974, is located to the south.

The master plan for the site shows a keen sense of the ecological through the relationships between natural systems and the building form. Two parallel buildings run north–south; the building on the east forms the guest accommodation, while that on the west contains the hotel service facilities. Public courtyards used for visual and environmental purposes – daylight and passive cooling – separate the two buildings. The train track and road on the west side are a source of noise and pollution, so using the service buildings to buffer the guest spaces is central to the operation of the hotel.

MATERIAL SYSTEMS

The materials proposed for the original building included roofs of coconut thatch and floors of raked sand. In the final buildings the roofs are made from local materials, such as clay tile, and floors are terracotta.[6]

LIFE SYSTEMS

The original Stage 1 buildings were designed with a highly shaded façade and verandas, complemented by the use of passive cooling from the sea breeze, which is channelled through the private courtyards to the living and sleeping areas. The masonry construction and terracotta floors create heat sinks, which moderate temperatures in the buildings, providing thermal comfort for the occupants. These principles were not fully realised in Stage 1; noise problems from the corridors compromised the strategy of natural ventilation, and so air conditioning was installed.

In Stage 2, Bawa addressed this problem, creating a new plan that moved the private courtyards to the west, providing a buffer space between access corridors and the guestrooms. The use of lattice screens allows breeze to flow though these buildings while still providing acoustic privacy.

In a tropical climate such as Sri Lanka's, providing the option for passive cooling is a way of creating the tourism experience. Thermal comfort by natural means is one of many factors that influence the human sense of health and well-being in a building. In this case Bawa has added more, creating a rich experience through sensitivity to the interplay of many building elements and the natural environment.

The courtyards in Stage 2 are a case in point. These small, intimate spaces, although seemingly useless from a functional point of view, provide an opportunity for planting frangipani trees, which create shade, silhouettes and scent. It can be argued that the existential quality of the building drawn from ecological principles assists in creating the sense of delight. This humble guesthouse is now a sought-after resort hotel.[7]

3 Serendib hotel. **Above**. Stage 1 buildings shows the use of passive strategies such as covered deep balconies and extensive use of shading. **Right**. Stage 2 buildings show a refinement of this approach to increase ventilation and diffuse daylighting through linking courtyards to the east and west.

environmental technology drives the improved environmental performance of these buildings. This means that green buildings are only superficially green; they express the environmental science that underlies their design, but do not draw deeply from ecology in terms of their concept and form. He argues that it is a question of fusing art and environmental technology: that a green architecture is not simply the sum of its environmental technologies, photovoltaic systems and other environmentally friendly services.[8]

Examining the nature of ecology can extend this argument. Ecology was established as a study of the relationships and interactions between individual organisms and their natural as well as developed environments. Green architecture is concerned with these interactions and relationships as a fundamental design premise. Yet this is not an easy task, given the complexity of the relationships in nature.

Green design can be regarded as the adoption of ecological principles to underpin the architecture. These principles are evident in the work of modern regionalist architects who have tried to respond to the local environment and local culture in their work. In the context of Wines's argument, the emergence of the principle that *form follows environment* can be seen. In this design approach, the function of the building plays a role in the design but it must be measured against environmental considerations, whereas present design approaches often consider func-

tional, social and economic factors but forget environmental issues. The example of the Serendib Hotel by Geoffrey Bawa is given to illustrate the concept.

Form follows environment: the work of Geoffrey Bawa
The work of Geoffrey Bawa has made him the master of resort design in Sri Lanka. The rich and diverse nature of the environment in Sri Lanka has made it an ideal location for tourism. It has a range of climate zones, which produce different flora and fauna; furthermore, the topography is varied, from a mountainous centre with dry arid zones to tropical coastal plains. Bawa recognized the potential of the natural environment and the ways this could be linked to the creation of the tourism experience. The importance of site and climate as sources of ideas for his design work is evident, but there are also ecological factors in the shaping of his buildings.

The ecological design factors can be categorized into three abbreviated versions of the ecological cycles that form the natural environment – site and climate, life systems, and material systems:

- site and climate that form the context to the building;
- life systems that address issues of human comfort in the context of water, air, scent, sound and light; and

5

- material systems that address the degree of manufacture, which ranges from primary materials such as stone, timber or earth, through secondary materials that have been recycled or re-used, to tertiary materials, including components and complex construction systems that have been industrially produced.[9]

Any study of the workings of the Bawa office will recognize that its vital ingredients were the talented architects he employed and the 'Bawa method' he used to create the buildings. It is the combination of method with consideration for site and climate that seems to have evolved this form of modern regional architecture.[10] Part of that method may have been the delight he had in the 'planning and construction of the building, which creates an experience which cannot be explained in words'.[11] It can, though, be understood with regard to the principles and methods he used; the delight that he had in planning is then expressed in the delight that is experienced by guests in the buildings he designed.

It can be argued that the definition of green design is understood first from the principles and methods used to create the architecture, and second, through the ways that it provides for the occupants an existential sense of delight in the relationships the building makes with the ecological systems. Advancing green design requires examination of the process, as well as the experience created by the building.

Exploring the green design process

Opportunities for exploration focus on the use of specific tools and methods for different parts of the design process. These are called *pathways*, for convenience, although each part of the design process has an affinity with a particular tool and method. Matching tools and methods to stages in design creates a system as follows:

- pre-design – environmental briefing systems;
- sketch and design development – rating and benchmarking systems; and
- post-construction – blueprinting systems.

Chapter 3 provides an overview of the tools and systems and some of the arguments for how and why they are appropriate for green design. Subsequent chapters will examine the tools and methods in detail.

Pre-design: environmental briefing

The brief is one obvious and important part of the design process that can be used for advancing green design.

The environmental briefing paradox

The Code of Practice of the Royal Institute of British Architects has started to challenge the generally poor understanding of sustainable development by clients and the conflicts that it creates in design. The Code states that, while an architect's primary responsibility is to the client, they should have due regard for their wider responsibility to conserve and enhance the quality of the environment and its natural resources.[12] Hyams, in his book on briefing explains:

> This statement neatly summarizes the paradox that lies at the root of the notion of sustainable development. The prevailing culture sees land and nature as resources to be exploited for gain, but the environmental degradation caused by development has clearly brought us up against the limits of exploitation. Clients build primarily for economic gain, generally working within the accepted norms of economic life, including the exploitation of resources such as land, forests, energy and water. Even the smallest conventional construction project uses resources and generates pollution, so how can architects serve their clients while at the same time conserving and enhancing the quality of the environment?[13]

The paradox has led to an argument that promotes the environmental brief, not only as a design tool, but also as a set of reasons and measures for advancing green design. The arguments centre on the transformation of the building industry through green design and, more importantly, on using green design as a tool for improving costs and saving money.

The design brief as an environmental tool

The internal issues of design and building procurement are concerned with how buildings can be tuned to deliver environmental improvements. This notion comes from a range of sources and from the growing body of standards focused on efficient management and process control.

Why should there be such a focus on the brief as an agent of change?

David Hyams argues that 'the briefing exercise is the single most important function in the construction process'.[14] Yet how committed are designers to the brief as a tool in the procurement process?

Wittman, in 1998, surveyed 650 architects registered with the Royal Australian Institute of Architects to assess their values and attitudes to green design; this involved issues concerning the design process and implementation of green design. With regard to the design process, Wittman reported that nearly 70 per cent of respondents considered the brief to be the most important factor in commissioning a new project, yet only 30 per cent rated energy efficiency as important. Furthermore, the budget was second in importance to the brief for commissioning the project. The logical outcome of this finding is that architects need to address these problems within a project from the outset; clearly, the budget and the brief are two of the main parameters that shape the design.

The survey also canvassed the commitment of architects to green design. Findings revealed that nearly 60 per cent of the survey sample reported low commitment to energy efficiency and ecological design.[15]

Wittman concluded from the survey that there were barriers to the implementation of ESD. Significantly, she asked the respondents to report the most important factors that define good design. The factors of function, aesthetics and context were rated higher in importance than environmental considerations, revealing that one of the barriers could be the value structure of the architects surveyed.[16] Cheshire argued that this attitudinal barrier could be addressed using a number of strategies, one of which is to establish a brief with a greater environmental focus.[17] Hyams supports this concept and has included one of the categories in his checklist for the briefing process. Hyams, in his *Construction Companion to Briefing,* argues the importance of the brief:

Building in Britain costs up to a third more than in America or the rest of Europe. Not only does this place a heavy burden on the economy and hinder adaptability and change, but also the resulting buildings are often inappropriate and inconvenient for their users. Sir Michael Latham, in his report on improving the efficiency of the building industry, identified various factors that contribute to the high cost and poor user satisfaction of new buildings in this country. Poor briefing came high on his list. Time spent deciding what is required before designing is infinitely less expensive and more effective than changes made during design, let alone during or after construction. The closer a project comes to construction the higher will be the cost of change, and the smaller the opportunity to revise decisions. Architects in Britain have always taken instruction from their clients, but rarely systematically.[18]

The drive to more systematic approaches to the design process comes from outside the design professions. Chapter 4 describes the environmental briefing system developed by the authors as a way of using the design brief as a tool for green design; it is discussed with reference to a case study. Designers who wish to write an environmental brief may find this practical tool interesting.

Sketch and design development: rating and benchmarking tools

International environmental standards

International standards for environmental protection have evolved through research. The main systems available to the designer are international standards such as the ISO 14000 series on environmental management and ISO 9000 for quality management.[19] These standards are frameworks that have been adapted for particular uses within industry and have spawned a number of tools for the design and operation of buildings.

Building environmental assessment tools (BEA)

These tools have been developed as a way of providing a set of environmental criteria, common to all, for the design and operation of a building. The tools can be regarded as a standard for most purposes, since they represent a metric against which projects can be evaluated. There are three main arguments for adopting this approach.

First, the standard provides a clear set of environmental criteria – both qualitative and quantitative – for a green building. Second, the predicted or actual performance of a building can be assessed against the standard. Third, standards can be delivered by way of ratings or benchmarking tools. This enables high-performance projects to be rewarded through an eco-label system.

Without development standards such as these it has been difficult adequately to compare and predict the environmental performance of buildings.

Developing design phase and building operational tools

There is a growing trend to identify different BEA tools for different parts of the design process. For example, a distinction is now made between *design phase tools* – those that simply assess the design of the building and its construction (e.g. Green Star for offices,[20] Green Globe Design and Construct Standard[14] for tourism projects) – and *post construction tools* for building operations (NABERS and Green Globe Company Standard).[21,15] The former examine the potential environmental impacts of the design and the latter focus on the environmental management of the building during its life cycle.

The argument for design phase tools is emerging. Experience has taught us that good green design deserves good management, but poor design is impossible to manage from an environmental standpoint. Furthermore, more designers can work from environmental principles, and by utilizing a design standard for green design the current barrier between design and operation can be removed. Without both processes, green design can be self-defeating.

In summary, there are two main issues with selecting a tool and a method: first, deciding in which phase of design it will be used – in design or in the operational phase post construction; second, realizing that particular tools and methods have been developed for various building types – offices, houses and hotels.

Rating tools and benchmarking tools

A more detailed examination of how rating tools and benchmarking tools have evolved is provided in Chapters 5 and 6, where meshing these with the design phase is discussed. Many rating tools have checklists, which are ideal for integrating into the sketch design phase; also the environmental criteria from these tools can be integral to the pre-design stage.

Post construction: blueprinting

The use of the post construction phase is often seen as a neglected aspect of design, and this is often because of the fee structure for projects, which is focused on the earlier phases. It is argued that this is an area of opportunity that designers can expand and use for commercial and environmental purposes.

Blueprinting: making more from the post construction phase

An important tool has emerged from research: the use of projects already built as a way of advancing green design. Learning from completed buildings is a traditional way for designers to advance the discipline. There are issues, however, concerning the way in which broader generalizations about the design of building types can be made from these specific cases. From this concern arise questions of context: for example, how useful to Australian practice are case studies of specific buildings in the UK?

Blueprinting is a way of documenting examples of building projects, and learning from them in a way that respects context. International Energy Agency Task 28 in Solar Sustainable Housing demonstrates how blueprinting can be used to extract information from the post construction phase. This has involved the identification of a number of demonstration projects that include innovative concepts for green design.

Demonstrating workable solutions

The demonstration projects have promoted a range of analytical studies to explain the technical synergies that have evolved in solar sustainable housing. These have led on to the development of climate-specific 'generic solutions'. A notable project is the International Energy Agency Task 28 on Solar Sustainable Housing, which features solution sets from a number of countries. The Hybrid-Z Zero Energy house from Japan uses a combination of solar electrical generation, direct gain systems and energy-efficient heating systems. Developed by the mass-housing builder Misawa, the system utilizes many of the synergies found in the European examples, high levels of insulation, high-performance windows and low infiltration.

Other solution sets have evolved to develop row houses in Sweden without heating systems, and a detached cost-effective and energy-efficient house in Scotland. Specific solution sets have evolved for counties such as Italy, where there is a need to retrofit existing houses to improve energy efficiency. The Saline housing proposal applies an external skin to the building to improve the insulation and passive performance. The effect will

4 Serendib Hotel. **Above**. New wing with courtyards that provide diffused light and ventilation to the guest accommodation. **Top left**. Internal layouts are designed for ventilation; the bathroom walls are angled to facilitate airflow from the courtyards to the sleeping area. Air conditioning was retrofitted but the thermal mass of the building moderates temperatures. **Left**. Frangipani trees planted in the courtyards add to the life systems with fragrance and silhouettes.

be to reduce running costs while improving the comfort of the occupants, which is particularly important for many who have low incomes and for whom energy costs can be a significant part of the weekly budget.

Monitoring performance

The significance of work on the solution sets is that the ideas within the solution sets can be applied to other projects with similar levels of technological development, climate and housing need. While the IEA blueprint works at the technological end of the design process, some projects have focused on the green design principles as a starting point. In addition, the work draws on the need for the monitoring of existing building to show improved performance.

Promoting green design

Finally, an important aspect of blueprinting is that it facilitates the marketing and promotion of green design, which is weak currently because of insufficient skills and knowledge. A case study of the Your Home project in Australia shows that it is a success story in promoting green housing.

Chapter 7 provides more detail of the blueprinting process used and the issues associated with this work.

Approaches to green design: case studies

Transforming the building industry to reduce environmental impact

A number of issues about the transformation of the building industry can be drawn from initiatives and developments made in response to the environmental imperative. In some cases these represent barriers to reducing environmental impact; in others they represent opportunities for improving the environmental performance of the industry.

Addressing the myths

In recent years a number of myths have evolved concerning the application of green design and building. They have arisen for many reasons, but mostly act as barriers to the implementation of green design.

An important myth relates to the 'info glut' concerning green design; a large number of tools and system have been developed, but their application is still not a matter of common knowledge. This absence of knowledge also contributes to the second myth: the notion that green buildings are expensive.

Much work has been carried out to advance the business case for green design, and it is now usual for the design process to include life cycle costing studies that articulate both cost and environmental benefits. This second myth implies that there is little incentive for clients and developers to build green; it is being addressed by providing information on social benefits, such as the productivity of the occupants and improved risk management for the developers' property.

The final myth concerns the use of environmental technology, which is seen as a 'fringe technology', unreliable and expensive to operate. Solar hot water heaters once suffered from such a label, but this misconception has since been corrected.

Solution sets

Solution set research is a way of addressing the 'fringe technology' myth. The debate is increasingly about the way passive and active systems and associated technologies are integrated, and about the related need to create synergies between technical systems and human systems of management. Industry design standards are crucial in driving this form of transformation.

The development and adoption of environmental design standards by industry sectors

As yet, the provision of appropriate technology is only a part of the prescription for transforming the industry; working with human systems to effect change is equally important. To this end, some industry groups have developed and adopted industry design standards that include environmental criteria. The tourism industry is a one such group; it has developed operational and design standards for its infrastructure, including a range of tools for assessing buildings.

Reshaping the design process

The adoption of industry standards has provided the potential to reshape the design process for green design. Many opportunities exist for improving the design and delivery of buildings; these include better use of the design brief, applying building environmental assessment tools, and tapping into the post construction knowledge base for design research, performance evaluation and promotion. Chapter 8 is a summary of the design-orientated aspects of transforming the building industry using these pathways.

The application of the tools and discussion of how designers have evolved this into a workable design approach is provided in Part 3. This is structured around particular building types: housing, hotels, resorts, interpretation centres and offices. The reason for this is that it gives some indication of the system used for each building type and how the designers applied the tools and systems.

Housing

Seven housing projects were examined:

1. Yeang EcoHome, Malaysia;
2. BedZED, London, UK;
3. Cairnlea EcoHome, Melbourne, Australia;
4. Ostia Antica Housing, Italy;
5. Lindås Housing, Sweden;
6. Peterculter House, UK; and
7. Misawa House, Japan.

The first three projects were examined with regard to the EcoHomes rating tool; in the case of the Yeang EcoHomes, Malaysia, the rating tool was used to inform the environmental brief that was developed for this project. The remaining projects are demonstration projects from the blueprinting work of IEA SHC Task 28.

Standards as a useful method of defining 'green design'

The first case study, the Yeang EcoHome (architect Ken Yeang, Kuala Lumpur, Malaysia; see Appendix 2), demonstrates the use of an environmental standard, as found in the EcoHomes rating tool, to define green design. This tool has a checklist of environmental criteria that were used in conjunction with the

Environmental Briefing system to shape the project brief. In this way the original bioclimatic brief was expanded to include a wider range of environmental criteria in the project.

Using rating tools post construction

The Cairnlea EcoHome demonstration home (see Appendix 2) shows how green design principles can be applied to a project home in Melbourne. Project homes in Australia are cost-effective housing for low- to medium-income groups; attempting to build an EcoHome with cost constraints is a particular issue with this project.

This project is evaluated post construction, using criteria from the BRE EcoHomes rating tool. The objective is to demonstrate how these criteria can be used at the post construction stage to provide a standard to evaluate the building, as well as to give insight into how the tool might be developed. The EcoHomes tool seems to be aimed at the UK housing industry, but has some broader relevance for countries that do not have such tools; some guidance is provided on how to interpret specific criteria in a broader context.

Cost-effective green design for housing is seen by the developer of this project as a marketable commodity. Many green technologies cost extra and the benefits are not immediately visible, for example avoiding PVC in plumbing and wiring. Chapter 9 provides information on how best to address cost and promotion issues concerning housing, and examines issues of perceived value adding and evidence of higher economic value for EcoHomes. The use of solar energy is a key strategy for cost-effective EcoHomes.

Following the 'soft energy path': renewable energy

The case studies from the blueprinting work offer solution sets for energy-efficient houses that rely on creating synergies between the active, passive and biophysical systems in the house. The underlying principle is to use renewable energy where possible, in conjunction with a highly effective envelope. The Lindås Housing demonstrates that cost-effective row housing can be provided without a normal heating system, even in cold climates; it uses waste heat from the internal functions of the house to provide inside air temperatures within the comfort zone in winter. Zero heating designs such as the Lindås Housing can also be achieved in detached houses like the Peterculter House, Scotland (see Appendix 2). In both cases the cost of green

design features is traded off against other elements in the house to keep within the client's overall budget.

The Hybrid-Z Zero Energy home, created by Misawa Homes Institute of Research and Development in Japan (see Appendix 2), provides a blueprint for a semi-autonomous all-electric houses. This house balances energy from the grid with that derived from solar sources to give a net zero energy consumption, eliminating CO_2 emissions and reducing fossil fuel use. Added benefits include the provision of a comfortable environment for an aging population as well as reducing energy consumption to 40 per cent of that of a traditional home.

As a final example, the Ostia Antica Housing in Italy demonstrates the use of over-cladding to improve the quality of the building envelope of existing housing. A passive heating and cooling system is integrated with the envelope; it not only improves the insulation and window performance but also provides heating and cooling from renewable energy. This feature is particularly important to the occupants of the housing, as many have low incomes and presently pay relatively high energy costs. Mitigating energy losses by over-cladding keeps the occupants in their own homes, increases comfort and reduces costs, as well as reducing environmental impact.

However, the availability of the technologies used in these kinds of demonstration project can be a problem. This has been solved in the case of the Beddington Zero (Fossil) Energy Development (BedZED) project, which aims at greening the supply chain, providing an easily assessable green kit of parts for housing.

Greening the supply chain

The supply chain is the materials, components and systems that are used in the manufacture and construction of the building. Building designers are crucial to this; in conjunction with their clients, they select and specify from the supply chain. The BedZED project demonstrates the way that the environmental credentials of the materials, components and systems can be assessed. Case studies of the materials are made, and design options for different components examined, so that cost considerations and quantifiable information on environmental benefits can be weighed up. Research on quantitative environmental benefits uses life cycle analysis and eco footprinting to create an environmental profiling system for materials.[22]

Hotels and interpretation centres

The case studies of hotel and interpretation centres include a number of projects assessed under the Green Globe Benchmarking system, developed specifically for the travel and tourism industry (see Chapter 5). The last project listed below has been submitted for LEED Certification (See Chapter 6).

The projects include:

- Novotel & Ibis Homebush Bay, Australia;
- Sundancer Spa and Beach Resort, Lombok, Indonesia;
- Tramping Huts, New Zealand;
- Lark Quarry Trackways Building, Australia;
- Heron Island Redevelopment, Australia; and
- Pittsburgh Glass Center, USA.

Precinct master planning to improve building environmental performance

Many of the case studies are blueprints for the environmental performance of a single building. There are also advantages in examining potential improvement of the environmental performance of clusters of buildings, such as those found in tourism and commercial precincts, which are often mixed-use developments comprising many types. The advantages of this type of development are seen in the BedZED project, where a mixed-use development can provide social and economic benefits as well as improvements in environmental performance. The benefits in terms of building-related performance can be seen in this case study.

The Novotel & Ibis in Sydney is termed the 'Green Hotel'. It was constructed for the 2000 Olympic Games, and a number of initial strategies made this building a benchmark for environmental design. The building is set in the precinct of the Olympic Park at Homebush Bay: it was developed as a green precinct, including environmentally designed roads and a grey water main. The precinct also introduced management systems, such as the adoption of green leases for buildings and the use of the ISO 14000 standard for environmental management. This road map approach provided a suitable framework to support the environmentally sustainable hotel.

Building environmental assessment tools and high ecological value environments

The development of tools for assessing the impact of buildings in environments that have high ecological value requires specific design and construction practices. The Lark Quarry Trackways Building and Shelter, the Tramping Huts (see Appendix 2) and the Heron Island Redevelopment (see Appendix 2) demonstrate the need for environmentally sensitive building practice. In these kinds of projects, the builder needs to have knowledge and experience of environmental issues and has to be involved at an early stage with the design and with the strategic thinking about construction methods and systems. In many cases transportation costs, and the environmental impact from that aspect alone, can be significant. The Green Globe Design and Construct Standard is a framework for the design and assessment of buildings in these situations.

Environmental standards and the building context

First, different building types create different environmental problems, and so the criteria used in a given standard may not match the types specified.

Second, the performance benchmarks for buildings vary with climate and site, thus further complicating assessment of the project against a standard.

Third, the building programme and location may present differing environmental design challenges, which may not be addressed by the standard. The PNC Center in Pittsburgh is a case in point; this financial centre required large floor plates of 2,000 m^2 for functional reasons. This posed a significant challenge in terms of trying to create a green building.

Other case studies have helped focus discussion on various issues concerning environmental standards for buildings. The Cairnlea EcoHome demonstration home shows how green design principles can be applied in a low-cost house in Melbourne. This project is evaluated against the BRE EcoHomes standard, giving insight into how this standard may evolve for low-cost buildings in cool temperate climates.

Bridging professional disciplinary boundaries

A further feature of green design is the bridging of professional boundaries, which appears in many of the case studies. Lark Quarry Trackways Building and Shelter, a project of Gall Medek

Architects, is an illustration of this. The design for this conservation and interpretative centre for dinosaur tracks set the example of selecting the team to build the project rather than simply to satisfy some economic criteria. The architect, Jim Gall, is trained in the environmental sciences and in architecture. He brought together a team of experts from a range of disciplines to make this project possible.

Lark Quarry Trackways is located in a remote and fragile desert ecology, making the project logistically and environmentally challenging, and necessitating the bridging of professional boundaries. The shape and direction of the project were assisted by a working group of interested government organizations convened by the client. This group established a strong policy framework for green design from the outset, which helped make this project possible.

Starting with policy to guide green design

A clear policy for green design appears to be crucial to the start of complex projects, with multiple stakeholders in locations of high ecological value, if they are to achieve sustainable goals.

Heron Island Research Station Redevelopment, on the Great Barrier Reef, Queensland, and the Tramping Huts, McArthur Ranges, designed for the Department of Conservation in New Zealand, are successful projects that demonstrate the way a strong, united policy initiative for green design is essential for minimizing environmental impacts in areas of high ecological value. The structure of organizations such as the Department of Conservation in New Zealand enables them to assemble disparate stakeholder groups to contribute to a project. The Tramping Huts project in the McArthur Ranges involved stakeholders from tourism and conservation, with the result that areas of scenic beauty were preserved even while the public were able to access the area.

Building reuse as a green design point of departure

Some projects started with the environmental brief as a concept generator. Others used the brief as a point of departure, promoting a range of conceptual thinking. The Pittsburgh Glass Center (see Appendix 2) is a good example.

This project involved recycling an existing building, and so the design process dealt with a range of recycled and reused building elements. These elements comprised the design palette available to the architect and builder to create an experience for the users of the building in a cost-effective way. The result was a collage effect that afforded a unique visual experience, as well as an environmentally friendly project. The multidisciplinary design team on the project forged strong links that gave rise to particularly creative synergies between the designers, the builder and the client.

BEA and making the business case

Many projects focus on the need to make the business case for green design and to use this to market sustainable buildings. A prevailing myth is that green buildings cost more, and a range of initiatives has emerged to counter this misperception. Notable projects that have addressed this problem include office buildings, where the economic imperative often prevails because of currently favoured development models.

The Sundancer Spa and Beach Resort on the Island of Lombok, east of Bali, Indonesia, exemplifies the design of a five-star, low-impact project. In this case the use of best practice green design saved significant ongoing operational costs. BEA (building environmental assessment) tools assist with demonstrating the environmental and social benefits of a project but still do not adequately address the economic issues of projects such as this. Work is needed to include cost–benefit calculators into these tools, to assist with economic, social and environmental decision-making.

Offices

The projects in Chapter 11 examine the use of the environmental briefing system and BEA tools, such as GBTool (Canada) and LEED (Leadership in Energy and Environmental Design, USA), and pilot projects using the new Green Star rating tool in Australia:

- EPA fit-out, William McCormack Place, Cairns, Australia;
- CH_2, Melbourne, Australia;
- Reservoir Civic Centre, Melbourne, Australia;
- PNC Firstside Center, Pittsburgh, Pennsylvania, USA;
- Wessex Water Operational Centre, Bath, UK; and
- Philip Merrill Center, USA.

The importance of the environmental brief

Projects undertaken with a clear vision for green design shared by the client and the design team seem have the opportunity to deliver the best performance.

Many of these projects employed a briefing exercise in the broadest sense, with no particular pattern. In some cases, for example the Yeang house in Malaysia, the brief was used to test some of the conceptual ideas developed by the architect. The BRE EcoHomes standard was used as the basis for testing and developing the design ideas.

Other projects have followed a more structured process as developed in the Environmental Briefing system. William McCormack Place is an example where the needs for fit-outs created an important priority in the building design phase, by way of a policy of including environmental criteria in the briefing process. In this case a government office building was destined to accommodate environmentally conscious tenants. The brief was used as a vehicle to help shape the design of the structure, envelope, services and fit-out of the building.

Environmental criteria: the project brief

Council House 2 (CH$_2$) is a proposed new civic building in Melbourne, Australia, while Reservoir Civic Centre (see Appendix 2) is another example in Melbourne. These projects have been used to pilot the new Green Star rating tool (see Chapter 6.)

CH$_2$ has been designed to demonstrate best practice green design, and a range of design and innovative environmental technologies have been specified, including sewer water mining and phase-change materials to improve thermal performance. The rating scheme was used from the outset to inform the brief, and becomes a 'road map' around which the design team structures their discussions.

The charrette as a starting point for green design, the brief as a living document

The Philip Merrill Center, USA was assessed through the LEED and GB Tool system. The building is the operational headquarters for the Chesapeake Bay Foundation. The LEED rating tool was instrumental in conveying the importance of environmental criteria to the client, yet this way of communicating can be highly didactic and prescriptive. In this case the architects used a charrette process, which involved brainstorming using the LEED

tool as a framework or checklist of possibilities. In outcome form, the process was to use the tool to inform the brief for the building and to evolve its character through the design phase. In this context, the project brief can be thought of as a living document that is non-prescriptive and open to reinterpretation throughout the design phase.

Two tools were used: the LEED tool for the design phase and the GB Tool post construction. The GB Tool allows ongoing improvement of the building during operation and management, maintaining the links between the design and management team post construction.

Interpreting results of the rating and benchmarking scheme

An additional study of the Philip Merrill Center demonstrates the differences in output from the two tools used. It is of interest to note that the GB Tool provides different output to the LEED rating tool; the former provides benchmarking of the performance against individual criteria, while the latter simply gives a score for each criterion. Of the two systems, the GB Tool gives more illustrative indications of the environmental performance measures; the strengths and weaknesses of the building against each of the criteria can easily be seen, giving a comprehensive understanding of how the building met the standard.

This demonstrates the potential of these types of tools, not only for the eco-labelling purpose for which they were developed, but also for ongoing research and post occupancy study. The documentation needed to determine the ratings is extensive; while some tools are less hungry for data and documentation, significant time and resources are always needed for the assessment.

A useful part of the LEED process is the section that addresses innovation. Making more use of this information in a blueprint exercise for post construction analysis is a possible way to move forward. As with the IEA SHC Task 28 work, questions arise as to what patterns can be found in the innovative solution sets used in these buildings. How can innovation in green building design trickle down from best to common practice?

Innovation and design process

The PNC Firstside Center (see Appendix 2) demonstrates some of the difficulties of achieving high ratings in buildings with complex programmes and constrained urban locations. In this case, the need for relocation to improve corporate organizational efficiency created the demand for the building.

The organization was fragmented, being accommodated on many sites; rationalizing and relocating into one large flexible green building was seen to have numerous advantages for the organization and for the environment. The LEED rating tool was used to assess this building. The strategies for innovation in the assessment are as follows:

- plug-and-play office systems and carpet tiles with releasable adhesives to allow low-cost reorganization of the fit-out of the building;
- development of a hybrid HVAC (heating, ventilating and air conditioning) system, which could be refitted and would respond easily to fit-out, reducing churn costs and waste; and
- partnership between public and private transportation organizations, enabling the relocation of the building from

Chapter 1: Overview - Defining the Environmental Brief

PART 1:
THE CONTENT

Chapter 2: The Environmental Imperative

Chapter 3: Principles, initiatives and responses

PART 2: PATHWAYS

Chapter 4: Advancing Green Design - defining the pathways

Chapter 5: Environmental Briefing - The Environmental Brief System	Chapter 6: Benchmarking - Green Globe 21, GBC Systems	Chapter 7: Rating - Green Star BREEAM EcoHomes, LEED Systems	Chapter 8: Blueprinting - IEA Task 28

Chapter 9: Transforming industry, reducing environmental impact and addressing the myths

PART 3: APPLICATIONS

Chapter 10: Case Studies *(projects in italics are available on the World Wide Web)*

HOUSING	HOTELS AND INTERPRETATION CENTRES	OFFICES
Environmental Briefing Project	**Green Globe 21 Projects**	**Environmental Briefing Project**
Yeang EcoHome, Kuala Lumpur, Malaysia.	Novotel/Ibis, Homebush Bay, Australia.	EPA Fitout, William McCormack Place, Cairns, Australia.
EcoHome Projects	Lark Quarry Trackways, Winton, Australia.	
BZED, London, UK.	Sundancer Resort, Lombok, Indonesia.	**Green Star Pilot Project**
Cairnlea, Melbourne, Australia.	*Heron Island Refurbishment, Australia.*	CH2, Melbourne, Australia
		Reservoir Centre, Melbourne, Australia.
IEA SHC Task 28 Projects	*The Crows Tramping Huts, New Zealand.*	
Ostia Antia Housing, Italy.	**GBC & LEED project**	**BREEAM Project**
Lindus Housing, Sweden.	*Phillip Merrill Centre, USA.*	Wessex Water Operational Centre, Bath, U.K.
Peterculter House, UK.	**LEED project**	**LEED Projects**
Zero Energy House, Japan.	*Pittsburgh Glass Centre, USA.*	*PNC Centre, Pittsburgh, USA.*
Prosser House, Australia.		

5 Three-part structure.

15

a heavily developed section of the city to a less developed area, and providing the catalyst for improvement to the public transportation system and urban amenity though a new transport hub and the provision of public open space.

This demonstrates the need to bring innovation into the design process to make effective use of the intrinsic qualities of green design and realize its true potential.

Rating tools and best practice

Projects such as the Wessex Water office demonstrate the value of focusing the client's interest on the whole-of-life benefits and productivity gains to be had from using green technologies and design groups, such as the Building Research Establishment in the United Kingdom. This building was used as a best practice model, highlighting the use of the BREEAM rating tool.

The project demonstrates that it is possible to design an office building to operate at less than one-third of conventional energy consumption levels while being mindful of environmental, social and economic factors. The lessons learned first of all were that all members of the design team should commit to the sustainable agenda from the outset.

Second, early adoption of industrial or other targets for improved environmental performance assists with design development. For example, a target for energy consumption in use was established in the brief; this target was also matched with indoor environmental quality standards.

Third, the optimum use of passive strategies assisted in minimizing energy in use. This was complementary to giving users responsibility for controlling their environment to enhance their sense of well-being.

Fourth, during construction, optimization of the primary structural systems was used to reduce the amount of material used by some 50 per cent.

Fifth, management strategies were used to identify the value added by the sustainable components for life cycle benefits, helping to support the case for the selection of these systems. Using open-book accounting and a cost consultant assisted with this process and facilitated the decision-making process.

Finally, the construction process was managed to ensure sustainable construction, by including rigorous but realistic environmental management clauses in trade contracts.

Practical applications

Transforming the brief

Green design is a response to the new Age of Information and Ecology of the twentieth century. Wines argues that green buildings can be superficially green when they express the environmental science that underlies their design, but do not draw deeply from ecology in terms of their concept and form. He argues that a green architecture is a question of fusing art and environmental technology; it is not simply the sum of its environmental technologies, the photovoltaic systems and other environmentally friendly services. To achieve this a number of pathways are found for green design. These include opportunities for making more from the brief, utilizing new tools and using blueprints involving post occupancy work to feed forward in the design process to new projects.

Research into environmental briefing suggests that there has been a change in the design methods and process used by designers. The shift from the analysis synthesis evaluation model to a conjecture reflection model based on the designers' schema has profound influences on the design of green buildings. For green design the reflection process is seen to be crucial for examining the environmental effects of the project. Harnessing the reflection process has led to utilization of the pre-design phase of the design process through environmental briefing. Information from building environmental assessment tools can feed into this briefing approach in the form of criteria for design as well as information from post occupancy studies. Creating these studies as blueprints is instructive for the briefing process.

Reforming building environmental assessment (BEA)?

The BEA pathway has now been followed by a number of designers, and experience is feeding back to organizations such as LEED that operate this form of assessment. Some argue that reforming is needed as a result of this feedback:[23]

1 LEED costs too much;
2 point-mongering and LEED brain;
3 energy modelling is fiendishly complicated;
4 crippling bureaucracy; and
5 overblown claims of Green Building benefits are misleading.

It is clear that BEA is only one pathway to achieving green buildings and there are limitations with the performance model used by these tools. The systems are essentially predictive models of possible environmental performance. Modelling work is complex and uncertain; the complexity of green design as seen in many of the projects is growing exponentially as designers try to improve performance through innovation. More research work is needed on evaluation benefits of green buildings. Present studies are limited by the size of samples and comparative work to draw out objectively the lessons learned from projects. The post occupancy process has yet really to be adopted within the culture of the building procurement process. Finally, assessment is costly and there are calls for simpler checklist systems that are easier to use but may lack the rigour of certification systems.

Increasingly, the path of BEA is transforming within the political and social culture. Figure 0.6 shows the relationship between major organizations and their stance on social and economic equality and environmental impacts. Clearly major organizations are not transformative, or reforming, and are still at a status quo level with the social and political milieu.

To change this BEA needs to shift focus to the planning and development level of cities, rather than the building level. Many of the social and economic benefits that come from green design are found at this level. Case studies such as the Novotel

at Olympic Park in Sydney and the BedZED project in the UK show these benefits. Both Green Globe and LEED are developing tools and standards for this level of environmental assessment that can nest within the master planning and design process, augmenting the planning process.[24]

Ongoing work

The application of the Environmental Briefing project and work on BEA is ongoing. Additional case studies are available on the following websites.

- Centre for Sustainable Design, The University of Queensland: www.csdesign.epsa.uq.edu.au/
- IEA SHC website: www.iea-shc.org/task28/

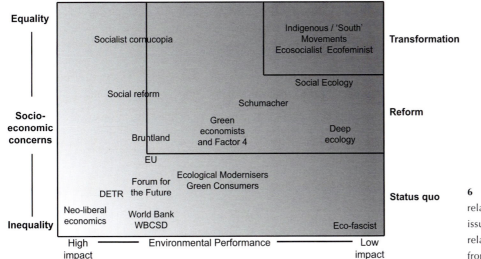

6 Mapping of organizations and their relation to transformative actions to address issues of social and economic equality in relation to environmental impacts. (Adapted from Mawhinney)

Part ONE

Context

1.1 Sunset, Munduk, Bali. The agricultural basis of the village has nurtured a cooperative economy that has evolved over hundreds of years. It is responding to the many environmental issues that are emerging as the area embraces development.

Chapter 1

The environmental imperative

Introduction

There can be little doubt that the environment and the ecological balance of the planet are no longer sustainable. Unless we learn to preserve and conserve Earth's resources, and change our basic patterns of consumption, manufacture and recycling, we have no future.[1]

Victor Papanek, in his book *The Green Imperative*, raised issues for building design professionals, arguing that they should adopt an ethical and ecological outlook towards the environment. That was in the mid 1990s, and the imperative remains as important today as it was then, although it has evolved to a broader environmental basis. The book presented to designers an ecological and ethical argument on the need to consider environmental issues as a first-order priority in design.

Papanek suggests three routes designers might follow to take up the environmental imperative. The first is through individual action: changing their behaviour, buying fuel-efficient cars, insulating their homes and so forth. Second, he advises individuals to join organizations that promote environmental initiatives, since through a collective means individuals can increase the scale of their efforts. Third, by taking action in the workplace through professional involvement, designers can change and adapt design thinking and processes to involve green issues. Papanek recommends that the central ethical question faced by designers should be 'What is the impact of my work on the environment?'

In addition, Lewis Mumford is reported to have stated that 'all thinking worthy of its name must now be ecological'.[2] If he is right, then where does it lead us? Can individuals or designers pioneer a path to reduced environmental impacts, or does the context in which they work demand a different course?

This raises questions about the models and methods designers might use as a basis for designing green buildings. This section examines some views about the environmental model that underlies the environmental imperative. Research work reported by David Yencken and Debra Wilkinson provides a more coherent model of the environmental impacts of humans on the planet. This, called the 'pressure–state–response' model (Figure 1.2), supports the imperative, backed by a body of scientific evidence.

The concept of sustainability is seen as the key to responding to the pressures that humans are placing on the planet's ecosystem. Yet definitions of sustainability can still be perplexing. Is sustainability a goal for designers, a process, an outcome or all of the above?

Views from the book by Mark Mawhinney, *Sustainable Development: Understanding the Green Debates*, suggest there is still a lack of resolution in the debate about the nature of sustainable development. How can designers work at a practice level when the theory has yet to evolve?

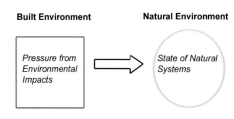

1.2   Pressure–state–response model.

1.3 Munduk, Bali. The agricultural basis of the village is changing with an increase in tourism and a shift in the crop types. Coffee has been one important crop, using coral trees for shade. In recent years there has been a shift to using clove trees for shade, and these also provide a better economic return for the villagers. Unfortunately the clove tree does not support such a wide range of biodiversity as the coral tree does. A new brand of coffee called 'Eco' coffee, grown under the remaining coral trees, has emerged as a niche-marketed brand supporting the local flora and fauna. **Bottom right**. Economic changes in Munduk have far-reaching negative impacts. Subsistence agriculture is giving way to year-round cash crops such as geraniums. This depletes the available water supply, which means loss of amenity in the short term and long-term damage to the biodiversity of the areas. **Top right**. Temples that were connected to the lakes are no longer connected and the emerging foreshore is indicative of the severely dwindling water supplies.

It has to be concluded that the present shift to ecological sustainable development (ESD) is in a transitional stage, and a number of contextual barriers have yet to be overcome. Integration of ESD into the building design professions is discussed in this chapter.

Pressure–state–response model (PSR)

PSR is a simplified model that describes present issues concerning pressures on natural systems caused by human population growth and development and indicates the responses that are needed to address these pressures. Many countries use a PSR model in providing frameworks for change in the nature of social and economic progress with respect to the natural environment.[3]

Pressure on ecological systems from environmental impacts

Each component of the PSR model can be examined in turn. First, in relation to pressures on ecological systems, the last 30 years has seen continuing and expanding research into the impact of human development on ecological systems.

Agenda 21, established at the 1992 United Nations Conference on Environment and Development (or 'Earth Summit'), in Rio de Janeiro, Brazil, has been widely adopted, by governments and organizations as well as by the general public, as a blueprint for sustainability in the twenty-first century. This document is crucially important, not least because it expresses a commitment to sustainable development by many of the world's governments. It addresses the development of societies and economies while conserving and preserving natural resources and the environment.

The importance of this document is often misunderstood. First, it provides an international framework that enables the creation of transnational standards for sustainable development. Second, it lists categories of environmental impact that are to be reduced as part of the development process. The areas are as follows:

- air pollution;
- deforestation;
- biodiversity loss;
- health;
- overpopulation;
- poverty;

- energy consumption;
- waste production; and
- transport issues.[4]

The state of natural systems is one of the prevailing concerns about pressures from human activity.

State of natural systems

The state of natural systems needs no introduction; there are frequent news items about the loss of particular species, the destruction of the Amazon rainforest and attempts to save natural systems. Since the beginning of the industrial revolution there have been disturbances to the equilibrium of the material and thermodynamic systems that comprise the earth's ecology. The main argument is about the effects of these disturbances and their consequences for humans. The disturbances can be summarized as follows:

- Disturbances to the carbon cycle appear to be linked to global warming in the atmosphere (1998, for example, witnessed a temperature increase of 0.17°C).
- Disturbances to the nitrogen and phosphorus cycles are attributed to increased fertilizer use.
- Hydrological cycles are being disturbed, which has an influence on climate changes.
- Changes in sulphur cycles are affecting regional air-sheds and air quality.[5]

The debate continues as to the line of causation. Are the changes the result of the disturbance from humans alone, or part of a more complex process within the earth?

Parallels can be found in history, and the international community has been likened to the passengers on the *Titanic*, who were reportedly preoccupied with rearranging the deckchairs before the vessel sank.

Responses to environmental impacts

A number of responses can be identified within the PSR model. One significant reaction has been to try to define policies on sustainable development. This involves debating the components of sustainable development and how they can be addressed. Another significant response is devising ways to resolve the current momentum for unsustainable development that has built up in recent years. There are very real stumbling blocks, called contextual barriers, to resetting the compass and changing society's current direction.

Conceptualizing sustainable development

Resetting the compass

Current accepted wisdom is to respond to the phenomena; a change of direction is needed otherwise you are liable to 'end up where you are heading' (Lao-tzu). Our present direction is taking us into an era of uncertainty; many consider sustainability is the lifebelt. In their book *Resetting the Compass: Australia's Journey to Sustainability*, David Yencken and Debra Wilkinson develop two important themes for taking steps toward sustainability: first, the metaphor of the journey; and second, that sustainable development is not a static condition but an ongoing metamorphosis.

Four pillars of sustainability

Yencken and Wilkinson suggest that sustainable development should be seen in the context of four sets of issues: environment, society, economy and culture. Their reason is that, in order to effect a coherent response to the pressures on the environment, most, if not all, of the components of society need to come into alignment. This makes the challenge of sustainable development one of the most complex and challenging paths, particularly in the design area.

The questions arise, what use are these four pillars, and how do they assist in resetting the compass? Unfortunately, the four pillars merely provide the cornerstones around which to frame the sustainable development debate; they are less useful in providing a line of enquiry.

1.4 The Plastic Pyramid, Munduk, Bali, Indonesia. The villages erected this plastic pyramid as a symbolic comment on the way plastic has been used in the country, in particular the way that waste material from packaging has contributed to visual as well as physical pollution. Pollution is unwanted waste and contributes significantly to the reduction in the natural capital on which much of the tourism industry relies. In Bali 60 per cent of employment is from tourism, which relies on areas of natural beauty such as are found in Munduk. The pyramid is made of waste plastic recovered from discarded packaging and formed into bricks using cement; unfortunately the two materials do not bond together and decay is inevitable.

Sustainability and sustainable development: a definition, a goal, a process, an outcome or all of the above?

Sustainability, and its attendant discourse, appears to have developed out of the discussion over the limits to the growth of economies in the 1970s. Yet there is still debate about the notion of what sustainability comprises: is it a goal, a process or an outcome? Mawhinney describes this as the sustainability debate.[6]

Sustainability as a social goal

Sustainability is a theory concerning the desirable outcomes of interaction between humans and the environment. A common definition is:

> The ability of this generation to cater for its needs without reducing the ability of all future generations to cater for their needs.[7]

While this definition contains a guiding sentiment and can hold a model for action, inevitably societies choose how sustainable they will be while satisfying their present needs. A more precise and practical definition is required for specific sectors of society and the industry groups within it. For example, it can be argued that green architecture has evolved as the practical application of sustainability within the building industry.

Sector-specific definitions appear to locate sustainability within the PSR model, and broad recommendations for action are contained within these definitions.

For example, the World Wide Fund for Nature (WWF) sees sustainable development within certain boundaries – maintaining our present flora and fauna ecosystems. Biodiversity is a low priority when it comes to development, and the WWF agenda is to elevate it to one of the highest places in the priority list for sustainable development. Their pioneering work on developing alliances with building sector groups is an interventionist approach. WWF alliances in the UK and Netherlands, through eco-labelling schemes and with the Accor hotel group, for example, are significant.[8]

Sustainability as a journey (process), not a destination

The Brundtland Report set a context for environmental conservation; it is often referred to as a watershed document, because it brought to the attention of the world the need to make rapid progress towards economic development. The report provides a key statement on sustainable development;[9] it was produced by a leading international group of politicians, civil servants and experts on the environment and development, and became a key policy document for change to a more sustainable future. The key issues in the Brundtland Report are:

- securing global equity; and
- redistributing resources towards poorer nations while encouraging their economic growth.

The report also suggests that:

- Equity, growth and environmental maintenance are simultaneously possible.

- Each country is capable of achieving its full economic potential while at the same time enhancing its resource base.
- Sustainable growth will require technological and social change.

The major thrust of the report was to develop relationships between the fundamental aspects of development:

- environmental protection;
- economic growth;
- social equity.

The environment should be conserved, and our resource base enhanced, by gradually changing the ways in which we develop and use technologies. This relationship has come to be known as the 'triple bottom line'. With unsustainable development, profit – an economic criterion – was usually the only measure of success. Sustainable development using the triple bottom line means that projects aim equitably to meet environmental and social criteria as well as economic ones. Many questions arise as to how this can be achieved.

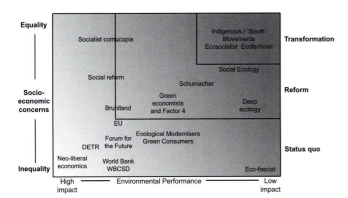

1.5 Mapping the views of major world organizations concerning sustainable development in terms of whether they are transforming, reforming or simply supporting the status quo. A triple bottom line framework is used to assess the organizations. (Adapted from Mawhinney)

Sustainability as an outcome

If the development of sustainability is in process, then how far have organizations progressed towards this goal?

Mapping the views of organizations involved with sustainable development has helped to define the context for designers and, to some extent, the limits to which development can be achieved within various countries and organizations.

Organizations that prioritize environmental issues are *perceived* as being more transforming, while those that are driven more by economic concerns appear entrenched in the status quo. Hopwood and Mawhinney have carried out useful mapping work on the views of major organizations.[10] They propose that there are two polemics – socio-economic and environmental. The organization's values toward social and economic equality are assessed as falling within the socio-economic dimension, while the environmental dimension spans both technologically orientated and purely environmental development. The mapping process is based on policy statements and the expressed views of the key players in sustainable development.

Three categories are identified:

1 *Transforming.* Organizations that are concerned with transforming society to a more sustainable future give a high priority to environmental values. Typically, they have little concern for economic or social values, and hence take a single agenda view of the move to sustainability.
2 *Reforming.* Reforming groups of individuals, who occupy a centre position, attempt to balance social, economic and environment factors.
3 *Status quo.* This group makes claims about sustainable development but is actually neither reforming nor transforming.

Using this categorization as a sieve, it is interesting to see where major change organizations fall. The 'status quo' group comprises organizations such as the Word Bank and the World Business Council for Sustainable Development.[11] The approach of this group is driven by an emphasis on the corporate and commercial needs of industry.

The World Business Council for Sustainable Development has set an agenda for development based on social, economic and environmental criteria. These three areas make up the triple bottom line and reflect a move away from economic rationalism to a multifaceted environmental approach. The Council has also coined a language of terms for corporate sustainability that correlates with economic limits to sustainability. *Eco-efficiency* is one such term; the object of eco-efficiency is to maximize value while minimizing resource use and adverse environmental impacts. In simple terms it means 'doing more with less'.

The World Business Council for Sustainable Development has identified seven components of eco-efficiency:

- reduce material intensity of goods and services;
- reduce energy intensity of goods and services;
- reduce toxic dispersion;
- enhance material recyclables;
- maximize sustainable use of renewable resources;
- extend product durability; and
- increase the service intensity of goods and services.

Eco-efficiency is achieved in a project by the delivery of competitively priced goods and services that satisfy human needs and bring about high quality of life, while at the same time, progressively throughout the life cycle, reducing ecological impact and resource intensity. In the building context, the term eco-efficiency has come to mean achieving the maximum environmental benefit for each dollar. This link between environmental and economic benefit is an emerging issue that underpins sustainable development.

Essentially this is a systems approach that aims to create boundaries around system operations to protect environmental and economic well-being. The scale and complexity of systems with large and extended boundaries makes environmental design and management much more difficult.

The path to sustainable development should theoretically reduce environmental impacts. Yet Hays, in his book *Main Currents in Western Environmental Thought*, reports:

> It was apparent to most people in the environmental movement that the goal of 'sustainable development' had been thoroughly subverted. The very term 'sustainable development' was thought by many to be an oxymoron. For others, the formulation was a cynical exercise to lend a fake legitimacy to full-on, 'business as usual', global environmental rapine.[12]

Contextual barriers

Evidence of the failure of sustainable development as a modus operandi is seen through the emergence of a number of political and social barriers. While the technical change that the Brundtland Report suggested was needed seems to persist as a prerequisite, changes in the social paradigm and political will are lacking. These have set up 'glass ceilings, walls and floors' as a response to the environmental imperative.

Economic rationalist policies

An emerging trend, which undermines the ability of individuals to respond to the environmental imperative, is the bias inherent in the economic context. The needs of the environment are often neglected in pursuit of economic efficiency.

Clive Hamilton, of the Australia Institute, and Richard Dennis, carried out a study of the effects of the Australian government's transformation of the electricity-generating sector into a market-based system, in which electricity suppliers were encouraged to compete, 'to reduce prices'. The conclusions reached were that the 'implementation of competition policy in the electrical sector has resulted in a substantial increase in Australia's greenhouse gas emissions'.[13]

The increased volume of greenhouse emissions that have resulted from the National Competition Policy in the electricity industry is substantial. If Australia's 8 per cent Kyoto target were applied equally across emitting sectors, then the electricity sector's net emissions should increase by only 10.3 megatonnes. Yet, it is estimated that competition policy alone was responsible for an increase in emissions of 11 megatonnes in 1998.

One analysis by Hamilton and Dennis indicates that competition policy in the electricity sector will cost Australia almost A$1.5 billion in environmental damage over the period 1998–2005. This policy failure can be attributed to the fact that the National Competition Policy has promoted short-term cost minimization instead of economic efficiency; where significant negative externalities are associated with the production of a product, it cannot be assumed that price reductions will result in a more efficient allocation of resources. National Competition Policy has been based on the 'conflation of microeconomic reform and competition policy'.[14]

1.6 Munduk, Bali, Indonesia. The adoption of tourism into the economy of the village developed after the cooperative model of the agriculture. All share the water for the rice paddies, in the same way that all share in the tourism. **Left**. The accommodation is traditional low-impact low-cost developments supported as a cooperative within the village. The model has limited potential for growth but is sufficient to sustain the village community. **Top right** and **bottom**. Water from adjacent rice paddy fields is reused to create water features.

The above case is a classic outcome of the law of economic rationalism; the first-order decision is cost, and other decisions are secondary. Where a national culture is based on this premise, it is hard to see how design values concerning 'green buildings' can flourish. Hamilton and Dennis argue that this approach reduces the competitiveness of the renewable technologies that form the soft energy path.[15]

The obsession with the hard energy path

The concept of the soft energy15 path was developed by Amory Lovins, among others, in the 1970s, as an alternative route to 'hard technology', or energy systems based on extracting finite resources from the lithosphere. He contended that we should derive our energy from the ecosphere, that is, from solar, wind and water.

Lovins discusses this issue in the Schumacher lecture series of the 1980s. He argues for 'soft energy' paths on the basis of 'scale'; big power stations are high-cost pieces of infrastructure and when they fail, or when the grid fails, chaos is the consequence (grid failure caused massive power blackouts in the USA in the summer of 2003). Lovins suggests: 'if one of these 1000-megawatt plants dies on you it is embarrassing. It is rather like having an elephant die in the drawing room. You have to have another 1000-megawatt elephant to take the carcass away.'[16]

The social and cultural implication of the big systems approach based on non-renewable fuels, Lovins argues, is that it creates a lack of social responsibility in those who design the systems.[17]

Unlimited growth and the missed opportunity of micro-economic reform

The counter-argument to the soft energy path lies in the concept of economic growth. A question asked of Lovins at the end of his Schumacher lecture series was: 'Does the soft energy path include lower economic growth?' This is a stonewalling question, because there is no answer to it, since the soft energy path has not yet been seriously attempted.

Lovins tendered the ecological argument of 'keeping energy and material flows within the life cycle'. He argued that the hard energy path involves purchasing energy from outside the system – oil from overseas, for example, which drains resources. Going down the soft path, on the other hand, means there is very little drain on resources, since most stay within the system.

Lovins, and a number of others since, argued that the soft energy path can create economic growth but in a different context, that of sustainable development. The recognition that sustainable development is a viable form of micro-economic reform is still to be acknowledged.

Environmental impact assessment: lack of tools for the job

Ways of measuring the environmental impact of sustainable development are still evolving. Environmental impact assessment (EIA) methodology, much of which is now enshrined in national and local environmental impact legislation, remains selective and restricted to high-impact projects.

Ian Thomas has developed a relationship model of the various EPA procedures for assessing the impacts of development, which are:

- strategic environmental assessment (SEA);
- cumulative impact assessment (CIA); and
- environmental impact assessment (EIA).[18]

The SEA and CIA are primarily governmental procedures that feed information concerning impacts into planning and policy programmes. EIA is used on existing project-specific developments.

Comments on these current procedures are, first, that their scope is selective, primarily focused on ecologically sustainable development. Thomas quotes a number of authors who foresee a shift towards a new procedure called 'integrated impact assessment' (IIA), which includes social and economic factors. Second, EIA addresses specific projects and does not extend to all developments, examining only those projects that are likely to impinge on the ecological values of areas of high or pristine ecological value. It is likely that an argument for a broader range of tools, such as the environmental brief, could be used to address some of the existing limitations.

It is apparent that these forms of assessment are micro in scale as well as project-specific. Other tools are macro in nature and examine material flows and waste with regard to the main ecological cycle; the breadth of analysis accommodated by these tools varies. An example of such a tool is ecological footprinting (EF),[19] developed to evaluate ecological disturbance in terms of national land utilization, as a function of density –

persons per hectare. Attempts have been made to adapt this tool in order to assess the sustainability of settlements such as cities and communities, but it is recognized that it can only address a set of factors concerning ecological systems for a single sustainable community.

The benefit of such a tool, nevertheless, is that it can provide educational as well as research information on environmental impact. One interesting aspect of the tool is that it can assess the footprint of particular lifestyles. The calculator is intended to assess a person's present lifestyle in terms of the carrying capacity of the earth. It is not surprising to find out that if the entire world population followed a typical consumption-based lifestyle, approximately five earth-sized planets would be needed to support it. It is also interesting to see the kind of lifestyle the model predicts will stay within the carrying capacity. This requires, among other things, adopting a vegan diet, walking or cycling to work, sharing a house with at least four people, using renewable energy and recycling waste, and taking holidays locally.[20]

Missing factors in sustainable development

Mahwinney suggests that there are important factors in creating sustainable development that are often not fully understood or get lost in evaluation. These factors must be recognized if appropriate assessment is to be achieved and are as follows:

- *Scale.* The appropriate size and economic basis for a level of population retention.
- *Displacement.* Moving the problem, rather than addressing the problem.
- *Value judgements.* Experts often overlook mapping the effects of value judgments on development decisions.
- *Democracy.* Involving stakeholders in the development is essential for sustainable development, but has received little attention.
- *Efficiency.* Providing the best solution for the widest number of factors.
- *Space.* Space and use of land is a primary factor.
- *Population density.* Population density and migration are linked to sustainable development.[21]

Mawhinney argues that strong relationships exist between some of these factors. He suggests that space, population and effi-

ciency are powerful components in the matrix for a sustainable development.[22]

Interestingly, many of these factors are already important design considerations in the approach to building design and procurement. Different terms are applied in the case of a building project; for example, population density is expressed in terms of occupancy rate, and scale refers to the dimensions that are useful in terms of sustainable building development.

Schumacher developed a path that relates to this issue of scale. His maxim, 'small is beautiful', came from his experience with Swiss cantons, which are small self-contained and locally administered units. He saw this unit as an efficient and autonomous unit of development that could regulate its own destiny. His central argument asserts that sustainable building development can match this model; small steps taken at the local level and replicated worldwide can significantly influence global sustainability.

Schumacher's maxim can be the designer's creed. Because actions by designers control the form and scope of the design process, it becomes a point of action for many groups, associated with the design and building industry, who wish to use sustainability as a framework for development.

Amery Lovins's approach of looking for 'soft paths' to sustainability may give some direction; it can be linked with the concept of working at the local level, only with a global vision of sustainability, to provide an agenda for change. This can be summed up as 'think globally, act locally' – yet what does local action mean in physical terms? Schumacher suggested the units of analysis should be 'small'; does this mean a building, or a subdivision?

There has been discussion on the scale of sustainable building development – in particular, concerns about the character, size and function of building proposals. The ecological sustainable development of a precinct brings to bear a different range of green issues than does an EcoHome; the former is concerned with the range of social, economic and environmental needs of a community, while with the latter the dimensions of green design are those that relate to a family.

Consequently, one of the problems in applying green design is finding feasible units of analysis; deciding where to draw boundaries in terms of buildings types, size and scope of development is not easy. Sustainable development is not simply about material characteristics: there are also spatial and temporal parameters to consider. It is difficult to find a unit of analysis

Table 1.1 A simplified mapping hierarchy of the scales of sustainable building development in relation to available standards for tourism

Levels	Design phase	Operations phase
Level 1	*Sustainable cities/regions*	
Standards	None	GG Community standard
Level 2	*Sustainable communities/precincts/mixed use development*	
Standards	GG Planning and Infrastructure Design (proposed)	GG Community standard
Level 3	*Sustainable buildings*	
Standards	GG Design and Construction	GG Company standard

that is appropriate for research or for creating sustainable building development standards.

A broad hierarchy of sustainable developments for tourism (to include buildings and supporting infrastructure) is proposed. Three levels have been created that correspond to the increases in scale of development from buildings through cities to regions.

Further distinctions between the design and operations phases of the development are made to facilitate integration with the development process; at present most research and application activity is confined to the building level (see Table 1.1). The standards are currently marketed through Green Globe (GG).

At the building scale, the Healthy Home Project[23] demonstrates how a new, suburban house can achieve a high level of environmental sustainability through improved air quality, passive solar design, active solar systems and the selection of low-embodied-energy materials. It challenges existing norms of house design and legislation concerning the on-site reuse of resources such as water, and the collection, purification and use of rainwater.

This has been achieved in the form of a prototype environmental single residential dwelling constructed on the Gold Coast, Queensland, Australia. In addition, the project brings together cutting-edge environmental technologies, through partnerships with over 30 industry organizations and other collaborating groups. These groups have supported the project with an extensive range of products, services and contributions.

The scale of change in building development is a concern and also an opportunity. This phenomenon is closely linked to Alvin Toffler's concept of 'Future Shock'.[24] In his book with that title, Toffler describes the personal feelings of disorientation that

are associated with change. These can be felt when experiencing other cultures, but have most to do with the rate of change within cultures in the twenty-first century.

The book, written over 30 years ago as social history, seems to be more about the present than the future. Transience has become a permanent feature of the built environment, and the speed and scale of change demands re-skilling of those who do design work. The consequence of transience for the built environment is that it brings with it an opportunity for realizing ESD; some 10 per cent of the city of Melbourne is renovated each year, which means that the building stock is effectively recycled every ten years.[25] If this is a general phenomenon, it affords a major opportunity for environmental, economic and social progress.

The need for a model

Arguably, in addressing operational barriers, a model is needed to set a direction. During the design and development process, the model is often extracted from a particular project in which the barriers have been addressed. For example, the Vales's Autonomous House was designed so that the building could be serviced within the boundaries of the site, avoiding environmental impacts.[26] This could be a manifestation of a model for self-reliance and integration of the building with its immediate ecosystems. The Beddington Zero (Fossil) Energy Development in the UK, designed by Dunster Associates, could be taken as a model for comprehensive precinct development that mitigates impacts on the major ecological cycles – carbon, nitrogen, phosphorus, hydrological and sulphur – while providing strategies to deal with the social and economic dimensions of sustainability (see case study in Chapter 9).

Embracing a local action model: ecological sustainable development (ESD)

Sustainable development can be seen to apply across the economy from the manufacturing sector to the service sector, each sector providing its own challenges and responses to the environmental imperative. A particular approach to sustainable development as it is applied to building design and procurement processes is needed. Increasingly there have been calls to institutionalize ecological sustainable development (ESD) within the structural, legislative and managerial frameworks of communities.[27]

Within the building development sector, an agenda exists for assessing sustainable buildings that is concerned with the scale and complexity of the building process. Given the nature of building development, what is an appropriate model to ensure its ecological sustainability?

Defining ecological sustainable development

The concept of ESD has been integrated and institutionalized within professional groups, such as the Royal Australian Institute of Architects (RAIA) and the American Institute of Architects (AIA). The RAIA's current definition of ESD states:

> The goal of ESD is to achieve development that improves the total quality of life, both now and in the future, in a way that maintains the processes on which life depends.[28]

The objectives of ESD are to:

- enhance individual and community well-being and welfare by following a path of economic development that safeguards the welfare of future generations;
- provide for equity within and between generations; and
- protect biological diversity and maintain essential ecological processes and life support systems.[29]

In addition, these professional groups have taken steps to introduce design strategies and assessment processes for ESD (see Chapter 2).

The need for ESD: the case of Munduk, Bali

ESD strategies can be derived from studies of communities such as Munduk in Bali, Indonesia, where the current agricultural economy is shifting to one that is service-intensive, to support international tourism. The effects on local communities and their infrastructure are profound; principally, the cooperative approach to agriculture, which had been necessary to ensure equity in the use of natural resources, is changing.

The attraction of the tourism dollar is creating speculative rather than strategic building development, and cooperative ownership and management is being supplanted by individual ownership. Escalating house prices as a result of overseas investment mean that the opportunities for local tenure diminish and the responsibility for caring for the land is lost.

The inability of the population to adapt to changes is manifested in a number of ways:

- an inability to establish mechanisms to deal with waste – the plastic pyramid;
- the shifting to monoculture and the associated effects on biodiversity;
- utilization of new crops that do not fit the rainfall pattern, reducing water supply and amenity.

Yet the Balinese people have a sensitivity to design, and this does help to create opportunities for ESD. In the case of Munduk, the adaptive reuse of agricultural buildings for tourist accommodation results in a low-impact, low-cost development that gives a unique quality to the tourism experience. Although the opportunities for sustainable design are largely ignored at present, in both the developing and the developed worlds the growing concern for sustainability, particularly in cities, provides an opportunity for green design.[30]

Opportunities for green design strategies to enhance ESD

The opportunities for design strategies to improve ESD can be seen at differing scales of development.

Sustainable cities

The opportunity of improving the sustainability of cities is one of the challenging movements that could emerge from the institutionalization of ESD. Recent work by the RAIA on this challenge has been the establishment of a 39-step road map demonstrating how the design of the form and character of the city can assist in reducing environmental impact.[31] This document comments on the unsustainability claimed for the development practices presently in place. There is basic evidence that urban form has a bearing on environmental performance and that density alone is not the major factor.

The general proposition that denser cities are more efficient in reducing impacts is giving way to a more diverse typology of cities, with forms responsive to various situational factors. The growth of cities in the 200-kilometre coastal edge of Australia is becoming critical, increasing the population density on the coast strip. Indeed some coastal towns are capping population growth in order to maintain quality of life.

A picture of the existing main indicators of a sustainable city is emerging. One of these has to be the provision of a viable public transport system. Further indicators may relate to the ways by which the city can support a lifestyle that reduces each person's eco-footprint. This would call for a finer grain for design and development: one that centres on social and economic factors as drivers for improved environmental performance. The following are strategies that should be used:

- systems to support walking and cycling to local amities, transport nodes and work centres;
- transport nodes and systems that are adapted to these systems, i.e. cycle racks on buses;
- urban form that supports public transport systems and nodes;
- protection and enhancement of vegetation and biodiversity – landscape systems and public open space integrated with buildings; and
- urban form that supports a reduction in resources such as energy, water and the creation of waste.[32]

Sustainable precincts
ESD can be applied within the framework of sustainable cities, at the precinct level. Precincts normally include the development of substantial areas of land and involve the construction of multiple building types, consisting of residential and commercial properties. (Case studies in Part 3 demonstrate the advantages of ESD for larger projects.)

When the ESD boundary is defined around a large number of buildings rather than a single house or building, there is an advantage of scale. This offers a greater potential for cogeneration of energy, on-site water and waste treatment, and other high-performance components of the environmental infrastructure. For example, the Novotel & Ibis study of the Green Hotel in Olympic Park, Homebush Bay, Sydney, demonstrates the importance of sustainable design and its positive potential to produce buildings that perform well environmentally. To conserve water, the Olympic Park Committee installed a grey water main to serve buildings on the Olympic site. All buildings can access this main, significantly reducing their water consumption at very little cost. The use of a green lease enables effective design and operation to ISO 14000 standards.

EcoHomes and EcoHome renovations
Another approach to achieving ESD is to start at the other end of the problem, attempting to apply ESD principles at the scale of new and existing houses. A number of EcoHomes have been built across the world that demonstrate the availability of the technology and the consequent benefits to occupants and the environment. Lessons learned from some of the case studies in Part 3 demonstrate that small changes to the form and fabric of the building, as well as use of green technologies for servicing, can result in a significant improvement in environmental performance. Benchmarks of 60 per cent saving on water, 25 per cent saving on energy, and on-site waste recycling to minimize landfill waste have been obtained. The use of permaculture landscape, or local indigenous dry-season-tolerant plantings, lowers the impact on the hydrological cycle.

In many cases there is a lack of incentives for individuals or developers to implement the EcoHomes strategies in new buildings or renovations. As will be seen in later case studies, the economic benefits for individual owners are small, yet the environmental benefits are large when multiplied across the housing stock of a city.

Summary

The PSR model provides a framework for understanding the environmental imperative and is based on three axioms.

- With the size of the human population, changes in technologies and consumption are creating impacts.
- These impacts are disturbing the ecological cycles, which support humanity and also all living things.
- It is possible to reduce these pressures, using ecological sustainable development (ESD) through local actions.

There are reasons for using local action in the form of ESD. First, much building development is piecemeal, locally based and in response to local needs. Developers, and the opportunity to develop, have largely shaped the scale and character of building development in recent years. This has conventionally been seen as part of the problem and not part of the solution to ESD. As seen in the PSR model, since local actions create environmental impacts that are global, there is a need to include the developer and associated communities within the mission and scope of ESD.

Second, tools, codes and environmental standards that work in the local context can be used to measure environmental per-formances. The metric of these tools reflects the global problems identified in the PSR model, so global needs can be addressed by local action.

Third, contextual barriers for implementing ESD are well documented. One argument for addressing these barriers is that it will lead to the institutionalization of environmental principles within the mainstream social, economic and political framework of society. Professional building design groups are integrating ESD; the groups examined in this chapter include the RAIA and AIA who have taken steps to integrate environmental principles within their organizations. This proactive approach addresses the need for ESD and strategically places the design professions in a position to take up the opportunities as society moves towards creating sustainable cities, precincts and homes. The next chapter examines some of the principles underlying ESD, and initiatives that have been taken to move it into the mainstream, as well as listing further steps that need to be addressed.

2.1 Rocky Mountain Institute. A demonstration building for green design.

Chapter 2

Principles, initiatives and responses

Introduction

The main argument of the preceding chapter was a call for more support for establishing the environmental imperative as a context for building design professionals, by institutionalizing ecological sustainable development (ESD) within their professional groups. ESD is in a transitional stage of introduction and still lacks the necessary micro-economic reform and associated legislation that it will need in order to be classed as mainstream. A number of contextual barriers remain in place, but fortunately the move to ESD is progressing on a broad front, through a range of initiatives, specifically green design, or sustainable design as it sometimes called.

The aim of this chapter is to examine some of the principles that underpin the drive to ESD, with some examples of the initiatives used to push and pull building development. Finally, the responses emerging from the building design and procurement process are examined with a view to improving green design.

Principles

In recent years, principles for addressing the environmental imperative have shifted from mainly ecological issues to a synthesis of other issues, such as economic and social factors. Hence a number of principles have emerged mostly following this theme, some of them favouring greater emphasis on a social rather than a technical agenda as a means of change. Four useful principles can be found in the literature, and these will be discussed in turn.

Polluter pays

Collins[1] argues that one of the main principles for sustainable development is that the polluter should be given some form of penalty for creating adverse environmental impacts. He cites the case of Europe, which is more than ever characterized by its urban fabric; 50 per cent of the population lives in cities. Most cities face similar futures: 'decay of the urban environment through congestion, water and air pollution, deterioration of housing and derelict land and the disappearance of useful open space'. Addressing this future has been a major commitment of the European Parliament, which published a Green Paper in 1990.[2]

Unfortunately, since then little has been achieved, and Collins argues that a new model of development is needed that is 'more environmentally friendly, creates and sustains more jobs and which takes into account quality of life'. He argues that a new measure of architectural design should be based on this model.[3]

Edwards suggests: 'Architects have a larger share of responsibility for the world's consumption of fossil fuel and global warming gain than any other professional group.' He reports that two principles, enshrined in EU Law, place this responsibility firmly in the hands of the environmental providers; in the case of sustainable building development, it is in the hands of the construction industry. One major principle is that the 'polluter pays'. This is exposing not only developers, but also their design teams, to litigation risks. While there is thorough, extensive environmental protection and EIA methodologies legislation in place that addresses this principle, the general increase in the level of pollution and environmental impact is a growing concern.

The difficulty is that attacking the general level of pollution through management and design is hardly a viable strategy. In the extreme case, developers and their design teams would risk financial penalties for creating unsustainable development, but unless the case involves infringement of environmental protection legislation this is hardly likely to occur in the present system. An alternative strategy for applying this principle is the use of information to create 'informed choices' within the development process to avoid pollution and minimize impact. The rule of reason in development may be an alternative to the rule of law in safeguarding the environment. An extension of this thinking is seen in the second principle: that pollution should be dealt with at source.

Pollution is dealt with at source

In the case of the building industry, the application of this principle means more environmentally effective buildings.[4] If 'pollution' is taken to be equivalent to environmental impact, then support for Edwards's argument is seen in the extent to which buildings contribute to urban decay and negative environmental effects. He states that buildings and their construction are responsible for 40 to 80 per cent of society's environmental impacts in the United Kingdom, in the following proportions:

- energy use 50 per cent;
- raw material use 40 per cent;
- ozone depleting chemicals 50 per cent;
- land lost to agriculture 80 per cent; and
- waste use 50 per cent.[5]

Edwards has suggested that designers, and indeed the whole construction industry, need to develop policy and guidelines for reducing the environmental impact of buildings. An extension of this thinking is to use initiatives in the design phase of building development to ensure that pollution – that is, environmental impact – is minimized. The outcome of this would lead to better quality of life for users of buildings. This third principle exists at a number of levels.

Quality of life

The third of the principles addressing the environmental imperative is to use sustainability to improve the quality of life of the citizens of an area or country or, at a micro scale, the users of buildings.

The UK government, through its policy 'Quality of Life Counts', has embraced this goal.[6] This policy was developed to establish a reporting method for the shift towards sustainable development. John Prescott, Deputy Prime Minister, suggested in this document that 'Improving the quality of life for the people of this country is perhaps the most important duty of Government.'[7]

However, 'quality of life' is not easily quantified and may mean different things to different people. A survey in 2001 explored what issues are most important to people and most affect their quality of life. It then explored how they rated their quality of life and their optimism for the future.[8]

Exploring the factors affecting quality of life in the UK context requires a methodology for assessing the regions in the UK. The Department for Environment, Food and Rural Affairs has published an update to its leaflet *Quality of life barometer*. This contains new figures released since the launch in February 2003 of the government's third annual report on sustainable development, *Achieving a better quality of life*. This new data is updated to 2002.[9]

Seven headline indicators are used as follows:

- economic output;
- investment;
- climate change;
- air quality;
- road traffic;
- land use; and
- waste.[10]

Applying quality of life at the sustainable building level needs a separate set of indicators relating to community issues. These issues can be seen in the case study of the BedZED project in Part 3. This example has created an integrated approach to a range of quality of life issues. At the heart of the quality of life indicators are found the three core factors of economics, social improvement and environmental concern. The fourth principle is aimed at balancing these factors.

2.2   The 'Zed Challenge', developed by Bill Dunster Architects, shows the range of issues that relate quality of life and the environment. The Zed challenge asks how we can increase our quality of life while reducing our environmental impact.

Table 2.1   Applying the triple bottom line

A model of the triple bottom line

1 The triple bottom line
The three lines represent society, the economy and the environment. Society depends on the economy – and the economy depends on the global ecosystem, whose health represents the ultimate bottom line.

2 Instability
The three bottom lines are not stable; they are in constant flux, as a result of social, political, economic and environmental pressures, cycles and conflicts.

3 Continental plates
Think of each bottom line as a continental plate, often moving independently of the others.

4 Shear zones
As the plates move under, over or against each other, 'shear zones' emerge where the social, economic or ecological equivalents of tremors and earthquakes occur.

ECONOMIC/ENVIRONMENTAL
   In the economic/environmental shear zone, some companies already promote eco-efficiency – there are greater challenges ahead, e.g. environmental economics and accounting, shadow pricing and ecological tax reform.
   Eco-efficiency reporting is a method for examining this area.

SOCIAL/ENVIRONMENTAL
   In the social/environmental shear zone, business is working on environmental literacy and training issues, but new challenges will be sparked, e.g. by environmental justice, environmental refugees, and the inter-generational equity agenda.
   Social reporting is a key mechanism in addressing this relationship.

ECONOMIC/SOCIAL
   In the economic/social shear zone, some companies are looking at the social impacts of proposed investment, but bubbling under are issues such as business ethics, fair trade, human and minority rights, and stakeholder capitalism.
   The business case for these developments is crucial.

Balancing the triple bottom line

Definitions abound of the triple bottom line (TBL) and its focus. SustainAbility, a group founded in 1987 (and hence the longest-established international consultancy specializing in business strategy and sustainable development), defines the TBL on the basis of environmental improvement, social equity and economic development, as follows.

> The triple bottom line (TBL) focuses corporations not just on the economic value they add, but also on the environmental and social value they add – and destroy. At its narrowest, the term 'triple bottom line' is used as a framework for measuring and reporting corporate performance against economic, social and environmental parameters. At its broadest, the term is used to capture the whole set of values, issues and processes that companies must address in order to minimize any harm resulting from their activities and to create economic, social and environmental value. This involves being clear about the company's purpose and taking into consideration the needs of all the company's stakeholders – shareholders, customers, employees, business partners, governments, local communities and the public.[11]

Accordingly, this final principle involves balancing the three pillars of sustainability: economic, social and environmental factors. Businesses are now trying to utilize this method of reporting to demonstrate a balanced view towards sustainable development. Yet the challenges for this are apparent.

SustainAbility argues that the balancing of these three factors is a problem for companies, likening them to three tectonic plates. The key issue with this principle is to establish what constitutes 'balance' between these three factors.

At the sustainable building level, eco-efficiency reporting is useful for selecting components and solution sets and is discussed in Part 2. Examination of the social/environmental shear zone is necessary in projects that have a significant social dimension such as housing; this appears to be a largely a research activity.[12] Business case reporting is growing in the promotion of green building, as a mechanism to dispel myths about the added costs of this type of building compared with traditional methods. These procedures have found their way into a range of initiatives to help decision-making in response to the environmental imperative.

The initiatives for change: the push and pull taxonomy

The different types of initiatives can be categorized in a simple way in a 'push and pull' taxonomy: the 'push' approach is exemplified by legislation making the polluter pay, and the 'pull' approach by the offer of a range of incentives to encourage the construction industry to improve its environmental performance. Governments seem to favour the latter approach over the former because of the political hurdles that need to be overcome to change the present system. Pull initiatives in the UK include:

- the Construction Task Force presenting business cases;[13]
- the Strategic Forum on *Accelerating Change*;[14]
- *Sustainable Communities: Building for the Future*, ODPM, February 2003;[15]
- Rethinking Construction approach, 1998;[16] and
- Building Research Establishment development of environmental assessment tools.[17]

Push initiatives in the UK include:

- Building Regulations;[18,19]
- Planning and Compulsory Purchase Bill, January 2003, ODPM;[20] and
- Energy White Paper, February 2003, DTI.[21]

A number of examples are presented as small case studies to illustrate the types of approach used in three countries: the UK, USA and Australia. The first approach involves measures to create self-regulation of sustainable construction of buildings in the UK, mainly pull initiatives. The second centres on the emerging role of trans-professional groups, such as the US Green Building Council in the USA, which tend to use the prevention principle, attempting to reduce pollution and environmental impact at source and at the building level.

Construction industry self-regulation in the UK

The policy landscape in the UK has changed in recent years in response to the environmental imperative. Two of the main pull initiatives are the Rethinking Construction project and the Construction Task Force.

2.3   Beddington Zero Energy Development (BedZED). Bill Dunster Architects. A project demonstrating how councils can implement sustainable development within the present unsustainable culture, through interventions at the precinct as well as the building level. The mixed-use development in the project assists with the economic case for sustainable housing; rental from the business accommodation offsets housing rental costs. The improved quality of life that comes from the environmentally sustainable master planning is an added benefit.

Rethinking Construction is an approach to self-regulation of the construction industry in the UK, which comprises some 1,000 construction organizations; it aims to achieve radical improvements in the design, quality, sustainability and customer satisfaction of UK construction. Furthermore, it aims to assist the industry to recruit and retain a skilled workforce by improving its employment practices and health and safety performance.

The Construction Task Force has a more specific aim: to provide a model for sustainable construction. This presents for consideration a number of 'drivers', 'processes', 'performance indicators' and 'targets', with the goal of creating a new industry standard for environmental performance.

The important outcome of these initiatives is first to provide a business case for sustainable construction, to remove one particular barrier to self-regulation of the industry. Second, a collection of demonstration projects has been created, which provides a set of blueprints for developers, designers and construction companies. These projects aim to go beyond prescriptive lessons on sustainable construction methods and techniques, instead looking to trigger a groundswell of change towards better environmental performance in the construction industry.[22] A checklist is provided to guide the creation of further demonstration projects. It follows a triple bottom line approach that considers the economic, social and environmental performance of a project.

The triple bottom line approach enables companies to track construction performance with respect to the sustainability strategies and techniques used in the building. A useful example is the case of the Sutton local council, which through its policy of responding to the environmental imperative established a demonstration project called BedZED (Beddington Zero Energy Development). Examination of the evolution of the policy landscape of this council, and of the demonstration project, provides an insight into the important links at the local level between policy, strategies and improved environmental outcomes.

Making the business case for sustainable construction
A key initiative of the Sustainable Construction Task Group comprises the arguments it has successfully advanced to support the business case for sustainability. As it claims:

A company that places sustainability at the centre of its management and operations is in a far healthier position than its competitors who still choose to operate in a risky and increasingly outdated fashion. The benefits for those companies that take up the challenge of sustainability cannot be over emphasized.[23]

Organizations and task force groups need to develop clear arguments in favour of sustainable construction to convince stakeholders; the key concern of these groups can be allayed by successfully arguing the business case for sustainable development. Such arguments are put forward in the conclusion to a report by the Sustainable Construction Task Group. This group includes industry leaders, and was established to investigate and make recommendations on improving the take-up of sustainable development strategies by the construction and property sectors.

The Group has pointed out the significant economic strength that property represents, with assets of GB£72.3 billion; it argues that economic strength carries responsibilities, and that the property sector can no longer afford to allow itself to hide behind the 'circle of blame' that has dogged the sector for many years. In the circle of blame, each sub-group of stakeholders blames the others for lack of leadership in sustainability in the property market. Key arguments in the circle of blame are exposed in the Group's recommendations (see Table 2.2).

Ironically, the Group argues that *all* parties would benefit individually by making a definite policy shift to sustainable development. The benefits are:

1   *Environmental performance*. The construction and property sectors currently under-perform in terms of environmental impact, so that a modest effort would be seen to yield large benefits. Key possibilities lie in the use of brownfield sites and in establishing sustainable waste management systems.

Table 2.2 'Circle of blame': a model of the development process

---

Arguments for lack of action in the development process – 'circle of blame'

Investors see no demand by occupiers for environmentally efficient buildings.

Developers would ask for environmentally efficient buildings, but investors won't pay for them.

Occupiers would like more environmentally efficient buildings, but there is little choice available.

Contractors would build environmentally, but developers don't ask them to.

---

2   *Mitigating risk*. Providing for the consequences of environmental degradation are a way of future-proofing buildings. Global warming is expected to create greater extremes of climate – drier summers and winter flooding – which will have a significant impact on property and create foreseeable risks.[24]

3   *Social responsibility*. For the property sector, sustainability can bring regeneration, job creation in the building sector, and better workplace health and safety for the construction workforce. The Construction Industry Training Board in the UK suggests 370,000 new employees are needed if the sector is to grow. Recruitment is likely to remain low while poor workplace health and safety standards in the construction industry remain a matter of public record.[25] Some 30 per cent of non-domestic buildings in the UK exhibit 'sick building syndrome', which contributes to the large number of workdays lost through sickness. This social aspect of sustainability is central to the business case for sustainable construction. It may be that tougher health and safety laws are necessary to compel corporations to act as good 'corporate citizens' and provide safe workplaces for their employees. It can be shown that once this responsibility is taken up at the highest corporate level, the benefits then translate into more profitable outcomes.

Building the *economic argument* for sustainability is central to the interests of business. Social and government pressures are likely to grow, forcing companies to change as environmentally minded customers take business away from them. Companies need to be seen to be environmentally friendly and this perception must be backed up by substance. The Dow Jones Sustainability Index demonstrates that companies that embrace environmental issues out-perform conventional companies.[26] This sustainability index method of profiling companies lifts their status, and improves ratings and their relationships with consumers.

Operation benefits accrue through the use of environmentally friendly strategies, which include:

- cost savings from material efficiency (recycling);
- green homes that produce less greenhouse gas and incur reduced energy bills;
- improved habitats under the Climate Change Levy (CCL);[27]
- reduced landfill disposal costs;

- reduced transport costs and better fleet efficiency;
- reduced risk of fires from adverse environmental effects; and
- more flexible building systems.

Many of the elements of the business case have now been incorporated into projects that serve as case studies for the industry's commitment to self-regulation.

Demonstrating sustainable construction

The UK government set out its commitment to sustainable construction in a number of documents from 1989 onwards. The Building Research Establishment (BRE) and the Department of Trade and Industry (DTI) set about examining the many examples of sustainable development in the UK. Their report, Demonstrations of Sustainability, carries a review of policy developments that underpin the move to sustainable construction.[28] The programme collects together projects from every part of the construction industry, providing exemplars that demonstrate innovation and change, which can be measured, evaluated and shared. There are several types of project: some are site based and involve buildings; others are organizational change projects in which organizations have restructured their operations to improve their environmental performance.[29]

The programme uses two methodologies:

1. base line survey; and
2. case studies of demonstration projects.

The *base line survey* involves collecting data on existing construction organizations and their projects, bringing together projects carried out by construction-related companies and examining them against a set of 12 key performance indicators (Table 2.3). The indicators are based on economic factors as well as other social criteria.

The base line study involves a 'management by measurement' philosophy, through these 12 key performance Indicators ('Kepi's') for the construction industry.[30] The DTI collects data from industry annually, enabling a comparison to be made between industry performance and that of the Rethinking Construction demonstrations. The report states: 'The projects substantially outperform the average of the UK industry against the

Table 2.3 Base line study of sustainable construction: use of 12 key performance indicators

Indicators	Benchmarks
Client satisfaction	
• product	80 per cent
• service	80 per cent
Defects	58 per cent
Safety	Mean accident rate per 100,000 employed
Cost predictability	
• design	On target or better
• construction	On target or better
Time predictability	
• design	On target or better
• construction	On target or better
Profitability	Medium profit on turnover
Productivity	Mean value added/employee (GBP000)
Cost	Change compared to 1 year ago
Time	Change compared to 1 year ago

key indicators.'[31] In this way 'best practice' demonstration case study projects can be identified in relation to the industry norm.

An additional checklist is used to gather information for the demonstration programme and for creating *individual case study projects*. This checklist is based on the Sustainable Construction Action Plan and the Sustainability Index. It utilizes the outputs of all the working groups in seeking the latest theory and practice of sustainable construction. The National Strategy Panel is making this checklist available to all new demonstration projects, to provoke thought and further innovation.[32] For convenience of explanation, the checklist has been separated into three parts, covering the economic, social and environmental factors relating to sustainability.

There are more than 400 projects the programme, with a total value of over GB£7 billion. They provide examples of off-site construction, standardization, new technology, respect for people's activities, partnering and supply chain integration, and other areas of process improvement. Collecting these demonstration projects has created a measurement of 'culture of performance' as the primary way to verify innovation and improvement.[33]

The information has been assembled into checklists, which are useful for designers wishing to create sustainable projects. The checklists cover four main areas:

- planning;
- design;
- construction; and
- finished product.

Planning issues concern the selection and planning of the buildings on the site. This recognizes that the characteristics of the site determine transport opportunities and users' environmental impacts. Sites with multiple transport options, including public transport nodes, will allow for less environmental impact than those sites that are only serviced by cars. Reuse of brownfield sites that have been previously developed saves the natural landscape of greenfield sites. Also, smaller building footprints leave more space for natural habitats and biodiversity.

Design of the buildings affords the main opportunity to limit impacts on the environment. Design is a complex process with many overlapping considerations; for example, the envelope design affects a range of management, energy and environmental quality issues, and an integrated solution will yield the best environmental outcome. Design checklists are useful, in a limited way, as a starting point and as a finishing point for the designer; at the start they are a list of things to consider and at the end they serve as a reminder of things that should have been included. A checklist is often looked upon as a designer's conscience.

Sustainable practices must apply to the construction process. There is considerable room for improvement on most construction projects and it is the builder's responsibility to implement appropriate strategies. Unfortunately builders are motivated by profit and this can conflict with the need for sustainable construction, so it is sensible practice to include the requirements for sustainable construction in the terms of the contractual agreement with the contractor. This will require auditing and cleaner production techniques to ensure compliance, so part of the client team will need to take responsibility for overseeing these processes.

The Rethinking Construction group (see page 38) recommends the use of a checklist by all applicants to help with project design, and this is provided to all regional coordinators and to applicants for new demonstration projects. Rethinking Construction encourages applicants to consider all aspects of sustainability (economic, social and environmental) and to guard against undermining one section for the benefit of another.

Holistic environmental assessment tools have been developed, such as SPeAR$_{TM}$; BREEAM (offices, retail and industrial); EcoHomes; CEEQUAL (civil engineering); Bespoke BREEAM for one-off projects; and the 'Sustainability Checklist for Developments'.[34] If a demonstration project is using such a scheme or an equivalent, it is deemed to pass the environmental section of assessment. If such assessment should be found inappropriate in a particular instance, the environmental performance indicators (EPIs) benchmarks for site and building performance, or the Design Quality Indicators (DQIs) may be of use for design assessment.

The Building Research Establishment (BRE) in recent years has become a key group, through its work in the Rethinking Construction initiative. It has pioneered many other initiatives including a range of environmental assessment tools (see Part 2). Its mission is as follows:

The BRE is the UK's leading centre of expertise on buildings, construction, energy, environment, fire and risk. We provide research-based consultancy, testing and certification services to customers worldwide. BRE is owned by the Foundation for the Built Environment (FBE), a registered charity with a mission to champion excellence and innovation in the built environment.[35]

The London Borough of Sutton is an example of a successful project application by local government that progressed from formulation of policy for sustainability through to successful environmental practice by setting up a demonstration project.

The London Borough of Sutton and its demonstration project: policy strategy, demonstration
Sutton is known as 'The Greener, Cleaner Borough'. It is located 25 minutes from central London by train and has a tree as its logo.

Northern areas of the borough have similar characteristics to inner London, with areas of significant deprivation and unemployment. Its southern boundaries border on open fields and the North Downs. The 180,000-strong community has a vibrant economy and a quality of life that has attracted many major employers. Unemployment is low, with jobs mainly in the service, professional, light industrial and retail sectors. There is a substantial cohort of commuters. Prosperity is evident in the town shopping centre and in the district centres of Cheam, North Cheam, Worcester Park, Rose Hill, Carshalton and Wallington.[36]

Sutton is facing similar challenges to other London boroughs and has led the way in creating a sustainable future for its residents. Areas of deprivation within the borough have been attacked through a massive regeneration project, one of the largest in the country. The Roundshaw Estate is undergoing redevelopment, from 1960s concrete-deck terraces, to new low-rise houses with gardens and off-street parking, and regenerated community facilities.

Projects of this kind require a partnership approach to achieve a sustainable outcome and Sutton's Regeneration Partnership involves the council, housing associations and private sector partners working together. This highly successful project, creating new homes, jobs and schools for local families, is now well under way and involves GB£30 million of funding.

Underpinning the borough's regeneration project is an EMS[37] approach, which means implementing policies aimed at continuous improvement of environmental performance in all areas and complying with all relevant environmental requirements including the partnership's Local Agenda 21 goals. These policies exist to ensure that all suppliers to the council recognize and address environmental matters relating to their products and services.[38]

SUTTON'S ENVIRONMENTAL POLICY
The council has a sustainability policy, which encompasses a range of issues over six main areas. These areas involve developing aims and goals, creating actions and campaigning, presenting promotions, providing encouragement, monitoring progress and producing outcomes. The details are as follows.

1   *Aims*
   • discourage waste and encourage the recycling of materials and use recycled materials wherever practicable;
   • improve energy and water conservation in council buildings and encourage this elsewhere;
   • protect the public from dangers incurred through the use, transport and storage of dangerous and toxic substances, e.g. asbestos and radioactive materials;

   • seek to minimize the impact on the environment in terms of materials used in the pursuance of the council's function;
   • reduce and discourage litter as part of the 'Greener, Cleaner Borough' campaign.

2   *Actions and campaigns*
   • against pollution, e.g. of air and water;
   • against anti-social levels of noise.

3   *Promote*
   • development and implementation of renewable energy sources;
   • protection and enhancement of the open spaces, waters, trees and hedges under its control, to meet the needs of the Sutton Nature Conservation Guide;
   • allotments and horticulture.

4   *Encourage*
   • healthy eating – provide the widest circulation of information on the subject, and discourage the use of unnecessary additives, particularly within the Council's services;
   • the use and improvement of public transport – provide improved facilities for disabled people, pedestrians and cyclists;
   • consideration of favourable employment that enhances the borough's environment;
   • a responsible and informed attitude to the use of artificial fertilizers, pesticides and herbicides on council-owned land and elsewhere, and aim to reduce the use of artificial fertilizers;
   • community participation in this programme, and work with other organizations committed to the same goals;
   • a positive attitude to the local environment from individual residents, groups and organizations – encourage the expansion of environmental education.

5   *Monitor*
   • the rate at which green areas are diminishing in the borough and endeavour to compensate for this.

6   *Produce*
   • an annual report on the state of the environment so that the implementation of these policies can be monitored;

• where necessary, new planning policies to support these aims.

One particular project that demonstrates the realization of this policy is the BedZED, or Beddington Zero (Fossil) Energy Development.[39] BedZED is a pioneering green village, built on a brownfield site in Hackbridge. A key economic feature of the project is its break away from central government policy on land prices. It is the first local authority approved to sell land below market price as a way of creating equity for sustainable development. Further partnerships with a social housing provider, the Peabody Trust, enabled the construction of an 82-home sustainable housing scheme – the BedZED scheme – located on the four-acre site.[40]

What is so special about the BedZED project? A core argument by the architect, Bill Dunster, is that the scheme creates zero carbon emissions. He explains: 'BedZED will only use energy from renewable sources generated on site. It is the first large-scale "carbon neutral" community – i.e. the first not to add to the amount of carbon dioxide in the atmosphere. BedZED shows how housing can be built without degrading the environment.'[41]

Edwards explains the reason: 'Energy remains a major consideration, especially the impact urban development has on fossil fuel use and resulting levels of carbon emission.'[42] He argues that there is a direct relation between energy use that impacts on the resources within the environment by, for example, fossil fuel depletion, and global warming, which harms the ecology. Continued fossil fuel use contributes to global warming, which raises ocean temperatures, threatening to obliterate some of the world's most significant ecosystems such as the Great Barrier Reef. It is essential to shift urban development toward zero carbon emissions.[43]

Bill Dunster explains:

BedZED is a 'zero energy' development – it will not use more energy than it produces. Everything about the scheme, from the layout and the building materials to the heating supply, has been designed to cut energy consumption. By avoiding fossil fuels, BedZED will generate zero net carbon emissions. We believe it to be the first large-scale 'carbon-neutral' development – that is, one that will not contribute to global warming.[44]

The arguments that emerge from the demonstration project are twofold. First, Elizabeth Whatmore, DTI Director of Construction, comments:

BedZED made the case for sustainable development not by its innovative technologies, or in its ability to collect industry awards, but in its success in building low energy homes that people genuinely want to live and work in. The Carbon Neutral Toolkit could, potentially, be key in convincing the wider construction industry, and crucially clients, that by following the BedZED example a profit can be made on sustainable development and that a significant market opportunity exists not to be missed.[45]

Second, the business case for CN (carbon neutral) development appears to be based on three arguments in the UK:

1   The reduction in carbon dioxide emissions and its effect on climate change means that councils can award incentives to developers in return for environmental improvement.
2   Buyers are willing to pay a cost premium for CN development, presumably for quality of life issues (17 per cent more on average).
3   Build cost would be further reduced through economies of scale, as more CN developments are built.
4   DTI will provide financial support for the research and development to carry out similar projects.[46]

Meanwhile, development in the UK continues apace. The Department for Environment, Food and Rural Affairs estimates that an extra 3.8 million new homes will be needed by 2016 – a 10 per cent increase in the number of UK households since 1991. As Lord Rogers's Urban Task Force points out, if these new homes were built at current densities they would cover an area of land larger than Greater London. (In 1998 Richard Rogers was invited to chair a Government Task Force charged with translating sustainable urban development principles into strategic advice for planning authorities in England. The Urban Task Force was faced with three specific urban challenges: decline of regional inner-city areas and communities; an official prediction of a requirement for 4 million additional households; and suburban sprawl consuming greenfield sites at an alarming rate, causing social and economic decline within inner-city areas – see www.richardrogers.co.uk).

The local action model espoused by Schumacher is realized in the initiatives taken in Sutton. The borough has a structured approach that embraces Collins's new model for sustainable development through environmentally friendly design, creating jobs and taking account of the quality of life. The success of this approach comes from a clear policy direction, prudent environmental management, successful partnerships with industry and creative architectural and engineering design.

Greenhouse abatement initiatives

The Australian Greenhouse Office (AGO) has tried to apply the 'polluter pays' principle to its initiatives for greenhouse gas emissions.[47]

This organization is claimed to be the world's first government agency dedicated to cutting greenhouse gas emissions. It has only been recently established, in 1998, to act as a separate agency within the environment portfolio providing a 'whole of government approach to greenhouse matters'.[48]

The Commonwealth Government allocated funding of A$1 billion dollars for climate change abatement though initiatives such as 'Safeguarding the Future: Australia's Response to Climate Change', and measures for a 'Better Environment' announced as part of Australia's new tax system in 1999. Australia has yet to sign the Kyoto agreement, but these measures are designed to arrest the probable causes of global warming. As AGO suggests:

Climate change is an issue of major significance for all of us. Most of the world's leading scientists agree that global warming caused by human activity is occurring. New and stronger evidence that humans are having an influence on the global climate through greenhouse gas emissions is presented in a report prepared by the Intergovernmental Panel on Climate Change in 2001. ... The ultimate objective is to stabilize greenhouse gas concentrations in the atmosphere at a level that will prevent dangerous human-induced interference with the climate system.[49]

The Australian government's agenda targets emissions abatement on many fronts, including the following initiatives:[50]

- boosting renewable energy initiatives and pursuing greater energy efficiency;
- investing significant resources into greenhouse research and monitoring Australia's progress towards its Kyoto target through the National Greenhouse Gas Inventory;[51]
- studying the landscape of Australia through the National Carbon Accounting System;[52]
- investigating the possibility of a domestic emissions trading scheme;
- encouraging industry, business and the community to use less greenhouse-intensive transport;
- fostering sustainable land management practices; and
- providing impetus for greenhouse action through the Greenhouse Gas Abatement Program.[53]

The AGO recognizes that global warming presents challenges to the way we live and work. It recognizes that collaborative action by industry, by governments at all levels and by the community at large is necessary to meet this challenge.

The housing sector is identified as an important one by the AGO, which argues:

One-fifth of Australia's greenhouse gas emissions come from households. There are 7 million households in Australia each producing more than 15 tonnes of greenhouse gas emissions every year (1 tonne of emissions would fill a family home). Energy use, car use and waste are the largest sources of household emissions.[54]

A key argument is that small but significant strategies can be used, which when added together make an important reduction in greenhouse gas emissions. The Australian Greenhouse Office promotes a range of initiatives to enable communities and households to reduce their greenhouse gas emissions:

- Household Greenhouse Action (HGA)[55] is working to reduce emissions from households by focusing on home heating and cooling, refrigeration, lighting and water heating.[56]
- Cool Communities[57] is providing information, support and financial assistance to help communities take easy, practical actions to reduce household greenhouse gas emissions.
- Cities for Climate Protection$_{TM}$ (CCP$_{TM}$)[58] Australia is assisting over 160 councils throughout Australia to develop

and implement greenhouse reduction action plans, in both their corporate operations and within their communities.

Improvement of the energy efficiency of homes and appliances is one of the most effective ways of reducing greenhouse gas emissions. The Commonwealth, in partnership with State and Territory governments, is working to improve the energy efficiency of domestic appliances. Key publications from this work are *Global Warming Cool it – A Home Guide to Reducing Energy Costs and Greenhouse Gases* and *Your Home*, which has a suite of design guide materials for creating stylish, comfortable, energy-efficient and environmentally friendly houses.[59]

This literature contains advice on the use of a range of rating tools. Some aspects of building performance that can be rated include:

- energy performance of the building envelope;
- energy efficiency of appliances and services;
- performance of individual components (e.g. windows, insulation, wall construction);
- life cycle environmental impact of the materials used, in terms of emissions and depletions; and
- environmental impact of whole buildings.

The energy rating of appliances is mandatory for all of the following electrical products offered for sale in Australia. They must carry an approved energy label:

- refrigerators and freezers;
- clothes washers;
- clothes dryers;
- dishwashers; and
- room air conditioners (single phase).[60]

Accordingly, the AGO has a range of information to help designers with decision-making regarding environmental impacts of buildings.

Trans-professional groups

The role of trans-professional groups has grown in recent years. An example of a trans-professional group is the US Green Building Council. It is described as 'the nation's foremost coali-

tion of leaders from across the building industry working to promote buildings that are environmentally responsible, profitable, and healthy places to live and work'.[61]

The Council was founded in 1993 as a national non-profit organization based in Washington, DC, USA, and has become a centre for the debate and action on environmental issues facing the industry's multiple interests. It has grown to include more than 2,000 international organizations. The Council's purpose is to integrate building industry sectors, lead market transformation and educate owners and practitioners. The governance of the Council comes from a diverse membership of organizations, which is primarily consensus-driven. A committee-based product development system is used to develop and administer tools, such as the LEED$_{TM}$ Green Building Rating System.

Hence the work of this group is in promoting and developing standards for green design and applying these though a rating tool. These tools, called building environmental assessment (BEA) tools, are a key component of the US Green Building Council.

Similar organizations to the US Green Building Council are emerging in other countries, and a world organization has been developed. The World Green Building Council was launched in Austin, Texas, USA. Delegates from nine founding countries – Australia, Japan, India, Korea, Brazil, Mexico, Canada, Spain and the USA – ratified the formal incorporation of the organization.[62] The Green Building Council of Australia is one of these new groups that recognizes the significant environmental impact existing buildings have on the environment. Its mission is the development of performance rating tools for existing buildings. Tools for other building types (industrial, residential, retail, etc.) and phases will be developed in a staged process.

The Green Star tool is based on Australian and international research on the measured environmental impact of buildings. It has been used to determine the categories and criteria, and the weightings of each of the criteria. The development of the tool includes recognition of

the diversity of the property industry players and split incentives. A building's life spans its planning, its design, construction and operation; and its ultimate re-use or demolition. Often the entity responsible for design, construction, and initial financing of a building is different from those operating the building, meeting its operational expenses and paying employee salaries. However, the decisions made at the first phase of building design and construction can significantly affect the costs and efficiencies of later phases.[63]

One of the main barriers noted by the Council is that property is regarded as a long-term asset class, but is financed using short-term economic models. This bias in the financing methodology is a contradiction in the property business. It has an immense impact on the character and quality of the built environment and its environmental impact. The Council's mission is to promote 'green design' as a way of shifting thinking in the property sector away from this short-term financing model. The adoption of a rating tool to establish a design standard for sustainable building is a step towards development by the property industry of a workable sustainable development policy. Brendan Crotty, Chair of the Green Building Council, points out:

> The benefit of an industry based rating tool is that it reflects the realities of the market. Not only will it reflect the realities of the market today but also the realities of the market tomorrow. What the Green Building Council members and particularly the Board – both government and industry representatives alike –understand is, that unless there is some economic benefit in environmentally sound design practices they simply will not be implemented.[64]

Green Star aims to provide a 'comprehensive industry-owned national voluntary environmental rating system, which evaluates the environmental performance of buildings'. It will have rating tools for different phases of the building life cycle (design, fit-out and operation) and for different building classes (office, retail, industrial, residential, etc.). The tool has evolved from existing tools in overseas markets such as the British BREEAM (Building Research Establishment Environmental Assessment Method)[65] system and the American LEED (Leadership in Energy and Environmental Design)[66] system, setting individual environmental measurement criteria with particular relevance to the Australian marketplace and environmental context. Additional features of the tool include:

- use of the 'ESD Guide' developed by the Melbourne Docklands Authority[67] that has been provided to the Council to assist in the development of a local system;

- use of the best regulatory standards to encourage the property industry to improve the environmental performance of development;
- recognition and reward of best practice, Australian and world leadership.

The GBCA is currently piloting the Green Star rating tool for the design phase for new development, or basic building refurbishment, of office buildings. The tool's purpose is

> incorporating green building practices into the project during the design phase, which are viewed as critical for the making of green buildings. Decisions made during design set the project direction and an integrated building design is the cornerstone for developing green buildings.[68]

Green Star is:

- a design guideline for sustainable construction and operation;
- the standard for certification and recognition for green design, construction and operation;
- a green building design training programme to encourage best practices and provide support to the Australian property industry; and
- [It] supports and advances the Council's mission and is consistent with the governing principles, goals and objectives.'[69]

Other groups focus on the business and sustainable development issues of green design. The Rocky Mountain Institute (RMI) is one such group. RMI is a multidisciplinary 'Green Think Tank', located at Snowmass, Colorado.

> Rocky Mountain Institute is an entrepreneurial non-profit organization that fosters the efficient and restorative use of natural, human and other capital to make the world more secure, just, prosperous, and life-sustaining. We do this by inspiring business, civil society, and government to design integrative solutions that create true wealth. Our staff shows businesses, communities, individuals, and governments how to create more wealth and employment, protect and enhance natural and human capital, increase profit and competitive advantage, and enjoy many other benefits –

ROCKY MOUNTAIN INSTITUTE (RMI) HEADQUARTERS BUILDING

Architect: Steve Conger, AIA of the Aspen Design Group
Construction: Amory and Hunter Lovins, 12 professional builders and artisans, and over 100 volunteers

The building is located in Snowmass, Colorado, USA. It is approximately 400 m² (4,000 sq. ft) and was completed in 1984. The building has relevance today as a demonstration building. It has been continuously updated and remains a showcase of energy-efficient design and construction techniques. The main strategies include energy- and resource-efficient technologies, and environmental quality such as natural lighting, good indoor air quality, plants, natural ventilation, and natural sounds such as water.

'The original RMI building has three functions: a house for Amory and Hunter Lovins and their guests; a year-round growing space for fruits, vegetables, herbs, flowers, and fish; and a research center whose use is donated as the headquarters of RMI, a nonprofit resource policy center.'[70]

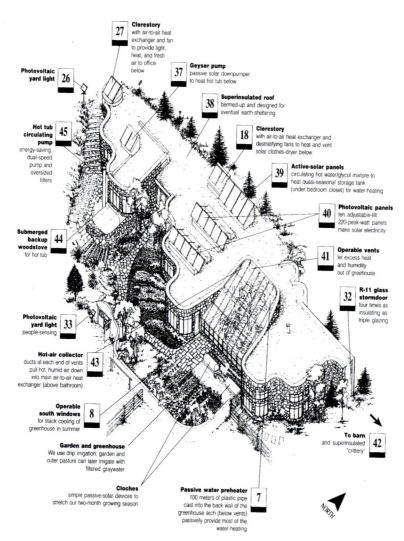

27 **Clerestory**
with air-to-air heat exchanger and fan to provide light, heat, and fresh air to office below

37 **Geyser pump**
passive solar downpumper to heat hot tub below

38 **Superinsulated roof**
bermed-up and designed for eventual earth-sheltering

18 **Clerestory**
with air-to-air heat exchanger and destratifying fans to heat and vent solar clothes-dryer below

39 **Active-solar panels**
circulating hot water/glycol mixture to heat quasi-seasonal storage tank (under bedroom closet) for water-heating

40 **Photovoltaic panels**
ten adjustable-tilt 220-peak-watt panels make solar electricity

41 **Operable vents**
let excess heat and humidity out of greenhouse

32 **R-11 glass stormdoor**
four times as insulating as triple glazing

26 **Photovoltaic yard light**

45 **Hot tub circulating pump**
energy-saving, dual-speed pump and oversized filters

44 **Submerged backup woodstove**
for hot tub

33 **Photovoltaic yard light**
people-sensing

43 **Hot-air collector**
ducts at each end of vents pull hot, humid air down into main air-to-air heat exchanger (above bathroom)

8 **Operable south windows**
for stack cooling of greenhouse in summer

Garden and greenhouse
We use drip irrigation; garden and outer pasture can later irrigate with filtered graywater

Cloches
simple passive-solar devices to stretch our two-month growing season

7 **Passive water preheater**
100 meters of plastic pipe cast into the back wall of the greenhouse arch (below vents) passively provide most of the water-heating

42 **To barn**
and superinsulated 'crittery'

NORTH

2.4 Bird's-eye view of the Rocky Mountain Institute (RMI) HQ building showing the strategies used in this demonstration.

2.5   Rocky Mountain Institute (RMI) headquarters building. Site response allows for a passive heating system that enables tropical plants to grow. The building is partly earth-integrated, which is an effective strategy in a climate such as Colorado's, with its extreme temperatures characteristic of the continental climate.

largely by doing what they do far more efficiently. Our work is independent, non-adversarial, and trans-ideological, with a strong emphasis on market-based solutions.[71]

The Rocky Mountain Institute was pioneered by Amory Lovins and has steered initiatives into many areas of sustainable design. Much of the ethos of the group is manifest in Amory Lovins's own home, the former office of the Institute in Snowmass. Visits to the Institute are not complete without a tour of this building. Designed at a time when green design was emerging into the construction landscape, this experimental house demonstrates the capability of green design to reduce environmental impacts. The building was completed in 1984 and has been continuously updated since, so that its many innovative features are as up to date today as they were when the home was first built. This building is described in detail on the Rocky Mountain Institute website.[72]

The Institute's emphasis is on making the business case for sustainability. Ideas and arguments in support of sustainable design appear in the current book, *Natural Capitalism*.[73]

Another key direction of the Rocky Mountain Institute is to promote the business case for sustainability through partnerships. One project that is presently evolving is 'The Natural Edge Project'.[74] This project has formed international partnerships and has launched a companion website highlighting current pioneers and future directions for sustainability in the Australasian region.

The core strength of this not-for-profit project is the emphasis on collaboration with peak bodies like the Institution of Engineers Australia (IEAust); Commonwealth Scientific and Industrial Research Organisation (CSIRO); the World Federation of Engineering Organizations (WFEO); Australian Green Development Forum; environment–industry advocates and members; government agencies, and acting in partnership with the Rocky Mountain Institute.

Table 2.4   Key leverage points in the design process to introduce sustainability standards

Leverage points	Purpose
Site and building master planning	Environmental impact assessment and building siting/land use to green planning guidelines
The building design brief	Specification of green design standards and costing planning resolved
Council design approval and third party certification	Meet baseline government standards and 'Certification of Best Practice'
Construction and third party certification	Sustainable building and 'Certification of Best Practice'
Post construction and third party certification	Evaluation of design and continued environmental management of the project

FLOORPLAN

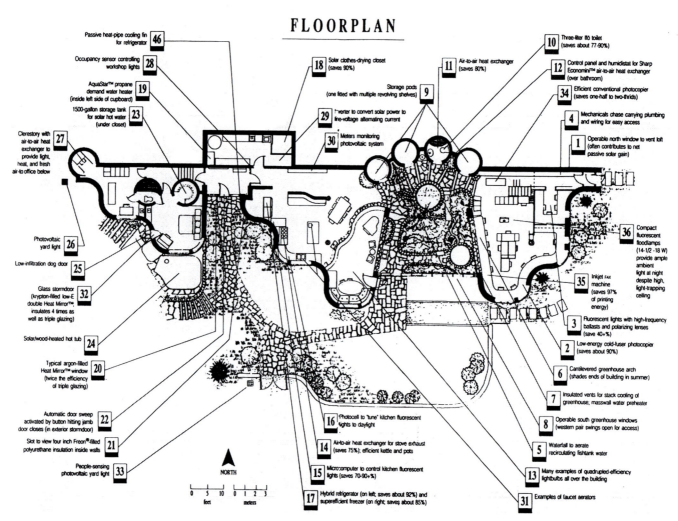

46 Passive heat-pipe cooling fin for refrigerator

28 Occupancy sensor controlling workshop lights

19 AquaStar™ propane demand water heater (inside left side of cupboard)

23 1500-gallon storage tank for solar hot water (under closet)

27 Clerestory with air-to-air heat exchanger to provide light, heat, and fresh air to office below

26 Photovoltaic yard light

25 Low-infiltration dog door

32 Glass stormdoor (krypton-filled low-E double Heat Mirror™ insulates 4 times as well as triple glazing)

24 Solar/wood-heated hot tub

20 Typical argon-filled Heat Mirror™ window (twice the efficiency of triple glazing)

22 Automatic door sweep activated by button hitting jamb door closes (in exterior stormdoor)

21 Slot to view four inch Freon®-filled polyurethane insulation inside walls

33 People-sensing photovoltaic yard light

18 Solar clothes-drying closet (saves 90%)

9 Storage pods (one fitted with multiple revolving shelves)

29 Inverter to convert solar power to line-voltage alternating current

30 Meters monitoring photovoltaic system

11 Air-to-air heat exchanger (saves 80%)

10 Three-liter ifö toilet (saves about 77-90%)

12 Control panel and humidistat for Sharp Economini™ air-to-air heat exchanger (over bathroom)

34 Efficient conventional photocopier (saves one-half to two-thirds)

4 Mechanicals chase carrying plumbing and wiring for easy access

1 Operable north window to vent loft (often contributes to net passive solar gain)

36 Compact fluorescent floodlamps (14-1/2 -18 W) provide ample ambient light at night despite high, light-trapping ceiling

35 Inkjet FAX machine (saves 97% of printing energy)

3 Fluorescent lights with high-frequency ballasts and polarizing lenses (save 40+%)

2 Low-energy cold-fuser photocopier (saves about 90%)

6 Cantilevered greenhouse arch (shades ends of building in summer)

7 Insulated vents for stack cooling of greenhouse; masswall water preheater

8 Operable south greenhouse windows (western pair swings open for access)

5 Waterfall to aerate recirculating fishtank water

13 Many examples of quadrupled-efficiency lightbulbs all over the building

31 Examples of faucet aerators

16 'Photocell to 'tune' kitchen fluorescent lights to daylight

14 Air-to-air heat exchanger for stove exhaust (saves 75%); efficient kettle and pots

15 Microcomputer to control kitchen fluorescent lights (saves 70-90+%)

17 Hybrid refrigerator (on left; saves about 92%) and superefficient freezer (on right; saves about 85%)

NORTH

0 5 10   0 1 2 3
feet   meters

2.6 Rocky Mountain Institute (RMI) headquarters building. Floor plan showing strategies used in this demonstration project.

Building environmental assessment (BEA) and creating environmental standards

The Institute has a section dedicated to green building projects and building environmental assessment. It supports developers who wish to follow the green development path. Discussion with Huston Eubank, Director of Green Development at RMI, points to the work carried out by the Institute. A key aspect of this work is that done by such leaders as Bill Brown and Bill Godfrey on the development of environmental standards such as those that underpin the LEED rating system. Eubank argues that these standards form a cornerstone to green development and a basis from which best practice can evolve. The Institute is working with the ASHRAE committees to develop new standards for energy efficiency and thermal comfort.

'Leverage points' in design

Eubank suggests there are 'key leverage points' in introducing environmental standards as a cornerstone of the development process (Table 2.4). One of these points is the design brief, which is why standards like LEED need to be factored into the project at the feasibility stage.

The term 'leverage point' here is derived partly from financial usage, but also partly from its structural meaning in terms of green design. The term refers to opportunities in the progress of a project's scope, shape and form where principles of green design can be applied that will have significant impact on the building's operational performance. An example of a leverage point is seen at the master planning stage of design where the designer has control of the overall orientation and form of the buildings for micro-climate control. If good passive design principles are not applied at this point, a range of energy-efficiency benefits can be lost. Similarly, with the design process there are points where checks and balances can be made to facilitate the application of green strategies. Further analysis shows a range of opportunities for leveraging green design.

Interestingly, this analysis implies a high degree of control of the design process, and the extent to which design professionals can take advantage of this remains to be seen. An incentive for this kind of control can be found in the use of certification systems for green buildings.

Certification of green buildings

Creating standards and examining how these can be implemented cannot be complete without some method of compliance auditing, so a key outcome of much of this work on standards was the creation of a 'third party certification approach' that makes use of tools such as LEED. This is seen as a way to enhance the design in the same way that quantity surveyors have exercised cost control over building budgets. It espouses the well-known saying, 'If you 'can't measure it you can't manage it.' Environmental performance can be managed through auditing and accounting, in a similar way to costs.

Plugging the green knowledge gap

The link between green design and management appears as an emerging trend in the work of these trans-professional groups, and this link has revealed that the building industry is still grappling with a huge knowledge gap, not only in what green design is, but also in how to build and manage these buildings throughout their operational cycle. As nature abhors a vacuum, the role of the trans-professional groups has been to fill the knowledge gap.

Professional groups

Professional groups such as the American Institute of Architects (AIA) and the Royal Australian Institute of Architects (RAIA) have embraced ESD through a number of initiatives.

Sustainable design
ETHICAL AND EDUCATIONAL MECHANISMS

Much of the work in this area by building professional groups has been to create ethics statements embracing ESD, which have then evolved into educational programmes about ESD in liaison with allied groups.

The American Institute of Architects, for example, through its Committee on the Environment (COTE), has developed a number of initiatives to facilitate environmental improvement, stating that 'the suggestion that green design in the USA is only about environmental management underplays the capacity of inspiring designers to think creatively about environmental issues'. The Institute's mission is 'to sustain and improve the environment by advancing and disseminating environmental knowledge and values, and advocating the best design practices to integrate built and natural systems to the profession, industry, and public'.[75] It has five main goals:

1 Educate architects about the environment and the energy-related impact of design decisions and encourage active membership participation in these activities.
2 Communicate the AIA's environment and energy-related concerns to the public and private sectors and influence the decisions of the public, professionals, clients, and public officials on the impact of their environmental and energy-related decisions.
3 Foster leadership among architects in all facets of environmental decision-making.
4 Establish and maintain alliances with environmental organizations such as the US Green Building Council, Urban Land Institute, American Solar Energy Society, Sustainable Buildings Industry Council, and UIA World Congress of Architects.
5 Promote implementation of a sustainable design programme in architecture schools.

In 2003, the COTE organized an annual design competition to identify and recognize the benefits of a high-performance, sustainable design approach, and to educate the architectural community and the public about the enhanced value that sustainable design delivers to developers, building owners and occupants. It acknowledges architects as experts in the creation of energy-efficient and environmentally responsible design solutions.[76]

SUSTAINABLE DESIGN TOOLS

The RAIA has developed a number of sustainable design tools to support ESD.[77] The first of these tools is used to implement this approach by reshaping the design process (design phase tool); the second assesses the results of the product of the process though an awards system for ecological sustainable development (post-construction assessment).

The design phase tool is driven directly by the RAIA Environment Policy and consists of identifying sustainable strategies to be applied during the phases of design.[78] The objective is to implement sustainable design practices. In order for architects to meet the objectives, they should consider the four following interrelated tenets of environmental sustainability at every stage of a building's life:

- *Bio-diversity*. Protect and restore ecological diversity, health and functionality.
- *Resources*. Optimize their use, especially non-renewable resources.
- *Pollution*. Minimize pollution of soil, air and water.
- *Quality of life*. Improve the health, safety and comfort of building users.[79]

The strategies are categorized according to environmental impact criteria and are related to the stages of the design process. Although this document is called a 'Note', it is a tool aimed at backing up the RAIA Environment Policy. The intention is to create a, 'checklist of ESD issues that should be considered during the creation and use of buildings'.[80]

The post construction tool is called the Ecologically Sustainable Development Award Checklist, and provides a set of ESD criteria for evaluating the building. A scoring system is used to evaluate the building according to each of the criteria. Experts carry out the assessment.[81] The impression gained from the checklists is that there is an intention to reshape the design process through policy and the application of ESD strategies, and that the policy should apply to all buildings.

Additionally, the strategies are cross-referenced to further detailed advice in the Institute's Environmental Design Guide.[82] This approach aims to assist architects to provide appropriate professional advice in the context of sustainable design.

A question arises as to how these tools and their associated advocacy systems compare and complement initiatives being developed by other groups. The trans-professional groups such as the Green Building Councils have developed tools for assessing buildings that are also shaped around the green design process. How can harmonization be achieved between these emerging tools and systems, and how can this help to avoid the present confusion in the industry?

Responses

The responses to the need for ecological sustainable development can be summarized as a number of changes to design thinking and practice, as they are viewed by the main stakeholders in the ecological development process. Research from the UK seen previously identifies an inertia in the market. The primary stakeholders in the present development process are the investors, developers, occupiers, contractors and other participants in the building design and process. The argument mounted is as follows.

- First, investors and developers see no demand for environmentally efficient buildings and won't pay for them.
- Second, occupiers would like more environment-efficient buildings but find that there is little choice available.
- Third, building design professionals and builders would design and build environmentally, but developers don't ask them to.

This is about making the environmental case. The development process needs champions for ESD: building design professionals are in an ideal position to be those champions.

Addressing this inertia has meant developing cases for green buildings that respond to the needs of each stakeholder group. For investors and developers, the focus is on creating the business case for green buildings; for occupiers, it is about the social order and milieu (although more research is needed to argue this strongly). Finally, the environmental case can be argued with building design professionals and builders, in the context of the development process. How can the environmental case be up-streamed to a core issue in the minds of the other stakeholders?

Table 2.5 List of benefits of green buildings[83]

US Green Building Council arguments for 'building green'

Environmental benefits:
- enhance and protect ecosystems and biodiversity
- improve air and water quality
- reduce solid waste
- conserve natural resources

Economic benefits:
- reduce operating costs
- enhance asset value and profits
- improve employee productivity and satisfaction
- optimize life cycle economic performance

Health and community benefits:
- improve air, thermal and acoustic environments
- enhance occupant comfort and health
- minimize strain on local infrastructure
- contribute to overall quality of life

Components of the business case

Definitions and benefits of green building

Some of the main outcomes from the initiatives to promote green design are simplification of the definition of green buildings and articulation of their benefits. The motive for these is that developers and clients are unlikely to embrace green design without a clear and concise understanding of green buildings and their benefits (Table 2.5).

The US Green Building Council has developed a definition of green design, which is focused on the need to design buildings to reduce environmental impact. The main argument is that the built environment has a profound impact on our natural environment, economy, health and productivity. For example, in the United States buildings account for the following impacts:

- 36 per cent of total energy uses, in particular 65 per cent of electricity consumption;
- 30 per cent of greenhouse gas emissions;
- 30 per cent of raw materials use;
- 30 per cent of waste output, involving 136 million tons annually;
- 12 per cent of potable water consumption.[84]

The main strategy is to take advantage of 'breakthroughs in building science, technology and operations which are available to designers, builders and owners to ... maximize both economic and environmental performance'.[85] The benefits are not just confined to environmental issues.

At the heart of the problem are the economic barriers to green design: 'There is an enduring and widespread perception in the industry that green buildings inevitably carry a higher cost premium for design and construction.'[86]

First cost, least cost or value adding

The main design premise used for many buildings is to consider the capital cost of the building as the first order, and only, decision-making criterion. This has come to be called the 'first cost' or 'least cost' issue, a single criterion approach to designing buildings, in its crudest form suggesting that the only decision is about cost. This is not only simplistic but also unintelligent, since it reduces the procurement process to operating by the rules of the bazaar.

First cost can be countered by many arguments, at both policy and strategy levels. The US Green Building Council sees important counter-arguments emerging from the social imperative for a change to green building: first, by promoting green design as innovative, since innovation in design is seen as very important; and second, by characterizing companies that build green buildings as 'progressive organizations', which is equally important. These two factors, it is argued, comprise a social imperative for change.

Research by the US Green Building Council has also indicated that, although sustainable design may increase the capital or first cost of a development by 1–3 per cent, this depends to a large extent on the level of reduction in environmental impact. Some ways to progress beyond the first cost barrier by promoting value adding of green buildings include:

- adjusting budgets incrementally, to add 'green design strategies' progressively;
- increasing design fees to demonstrate life cycle benefits;
- utilizing government grants to support costs;
- using performance contracting to fund additional first costs; and
- trading-off first costs with life costs.[87]

Life cycle thinking and worker productivity

Adopting the 'life cycle perspective' is the second major step in implementing green design. Life cycle thinking is a central part of green design because it shifts priorities to a more holistic view of building performance. So what is life cycle thinking?

Studies of productivity analyse the performance of the building during its lifetime. As an example, effective daylighting design can result in real performance benefits: studies of the academic performance of school students have shown the benefits of using daylight. The Heschong Mahone Group reports:

Controlling for all other influences, we found that students with the most daylighting in their classrooms progressed 20% faster on math tests and 26% on reading tests in one year than those with the least. Similarly, students with the largest window areas were found to progress 15% faster in math and 23% faster in reading, than those with the least. And students that had a well-designed skylight in their room, one that diffused the daylight throughout the room and which allowed teachers to control the amount of daylight entering the room, also improved approximately 20% faster than those students without a skylight.[88]

The social case: more research is needed

Health and well-being

An argument that is currently under scrutiny is based on statistics concerning the proportion of time people spend indoors and the deterioration of people's health attributable to building-related factors. The US Green Building Council has cited a range of research findings that point to the present building stock as contributing to many new health complaints from users.[89] The evidence is still circumstantial but it points to serious reasons for concern.

Americans on average spend more than 90 per cent of their time indoors.[90] New chemicals have grown in number – 4 million since 1915, with 1,000 new chemicals added every year.[91] The number of asthma sufferers in the US is more than 17 million.[92] There has been an increase in the incidence of asthma of 75 per cent[93] from 1980 to 1994. The annual US direct health-care cost for asthma is more than US$9.8 billion (plus indirect costs from lost productivity of $2.8 billion).[94] In the US 38 per cent of people are affected by allergies.[95] These figures mean

that about one-third of the workforce is sensitive to airborne particulates and chemicals.

Given the high levels of indoor occupancy, a shift in design priorities is needed to avoid significant loss to productivity of the workforce. *Environmental Building News* suggests:

Our health and well-being are inextricably linked to the buildings in which we spend the vast majority of our time. The resources expended and productivity lost due to indoor environmental quality problems have a huge impact on our economy and the well-being of millions of people. A systems approach to solving these problems is needed, in which architects, builders, building managers, building scientists, and medical professionals work closely together. We need to begin using the best current practices for ensuring good indoor environmental quality, and we need to develop a comprehensive research agenda so that we can gain a better understanding of how buildings influence occupant health – and what to do about it.[96]

Worker productivity and indoor environmental quality

One of the main benefits of green design was identified in the early 1970s with the design of the NMB Bank Headquarters in Amsterdam. This green building delivered life cycle benefits, and demonstrated the importance of the work environment for worker productivity.[97] Although a direct correlation between environmental quality and the output of workers is yet to be conclusively proven, there is growing evidence that poor environmental quality leads to poor performance and is manifest in absenteeism.

The US Green Building Council cites an estimated US$29–168 billion in national productivity losses per year. For buildings that have a high population of employees, salary costs are the major component of their budgets.[98] Small increases in productivity can mean considerable savings in running costs and make it financially viable, from the life cycle perspective, to use green strategies.

Up-streaming the environmental case

Establishing a road map

The major difficulty in making the environmental case is the changing context of each organization and design project. Green design appears complex, and raises the questions of where to start and how to change. These are prevailing questions faced by clients and designers.

The US Green Building Council has established a schedule of ten steps for starting a 'Green Building Program'. The ten steps are as follows:

1   Creating the policy context with a framework of sustainable development.
2   Assessing opportunities and barriers.
3   Using best start-up practices for working within the political, social and environmental realities of the area.
4   Capitalizing on organizational resources through partnerships.
5   Working with key decision-makers.
6   Developing 'green guidelines'.
7   Adopting, adapting and supplementing the LEED rating tool to avoid 'Green Washing' criticism and to add rigour to the programme.
8   Using incentives to address the first cost barrier.
9   Developing training and outreach programmes to up-skill design teams.
10 Creating exemplary or showcase buildings to address the life cycle costing barrier.

The basis of the LEED system, which forms the environmental model underpinning the Council's work, is discussed in subsequent chapters. Other initiatives involve use of the work of the US Green Building Council and the Rocky Mountain Institute (RMI).

Reshaping the design process

In order to make a case to developers and investors for environmental benefits, there is a need to examine closely the capacity within design organizations to deliver green buildings – without this capacity it is difficult to make arguments for green design. This procedure includes reshaping design and procurement processes. Professional groups such as the RAIA have established mechanisms such as education, design guidelines, award systems for green buildings and checklist strategies for reshaping the design process. Design practices therefore need to adopt and adapt these available systems to build capability.

There is also a need to be aware of the issues of harmonization and standardization of various BEA tools and systems. The current plethora of tools is perplexing, and part of the reshaping of the design process means examining the appropriate tool for the project and advising investors and developers accordingly. This raises the challenge for professional groups such as the AIA and RAIA to harmonize the other BEA tools within the industry to present a cohesive approach to green design.

The design approval (DA)

Investors and developers are beginning to appreciate the use of green design and associated BEA tools as a method of fast-tracking through the governmental DA process. The reasons for this are similar to those for other environmental impact tools (EIA). The onus is on the developer to demonstrate appropriate environmental performance – not just for the initial impact of the project, but including impacts of the building during construction and during its life. BEA tools represent an easy-to-apply standard of environmental performance.

Summary

The need to respond to the environmental imperative has led the development of principles for creating ESD. These principles can be applied through various initiatives; some are legislative and push change forward, while others are pull initiatives, using incentives. The application of this approach can be seen in the UK, which has developed a combination of initiatives to support the move to ESD. Similarly, in Australia, a similar pattern is emerging. In the USA the emergence of trans-professional groups, combinations of architects, engineers, developers and other building design professionals, have shifted practice though voluntary action. A range of mechanisms have been developed – education, design guidelines, BEA tools, training and advice – and are now available. Professional groups that represent architects have developed their own approach. The response to the environmental imperative can be summarized in the way a number of cases – business, social and environmental – have been made for green buildings.

The next part of the argument is structured around the need for advancing green design by using tools and methods to assist with reshaping the design process. The following chapter provides details of specific tools and systems.

Part TWO

Pathways

3.1 Healthy Home Project. Architects: Richard Hyde and Upendra Rajapshka.
Advancing green design involves solving existing problems in new ways.

Chapter 3

Advancing green design

In the preceding chapter a picture emerged that shows that designers are working in a changing context. Yencken and Wilkinson speak of the movement towards sustainability as a journey, yet in reality sustainability is an outcome of the way in which society lives and works. If sustainability is the destination, then green design and green buildings are aspects of the journey for building designers.[1] If this is so, what is the green approach to design?

The aim of this chapter is first to expand the definition of green design developed in the Introduction; second, to define the tenets of a green approach to design, giving consideration the complexity of the process; and third, to identify some of the opportunities for advancing green design within the design process, in particular the use of tools and methods. Reference will be made in the discussion to the Healthy Home Project in Australia, which is a demonstration project that used a green design process (see Figures 3.1 and 3.2). The opportunities for advancing green design are defined as three pathways, and the arguments for using these pathways are examined.

Defining green design

The argument developed in the Introduction suggested that green design is a response to the new Age of Information and Ecology of the twentieth century. While green design can mean utilizing ecological principles in design, a substantive dilemma arises if green buildings do not provide improved environmental performance in their operations. *Form follows environment* is a simplified description of the approach, yet there is a substantive

requirement for green buildings to provide both a meaningful expression of the ecological principles on which the design is based and a high level of environmental performance in operation (subject to appropriate management).

Form without substance

Examining the nature of ecology can extend this argument. Ecology was established as a study of the relationships and interactions between individual organisms and their natural as well as developed environments. Green architecture is concerned with these interactions and relationships as a fundamental design premise. Yet this is not an easy task, given the complexity of the relationships in nature. What approach should designers take to achieve this goal?

This is essentially an argument about *substance*, that is, environmental performance, versus *form*, the meaningful architectural expression of the ecological concepts that created the building. In essence the term *form* can mean a number of things: giving users a sense of being closer to nature; using the forms in nature to generate the building form. *Substance*, on the other hand, can be thought of as taking from nature and also giving back. Put another way, it is an argument about how green buildings may use nature to provide the wellspring of design ideas but also assist with repairing its ecological cycles that are damaged by humankind. Creating a green design approach is central to this definition.

3.2 Exterior view of the Healthy Home Project showing the lightweight construction.

Creating a green design approach

Creating a green design approach has involved addressing a number of major issues: first, how to tap into the green design knowledge base – there are many sources of information but those that are most useful are well-structured and coordinated; second, how to better engage the client and users in green design by developing a design process that provides a better understanding of the issues, and hence contributes to more confident decision-making; and third, how to better encourage and assist the builder and the manufacturing process to deliver a more environmental building – for example, many plumbers lack familiarity with solar hot water heaters, and green design involves addressing this barrier. The overview of the Healthy Home Project given in the box below details some of the measures for addressing these issues primarily in terms of working with the site, climate, life and material systems to improve environmental performance. Central to this project was tapping into the green design knowledge base.

Tapping into green knowledge

Many of the professional organizations that represent building designers have addressed green design issues by changing their mission statements and charters of professional ethics. These are a useful starting point for design professionals seeking a green approach to design.

One useful example is that developed by the Australian Council of Building Design Professionals (BDP). The BDP is a body of professional associations of architects, engineers, quantity surveyors, landscape architects and planners united to achieve better practices, policies, legislation and regulation for the design of the built environment. The BDP's major initiative is the development of the BDP Environmental Design Guide, which aims to further building design professionals' understanding of the importance and nature of ecological sustainable development (ESD) as it applies to the built environment. The Design Guide 'consists of five principles: consciousness raising; education and information; increasing the sophistication of the debate; catalyzing new thinking; and broadening society's understanding of the role of ESD'.[2]

The BDP Guide has been designed to link to each stage of the design process to provide information for the specific tasks of each design issue. Table 3.1 is a model of the BDP Environmental Design Guide process of design for sustainable development.

A matrix has been developed to match information about environmental issues related to the design process.[3] Underpinning BDP are a number of ethical principles that are used to promote sustainability in the following ways:

- maintain and/or restore biodiversity and biophysical ecologies;[4]
- maximize resource-use efficiency and reduce or eliminate unsustainable consumption of resources;
- minimize adverse emissions to air, soil and water;
- maximize the health, safety, comfort and productivity of people and places;
- integrate ESD objectives into all projects and all project design, development, delivery and commissioning processes;
- minimize negative cumulative impacts and generate positive cumulative impacts within and between artificial and biophysical environments over time;

OVERVIEW OF THE HEALTHY HOME PROJECT

The house is of lightweight timber construction. An innovative glue-lam portal frame construction has been utilized. This is common in industrial and commercial buildings but is new in the design of single dwellings. The portal frame allows a great degree of flexibility in the design of the internal spaces of the house. It frees up the structure internally, allowing large volumes, the promotion of stack ventilation and large numbers of openings to allow cross ventilation.

SITE AND CLIMATES

The location of the house 200 metres from the Pacific coast, with the Australian continent to the west and the ocean to the east, determines a distinctive warm temperate climate and weather pattern. In summer the site experiences wester-lies in the early morning. The wind swings around through the south during the day, to be easterly in the afternoon and evening. It then swings back through the south to the west overnight. This is a land breeze/sea breeze combination typi-cal of a coastal location. In winter the conditions are dominated by prevailing winds from the south and west.

The site has almost unobstructed solar access throughout the year. However, to the east and south-east are two large two-storey dwellings and a large jacaranda tree. These objects cause the winds at a low level to be redirected.

LIFE SYSTEMS

The house is analysed here in terms of its performance during the extreme seasons of winter and summer. The tempera-ture measurements from a height of 1,800 mm above the downstairs floor level are used in all comparisons between exter-nal and internal temperatures.

The average maximum air temperature for summer conditions was reduced internally by 2.0°C. This reduction places the average maximum within the acceptable summer comfort zone. External air temperatures in the shade measured over the 92 days of summer revealed that only 15 days had a maximum within the comfort zone. Internally, on the other hand, air temperatures show an improvement; 53 days were measured to have a maximum within the comfort zone.

Moreover, on extreme days with external temperatures of 40° or more the internal temperatures were reduced to by 7–8°. During these very hot days the house is sealed; windows are closed and, as heat gains are minimal because of the highly efficient envelope, the internal temperatures remain below external temperatures.

MATERIAL SYSTEMS

The project is an attempt to demonstrate how a new, suburban house can achieve a high level of environmental sustain-ability by employing, among other environmental strategies, improved air quality, passive solar design, active solar sys-tems and a selection of low-embodied-energy materials. It challenges existing norms of house design and legislation concerning the on-site reuse of resources such as water and the collection, purification and use of rainwater. This has been achieved in the form of an environmental prototype; a single residential dwelling has been constructed on the Gold Coast, Queensland, Australia.

Table 3.1 Framework used by Building Design Professionals (BDP) for relating environmental issues to the design process

BDP design stages	Energy	Water	Waste	Biodiversity	Materials	Transport	Indoor air quality	Health and comfort
Pre-design	✓	✓	✓	✓	✓	✓	✓	✓
Planning	✓	✓	✓	✓				
Siting	✓	✓	✓	✓	✓	✓		
Concept design	✓	✓	✓	✓	✓	✓	✓	✓
Detailed design					✓		✓	✓
Documentation					✓	✓	✓	✓
Construction	✓	✓	✓	✓	✓	✓		
Construction management	✓	✓	✓	✓	✓	✓		
Building operation and management	✓	✓	✓	✓	✓	✓	✓	✓

STRATEGY SELECTION PROCESS USED FOR THE HEALTHY HOME PROJECT

The following strategies were considered in the design:

- spatial organization that provides thermal delight and environmental connectivity while meeting user needs and lifestyle choice;
- small building footprint to minimize the site utilization and maximize existing vegetation;
- north orientation and shading to maximize breeze in summer, and provide solar access in winter and solar exclusion in summer;
- lightweight north-eastern-orientated building skin to provide rapid heat gain in winter;
- ground-connected mass construction to lower storey to provide 'cool pools' for daytime living in summer and 'warm pools' for evenings in winter;
- pavilion plan form with open section to provide cross ventilation for summer cooling;
- utilization of servant spaces to buffer served space from westerly sun and heat gain;
- use of a breezeway and water feature to promote ventilation and evaporative cooling between pavilions through the venturi effect;
- use of an atrium space to promote the convective cooling of internal spaces in summer calm conditions and provide light to deep plan spaces;
- utilization of a skeletal frame system that has low embodied energy, and is factory-made and prefabricated to high quality, to provide moment joints to resist racking loads, give internal planning flexibility and maximize openings for ventilation;
- utilization of smart window technology to reduce glare and solar gain to interior spaces;
- utilization of materials that have minimum of off-gassing and effects on human health;
- provision of storage and hydraulic systems for rainwater and wastewater for recycling and site irrigation, thus minimizing mains water usage;
- utilization of water feature to provide white noise and feeling of calm in the home;
- cool colour scheme and landscaping to promote psychological comfort;
- installation of grid-connected PV (photovoltaic) system to export power to the grid during the day and import power at night;
- selection of energy-efficient appliances that minimize power utilization;
- automated building monitoring system to audit performance and security; and
- use of gas fuel for heating to reduce carbon production.

3.3 Healthy Home Project. Green design is concerned with the supply chain, selecting materials and energy systems. Rapidly renewable materials like timber combined with radiant barriers to form composite lightweight construction gives a cost-effective and high-performing solution set in warm climates.

- reflect and respond to global, regional and local impacts of local actions and practices;
- promote equity within and between generations;
- embody a precautionary approach to the environmental consequences of decision-making;[5]
- leverage multidisciplinary teams and skills and incorporate stakeholder and community input.

Involving the client and user

A major issue that has emerged is the relationship between the client, the user (if they are not the same) and the designers. Experience has taught that by and large the client sets the level of the sustainability within a project. There are some basic reasons for this.

First, the brief for a project originates with the client and it is at the inception of a project that the level of sustainability is established. It is important in the green approach to design to involve the client in the discussions of environmental issues from the start.

For clients, particularly clients who have not previously procured a building, the concept of green design is elusive, so a set of activities has been devised to assist both the client and the design professional to realize the environmental aims of the project. Defining principles, developing strategies, and examining performance improvements in terms of comfort and reducing environmental impacts can be core elements of the discussion with clients and users in green design.

Defining principles as a way of understanding sustainability

Principles are guidelines or rules by which a building should be designed. The Vales[6] were among the first architects to frame sustainability as a set of principles and they developed six principles of green architecture:

- minimizing new resources and recycling existing resources;
- conserving energy in the life cycle of the building;
- working with climate to utilize the available resources generated – from wind, water and sun;
- respect for the site and for impact on the environment;
- respect for users and their health and well-being; and
- holism.

The last principle, holism, is often misunderstood and is the understanding of the building as an interconnected part of a larger environmental system.

3.4 Healthy Home Project. Interior of the first floor of the home. The interlinking spaces for ventilation and daylight demonstrate the benefits of green design. The underlying brief of this house was to be healthy for the user and healthy for the environment, and this became a central part of the design thinking.

Developing strategies

Accommodating the issues of holism within the discussion has led to some confusion as a result of the increased complexity of interactions and implications that this creates. It has therefore become necessary to scope a project in terms of the strategies and techniques that can be used to improve environmental performance. Tools such as checklist are good starting points for this approach. Table 3.4 shows the selection of strategies that were used in the Healthy Home Project. Some strategies were eventually realized; some were not. The use of strategic thinking about green design can mean at worst a shopping list of green technologies, and at best an opportunity for brainstorming and creative speculation on what can be achieved.

In this context the concept of holism has been expanded to represent a 'performance view' of building design. It is necessary to link design to measures of performance and this is done by developing and using performance indicators.

Enter the era of the 'indicator'

A third point of dialogue, apart from principles and strategies, is to gauge the predicted performance of the building once it has been built and is in operation. The performance approach to building design revolves around finding meaningful indicators of building performance that reduce environmental impacts. This raises questions of what indicators are, and how they are to be linked to some of the larger-scale problems of environmental impact such as ozone depletion and loss of biodiversity. Further questions arise as to how to link this back to the design issues that are familiar to building designers.

The term 'indicators' is rapidly becoming a key construct for assessing the performance of green buildings. The assumption behind this trend is that performance can be measured, and so some manageable method of measurement is needed. For example, 'energy use' can be expressed as a measurement calculated in kWh/per year.

The data needs to be easy to identify and a methodology is needed to collect and analyse it. It may be easy to favour the performance view, but a number of problems are still to be resolved. In the Healthy Home,[7] the quantitative indicators were converted to qualitative indicators and applied to design issues. Having passive design strategies in place with the appropriate techniques was found to be a significant indicator of sustainability during the design process. With these in place, the predicted heating and cooling energy use of near zero kW/h per year can be achieved. This is not to say that performance is not an ongoing issue: the Healthy Home undergoes continuous performance assessment to monitor the sustainability of the building in use.

Selecting sustainable techniques, a supply chain and the solution set

The third set of issues in developing a green design approach concerns selecting materials and construction systems that are environmentally friendly. The term 'supply chain' has been developed to focus attention on the wide range of materials and production systems that make up the building procurement process. The search for green materials has been hampered by lack of research into the life cycle assessment of materials and the translation of this information into usable data for designers and their clients. Some fundamental questions have been raised about how to utilize design strategies and techniques in building design to successfully deliver improved environmental performance when the information to support decision-making is not available. This raises questions of professional boundaries and extends the responsibilities of building designers.[8]

An important role of the designer is to select the strategies and techniques used to realize the building. Sustainable design requires components to be sourced locally where possible, yet it is necessary to be suitably circumspect about this so that a number of manufacturing companies can be considered in order to allow for commercial competition. This can be a major problem, which we call the barrier of the 'supply chain'.

One of the major reasons for the design of the Healthy Home was to help define the supply chain and to assist in locating some 30 companies, which supplied the environmental materials, components and systems for the house. The issue of creating a supply chain of materials, components and systems is being addressed as new websites are emerging that link designers and manufactures and help create a supply chain.

Navigating the complexity of green design

The development of green design in practice involves additional complexities and uncertainties about the process issues. These centre on the belief that to improve environmental performance the process by which buildings are designed should be more accountable in terms of the measure taken to address environmental issues. An emerging debate concerns how to better use both the design phase and the operational phase of the building. Conventional design thinking has separated these two phases conveniently into the design phase, which is prior to construction, and the operational phase after construction. A prevailing complexity is how to reconcile these two phases into a meaningful whole.

The design phase versus the operational phase

Some favour using the *operational phase* of the building to address environmental performance issues. A process of monitoring and auditing buildings is advocated, such as the collection of data on the amounts of energy and water used and types and quantities of waste produced. Measures are then put in place to reduce impacts over time. A central part of this view is that continual improvement is the way eventually to achieve a reduction of environmental impacts.

Another view is to work back up the building life cycle to the design phase and apply similar thinking there.

Working with the design phase

The *design phase* of a building can be viewed as having four steps (see Table 3.2), each with particular documentation outcomes:

- pre-design, which produces the brief;
- schematic design, which produces the preliminary documentation;
- detail design, which produces the completed documentation and construction; and
- evaluation, which is usually done post construction.

It would be wrong to view this classification as a design process. It is simply a series of steps to arrive at specific points in the resolution of the building. A number of tools have been developed to help building designers integrate sustainability issues within the design phase. The last ten years has seen a

Table 3.2 Design phase classification[9]

Stages	RIBA	AIA
1 Pre-design	Inception Feasibility Outline proposals Scheme design	Programming
2 Sketch		Schematic design
3 Detail	Detail design Production information Bills of quantities Tender action Project planning Operation on site Completion	Design development Construction documentation Bid Construction supervision Commissioning
4 Post occupancy	Feedback	Post occupancy survey

plethora of ideas and systems, which are the product of considerable thought and research.

It is beyond the scope of this section to define all the tools available to designers, but Watson provides a useful summary:[10]

- goal setting;
- checklists;
- computer-based guidance;
- case studies;
- principles;
- preference lists;
- manuals for sustainable building;
- life cycle assessment information;
- scoring systems such as rating systems; and
- eco-labels.

The next section examines how these tools have evolved into methodologies or pathways to enable designers to apply sustainability.

Three pathways that can be utilized in design have been identified by matching the tools to the various stages. While there are many permutations of the matching process in practice, and different design approaches will use different combinations of tools for different phases, it is possible to make certain generalizations as some tools are particularly suited to particular stages in design.

1 *Making greater use of brief.* This is called the environmental briefing systems approach, noted for integrated goal-setting, checklists, preference lists and principles in its frameworks.
2 *Applying performance assessment.* These are called environmental assessment systems and are noted for utilizing scoring systems, eco-labels and life cycle assessments. They are commonly integrated into rating or benchmarking systems and assist with measuring the environmental impact of the building.
3 *Learning from existing high-performance buildings.* These can act as exemplars or blueprints for further projects. They are called blueprints since a case study methodology is used. This approach is often carried out post construction and the outcome provides the designer with knowledge to feed forward to the next project.

The pathways for green design have arisen from mapping the tools to the design phase classification. These pathways are conceptualized as lines of enquiry involving tools and systems that progress green design (see Table 3.3).

The Healthy Home followed the first line and third line of enquiry. At the pre-design phase goals and objectives were defined in the beginning and the design advanced through a number of charrettes. Although no explicit brief was established, the design team used a number of green principles to inform

Table 3.3 Matching tools to design stages to create pathways for green design

Pathways	Stage 1: Pre-design	Stage 2: Sketch design	Stage 3: Detail design/ construction	Stage 4: Post occupancy
1 Environmental briefing systems	Charrettes Briefs Reports Principles	Analytical studies		
2 Environmental assessment systems	Checklists Pre-assessment	Design phase rating systems Design phase benchmarking systems		Operational phase rating systems Operational phase benchmarking systems
3 Blueprinting systems				Case studies Surveys of buildings in use Monitoring Analytical studies

Table 3.4   Strategies used in the Healthy Home Project

Strategies
Spatial organization that provides thermal delight and environmental connectivity while meeting user needs and lifestyle choices.
Small building footprint to minimize site utilization and maximize existing vegetation.
North orientation and shading to maximize breeze in summer, and provide solar access in winter and solar exclusion in summer.
Lightweight north-eastern-orientated building skin to provide rapid heat gain in winter.
Ground-connected mass construction to lower storey to provide 'cool pools' for daytime living in summer and 'warm pools' for evenings in winter.
Pavilion plan form with open section to provide cross ventilation for summer cooling.
Utilization of servant spaces to buffer served space from westerly sun and heat gain.
Use of breezeway and water feature to promote ventilation and evaporative cooling between pavilions through the venturi effect.
Use of an atrium space to promote convective cooling of internal spaces in summer calm conditions and provide light to deep plan spaces.
Utilization of a skeletal frame system that has low embodied energy, is factory-made, prefabricated to high quality, provides moment joints to resist racking loads, and gives internal planning flexibility and maximizes openings for ventilation.
Utilization of smart window technology to reduce glare and solar gain to interior spaces.
Utilization of materials that have minimum of off-gassing and effects on human health.
Provision of storage and hydraulic systems for rainwater and wastewater for recycling and site irrigation, thus minimizing mains water usage.
Water feature to provide white noise and feeling of calm in the home.
Cool colour scheme and landscaping to promote psychological comfort.
Installation of grid-connected PV (photovoltaic) system to export power to the grid during the day and import power at night.
Selection of energy-efficient appliances that minimize power utilization.
Automated building monitoring system to audit performance and security.
Use of gas fuel for heating to reduce carbon production.
Healthy Home Project: strategies that evolved as part of the charrette process used in the design of the building.

the design. These are derived from the work of Brenda and Robert Vale, through their book *Green Architecture*. A number of analytical studies were carried out during the design stage to validate the design. These included:

- water flume testing for ventilation;
- shading study;
- embodied energy study;
- lighting study; and
- water balance study.

The building has since been used as a blueprint and has been documented. At the post occupancy stage the building was written up as a case study using data from a survey of occupants to gain feedback on the building performance. A life cycle cost study was undertaken as well as monitoring of building to provide a demonstration of the design and technical strategies used.

Yet what are the advantages and disadvantages of these pathways?

Pathways

Arguments for environmental briefing

Building designers consider the design brief to be the most crucial part of the design process for achieving high-quality buildings. Environmental design strategies are accorded less importance.[11] It is argued that the use of an environmental brief – that is, a brief that combines both architectural and environmental issues to drive building design – could be extremely effective in producing high-level environmental performance. Using the briefing stage to set out environmental criteria will allow for assessment of the building's performance throughout the various stages of the design process. This can be effective in ensuring that environmental design strategies are not compromised. The implementation of the environmental brief could be more important in achieving a high level of environmental performance than the environmental design strategies themselves.

The Royal Australian Institute of Architects' Practice Notes define a design brief as

> a written statement, which details the client's expectations and the functions of a proposed building. It should describe the facilities to be provided and the activities to be performed and also clearly identify the broad policies within which these are to be achieved in respect of time, cost and quality of the facility.[12]

At present, two approaches to implementing green design are available. The first is a 'top-down' system where the client sets the environmental goals and objectives. The second is a 'bottom-up' system in which the designer initiates the environmental strategies. Research has shown that both approaches are fraught with problems.

In a survey of architects, Wittmann found that designers have a poor track record in understanding an environmental approach to design and often cannot implement the top-down system. In the case of the bottom-up approach, the designer may have an understanding of environmental issues but the client does not have a similar interest or the resources are not available to achieve the goals.[13] The Wittmann survey pointed to the importance of the brief as a way of increasing the knowledge of environmental issues of both the client and the architect. The main proposition of Wittmann's research is that the brief can be used

to influence the level of sustainability in a project, and that this sets the direction for implementation of sustainability in subsequent stages of the design.

Further investigations into the Wittmann hypothesis have led to the development of a design-phase framework for integrating environmental issues in to pre-design.[14] An environmental briefing tool developed from this framework has been created and testing has been completed. This research involved working with designers through a research-in-action methodology. The briefing tool assisted with the design of four buildings: three houses and one office fit-out (see Part 2).[15]

From this work four main arguments have emerged for this approach, supported in part by the literature but also from focusing on the brief as a way of controlling the level of sustainability in a building project. The four are:

1　building design paradigm;
2　front loading theory;
3　transferring expert knowledge to non-experts; and
4　challenging the norms.

Building design paradigm

Briefing – or programming, as it is called in the United States – takes place in the early stages of the design of a building when client and designers make decisions that concern the inception and feasibility of the project. The activities in the architect's plan of briefing work include preparing the general outline of requirements, planning future actions and providing the client with an appraisal of the requirements to identify the form and scope of the design work.[16] Similarly, in the United States the programming phase is seen as setting the size, use and budget of the building.[17]

In recent years the functional complexity of buildings and performance requirements have increased, in turn increasing the conceptual and technical sophistication of building design. In addition, new knowledge domains are needed such as that of environmental issues arising from cultural changes to sustainability. The building designer is a generalist by training, and is surrounded by specialists and experts.

Research has been done into the way generalists deal with complexity and specialization through investigation of the models of design for building professionals. There are many models of design and much discussion as to which is an appropriate

3.5 Healthy Home Project. Located 400 metres from the beach on the Gold Coast, Australia. Images from the virtual tour. Information technology is used to promote green design and help designers tap into information on the project.

representation of design activity. Early models of design suggest an analysis/synthesis/evaluation set of activities (called the ASE model), where goals are set, problems identified and solutions explored and evaluated.[18] This approach is characterized by investigation of the parts rather than appreciation of the whole.

In recent years a different model is proposed that focuses on the whole rather than the parts. New designs are seen in terms of existing solution types or solution subsets, principles and strategies. Designing is seen as a conjectural and reflective activity.[19] Design is about examining which solution set, principle or strategy is appropriate in a particular design scenario. This model is called the conjecture reflection model (CR model). Each model is seen as a separate paradigm with its own design culture and specific methodology. It is not the purpose here to investigate design theory but rather to examine the consequences of the shift to the CR model in terms of briefing.

Research into the use of briefing systems suggests the plan of work is based largely on office protocols and the ASE model. Briefing is seen as a largely analytical activity. The language is rhetorical and is about goal-setting, analysis of requirements and appraisal activities. The proposition advanced is that the environmental brief can accommodate the expert knowledge in the new environmental domain by redefining briefing as a more complex pre-structuring exercise, reflecting on alternative principles, strategies and solution sets to meet the needs of the design problem. In this way it can be more appropriate to the CR model currently used.

Front loading theory

The second concept, that of front loading, comes from the notion of defining performance standards 'early in the design process'.[20] Experience from practice has suggested that trying to apply performance standards after the building has been designed is fraught with difficulty. Generally, guidelines are used as a way of 'front loading' the design. Limited progress in the field has been made on developing methods to accommodate pre-structuring of design information. Absorbing environmental guideline information into the brief is critical if better environmental outcomes are to be achieved.

Transferring expert knowledge to non-experts

The third main argument for using the brief to control the level of sustainability in a building project comes out of research on sustainable housing. This has exposed the lack of uptake of sustainable design in the great majority of housing being produced.[21] It is an internationally recognized problem and one that concerns those governments that are striving to reduce their greenhouse emissions as outlined in the Kyoto Protocol. One particular barrier is that of creating awareness among house owners for the benefits of green design in terms of user needs. There are a number of initiatives that have been developed to address this barrier and to raise awareness of these benefits.

First, the International Energy Agency has addressed this barrier through its work on sustainable solar housing. Sustainable solar housing is an approach to designing houses that improves the environmental performance of domestic buildings by using sustainable design strategies. The slow uptake of this design approach worldwide has prompted the International Energy

Agency to define a research task called 'SHC Task 28'.[22] The outcome of the SHC Task 28 has been to identify demonstration buildings such as the Healthy Home Project (see Figure 3.6), to promote to house owners the benefits of sustainable design. Solution sets provide can be fed forward into the briefing process (see Chapter 7).

Second, in Australia the challenge of the problem of knowledge transfer has been taken up by the Australian Greenhouse Office (AGO), which has two initiatives. The AGO's first initiative is through the Australian Building Energy Council (ABEC). It has developed an environmental building best practice case study web site,[23] which is being promoted to the building industry in the newsletter *Blueprint*. The second AGO initiative is the *Good Residential Design Guide*[24] project developed and launched by the Institute for Sustainable Futures, University of Technology, Sydney. This is perhaps Australia's ultimate practical guide to sustainable residential buildings. The project includes a set of case studies, many linked to the work of ABEC. These case studies cover all price ranges and all climate zones. There is a marketing introduction to assist the lay person in making decisions.

The *Good Residential Design Guide* and the *ABEC Task Force*[25] assisted with establishing a case study approach for sustainable housing, and since then have worked on developing a way to synthesize the case study work and bring together some conclusive outcomes. This revealed that the strength of the AGO approach is a useful source of techniques and examples, but it falls short of providing design guidelines or briefing information. It does little to establish the extent to which designers can challenge the norms of domestic construction, what the cost penalties are and what the environmental benefits might be (see Chapter 7).

Challenging the norms, setting new benchmarks
Finally, from the work on the Healthy Home Project[26] a number of strategies and solution sets are found to be achievable. Two of the main strategies – improved radiant insulation and creating a supply chain of green materials – are shown in Figure 3.3. It has been possible to use this approach to create benchmarks for new housing. Examples of the benefits are as follows:

- Electricity consumption can be reduced by 40 per cent if a solar hot water system is used, for little extra capital cost and with a government subsidy.

- Zero heating and cooling energy is achievable using passive design with no extra capital cost.
- Using photovoltaic systems, up to 25 per cent of remaining electrical energy demand can be provided from non-grid, renewable sources at an additional cost of A$4,000 with government subsidy
- Using innovative water-wise strategies, 30–100 per cent of the water consumption can be saved (provided legislative barriers are removed), at a capital cost of approximately A$5,000.
- Using appropriate construction, embodied energy can be confined within the boundary of 1,000 MJ per m^2 with no extra cost beyond a small life cost for termite inspection and corrective maintenance. This is half the embodied energy of a conventional masonry home.
- Zoning the main electrical appliances that create electromagnetic radiation away from the main living areas and checking levels in the main habitable areas.

It became clear that an innovative approach is needed to promote the kind of building developed in the Healthy Home Project to a wider market. The project involved a large number of experts and extensive design time to implement because of lack of information on environmental strategies and cost information. It is not feasible to replicate this approach in every new building, so it seemed preferable to consolidate the experience and information into a briefing document. The briefing document could be expanded with knowledge drawn from other projects. This seemed a more plausible direction to take.[27] It became clear that research was needed into the form and nature of an environmental brief. One argument that emerged was to adopt benchmarks within the briefing process to establish quantitative targets to be met for the main areas of environmental impacts – energy, water and waste.

Finally, the Healthy Home Project addressed the national need to move to a sustainable Australia through transformation of building design and hence of the entire building industry. Environmental design is a complex synthesis of both the pragmatic and the poetic aspects of design that crosses the boundary between the science and the art of the discipline. At the same time, there is a significant trend for employing non-experts to design a large proportion of buildings, particularly houses. If we are to achieve a sustainable future there is an acknowledged need to skill building designers in environmentally sustainable design.[28]

3.6 Healthy Home Project. **Right**. Use of an atrium space in the centre of the building facilitates cooling. The bedroom spaces have louvres at high level to assist with cross ventilation to the atrium. **Top**. The master bedroom is located with its own roof ventilation system. The building has no flyscreens in the envelope to avoid reducing airflow. Insect control is used at the bed and through the landscaping. A permaculture garden is used to minimize mosquito-breeding areas.

A solution may lie in the use of design tools that can transfer expertise and knowledge in a simple and effective way. Research into design tools suggests the environmental brief has the potential to accommodate the complexity of environmental systems and meet the needs of practice (as found in quality management protocols such as ISO 9000[29] and ISO 14000[30]). It transfers expert knowledge gained through design research to non-experts, enabling them to design environmental sustainability into their output.

Arguments for environmental assessment systems for buildings

An environmental assessment system for buildings comprises a tool to evaluate the environmental performance of a building and a method of integrating the tool within the design procurement process. Commonly called Building Assessment Systems (BAS), the tool can be a rating tool, which has a scoring system to assist with measuring the performance of the building. Other systems use benchmarking tools, which do not usually have a scoring system but measure each environmental criterion separately. More details of these systems are given in Chapters 5 and 6.

In essence, BAS is a process control system for buildings. The use of environmental assessment tools in conjunction with design is seen as a path to facilitate green design. It is beyond the scope of this chapter to carry out an exhaustive review of the tools; rather, it will report on the findings of others who have carried out this kind of research with a view to their relation to design. A comprehensive review is found in the work of IEA-ECBCS 31,[31] which surveyed 27 tools from 12 countries.[32]

The main outcome of the survey was to make three comments. The first identified the need to carry out 'uncertainty analysis' to assess the rigour of a design tool to reduce environmental impacts. This concerns the environmental criteria in the tool and the model of environmental performance desired. The second concerned improving transparency so that the method used in the tools and systems is clear and easy for users to understand. The final comment was on the need to develop tools for the early part of the design process.[33]

Further research work has been carried out into how tools address the needs of the design process. The main arguments for using BAS are:

- assists with greening the design process;
- provides a multicriteria approach to environmental design; and
- rewards developers and designers for adopting a green design approach.

A review by Watson[34] argues that tools such as the Green Building Challenge, LEED or BREEAM system have been developed for and are usually applied post design. Todd[35] claims that tools such as the GBC are too abstract and difficult for designers to use. He argues that the LEED system is more effective, as the framework matches the process used by designers. The LEED system has developed a link between credits in the assessment and strategies in the building. A limitation of the environmental assessment approach is that it can be highly prescriptive and leaves little room for innovative design.[36]

The main conclusion is that these systems are best suited to design certification, that is, confirming that buildings meet some form of environmental standard once constructed. An Australian system called NABERS (National Australian Built Environment Rating System) has been developed to carry out rating of sustainability in housing and offices post construction during the operational phase.

A multicriteria approach

The argument for a multicriteria approach for BAS comes from the use of single criteria systems such as energy-based assessment. For some time energy has been seen as the main criterion for assessing sustainability.

Balcomb argues that a number of computer systems for early design work can be found. Of the analytical computer tools, many are concerned with energy performance or are tools for modelling thermodynamic phenomena within buildings – heat flow, wind flow, and daylighting.[37]

Williamson and Soebarto argue that a multicriteria assessment approach to building assessment is favourable for more comprehensive assessment of environmental factors. They use a program called Ener-Rate,[38] which is innovative for a number of reasons. It deals with a broader range of criteria, both qualitative and quantitative. It can be used for assessment during the design phase as well as post design for building evaluation. The BAS can address the need to validate a building during the design phase and post construction using a multicriteria approach.

Rewarding 'best practice'

The use of eco-labels in conjunction with BAS provides an opportunity to reward developers and design teams for their efforts in improving environmental performance of buildings. The eco-label is viewed as very important 'currency' in the eyes of the consumers, local councils and government. The provision of eco-label systems assists with differentiation of products (buildings) in a market that until recently has been driven by cost rather than quality. It remains to be seen to what extent the 'currency' will be accepted within the building procurement market.

Arguments for blueprinting

Another pathway addresses what Nibel reports as a current paradox in the quantitative application of BAS tools: 'an assessment tool can have the greatest impact in the early design phase ...', yet the designers 'only have a rough description of the building and the assessment is made on this basis'. Nibel concludes that the precision found in the assessment tool is not matched in the design.[39] The statement questions the value of the assessment and demonstrates the lack of fit between tools and the design paradigm.

3.7 Healthy Home Project. Additional studies of the building were carried out as part of the blueprinting process. This included an electromagnetic radiation study.

It seems, then, that current tools are criticized for not fitting the building designer's paradigm. Given the reservations about present assessment approaches, there is some support for examining the brief as a pre-structuring tool as it may present an innovative solution. Support for this idea comes both from theory and from practice.

There is an emerging emphasis in the field that stresses the importance of developing a 'green building design process'.[40]

In the C-2000 Larsson argues that one key aspect to this is that a client/team workshop approach should be used to set priorities and performance standards. This green design process was used in the Healthy Home Project,[41] and while it is possible on large buildings where there are many consultants, it is not practical for smaller projects and has some drawbacks even in larger projects.

Larsson suggests changing the design process, which adds to the cost of the project.[42] He proposes that 'researchers and designers are becoming increasingly aware that the potential performance is largely determined at the early phase of design or even in the pre-design phase'. In this quotation he is signalling a need for more work in the briefing phase and this may be a more cost-effective solution.

The idea of developing a 'green process' is appealing, but practising engineers warn of the difficulties of this approach. Bill Addis[43] from Bureau Happold suggests that, rather than expanding the process, it should work within the economics of practice, that is, giving the best service for the dollar. He advocates better staging of the design process, with different methods and tools used at different stages. This, he advocates, is the key to marketing environmental design to clients. He makes a strong case for including both qualitative and quantitative aspects of design within this approach.[44]

The arguments for using blueprinting spring from the comments of Bill Addis. A blueprint in this context means an exemplar or demonstration project that solves a particular problem in a particularly elegant manner. Of interest are both the end result and the process by which the designers have achieved their goal. The arguments for this approach come from the way that the case study:

- provides insight into the holistic resolution of specific design issues;
- demonstrates the way the design addresses both qualitative and qualitative environmental issues; and
- enables specific information found in the case study to be generalized to other design problems.

For these reasons it is commonly found that blueprints tend to educate and inform.

Whole systems thinking

Taking a 'whole of system' view of a building rather than focusing on its specific parts is the derived notion of holism found in the underlying principles of green design. The concept is based on thinking that any system is more than the simple sum of its parts. Hence in examining a building from a holistic perspective much of the discussion involves the interrelation of the parts to form the whole. For example, the energy efficiency of a building is often discussed in terms of the amount of insulation needed to resist heat flow. In reality this is only one of many factors that form the basis of the discussion.

The disadvantage of holism is that it takes discussion into increasing complexities of relations. Hence some form of analysis or framework is needed to make such studies workable. An example of this type of blueprinting study is found in the work of the Rocky Mountain Institute, through sponsorship from the US Department of Energy. The publication comprises 200 green development case studies, which provide examples of a range of building types including education, commercial/offices, retail and laboratory buildings.[45]

Qualitative and quantitative information

The value of learning from the post occupancy phase of design cannot be overstated. Through case studies designers can probe in depth the way the design intent has carried through to the selection of strategies and finally to performance. This type of study can provide qualitative information concerning design issues as well as data on a range of quantitative performances.

Information from case studies can be aggregated and broader patterns of building performance established. An example of this is the report from the International Energy Agency, *Design Insights from the Analysis of 50 Sustainable Solar Houses*.[46]

Information technology (IT), education and training

Finally, the education and training opportunities provided by blueprints are further recognized. The Healthy Home Project utilized information technology to provide information on the project through a website, which receives over 600 hits each month (www.healthyhomeproject.com).[47] This has been successful in communicating information through the blueprinting process. To promote green design, the Healthy Home Project website has a virtual tour of the building, which allows inspection of the quality of the spaces and also of the environmental systems used.

In addition, monitoring information provides data on environmental performance.

The future possibilities of improved IT interface capabilities between the user and environmental systems in the house or building have the potential to drive improved environmental performance through ease of access to control systems, and improved quality of life through better control of comfort (INTEGER Millennium House 2005[48]). The Australian Greenhouse Office has develop a more extensive website for education and training purposes. Called *Your Home*, it is based around a range of case studies that can act as blueprints:

> The case studies illustrate a range of real solutions to specific challenges faced by people wanting to design, build or buy a more sustainable home. It is important to note that none of them 'get everything right'. There are few major challenges that humans are unable to overcome but building a totally sustainable home is one important goal that still eludes us.[49]

Summary

Green design is a response to the new Age of Information and Ecology of the twentieth century.[50] Wines argues that green buildings can be superficially green when they express the environmental science that underlies their design but do not draw deeply from ecology in terms of their concept and form. He argues that green architecture is a question of fusing art and environmental technology; it is not simply the sum of its environmental technologies, the photovoltaic systems and other environmentally friendly services.[51]

A further substantive matter is that in some case the reverse is found: the buildings claim to be green in terms of their form but are weak in science – that is, they do not deliver improved environmental performance.

Part of the debate about the form and substance of green buildings lies in their connection to information technology. As the information concerning a building and its performance can exist in both the physical and the virtual world simultaneously, there is an opportunity to use this potential.

A virtual tour of the building can be used to promote green design. The future possibilities of improved IT interface capabilities between the user and environmental systems in the house or building have the potential to drive improved environmental performance through ease of access to control systems and improved quality of life through better control of comfort.[52]

Opportunities within the design phase can provide new pathways for design. These involve matching tools to the design process. The arguments for the tools have been provided. The next chapters examine the tools in more detail: Chapter 4 examines briefing, Chapter 5 benchmarking, Chapter 6 rating and Chapter 7 blueprinting.

4.1 Thomson Foy House, 1999, Brisbane. Architect: Mark Thomson. The environmental briefing system was developed using this building as a pilot project to inform the design.

Chapter 4

The environmental briefing system

Introduction

The reasons for using an environmental briefing system(EBS) were articulated in Chapter 3; they centre on a number of issues concerning:

- the nature of the building design paradigm;
- front loading theory;
- transfer of expert knowledge to non-experts; and
- challenging the norms.

The purpose of this chapter is, first, to describe the components of one system (EBS) that has been developed for environmental briefing, and second, to explain how it is applied in a project.

Components of EBS

Environmental briefing

Architects see the project brief developed by the client as the most crucial part of the entire design process as regards achieving high-quality buildings. It is argued that a brief that clearly articulates environmental issues is likely to be extremely effective in driving the building design and producing good environmental performance. It is further argued that the briefing stage should be used to the full, to set out environmental criteria that will allow assessment of the building's performance throughout the various stages of the design process. This approach can effectively ensure that environmental design strategies are not com-

promised. For these reasons the implementation of the environmental brief is seen as an important pathway to achieving a high level of performance of the environmental design strategies themselves. Table 4.1 demonstrates that of all the stages of the design process, the brief can be seen as the most important in ensuring the implementation of environmental strategies.

The EB system has been developed from theoretical work;[1] practical testing involved a number of pilot projects, one of which is shown in Figure 4.1. The components of the system, shown in Figure 4.2, are structured in a series of stages, using a general-to-specific framework. Stage 1 involves starting with goals and objectives; Stage 2 consists of parameters; Stage 3 concerns strategies; and, finally, Stage 4 provides recommendations. Stages 1 and 2 are largely descriptive, mapping the issues in the project. It is in Stage 3, strategizing, that the usefulness of the tool is most apparent, since its analytical framework supports decision-making.

The implementation of the EB system required adaptation of existing design and procurement processes. Table 4.1 shows an example of how the process, as used in Australia, can be adapted to emphasise the use of the brief as a tool for environmental design.

The main recommendations for implementing EBS are to include environmental standards and associated systems (such as a checklist from a rating tool) within the brief; or simply adopting the rating tool as a further environmental standard. Research into the application of EBS has shown that time spent on the briefing phase can be extensive, but it is argued that this has been of value, since it has helped shape the project at an early stage, before getting into extensive design work.

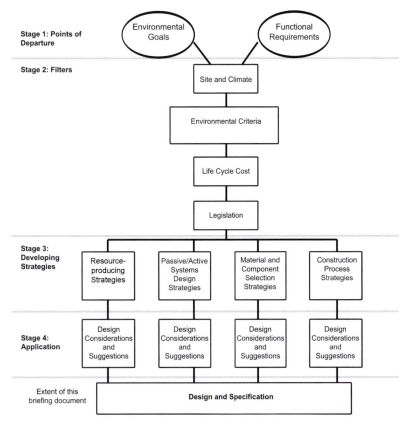

4.2 The environmental briefing system.

Table 4.1 Extending the briefing process through the environmental briefing system (key areas of change are in items 6 to 10)

RAIA briefing	Environmental briefing system
1 The client's vision statement for the project.	1 The client's vision will now incorporate, as one aspect, the desired environmental approach.
2 A definition of the scope and scale of the project including cultural, historical, technical and environmental requirements.	2 The scope of environmental considerations that will be incorporated within the scope of the overall requirements.
3 Identification of the site, any specific requirements and regulations required by local authority or other statutory bodies having jurisdiction, and demographics.	3 In relation to site requirements, detailed environmental analysis would be incorporated. Statutory requirements regarding the environment would obviously be made explicit.
4 A schedule of accommodation and equipment.	4 The schedule of accommodation and equipment will incorporate the environmental technology being used and the space required for it.
5 Function and functional relationships.	5 Functional relationships are integrated with passive design strategies.
6 Planning policies.	6 *Planning policies are also integrated with passive design strategies and with the use of active environmental systems.*
7 A project programme.	7 *The environmental strategies especially those relating to building construction are integrated with all others into the timing of the project. Approvals processes may take longer because of the non-traditional nature of environmental design at present.*
8 The project budget and how it was conceived, and life cycle costing methodology.	8 *Environmental strategies and environmental cost–benefit and life cycle costing for the environmental strategies are integrated into the budget.*
9 The client's management and administrative structure.	9 *Management procedures and operating manuals for the environmental technologies are integrated and incorporate environmental assessment.*
10 Quality assurance requirements.[2]	10 *Opens the possibility to implement environmental standards of ISO 14000 in addition to the quality standards of ISO 9000.*

Table 4.2 Environmental goals and functional requirements used in the Thomson Foy house: the aim of the environmental brief is to bring these two very different sets of requirements together

Environmental goals	Functional requirements
Principles	*Spaces*
Six principles of green architecture as set out by the Vales:	Kitchen – seen as the hub of the house – where Lyndal spends the most time – close relationship with the dining room, the family room and the laundry – on level access from the car.
1 minimizing use of new resources 2 conserving energy 3 working with climate 4 respect for site 5 respect for users 6 holism.	Laundry/utility room – seen as a possible work room or study, in which the laundry is reduced into a cupboard.
	Informal dining – linked to living. Informal living – linked to dining – separated spatially and aurally from the family room so that the children can be inhabiting the family room while there are visitors in the living room.
	Family/TV room – informal link to kitchen and laundry – possibly housing laundry within it as a cupboard.
	Disabled toilet at ground.
	Verandah – insect screened – strong connection to living spaces.
	Patio – connection to ground and undercover clothes drying – level access to the back yard.
	Master bedroom, robe and en suite – en suite may be linked to family bathroom via a shared toilet or some other similar arrangement.
Specific environmental criteria	
1 Minimize site impact – cut and fill	Three children's bedrooms – each with built-in cupboards and space for desks – one of which is larger and can accommodate two single beds.
2 Minimize operational energy use and CO_2 production	Family bathroom – may be linked to en suite.
3 Minimize embodied energy and CO_2 production	Linen cupboard – linen chute from upper to lower level if the house is two-storey.
4 Minimize virgin resource use – water, minerals, metals etc.	Studio – optional space – may double as home office or be under the house depending on spatial restrictions – may be fitted out at a later stage.
5 Maximize use of sustainable resources	Sewing/home office – same as utility space mentioned above – linked to laundry.
6 Maximize use of recycled and recyclable materials	Double car accommodation – level access into kitchen preferable.
7 Selection of environmentally safe materials	Bike storage – associated with car storage.
8 Maximize indoor air quality	Garden tool and equipment storage.
9 Optimize passive design	Fenced area for children's play, visible from house – especially kitchen and laundry.
10 Principles of Bau-biologie	
11 Minimize life cycle maintenance	Relationships – one-level living preferred.

Stage 1: Points of departure

The points of departure with the EB system involve a process of goal-setting. This is a complex issue, which is often a source of potential conflict in the brief. The successive stages seek to 'unpack' the core requirements in the project to facilitate discussion and decision-making. Two aspects facilitate the unpacking of the process; the points of departure include structuring the information into two areas. This involves setting environmental goals and function requirements.

Environmental goals

The setting of goals regarding the environmental performance of the project is a key activity that must take place at this early stage of the design process, even if they change throughout that process. These goals become part of the design problems to be solved; they may be prescriptive, such as the inclusion of specific environmental technologies or strategies, or they may be performance based, setting the desired levels of environmental impact, such as energy, water or material usage over the life of the building. Evidence that goals with regard to environmental performance have been set, either formally or informally, would indicate that environmental issues have been considered and that this is informing design decisions. The goals become the source of criteria that will facilitate the environmental decision-making throughout the rest of the design process.

Facilitating the setting of priorities

The raising of issues and the education of clients, through the process of creating a specific brief out of a set of generic issues, is, in essence, assisting clients to determine priorities for the allocation of their resources. The aim is that environmental issues will be raised in the list of priorities, on the assumption that the top priorities will get the greatest attention and have the highest chance of being achieved. As noted above, most clients intend to be environmentally responsible, though to varying degrees; this is reflected in the priorities that they set.

Functional requirements

Research on applying goal-setting in the briefing process has identified problems with the setting of priorities.[3] In many cases there are value conflicts between environmental and non-environmental issues.

The aim of the environmental briefing process is to facilitate the setting of priorities at the earliest possible stage of the design process. Where priorities have not been firmly established for a project, conflict tends to occur all through the design process, causing delay and angst between the clients and the design team. Once a set of priorities is established, specific environmental goals can be set for the project.

Typically clients bring a series of functional goals to a project. As part of the environmental briefing process, they are asked also to include their environmental goals. The designers bring to the process what is termed an 'environmental wish list', which includes an extensive set of environmental design issues for potential inclusion in the design. The briefing process then involves the 'marrying' of functional and environmental goals to form a set of overall goals.

A simple example of goal-setting informing design decision-making comes from one of the domestic residences, in which the clients had a goal to be self-sufficient in electricity usage. Part of the design problem for the roof of the house, therefore, was for it to be north facing at around 30° pitch, for the optimal installation of photovoltaic cells and a solar hot water system. In general, the results from the case studies showed that there was an acceptable correlation between the level of environmental performance set at the outset of a project and that achieved in the final design.

Logically, the same could apply to goals set for increased environmental performance. Such issues can possibly be incorporated into goals only through education and discussion about more stringent requirements for environmental performance. It must be noted that education and discussion will not necessarily lead to inclusion of these issues as goals, but inclusion will definitely not occur without them.

The brief as a bridge from generic to specific (the 'wish list')

It can be suggested, therefore, that the broadest possible range of issues should be raised in the briefing process, but it is also important to note that not all issues can be considered or taken on board. The brief acts as a bridge between the consideration of generic environmental issues and the specific issues that will be included in the project. The briefing process must facilitate taking unique project requirements into consideration and thus shaping the rest of the design process.

Environmental issues range from the global in nature, such as greenhouse gas emissions, to the very particular, project-specific issues, such as the health requirements of a client who may have asthma. Ultimately, though, the brief does not exist in a vacuum and the client's value structure is crucially important to decision-making.

Analysis of unique project considerations

All projects are unique, because of their clients, sites and relationships to the broader environment. Therefore, to be environmentally responsible, it is critical that there be as good an understanding of these parameters as possible when the structuring of the design problems takes place. If there is information missing at an early stage, design problems may be set and decisions made that will later require reversal when the information becomes available. Therefore, evidence that comprehensive analysis of these project variables has been done at an early stage is an indication that such issues are likely to be taken into account in the formulation of design problems. From the environmental perspective, this could include analysis of site conditions, macro- and micro-climate, soil, vegetation, local production or availability of materials, and transportation issues.

The client controls the level of sustainability in a project

It is arguably crucial for the client to set the performance criteria of the building. The environmental performance of the project can be regulated by the input of the client and the specific requirements that the situation poses. In addition to ethical issues, the client may demand other environmental criteria based on their lifestyle and health needs; for example, clients with respiratory problems may stipulate materials and finishes with minimal off-gassing. Performance criteria are then based on the client's ethics, goals and requirements. In other words, because the client invariably controls resources for a project, the ultimate level of sustainability is under the client's control. In order to improve implementation, however, this can only be

included in a goal – and therefore influence problem-setting – if it is raised as an issue.

The second stage involves examining the parameters surrounding the project goals achieved through education of the client and discussion of issues.

Stage 2: Applying filters

Parameters form filters to a project. Four main filters are identified:

- legislation;
- life cycle costing;
- environmental criteria; and
- climate.

Legislation

Governmental regulatory bodies specify environmental performance criteria of buildings according to their location. Differing standards occur in different locations and are regulated in a variety of ways. The BERS energy-rating scheme, based in Queensland, is an example of this; buildings are given a star energy rating determined by their environmental performance. This regulatory approach therefore affects building propositions and strategies in the early stages of design. Addressing design issues that the regulations may potentially impose at the onset of a project will influence development of the design during later stages.

Using BERS is an easy way to generate the necessary site information, based on the site evaluation, which can forewarn of the potentials and limitations of the project. The scheme bases its output on the micro-climatic data for the site and its surroundings that is of vital importance in generating the design.

Life cycle costing and environmental cost–benefit analysis

The second filter in the development of the brief is the cost-planning stage, where life cycle costing and environmental cost–benefit analyses are undertaken, particularly of resource-producing strategies that tend to add considerably to capital costs.

Table 4.3 Example of the simplified life cycle costing analysis for the resource-producing strategies[4]

Strategy	Capital cost	Life cycle cost–benefit	Environmental benefit
Photovoltaic (1.5 kW system)	$14,000	$420 per year	1,400 kg CO_2/year
Rainwater collection (22,000 litre system)	$4,500	$300 per year	350 kl of water per year (based on water cost of $0.85 per kl)
Solar hot water	$2,400	$280 per year	700 kg CO_2/year
Total per year		$1,000 per year	2.1 tonnes CO_2 + 350 kl water
Total life cycle*	$20,900	$25,000	105 tonnes CO_2 + 17,500 kl water

* assuming a 25-year period

The environmental cost–benefit analysis explains to the client what reductions of impacts on the environment might be made if the strategies are put in place. The quantitative data produced shows how the money spent will reduce the environmental impact of the dwelling. The life cycle costing process illustrates how larger capital costs that are due to the incorporation of environmental strategies would lead to a reduction in operational costs over the lifespan of the house.

Environmental criteria

As may be seen from the review of existing tools in Chapter 3, there is a plethora of assistance available, with various strengths and weakness depending on the application required. Part of the job of the front loading process is to draw on externally available information, as it is needed to inform the design process. Though there is a risk of having too much information, it is important to be able to source information in areas where the designers may not already have knowledge. In this sense, external documents or tools play the role of expert consultants. Evidence that such documents or tools are being consulted indicates that they are informing the setting of design problems.

Criteria from problem-setting are used in the error-elimination process
As part of the design process, criteria emerge, implicitly or explicitly, from the pre-structuring of the design problem. These criteria are then used in making assessments of design conjectures, as part of error elimination during the problem-solving process.

Hence, evidence that environmental criteria were coming out of the front-loaded design process would indicate that the process had the potential, at least, to aid in the decision-making process. Criteria taken from existing environmental assessment tools might also be included.

Reference to the environmental brief
In order that the front-loaded process and its products (the briefing document and the goals it contains) may have some bearing on the design decision-making process, there must be evidence that this document is being consulted throughout the design process.

Measuring conjectures
If there are criteria against which environmental performance of design conjectures can be measured, then there must also be evidence that these measurements have been made. Evidence that this is taking place might involve simple rule-of-thumb measurements, calculations from design drawings, or even advanced computer simulations of the design conjectures.

The final role of the environmental briefing process to be examined is the production of a record. Documenting issues considered, goals set and decisions made is valuable, not only for the project for which the brief is being developed, but also for future projects. Though environmental issues vary from project to project, dealing with their complexity will be assisted if a record is available of previous decisions made and the outcomes that resulted from them.

The practice of 'bringing forward' information, knowledge, experience or solution sets from previous projects for use on a project under consideration is termed *feed forward*.[5] Feed forward is critical to the iterative improvement of building design in general, but particularly, as in this case, for improving environmental performance. It is especially useful if knowledge gained from past projects can be used to inform the design process from the earliest stages, to forestall movement in directions already found not worthwhile and to avoid the need to repeat research groundwork. The feeding forward of knowledge and ideas had a large influence on the pre-structuring of design problems for the designer of the Thomson Foy house. As Hillier *et al.* state, a large part of pre-structuring relies on the designer's past experience.[6]

In order that the front-loaded process and its products – namely the briefing document and the goals it contains – will have a proper effect on the design decision-making process for an individual project, there must be evidence that they are being referred to throughout the design process. There was certainly evidence of this in the process of design decision-making in the case studies; however, the emphasis was on the environmental briefing process and on continued adjustment of the brief as a part of the design process, rather than on the importance of the brief itself as a record and as a resource document.

The process of recording goals in the brief cements issues in place for the designer and, perhaps more importantly, for the client. When design decision-making subsequently occurs there

---

THOMSON FOY HOUSE

The site is in Brookfield, a fringe suburb located south-west of Brisbane's city centre, in Queensland, Australia. The site has a steep slope with a maximum fall of one in three. The natural fall is to the northern boundary, the Boyd Street front. The long section of the site is orientated approximately north-east and south-west (Figure 4.3, top right). A park is situated on the opposite side of Boyd Terrace, where the ground continues to fall to a creek approximately 20 metres from the northern site boundary.

The neighbouring residences are built at a minimum of 1,500 mm from the side boundaries, with the boundaries themselves marked by rows of small shrubs. A concrete block retaining wall marks the rear boundary. The existing site cover was tall grass and there are three existing wattle trees in the south-west corner. Residences to the south, east and west are brick and tile construction project homes, setting the tradition of the remaining streetscape.

The preferred position for the proposed house from the inception of the design was the rear of the site, for many reasons. First, being high on the site gave more opportunity to catch prevailing breezes to passively ventilate the proposed house. Second, the outlook to the north could be appreciated from the top of the site. Furthermore, having the residence to the rear of the site presented options for future subdivision (Figure 4.3, bottom right).[7]

4.3 Site and climate analysis was a fundamental part of developing the brief for this project.

can then be a greater degree of confidence that correct decisions are being made relative to the project goals. An architectural brief should continue to evolve throughout the design process, and recording this evolution will assist in keeping a harmonious relationship with the client, as the designer attempts to fulfil the client's wishes. In those case studies where goals were not formally recorded, problems were encountered when it came to making design decisions. The brief serves as a starting point for assessing the design

If implementation of environmental strategies is to be achieved in the final design, there must be some way of monitoring the design as it evolves as part of the process criteria are developed, either implicitly or explicitly, from the pre-structuring of the design problem. It is these criteria that will be used for making judgements on design conjectures during the problem-solving process, as part of error elimination. Hence, evidence that environmental criteria did emerge from the front-loaded design process would indicate that the process at least had potential to support the decision-making process. In some cases, explicit assessment criteria can be taken from existing sources, or from rating or benchmarking tools. As will be seen in the following case study of William McCormack Place, the Green Building Challenge criteria supplemented the criteria developed for this building.

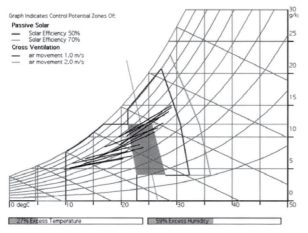

4.4 Bioclimatic analysis was used in the development brief to show favourable strategies to provide passive heating and cooling. In this case passive solar heating for winter and air effect in summer is appropriate in the Brisbane climate.[8]

The whole procedure can be depicted as a sequence of events leading from goal-setting through the design problem-solving process to the formation of criteria for assessing conjectures. The importance of the task of goal-setting in the front loading process is obvious: if no environmental goals are set they cannot be part of the design problem, and will produce no criteria for measuring conjectures. There would be no inputs to the error-elimination process and hence no influence on implementation of environmental strategies.

An important task for the environmental brief is to facilitate the linking of environmental assessment criteria to the particular goals set for a project. To this end there needs to be a certain degree of flexibility in the environmental assessment criteria in order to cater for unique project goals.

Site and climate

An important filter is the analysis of climate. From the environmental point of view, working with climate can provide resources to service the needs of the building and its occupants.

In the case of the Thomson Foy House, site and climate analyses were made as shown below. This involved a site study incorporating the following:

- site topography;
- slope analysis;
- mapping to locate sinks on the site for carbon and heat;
- geomantic survey;
- biodiversity assessment; and
- water balance study to establish water tank size.

During this process it is important to map the heat sinks and carbon sinks that are available on the site. In the case of the Thomson Foy house the following heat sinks were identified:

- Air-flow in summer provides a method of removing heat from the building.
- Trees are a valuable sink for carbon and retaining these on site is an important issue. Unfortunately the site had been clear-felled and hence this option was not available. Planting of trees was considered as a regenerative strategy to address this problem.

Bioclimatic analysis was done to give further understanding of the site in terms of the macro-, mesa- and micro-climatic conditions, so that strategies could be devised for providing thermal comfort. The raised position and the outlook to the north meant these strategies had potential.

The information from this process fed forward into the next stage of the briefing process. This provided considerable input to the testing of the design for ventilation.

Stage 3: Developing strategies

These first two stages – goal setting (points of departure) and establishing parameters (filters) – can be regarded as part of the existing briefing process. Subsequent stages are extensions to this process and involve developing strategies for the project and applying the brief. Moving forward with EBS means analysing and synthesising the information from these first two stages and developing environmental strategies related to every aspect of the design.

Client knowledge and the informed decision

Clients enter the design process as the party with control over the resources to realize the project, but the extent of their knowledge of environmental issues, and hence their capacity to make informed decisions about key strategies concerned with the project, is often unclear at the outset of a project. Research has been carried out into the clients' awareness of environmental issues. The outcomes showed that the clients differed in four key ways crucial to the eventual level of implementation of environmental strategies.[9]

In this research the clients all entered their projects with different perceptions of what is environmentally sustainable. Second, they each had unique sets of desires and priorities for the project. Third, they were open to different degrees to being educated on environmental issues. Fourth, they all had different budgets and hence different access to resources with which to work.

Among these factors, education cannot change the budgetary constraints, though it could change priorities within those constraints. This suggested the need to organize this stage of the briefing process as a discursive process, developing and evaluating strategies so that informed decisions could be made about

the project. The other three factors, however, may be influenced by education, hence the aim was to raise clients' understanding of the concept of sustainability and to change their desires and priorities so they would be more in favour of environmental considerations.

Evidence from research does not suggest that education of the client directly contributes to pre-structuring for the designer, but it certainly has an effect on problem-setting, because the client has to come to agreement with the designer as to what many of the design problems will involve. The education of clients is critical as an intermediate step towards implementation; its role is to change priorities in order to alter implementation. To this end, clarity of the presented information is of critical importance. Apart from educating clients on environmental issues, it is also important that these issues are always raised at the outset of the design process, even if all parties are fully aware of them.

Responding to goals and parameters

Responding to goals and parameters is organized into four main areas:

1 *Resource-producing strategies* – strategies that involving generation of energy, water, food and the treatment and/or reuse of waste.
2 *Passive and active design strategies* – strategic responses to climate, site and context aimed at minimizing impacts of the building while in use.
3 *Material selection strategies* – attempts to minimize the impact of the building before its use.
4 *Construction strategies* – on-site building practices aimed at minimizing the impact of the construction of the building.

Resource-producing strategies

Table 4.3 showed the analysis used to examine alternative strategies for harvesting the resources on the site, such as air, sun and water. The use of selected environmental technologies – solar electric, solar thermal, and water collection systems – were considered. Life cycle costing was used to evaluate the benefits of the systems. Grey water systems were not considered since local legislation prohibits this type of system.

4.5 Bedroom module showing the construction of the post and rail single-skin system and the hypar roof form.

Primary Structure

Issues

1. Minimising existing site disturbance
2. Minimising on site waste during the construction process
3. Ease of construction
4. Speed of construction
5. Future flexibility
6. Demountability
7. Minimise embodied energy
8. Materials from renewable/reused/recycled resources

Given these factors the following 4 structural systems are seen as the possible options:

- Timber Portal Frame – utilises small waste timber to produce larger elements
- Steel Portal Frame – higher embodied energy than any of the timber solutions and a non-renewable resource– steel is also harder to work with on site.
- Timber Pole Frame – on site construction not as quick or easy – elements are fabricated on site
- Post and rail (Guitar system) – more on site waste due to no prefabrication – longer construction period

Comparative analysis of strategies is given below

Structural Strategies	Site disturbance minimisation	Site waste minimisation	Ease of construction	Speed of construction	Future adaptability	Demoun-tability	Minimise embodied energy	Utilises renewable/ reused materials
Timber Portal Frame								
Steel Portal Frame								
Timber Pole Frame								
Timber Post and Rail Stud Frame system								

Recommended Selection – Primary Structure

The post and rail timber framing – this fulfils all of the criteria

All of the structural systems fulfil the criteria listed above although on site waste may not be as minimal with a timber frame system.

In terms of embodied energy rating the Timber Portal Frame performs well.

4.6 Developing strategies: Thomson Foy Residence. Example from the briefing process where strategies are compared. The part is taken from the Materials section and the sub-section on Primary Structure.

Passive and active design strategies

Table 4.4 shows the passive strategic responses to site and climate. The table is extracted from the EBS documentation for passive strategies. A number of diagrammatic sketches used to demonstrate the way that various approaches could address bioclimatic analysis are shown in Figure 4.4. This identified the need for ventilation to gain air effect for summer cooling and solar heating for winter.

Material selection strategies

Figure 4.5 shows the materials used in the Thomson Foy house and Figure 4.6 shows an extract from the EBS documentation for materials selection. In this case a number of primary structural systems were compared in terms of environmental criteria and this was used to select the system. The prefabricated post and rail system selected is shown in Figure 4.5. This timber single-skin plywood system has the advantage of very low material density but larger numbers of pad footings compared with other portal frame-type systems. Similar processes are used with a range of other issues.

Construction strategies

Figure 4.7 shows the type of construction process used. This resulted from consideration of the following issues:

- on-site waste management strategies;
- on-site pollution prevention strategies – water run-off;
- soil erosion – wind and water;
- dust prevention – wet cutting;
- noise prevention;
- on-site protocols – site disturbance;
- on-site education of contractors and subcontractors;
- modular construction;
- minimizing numbers of different trades;
- maximizing prefabrication;

Table 4.4 Strategies applied for the Thomson Foy house

Strategy	Reason	Insert diagram
Mass or lightweight materials	Potential to store or release heat	
Thin plan	Maximizes cross ventilation Gives high levels of natural light, avoiding dark areas	
Open section	Maximizes stack ventilation	
Windows facing equator Smallest building aspect to east and west	Solar access in winter Facing prevailing breezes in summer Reduced low-angle solar gain	
Use of tree canopy in summer Heat and glare dissipating planting Planting to allow solar access in winter	Shade to building but allowing breeze	
Use of verandahs	Rain and sun protection of walls Provide diffused light	

4.7   Construction of the single-skin post-and-rail framing system. This was prefabricated at the local training college, providing a useful training programme for apprentices.

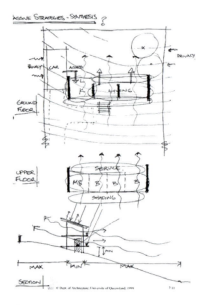

4.8   Thomson Foy House. Application of the Environmental Brief as a diagrammatic plan and section.

4.9   Final synthesis of strategies involves creating the environmental concept for the project. For the Thomson Foy house this can be seen in the section. One of the main ideas was minimization of resources, and hence reduced earthworks, through lightweight single-skin construction using rapidly renewable materials.

- construction of ancillary structures out of waste from the building process; and
- waste management plan, through the building specification.

The use of the lightweight system enabled the building to be manufactured off site by semi-skilled labour; it was easily transported to site and erected with a minimum of site disturbance.

Stage 4: Application

The final stage of EBS is the translation from brief to sketch design. This involves two activities: documentation of the decisions made and creating the environmental concept.

Documentation

A template called the environmental briefing record is used for documenting EBS. The primary aim of this document is to link the EBS approach to the ISO 9000 quality management protocols now used by building design professionals. Separating out the environmental features of the brief from the functional

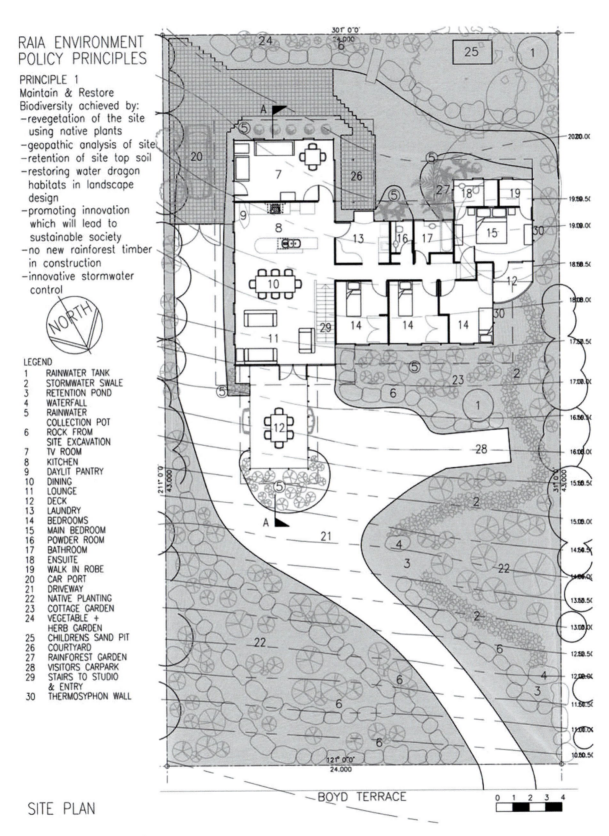

RAIA ENVIRONMENT POLICY PRINCIPLES

PRINCIPLE 1
Maintain & Restore
Biodiversity achieved by:
- revegetation of the site using native plants
- geopathic analysis of site
- retention of site top soil
- restoring water dragon habitats in landscape design
- promoting innovation which will lead to sustainable society
- no new rainforest timber in construction
- innovative stormwater control

LEGEND
1 RAINWATER TANK
2 STORMWATER SWALE
3 RETENTION POND
4 WATERFALL
5 RAINWATER COLLECTION POT
6 ROCK FROM SITE EXCAVATION
7 TV ROOM
8 KITCHEN
9 DAYLIT PANTRY
10 DINING
11 LOUNGE
12 DECK
13 LAUNDRY
14 BEDROOMS
15 MAIN BEDROOM
16 POWDER ROOM
17 BATHROOM
18 ENSUITE
19 WALK IN ROBE
20 CAR PORT
21 DRIVEWAY
22 NATIVE PLANTING
23 COTTAGE GARDEN
24 VEGETABLE + HERB GARDEN
25 CHILDRENS SAND PIT
26 COURTYARD
27 RAINFOREST GARDEN
28 VISITORS CARPARK
29 STAIRS TO STUDIO & ENTRY
30 THERMOSYPHON WALL

SITE PLAN

BOYD TERRACE

4.10 Thomson Foy House. Final plans.

Table 4.5 Thomson Foy House: materials and passive active systems selected

Materials	Benefits
Modular construction. A modular design grid has been adopted to minimize material wastage and promote standardization.	Cost-effective and efficient construction.
Low toxic finishes. All finishes in the project have been selected to create healthy living conditions, often utilizing natural alternatives.	Reduced volatile organic compounds.
PVC minimization. Non-PVC electrical and plumbing fittings have been selected to minimize the toxic environmental impacts of PVC.	No toxic smoke in the event of fire.
Innovative building structural system. The Guitar building system comprises laminated veneer lumber and plywood single-skin construction.	A low-embodied-process-energy rating is achieved.
Hypar roof design and construction. Hypar roof geometry provides functional and aesthetic features to the house construction.	Rollover low-maintenance gutters and barges possible.
Use of low-embodied-energy materials. Timber has been used from sustainable sources and high-energy-production materials have been minimized.	No rainforest timbers have been used in the project.

Passive and active systems	Benefits
Thermal zoning. The house has been thermally zoned to minimize heating requirements.	Reduced heating costs.
Recycling. Recycled materials and processes have been implemented throughout the project, including doors, structural elements and general building products and materials.	Reduced building cost.
Indoor air quality has been considered and maximized by optimum ventilation design and selection of materials minimizing volatile organic compounds.	Reduced risk of asthma for occupants.
Passive solar design. Eaves have been designed to allow infiltration of winter sun while excluding summer sun.	Maximum advantage is taken of natural resources.
Daylight maximization. Clerestories provide daylighting opportunities to all living spaces to minimize energy usage.	Reduced power consumption.
Ventilation optimization. University of Queensland water flume testing has been carried out to provide optimum ventilation design to all living areas.	Cool interior environment in summer.
Passive cooling design. Thermosyphon cavities in roof spaces assist in insulating the interior climate conditions.	Low-cost insulation method.
Energy-efficient appliances. All appliances have been chosen considering energy efficiency.	Reduced power consumption.
Electromagnetic radiation field control. All electrical appliances and wiring have been located and designed to minimize electromagnetic fields.	All electrical circuits are earthed and safe.
Living area orientation. All living and sleeping areas have a northern aspect to optimize local climate conditions.	Improved liveability and climate comfort.

aspects of traditional briefing enables analysis of environmental decision-making as early in a project as possible.

Creating the environmental concept

The environmental principles invariably become synthesized into a basic concept for the building – the basic organization of the building, without which it would not exist. The environmental concept is best expressed as a section (see Figure 4.9).

Packaging the brief and the environmental briefing record

The brief can be packaged in different ways for different users – clients, architects and builder – to achieve different outcomes. Briefing in its simplest form is a discourse between client and designer. Some discourse methods are highly structured, whereas others may follow a set sequence or checklist to define a project. The purpose of this document is to record the outcomes of the discourse at the briefing stage of the project.

The brief as a 'living' document

It is recognized that a brief should not be a static document; a rigid application of the brief has the potential to hamper the

Table 4.6 Thomson Foy House: resource-producing and construction systems selected

Resource-producing	Benefits
Roof water collection. Water conservation will be practised by collection and use of rainwater.	Reduced water charges.
Solar power. Solar hot water and photovoltaic power systems are to be incorporated in the design.	Reduced energy consumption.
Permaculture principles have been considered in the outdoor areas with landscaped elements to complement the natural flora and fauna.	Low maintenance and productive garden.
Water conservation. Toilet cisterns and garden irrigation systems use rainwater collected on site.	Reduced water consumption.
Stormwater quality control. All stormwater will be collected and dispersed on site and purposely oxygenated.	Stormwater entering the nearby creek will be free of site pollutants.

Construction	Benefits
Geomantic survey. Geo-biology has been considered in the building's location on the site to work with the natural geomantic effects of the area.	Reduced risk to geologically disturbed areas.
Project management. The project has been managed and supervised to monitor site issues and cost control.	Accurate time and cost control.
Training programmes. The project has been used to train tradespeople and university students, with the Construction Training Centre and the University of Queensland having direct involvement in the project.	Community benefits by employment and training.
Low-maintenance design. The project features various design features, such as a leafless gutter design to facilitate a low-maintenance building approach.	Reduced maintenance time during occupancy.

design process. The development of the brief is an ongoing process and should respond to the issues drawn out during the development of the design. In this state the brief becomes a 'living' document that responds to the detailed decision-making process and guides the development of the design.

Eco-efficiency achieved

One outcome of the briefing process is to arrive at an analysis statement of the eco-efficient measures used in the building. Tables 4.5 and 4.6 show these measures developed for the Thomson Foy House. Establishing in the brief a clear expression of the environmental goals for a project will relate to the building's overall environmental success.[10]

Summary

The RAIA Practice Notes define a design brief as 'a written statement, which details the client's expectations and the functions of a proposed building. It should describe the facilities to be provided and the activities to be performed and also clearly identify the broad policies within which these are to be achieved in respect of time, cost and quality of the facility.'[11]

The RAIA Practice Notes state: 'The operational success of a building is directly related to the clear identification of the functions to be performed in the proposed building, resolved through good design process.' By extension, EBS is seen as a

way of extending current briefing practice to acknowledge environmental factors more explicitly. The Practice Notes set out a comprehensive list of components required for a briefing document, and how this is extended through EBS; this can be seen in Table 4.1. The key areas of change are in items 6 to 10, which involve the implementation of the brief.

An environmental brief must ensure consideration of all of these aspects, while making explicit the environmental issues and/or goals in relation to each of the components. Furthermore, by including environmental criteria from other tools such as rating tools it is possible to include environmental standards in the brief. While this does not guarantee green design it nevertheless improves the potential at the front end of the design process.

The case studies that demonstrate the use of the EBS are:

- Yeang House, Kuala Lumpur, Malaysia; and
- EPA Fit-out, William McCormack Place, Cairns, Australia.

Acknowledgements

Michael Leo and Guitar building systems.

5.1 The Sundancer Resort, Lombok, Indonesia. Benchmarked under the Green Globe Design and Construct Standard

Chapter 5

Benchmarking systems

Introduction

Benchmarking systems are used to assess the environmental performance of buildings, both in the design phase and for assessing the operational performance post occupancy. Two systems are examined: the Green Globe (GG) system and the Green Building Challenge system.

The main components of benchmarking systems are:

- environmental criteria;
- database of performance benchmarks;
- benchmarking process that involves collecting performance data on the building; and
- assessment process, comparing the data from the building against the benchmarks.

The sets of environmental criteria originate from the European Environmental Press (EEP) model or, in some cases, from international tools such as Green Globe, derived from international policy on environmental impacts.

The name 'benchmarking system' originates from the way in which the criteria are used for assessment. The benchmarking data on building performance is collected through an extensive research activity, by examining either existing high-performance buildings or base-case building performance. For example, within a particular building type, the energy consumption for a range of buildings can be collected and norms for energy consumption calculated. From this a benchmark can be arrived at for best-practice energy consumption, which improves upon the norm.

A database is usually constructed for this kind of data, particularly with systems that have a wide range of categories and many quantitative criteria. Weightings are usually integrated into the criteria. Assessment involves comparing the data from the building under test against the benchmarks. In some systems targets are given to the designers to assist with the design process.

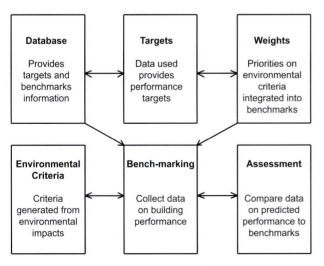

5.2 The general components of benchmarking systems.

Green Globe Design benchmarking

Overview

This tool has arisen from the need for a new industry design standard to support sustainability initiatives used to design tourism facilities. While there are many guidelines for the design of tourism infrastructure – buildings and other support infrastructure – there has been little work on creating a sustainable design standard or assessment methodology that could be easily adopted by industry. The Sustainable Tourism Collaborative Research Centre in Australia and its partner company, Green Globe Asia Pacific, in conjunction with the Universities of Queensland and New South Wales, have evolved a benchmarking system for the tourism industry.[1]

Research has built on existing work to develop a standard that comprises a range of measures, consistent not only with the early stages of design but also with Agenda 21 issues and Earth Check$_{TM}$ indicators. The standard is structured to minimize the cost to the design team and the developer of using a third-party assessment programme. This cost-effective approach, which works within the quality management (ISO 9000) process of design, makes for ease of integration with the building industry.[2]

Precepts

About Green Globe

Green Globe was conceived as a membership-based programme that travel and tourism (TT) companies could join to implement sustainable tourism practices based on Agenda 21 principles.[3] Around 500 companies (airlines, hotel chains, tour operators, travel agents) joined, and the organization gained a considerable profile within the industry, heightening awareness of environmental and sustainability principles.

Green Globe, as the only worldwide programme for sustainable travel and tourism, certifies companies and destinations against generic standards. Since the development of Green Globe, national and international research has proposed a number of instruments for eco-efficiency, by developing assessment tools and eco-efficiency agreement protocols and standards.

Assessment approach and design thinking

The assessment approach involves three stages:

- affiliation;
- benchmarking; and
- certification.

This approach is aimed at integrating with the design and construction process for a building and its associated infrastructure. It ensures not just that sustainable strategies and performance measures are employed in the building but also that sustainable construction practices are used to build it. The approach employs three levels of activity:

- design thinking;
- strategizing; and
- auditing.

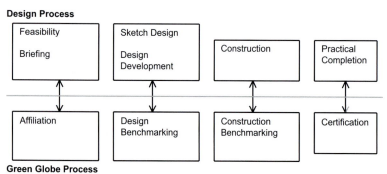

Design Process

| Feasibility | Sketch Design | Construction | Practical |
| Briefing | Design Development | | Completion |

| Affiliation | Design Benchmarking | Construction Benchmarking | Certification |

Green Globe Process

5.3 The Green Globe Design and Construct Process aligned with the Design process.

The assessment is based on an environmental standard specifically tailored for tourism infrastructure, such as hotels, interpretation centres and resorts servicing the travel and tourism Industry. The benchmarks used in the assessment are derived from environmental 'best practice' in the industry.

Background

In 2004, travel and tourism were expected to generate:

- US$5,490.4 billion of economic activity;
- 10.4% of total GDP;
- 214,697,000 jobs, or 8.1% of total employment; and
- 12.2% of total exports.[4]

The travel and tourism industry

Travel and tourism (TT), contributing US$5,490.4 billion (an estimated 10 per cent of world GDP[5]) in 2004, is the world's largest civil industry and is forecast by the World Travel and Tourism Council (WTTC) to achieve annualized real growth of 4.5 per cent in total travel and tourism demand to US$9,557.5 billion in 2014.[6]

The World Tourism Organization (WTO) estimates that the 689 million international travellers in 2000[7] will grow. WTO's *Tourism 2020 Vision* forecasts that international arrivals are expected to reach over 1.56 billion by the year 2020.[8]

In Australia, the National Visitors Survey (NVS) for showed residents aged 15 or older spent 297.4 million nights away from home and 160.3 million day trips were taken.[9] The International Visitors Survey (IVS) indicates that 4,459,500 international visitors travelled to Australia in 1999, staying 108 million nights.[10] This demand drives a continual need for new – and upgrading of existing – building and road infrastructure. Each new project creates opportunities to improve aspects of sustainability surrounding the facilities. The benefits of these opportunities are not only environmental but also economic. Research suggests that this approach does indeed provide benefits, at both broad industry and operation-specific levels.

The buzz that comes along with the idea of sustainability addresses the feel-good factor that can be used for marketing across the industry. It also enhances the credibility of claims by industry leaders for assistance from government for general impact and performance improvements aimed at shifting the tourism industry towards a more sustainable future. Unfortunately, industry-level advances in sustainability are hard to come by; specific operation-based initiatives have been the most successful in implementing sustainability in tourism development. These efforts focus on the *economic* benefits of sustainability and are driving change at grass-roots levels.

Tool development

The great growth in tourism brings a need for improved infrastructure facilities. Preliminary research, through a pilot study by the Collaborative Research Centre for Sustainable Tourism, reveals concern among stakeholders at the grass-roots level regarding the plethora of tourism bodies, the widespread range of assessment and accreditation systems and the cavalier use of 'eco-terminology' for marketing purposes. While broad design guidelines for tourism infrastructure do exist, little work has been done to relate these directly to environmental and economic performance indicators.[11]

Applications to design projects

There is an important link to be made between design considerations and the Agenda 21 principles. The design targets established in Table 5.1 are flagged in terms of these principles. It should be recognized that design issues can cover more than one principle.

Research

At present a number of internationally recognized 'whole building' assessment systems, such as the GBC building assessment tool, have been developed for the design and construction sector.[12] The GBC tool was tried out in the first year of this research project, Couran Cove being used as a case study to test the methodology. The results led to a number of conclusions; the GBC tool was found to be a useful basis for developing a framework for a standard for tourism buildings.

Work has since progressed on developing such a framework to suit the needs of the tourism industry. Without this tool, it would be difficult to link design guidelines and industry standards, and to carry out appropriate benchmarking of environmental strategies.

Table 5.1 Design issues and Agenda 21 principles

Design issues	Agenda 21 principles
Design approach	Policies for improvement
Siting	Land management Ecosystem conservation and management
Energy efficiency and conservation: Building materials and process	Energy efficiency, conservation and management Air quality protection and noise Energy efficiency, conservation and management
Protection of air, earth and water	Freshwater resource management Storage and use of hazardous substances
Construction	Energy efficiency, conservation and management Waste management and minimization Land management Ecosystem conservation and management Energy efficiency, conservation and management
Social	Improved social and cultural interactions

Development of the approach

During the development of the Green Globe Design and Construct Standard of buildings, it was realized that there was a significant difference between *design-phase performance* and *operational-phase performance*.

Design-phase performance is largely a predictive measure for a building, based on the design process prior to occupancy, while the operational phase monitors the post occupancy performance and is usually based on measured real data. In the case of Green Globe, the organization had developed standards for the operational phase performance assessment of companies and facilities. These standards had evolved from work on ISO 14000 systems, with developments to meet industry needs. The first evolution was undertaken with reference to ISO 14000, the international Environmental Management standard.[13]

ISO 14000

The ISO 14000 series standards provide organizations with tools that can be used to manage their environmental performance.[14] Rogers argues that there is an inherent problem with the approach used in ISO 14000:

ISO 14001 as currently written is limited in its ability to deliver improvements in environmental performance, because the emphasis is on improving the environmental management system, which in turn is expected to lead to improved environmental performance.[15]

He suggests that:

This Standard, known as Green Globe, sets definitive performance outcomes in terms of indicators in areas related to tourism. Certification to this Standard is possible and will be offered under similar rules to that currently used by the Joint Accreditation System of Australia and New Zealand. However, the system will contain improvements aimed at ensuring the maintenance of a high standard certification.[16]

The main limitations found with ISO 14000 are:

- absence of links with Agenda 21 and sustainable outcomes;
- emphasis on legal requirements as a basis for performance;
- limited involvement of interested parties (stakeholders) in the setting of performance outcomes;
- concentration on process rather than on actual outcomes; and
- perceived application of the standard to industrial rather than service sectors.

These criticisms may be too harsh; one of the key issues with developing any broad standard like ISO 14000 is that, in order to meet all needs, it is forced to be largely generic in nature. So the problem for users is mostly how to accommodate the intent of the standard and make it work with industry needs. There is an implicit assumption behind ISO 14000 that it will be adapted, and an adaptation can be seen as an industry adaptation.

In this context, one of the features of the Green Globe standards is that they develop and advance standards for the environmental improvement of the tourism industry that are linked to international policy on environmental impact.

WHOLE BUILDING RATING TOOLS AND ISO 14000
ISO 14000 refers to process. It gives a procedure to achieve environmental improvement that is relative to each organization.

Rogers observes:

An examination of ISO 14000 reveals no reference to this concept [environmental improvement] within these same sections of the Standard and the reference to environmental performance has been relegated to the definition of the term (3.8) and indirectly to continual improvement and some comments in the Annex. In fact, the Introduction to the Standard specifically discounts the need to consider performance beyond that set by legal requirements when it states *'It should be noted that this International Standard does not establish absolute requirements for environmental performance beyond commitment, in the policy, to compliance with applicable legislation and regulations and to continual improvement'.* [17]

Generally, the argument that emerges from this is that, while the ISO 14000 does not mandate absolute standards, it has a relativist approach to the context in which it is placed. In the development of the Design and Construct standard, one of the pilot projects, the Novotel & Ibis Hotel at Sydney Olympic Park involved the use of ISO 14000. This was for two main purposes:

1   to provide a legal instrument to ensure the building owners created and operated a building in line with the environmental guidelines of the Olympic Park precinct;
2   to provide an ongoing improvement to environmental impacts during the operation of the building.

Building assessment tools (BEA) tools have evolved as a voluntary rather than a legal basis for assessing both the design phase and operational environmental performance. The Design and Construct standard follows this pattern and provides targets and industry benchmarks that comprise an industry norm. Other tools have followed a similar pattern in recent years but use a rating process and can be called 'whole-building rating tools'. They attempt to extend the ISO 14000 methodology in a similar way.

Generally, with rating tools the standard is fixed but the criteria may change. Thus, in the LEED rating tool there are a set number of credits but some additional credits may be used. With energy rating tools, such as the Building Energy Rating System, which uses computer simulation, the building envelope can be manipulated to give an optimum energy performance. A number of assumptions are made about the building occupancy

schedule and thermostat settings. Criteria and benchmarks are fixed, for example a building is assumed to be air conditioned and a three-star rating is given if the predicted energy consumption is 30 kWh/m^2/year. Hence, with a rating tool the emphasis is on the rating how one building compares to another in a competition for environmental performance. Rating becomes equivalent to design performance.

However, the main question here is: How does the Green Globe approach differ from rating tools such as LEED and BREEAM?

Components of the Green Globe system

Examining the components of the Design and Construct standard and its part in the benchmarking system developed by Green Globe for tourism buildings might address this question. There are three main components to the system:

- environmental criteria and indicators;
- benchmarking process, which involves collecting performance data on the building, in relation to a database of performance benchmarks;
- assessment process comparing the data from the building against the benchmarks.

Environmental criteria

The environmental criteria for Design are organized into the following categories:

1   sustainability design approach;
2   energy consumption;
3   potable water consumption;
4   solid waste production;
5   social commitment;
6   resource conservation;
7   siting; and
8   waste water management.

The environmental criteria for Construction are organized into the following categories:

1   sustainability construction policy;
2   energy consumption;

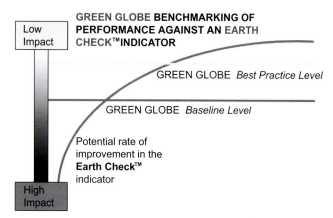

Low
Impact

**GREEN GLOBE BENCHMARKING OF
PERFORMANCE AGAINST AN EARTH
CHECK™INDICATOR**

GREEN GLOBE *Best Practice Level*

GREEN GLOBE *Baseline Level*

Potential rate of
improvement in the
Earth Check™
indicator

High
Impact

5.4 Benchmarking process leads to determining best practice. Green
Globe sets a baseline and best practice level.

3   potable water consumption;

4   solid waste production;

5   social commitment;

6   resource conservation;

7   site management;

8   waste water management; and

9   air quality protection and noise control.

Each category has a set of indicators to collect information on
the predicted performance of the building. These indicators are
used in the benchmarks.

Benchmarking

Benchmarking involves comparing the performance data from
building against predetermined levels. Benchmarks are established for all indicators. This is a complex process; a simple
explanation is that the benchmarks depend on the following variables:

1   Sector and sub sectors – for example, the hotels sector has
    four main sub-sectors: business hotels, accommodation
    hotels, motels, and hostels.

2   Quantitative indicators, such as energy, vary with the lati-
    tude and/or location and the sub-sector.

3   Other variables are taken into consideration, such as area
    under roof and occupancy rate, or 'guest nights'.

4   Qualitative indicators, such as meeting policy implemen-
    tation requirements, do not vary and apply to all sectors,

Collecting valid benchmarks is a time-consuming and expensive process, and hence for most benchmarking systems these
records are kept in a confidential database. The benchmarking
assessment is administered by a separate organization called
Earth Check$_{TM}$.[18] This makes it quite difficult to know what level
to aim for in improving performance to meet best practice standards. Since improved environmental performance can be
linked to cost, targets are provided to help designers complete
the benchmarking process. The benchmarks for the standard are
updated as part of an ongoing process of research into environmental 'best practice' for the travel and tourism industry.

Assessment process

Applying the Design and Construct standard involves three steps:
A, B, and C.

A: AFFILIATION

The developer becomes affiliated for the project with Green
Globe. Green Globe provides a pre-commitment questionnaire,
which assists with establishing whether the scope of the projects fits its standard.

B: BENCHMARKING ASSESSMENT

If the developer decides to proceed, Green Globe requires submission of documentation concerning the details of the environmental design and construction of the project that address
the environmental criteria. Green Globe provide the following
documents to assist with this process:

• handbook explaining the system;

• two spreadsheets – one for recording environmental design
  aspects and one for construction; and

• documentation list requesting specific additional information.

The data is evaluated by Green Globe and a benchmarking
report provided. If the project meets its standard, the benchmarking report authorizes the developer to use the Green
Globe logo.

5.5   Sundancer Resort. Passive design is assessed in the Green Globe Standard. High-quality envelopes with shading and natural-ventilation mixed-mode HVAC systems ensure operational savings in cost and energy.

C: CERTIFICATION

A further step can be taken that involves certifying the project fully, once construction is completed. This involves the appointment of a third-party auditor to review the benchmarking data and to validate the project. Green Globe has accredited assessors for this purpose.

Once certification is complete and accepted by Green Globe, the developer can use the Green Globe logo with a tick.[19] This is a simplified description of the process, and more details be found on the Green Globe website.[20]

A few questions are asked about this process: first, why the three steps and, second, why the benchmarking and certification process?

The three steps allow a staged approach to design-phase assessment that can operate within the design process. So, affiliation is recommended at the feasibility stage, to match the scope of the project with the standard. Benchmarking is at the sketch design stage, when strategies are being put in place to meet environmental criteria (interim assessment) and certification is at the post construction stage, once the project has reached completion, to assess the construction process and to check that the strategies envisaged at the sketch design stage have been adopted. Hence, the Design and Construct standard is a design phase benchmarking system.

Green Globe has further standards and systems to be applied once the building is occupied and functioning. The standards have been developed in a modular form, nested together to give a range of services for certifying environmental performance. The following examination of one part of the Design and Construct standard will give some insight as to the type of information that needs to be collected for the assessment process.

The Design and Construct standard

The Design and Construct (D&C) standard contains two sections: one with indicators for the design phase, the other with indicators for construction.

The Design standard

The Design section of the D&C standard has seven main categories, each with a set of indicators to measure predicted performance.

The first category deals with design approach and sustainable policy. Research has shown that the environmental briefing approach advocated in the standard needs support, so the first indicator is concerned with the spirit of the project brief. The standard requires the developer to brief the design team,

5.6   Sundancer Resort. The multidisciplinary team is crucial to green design. A member of the design team takes responsibility for providing assessment information for completing the benchmarking process.

from the outset, on the primacy of the environmental goals. This is perhaps the most important of all the indicators, since without an appropriate initial direction it would be difficult to expand the brief later to include environmental issues.

Moreover, it is recommended that a multidisciplinary team be used to implement this policy. A significant additional feature is an environmental management system, linking design and operational conditions, so that post construction environmental improvement can be pursued.

These are perhaps the most crucial parts of the standard, because should the requirements not be met then the likelihood of a successful 'green building' is drastically reduced. Ongoing environmental improvement depends on having policies in place in the main design documentation that will ensure the desired outcomes. Furthermore, implementing the Construction standard, by means of the Construction contractual system, will also link the builder into this policy framework.

DESIGN APPROACH

Indicators for design approach and sustainable policy are as follows:

- sustainability goals and vision in the design brief and undertaking of an effective environmental management system;
- an interdisciplinary and coordinated approach between all design professionals;
- an operational statement for post construction project assessment, operational control and, where appropriate, continual improvement of environmental and local impact;
- cost plan to include budget for sustainable strategies as non-negotiable measures; and
- contractual agreement with builder to include sustainable construction standards.

Subsequent indicators examine the outcomes of the activities of the design team. The selection of site and location of buildings has a major effect on biodiversity and habitat loss. For example, the sub-indicators for siting examine whether the project is built on a greenfield or a reused site, as well as the extent to which habitats are retained by reducing building footprints.

ENERGY EFFICIENCY

Energy efficiency and conservation require input from the engineering side of the design team, although architects can assess the passive design aspects of the scheme.

Energy consumption measures, for energy efficiency, conservation and reduction in emissions are:

- total predicted energy consumption kWh per area under roof (m^2);
- total predicted energy consumption CO_2 per area under roof (m^2);
- total predicted energy consumption breakdown, kWh and CO_2 per area under roof;
- use of passive design;
- use of efficient active design; and
- total predicted renewable energy use/total predicted energy consumption.

The predicted energy consumption can be derived by calculation or by simulation methods. This needs to be converted to CO_2 emission equivalents to assess environmental effects with respect to climate modification. A breakdown of energy for areas of the building is also required.

A priority is given to improvements over existing standards, such as ASHRAE. In addition, strategies are in place to achieve passive design and efficient active design. A checklist for passive design and a template for the life cycle analysis information with regard to active systems is provided. Finally, it is a requirement that a proportion of the energy of the project should be derived from renewable energy.

In the design of the Sundancer Resort, the master planning assists with optimizing the layout of buildings for favourable orientation. This provides guests with choices between natural ventilation and air conditioning for climate control. The savings in energy and running costs achieved by this approach are significant.

POTABLE WATER CONSUMPTION

Emphasis is placed on controlling the demand for water consumption and on harvesting rainwater. This indicator is linked to wastewater management so that recycled wastewater can be recycled for purposes such as irrigation, reducing the use of potable water. In the case of the Sundancer Resort, rainwater can be used for potable water but the seasonal cycle is unbalanced, with distinct dry and wet seasons. The indicators for potable water consumption are as follows.

- total predicted potable water (litres/year) consumption per area under roof (m^2);
- total predicted potable water consumption breakdown per area under roof (m^2); and
- use of water conservation and efficient appliances.

SOLID WASTE PRODUCTION

Waste management is seen as an important part of the standard. This is structured similarly to the energy section, with qualitative and quantitative indicators. The indicators for solid waste production are:

- predicted volume of solid waste to landfill per area under roof;
- use of on-site waste disposal and efficient appliances; and
- predicted non-biodegradable chemical use per area under roof.

The Novotel & Ibis at Olympic Park in Sydney has a waste compaction process, which reduces solid waste to one-sixth of

5.8   Sundancer Resort. Local brick manufacture reduces transport energy and utilizes local labour.

normal volume for export to landfill. In addition, it has a worm farm on site that deals with its 5 tonnes of organic waste. The resulting humus from the farm is so nutrient-rich that it cannot be used for fertilizing the plants on site. It is taken to a local nursery for reuse, mixed with other organic materials, as fertilizer.

The waste policy at the hotel is undergoing continuous improvement and there are plans to sell organic waste to a biogas energy generator to create 'green power' that the hotel can purchase back from the energy company. This interlinking of systems for waste recycling is aimed at maximizing waste processing on site and reducing the volume of waste to landfill.

SOCIAL COMMITMENT

The indicators for social criteria are:

- design measures to integrate contextual parameters;
- minimal impacts on native land and population; and
- enhancement of the 'user's' understanding and integration with the natural and social environments.

The social indicators are aimed at encouraging a 'stakeholder approach' to interaction between the building and the local community – trying to be 'good neighbours'. For example, in the

5.7   Sundancer Resort. Social indicators in the Green Globe standard include working with the local community.

Novotel & Ibis development the hotel plays a central role in the social activities of the Olympic Park community at Homebush Bay. The building also organizes events for community awareness of environmental issues and provides a 'good neighbour' attitude to Olympic Park and the city by providing an observation centre at level 17. In addition, the building acts as an airport beacon and a focal point on the site. The company has established a partnership with the leading conservation organization, WWF (World Wide Fund for Nature). The value of annual donations is based on the number of guests the hotel accommodates per year.

RESOURCE CONSERVATION

The indicators for resource conservation relate to criteria concerning the selection of building materials and processes and are:

- selection of green materials and processes for low environmental impacts; and
- eco-label products purchased and local materials used.

A rating system is used for assessing the materials selected, as well as emphasizing the use of local materials. In the case of the Sundancer Resort, there is no eco-labelling system for materials in Indonesia, so the extent to which local and recycled materials were used was the main indicator for the assessment.

SITING

Indicators for siting to reduce impacts through land management are:

- area of habitat conserved/total site area (m^2);
- siting suitability;
- building footprint/site area (m^2); and
- environmental siting attributes.

The target for habitat conservation could be as low as zero, with attempting to conserve existing habitats as a major priority. For example, in the Heron Island Redevelopment some or all of the existing footprint of previously established buildings was reused, helping to reduce the footprint of new buildings to avoid further reducing the bird habitats on the island. The siting suitability also examines the transport options that

service the site with a view to reducing emissions from this impact.

Environmental siting attributes are rated as follows:

- landscaping for micro-climate control;
- site-specific species selection;
- re-introducing plants native to the specific site;
- maintaining existing gene pool and existing natural vegetation protection;
- encouraging retention of adolescent planting and saplings;
- ensuring group plantings are diverse species;
- grouping plantings from similar habitats;
- implementing rainwater irrigation strategies (soakage pits, contour terracing and swales);
- minimizing area of non-native grass planting or eliminating it totally; and
- zoning areas of planting into high and low maintenance, and zoning higher-maintenance planting near buildings.

WASTEWATER MANAGEMENT

The indicators for wastewater management are:

- predicted wastewater treatment on site/total wastewater generated.

In the case of the Novotel & Ibis and Sundancer, all wastewater is treated on site. In the case of Olympic Park, it is recycled and a grey water main is provided on site for use by the buildings in the precinct.

Construction standard

The aim of the Construction standard is to reduce impacts of construction on site. This has a structure similar to that of the Design standard but examines specific construction-related issues for reducing impacts. Policy focuses on the builders' approach to construction management and whether they have appropriate policies in place. Considerable importance is placed on the need to measure and manage the resource consumption and waste outputs on site. To this end, a link is made to the Design standard where monitoring and measurement is mandated through the contractual process. Details of the main indicators are given below.

SUSTAINABILITY CONSTRUCTION POLICY:

- builders experienced in sustainable construction;
- appropriate sustainable construction management.

RESOURCE CONSUMPTION AND WASTE PRODUCTION:

- total energy consumption on the building site (MJ) per day/area of building site (m^2);
- total water consumed on building site (kl) per day/area of building site (m^2); and
- total volume of construction waste to landfill (m^3) per day/area of building site (m^2).

SOCIAL COMMITMENT:

- management plan for accommodating social and cultural issues in place; and
- workers living within 20 km of building site/total number of workers.

CONSTRUCTION RESOURCE CONSERVATION:

- appropriate building construction process and systems selection for location and site conditions.
- construction containment area/total site area (m^2);
- documented storage and use of environmentally harmful substances;
- total wastewater collected for disposal per day/water used litres/day;
- number of noise complaints per week; and
- number of air pollution violations per week.

Assessment reports and certification

Assessment reports are written at the benchmarking and certification stages. The benchmarking and certification processes have different objectives and occur at different points in the design process.

Ideally benchmarking occurs during the design process so that self-certification can take place. The design team can input data on predicated impacts of the design and can check whether they have sufficient strategies and measures in place to meet the standard.

In the case of certification, this occurs post construction. Data on the construction process is obtained and consistency between the as-built project and the standard is examined, val-idating the as-built design against the standard. This is very important, as during construction strategies are often edited from buildings and this could compromise the design in terms of meeting the standard. The assessment recognizes this; projects obtain a Green Globe eco-label for the benchmarking process and an eco-label with a tick if they achieve full certification.

Hence, the standard can operate at a number of levels, as a design phase tool as well as a post construction assessment tool. The tool also nests with other Green Globe standards, such as the post construction Operations standards that are concerned with the on-going environmental management of the facility.

Experience in practice

Applying the Design and Construct standard in practice has meant matching the different aspects to the design process for most effective implementation. The Building Design Professionals (BDP) group has identified a number of stages in the design process and argues that no one set of issues can be matched exactly to each stage (see Table 5.2).

Generally, though, for design phase assessment the design process can be matched with indicators in the standard. Thus in the pre-design stage we have consideration of sustainable goals evident in the brief and in bringing together the environmental team. Planning the project involves selection of appropriate passive and active systems; water and waste strategies are put in place, and green materials selected.

Conceptual design comes from the social and architectural context: for example, on Heron Island the building solutions interpreted the local tropical aesthetic quality of the island. Site selection and placement of buildings is a further key area.

Further realization of the project's systems and technologies is accomplished at the detail design stage, when it becomes possible to take an environmental, rather than a 'business as usual', approach to system selection. The selections are directly quantifiable at this stage. Finally, an EMS system should be included, to allow for ongoing improvement in the building operations stage.

Pilot projects

Development of the assessment systems involved a number of projects. These were:

Table 5.2   Matching GG Design and Construct indicators to stages in the BDP framework

---

Stages and indicators

Pre design

    A1 Sustainability goals and vision in the design brief and undertaking of effective environmental management system

    A2 An interdisciplinary and coordinated approach between all design professionals

Planning

    C4 Use of passive design

    C5 Use of efficient active design

    C6 Total predicted renewable energy use/total predicted energy consumption

    D3 Use of water conservation and efficient appliances

    E1 Selection of green materials and processes for low environmental impacts

    D5 Use of on-site waste disposal and efficient appliances

Siting

    B1 Area of habitat conserved/total site area

    B2 Siting suitability

    B3 Building footprint/site area

    B4 Environmental siting attributes

Concept design

    G1 Design measures to integrate contextual parameters

    G2 Minimal impacts on native land and population

    G3 Enhancement of the 'user's' understanding of, and integration with, the natural and social environments

Detailed design

    C1 Total predicted energy consumption (kW or GJ)/area under roof (m^2)

    C2 Total predicted energy consumption CO_2 /area under roof (m^2)

    C3 Total predicted energy consumption breakdown (kW or GJ)/ CO_2 /area under roof

    D1 Total predicted potable water (litres/year) consumption per area under roof (m^2)

    D2 Total predicted potable water consumption breakdown per area under roof (m^2)

    D4 Predicted volume of solid waste to land fill/area under roof

    D6 Predicted non-biodegradable chemical use/area under roof

    D7 Predicted waste water treatment on site/total waste water generated

    E2 Eco-label products purchased

Building operation and management

    A3 Operational statement for post construction project assessment, operational control and, where appropriate, continual improvement of environmental and local impact

---

- Lark Quarry Trackways Building, Winton, Australia;
- Tramping Huts, Department of Conservation, New Zealand;
- Novotel & Ibis Hotel, Olympic Park. Homebush Bay, Sydney;
- Heron Island Redevelopment, The University of Queensland; and
- The Sundancer Resort, Lombok, Indonesia.

With the Lark Quarry project and the Tramping Huts, we were able to develop the benchmarking indicators and also the construction standard. The Novotel & Ibis project was assessed post construction, and assisted with developing the standard for large-scale hotel projects. The Heron Island Redevelopment posed development challenges in an area of great natural beauty and in a complicated atmosphere where a group of stakeholders carried joint responsibility for the management of an environmentally delicate island.

Benchmarking and other systems

The main differences are found in the benchmarking approach, where the criteria are fixed but the benchmarks can change. For an international tool such as Green Globe this is of crucial importance, since a wide range of types of tourism projects are built in very different locations and climates. The pilot projects exemplify this, where at one extreme there are small tramping huts and, at the other inner-city hotels. There are projects built on fragile coral islands and others in desert regions. Furthermore, the projects offer different levels of service: some are five-star, some-one star, which sets different energy demands for the projects. A major question emerged concerning how to create a rating system for this wide diversity of projects.

The solution to this problem lay in establishing and using a multi-criteria performance model with adjustable benchmarks. The downside of this approach is the scientific information needed to drive it; data is needed to establish benchmarks for different sizes of project in different contexts of climate and location. Then there is the issue of implementation; this procedure calls for the use of a third-party certification process, calling for expert assistance to make sure that the desired outcomes are achieved.

In summary, the Green Globe approach has as its basis the implementation of international policy as found in Agenda 21. This gives a clear framework from policy principles to indica-

tors. The notion of continual improvement means that designers and operators can implement a life cycle approach through the design and/or operational phase that:

1 is specific to the tourism industry and is applied to tourism facilities, such as hotels and resorts, rather than offices or houses;
2 has a broad scope to accommodate a wide-ranging scale of projects, from small tramping huts to large inner city hotels;
3 is performance based, through a tiered approach of affiliation, benchmarking and certification, thereby enabling a phased approach to assessment that matches the stages in the design process;
4 has a single baseline standard to meet – there are no credits, ratings or levels, but projects are encouraged to meet best-practice level, which simplifies the system and makes it easy to operate;
5 boasts a large database of performance information on which the standard is based to assist with setting project- and context-specific benchmarks;
6 has an eco-label that is given for different stages – the Green Globe label for benchmarking (without a tick), and the label with a tick at the post construction point;
7 involves a third-party assessment that allows expert opinion to bear on the assessment process.

Acknowledgements

Dr Deo Prasad, The University of New South Wales
Shailja Chandri, The University of New South Wales
Melinda Watt, Earth Check Pty Ltd
Joyce Law and Sattar Sattari, The University of Queensland
Dr Peter Dux, The University Queensland
Mark French, formerly of The University of Queensland
Dr Ashley Scott, formerly Griffith University
Judy Kraatz, formerly Griffith University
Richard Moore, The University of Queensland

5.9 Couran Cove Development, South Stradbroke Island. Daryl Jackson Architects. The GBC process and tool for environmental assessment of this resort development through research with the CRC for Sustainable Tourism.

5.10 Couran Cove Centre complex. Careful selection of the structural system using primarily timber systems reduces site and environmental impact. **Bottom right**. Eco cabin design utilizes passive design and solar hot water to reduce energy consumption. **Top right**. An existing mango orchard was utilized as a religious centre.

Green Building Challenge (GBC)

A performance approach to design assessment

GBC '98 has presented a unique approach to performance assessments through its use of national/regional overlays on top of a global core system. Thus the framework recognizes the importance of regional factors related to climatic, resource, economic and even cultural conditions. The 'regional layers' have been developed by national teams and are usable by participating countries even now, for the purpose of developing local labelling systems. [21]

Introduction

The aim of this section is to examine the nature of the Green Building Challenge. The approach is led by Canada and centres on an international exercise in defining 'best practice' in buildings.

Green Building Challenge (GBC) is an international collaborative effort to develop a building environmental assessment tool, that exposes and addresses controversial aspects of building performance, and from which the participating countries can selectively draw ideas to either incorporate into or modify their own tools. The GBC process is managed by the *International Initiative for a Sustainable Built Environment* (iiSBE), whose website is www.iisbe.org. The task of organizing Sustainable Building conferences that include GBC presentations is now being carried out by iiSBE. [22]

As can be seen from this approach, one of the key issues with an international effort like this is reflecting local regional benchmarks and weightings as key factors.

Aim of the GBC approach

The aim of the GBC approach is to improve building performance in specific areas. The relevant areas include:

- reduction of Greenhouse Gases (GHG) by reducing emissions of CO_2 and other emissions with similar impacts;
- reduction of acidification (emissions of SO_2 equivalents);
- reduction of other impacts on ecosystems; and
- reduced use of scarce resources, such as non-renewable fuels, materials, land and water.

All of this is to be achieved while maintaining optimum conditions for human health. [23]

One of the main aims of the approach focuses on core environmental issues, but a range of other factors, such as economics, is also included in the framework. The reason for this is to facilitate cooperation with the industry sector.

Larsson argues that issues like energy efficiency have not been strong drivers for industry action during the last decade because of low fuel prices.

For commercial buildings, the main driver is economic gain, which means that first-order decisions are concerned with economic issues, and environmental issues become secondary. This in turn creates a central paradox in the area of environmental assessment-based systems, and leaves investors, developers and designers searching for economic gains from the use of environmental strategies. Their needs, however, are likely to be filled *indirectly* by the use of environmental strategies benefiting process improvements, indoor environmental air quality and life cycle costs. [24]

Therefore finding economic arguments for implementing environmental strategies is a challenge central to the GBC approach. It still remains a significant barrier to implementation, in that there are economic disincentives to implementation of green design.

In summary, the argument for the GBC approach is that green building guidelines and standards must address core environmental issues, but should also cover other issues of relevance to the industry. This is seen as a way to neutralize economic disincentives to green design.

Precepts

GBC working with the building context
The GBC approach is seen as nested within a broader range of industry-based initiatives aimed at neutralizing the economic disincentives to green design.

Design thinking, strategizing and auditing
A central part of the GBC is to ground the approach in the normal development process that includes:

- planning (of the area in which the building is located);
- site acquisition;
- financing;
- development permit;
- schematic design;
- contract documentation (drawings and specs);
- procurement;
- construction;
- operation; and
- demolition.

IMPACT OF DESIGN DECISIONS, PROCESS CONTROL AND BUILDING PERFORMANCE

Much of the theory underpinning the GBC approach concerns the relationship between design decisions and control over the design process, and its effect on the eventual building process.

Larsson argues that it is generally accepted that the impact of design decisions varies inversely with the time in the process at which the decision is made; this rule means that the cost of a decision varies directly with time. Experience suggests that early decisions are usually 'cheap' and have a major impact on the ultimate performance of the building, while later changes are often expensive and can be less effective in improving performance.[25] If this argument is accepted, it becomes clear that the very early phases of planning, site acquisition and financing must not be overlooked as potential points for encouraging environmentally high performance, and that the schematic design phase is of critical importance for incorporating green strategies. There is a question that arises from this line of argument: Is there a *green design process* that is different from the traditional methods of procuring buildings?

Towards a green design process

As part of the GBC development work, generic design steps have been developed (set out in C-2000 software C2k-P).[26] This sets out input at the key decision-making points in the design process. For convenience, these have been listed in three tables, with each table representing a stage in this process. From these, descriptions of the main activities that are central to design phase activity can be derived.

This design process has two main dimensions: first, activities that should take place with respect to green design; second, where these activities should be positioned in the process. The activities can be categorized and described as follows:

- strategizing, proposing, developing green strategies to reduce environmental impacts;
- auditing, checking, assessing, confirming, determining agreements to decisions regarding the strategies;
- documentation, preparing, summarizing outcomes of strategies and reporting.

The main steps identified are as follows.

1 pre-design;
2 sketch design;
3 design development; and
4 post construction.

Additional management issues have been raised with regard to greening the design process. These include:

- interdisciplinary work between architects, engineers and operations staff right from the beginning of the design process;
- discussion of the relative importance of various performance issues and the establishment of a consensus on these between client and designers;
- the provision of a design facilitator, to raise performance issues throughout the process and to bring specialized knowledge to the table;
- a clear articulation of performance targets and strategies, to be updated throughout the process;
- the use of energy simulations to provide relatively objective information on key aspects of performance; and
- documentation of major steps and issues raised in the process.[27]

Simple software design support tools have been produced to help design teams enrolled in the C-2000 programme. One outlines generic design steps and provides a simple way for designers to record their performance targets and strategies; another facilitates the client and design team in reaching a consensus on the relative importance of various issues. The C-2000 IDP process is now being used as a model for development of a generic international model, by Task 23 of the International Energy Agency, and discussions are under way with the Royal Architectural Institute of Canada (RAIC) to see whether the process can be accepted as an alternative form of delivery of professional services.[28]

RESEARCH BACKGROUND

Since the mid 1990s, considerable research has been focused on the development of systems to assess the environmental performance of buildings, GBC being only one of many. Lessons learnt from this are threefold.

The first is that it is possible to develop an eco-labelling system that indicates the building's approximate performance clearly to end-users. Larsson argues that it is better to view these as 'approximate', since building performance includes many factors, only some of which are measurable in an exact sense.

The second is confirmation of the merit of this approach, in that

researchers and government agencies are viewing performance rating and labelling systems as one of the best methods of moving the performance benchmarks in the marketplace towards a higher level of performance. There is a growing realization that a major jump in performance levels, at least in market economies, will depend on changes in market demand, and that such change cannot occur until building investors and tenants have access to a relatively simple method that allows them to identify buildings that perform to a higher standard.[29]

The third shows the way to more specialized schemes, such as those more closely tied to life cycle assessment (LCA), including ECO QUANTUM (Netherlands), ECO-PRO (Germany), EQUER (France) and Athena (Canada).[30]

GBC components

The main components of the GBC systems are as follows:

- international programme of collaboration;
- environmental criteria;
- benchmarking and weighting; and
- assessment process.

The GBC approach has evolved through a series of international collaborations to identify best-practice green building. The milestones listed below follow the presentation of the work on the sustainable building conference stage since 1998. These were the GBC '98 conference, Vancouver 1998; International Sustainable Buildings 2000 conference, Maastricht, the Netherlands; and International Sustainable Buildings 2002 conference, Oslo, Norway (GBC 2002). National teams from 16 countries participated in GBC 2002.[31]

This sequence of conferences has contributed to the development of an assessment framework, in the form of computer software (*GBTool*), which enables a full description of the building and of its performance and allows users to carry out assessments relative to regional benchmarks.

The international collaboration is set to evolve with the Green Building Challenge 2005 at the Sustainable Building 05 Conference (SB'05). This is a continuation of the GBC 1998 to 2002 process and of the multi-year period of review, modification and testing of the GBC Assessment Framework and Green Building Tool (*GBTool*). This round of the GBC process culminated in the presentation of the assessed buildings at SB'05 held in Tokyo, Japan, in September 2005, while intermediate stages and the preparation phase were to be discussed at the five regional conferences at SB'04.[32]

Environmental criteria

In the performance assessment framework developed for the international Green Building Challenge process, a complete range of Green Building issues is outlined in Table 5.3.

In the *GBTool* software, the parameters extend to two finer levels of detail: criteria and sub-criteria. The lowest level consists of scoring guide statements, which are intended to assist users to assign performance scores from –2 to +5, where 0 represents minimum industry practice, +3 best practice and +5 the best achievable without regard to cost-effectiveness.

Benchmarks and weightings

Benchmarks and weightings are set locally. In essence, the weightings for each country are developed from expert opinion decided by ballot. A critical feature of *GBTool* is that scoring is done relative to explicitly declared benchmarks. Each national team was requested to complete the benchmark values of a specifically designated section of *GBTool*, and these were subsequently automatically accessed and referenced in the analysis. The choice of benchmark value is therefore critical to the overall performance assessment; this is a feature that requires very clear direction on its selection and use within *GBTool*.

In addition to the relative measure of building performance, 12 environmental sustainability indicators (ESIs) are used as

Table 5.3 *GBTool* categories and indicators

Categories and indicators

Resource consumption
        Net consumption of delivered energy
        Net consumption of land
        Net consumption of potable water
        Net consumption of materials

Environmental loadings
        Emission of greenhouse gases
        Emission of ozone-depleting substances
        Emission of gases leading to acidification
        Solid wastes
        Liquid wastes
        Impacts on site and adjacent properties

Service quality
        Air quality and ventilation
        Thermal comfort
        Daylighting, illumination and visual access
        Noise and acoustics
        Flexibility and adaptability
        Maintenance of performance
        Controllability of systems

Pre-operations planning
        Construction process planning
        Performance tuning
        Building operations planning
        Transportation management planning

Economics
        Life cycle costs
        Capital costs
        Operating and maintenance costs

---

absolute measures of performance. These are absolute performance measures, which characterize sustainable building practices and facilitate international comparability. These indicators represent the environmental criteria used in the system.[33]

Assessment

Assessment is carried out using *GBTool*. Each national team customizes the tool in terms of its weights and benchmarks. The assessment framework for 2002 involved the following:

1   National teams obtain access to selected projects developed by a team of international experts under the direction of an International Framework Committee.

2   GBC provides the current GBC2002 version of *GBTool* in MS Excel format and an integrated manual available on line.

3   The core assessment framework is adapted by national teams to the conditions of their own countries and regions. The regionally adapted systems reflect issues such as regional energy and environmental priorities, cost-effectiveness and urban planning issues.

4   Buildings to be assessed are selected by national teams to represent 'best practice', and conform to key criteria of the assessment framework. National teams supervise the information-gathering process for these buildings, including a detailed characterization of the building, a description of the process followed in its design, construction and operation, and planned building operation procedures. The teams undertake energy simulations using accepted computer programs like DOE-2 or EE4 (in Canada).

5   A central quality-control mechanism ensures that national teams use relatively consistent assumptions. The heart of the process is the detailed assessment of two or more 'best practice' buildings from each participating country. The results are scored, weighted and graphically represented, all assisted by *GBTool* – a program developed especially for the purpose.[34]

Experience in practice

The projects

The GBC approach appears to operate at two levels. At the international level, the search for best practice buildings drives both the advancement of green design and the evolution of the assessment process as a reward system for high-performance buildings. The Philip Merrill Center is an example of a project that was part of the 2002 GBC process from the US team. At the commercial level, particularly in Canada, the process enters into a range of initiatives. Larsson argues

The commercial buildings industry is driven almost exclusively by considerations of capital cost and return on investments. This fact, combined with the very low cost

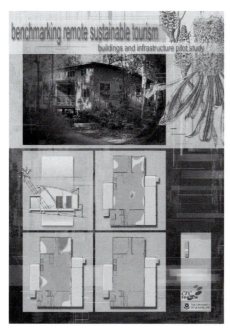 

5.11 Right. Couran Cove. GBC analysis shows the output from the GB tool. Left. Analysis of the eco cabins as part of the work on the GB tool.

of energy during the 1990s, made it difficult to move the industry towards high levels of energy-efficient perform-ance. Programs such as the C2000 Program from Natural Resources Canada are of relevance.[35]

In addition, the GBC process has identified broad policy ini-tiatives to advance green design through strategies for public sec-tor and private sector implementation.[36] Larsson argues that these initiatives are critical to greening the design process through greater synergy between professionals.

For designers, use of the Integrated Design Process encour-ages many engineers to become involved in the early design stage of buildings for the first time; and architects are learning valuable new skills. When this is combined with the incentives available, it is difficult to see any obsta-cles to widespread participation. When labelling systems are widely available, more definitive proof of the impor-tance of high performance will be at hand and poorly per-forming buildings will hopefully become a relic of the 20th Century.' [37]

The *GBTool* application of the GBC system was used in the Couran Cove project described in this section and in the Philip Merrill Center described in Chapter 11.

Acknowledgements

This section is reworked from papers written by Nils Larsson, Natural Resources Canada Ottawa, April 2000, and information developed by Ray Cole (see the iiSBE website www.iisbe.org).

6.1 The Environmental Building, Building Research Station, Garston, UK.
Architects: Feilden Clegg of Bath.

Chapter 6

Rating systems

The last five years has seen a profusion of new green building rating systems ... at first glance it might appear as if each tool performs the same function as the others, but closer inspection reveals they all cater to different markets, phases and building types. It remains to be seen whether the industry will embrace a 'one tool fits all' approach or pick and choose different systems for different uses.[1]

Introduction

The aim of this chapter is to examine the nature of rating systems using a number of examples. Rating systems by definition have three main components. First, a set of environmental criteria is created, usually derived from the negative impacts on the environment caused by unsustainable development. Second, a scoring system is developed for assessing whether the environmental performance is improved; this examines issues such as the predicted energy use and gives a score for the performance level achieved. Third, a system of weightings is usually

applied to the scores; for example, in some systems energy is seen as a very important issue, and hence energy would be given a higher weighting in the total score. There has been debate about ways of arriving at an appropriate weighting system.

As a result of the assessment and the weighting system, an overall score is given for the environmental performance of the building, which is then compared to the performance benchmark, or a set of benchmarks, or to a set level. Some systems use a star rating for performance benchmarking, while others set a 'best practice' level.

Three systems are examined here: the BREEAM system from the Building Research Establishment in the UK, the LEED system from the USA and the Green Star system from Australia.

Overview

Labelling is a well-established method for conveying to consumers important credentials on a product's performance. Rating systems are an extension of the labelling concept that enables the environmental performance of buildings to be defined or

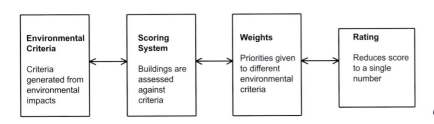

6.2 The general components of rating systems.

labelled using a common set of industry-agreed benchmarks and measurement methods. This allows for credible and transparent reporting of a building's environmental attributes and avoids ambiguous claims regarding green performance.

Support

Support for rating systems comes from various players in the property industry:

- developers;
- government;
- building designers;
- building owners;
- tenants; and
- investors.

Importantly, from an environmental briefing perspective, rating systems allow developers and owner-occupiers to specify easily the environmental performance requirements for a building, by simply stating the rating to be achieved. Developers are rewarded for this commitment by way of the label awarded to the building, which can be used for marketing purposes.

Governments often use rating systems to set benchmarks for their own buildings; for example, in the UK the government has specified that BREEAM environmental assessments must be undertaken on all new and refurbished government projects.[2] The BREEAM rating specified for these projects was increased from 'good' in 2001 to 'excellent' in 2003.

The support of rating systems by government has given these systems additional momentum. Since government is the largest player in the property industry, designers and contractors need to get up to speed with green design and rating systems to help win projects for this major client.

Most rating schemes are voluntary, often run by not-for-profit industry organizations such as 'green building' councils, which can now be found in many countries. Their intent is to recognize and reward best practice buildings, usually those in the top 25 per cent of environmental performance. This approach complements legislation, through which governments usually set minimum standards for environmental performance. Legislation sets the bar for all buildings to achieve; rating schemes provide an additional, higher performance, target. Put another way, legislation 'pushes' the bottom of the development market towards better environmental performance, while rating schemes 'pull' the upper end onwards and upwards.

Sometimes local governments and councils include imposed ratings in their planning conditions. This has the effect of bringing 'voluntary' rating schemes into the legislative ambit of the market – for which they were not intended. However, it is possible to use rating systems creatively in the planning process and still keep them voluntary by awarding developers with dispen-

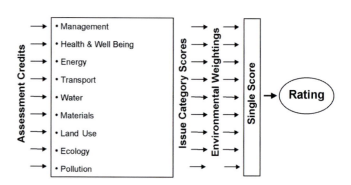

6.3 **Left**. The Environmental Building, Building Research Establishment, Garston, UK. Façade made from photovoltaic systems. **Above**. BREEAM rating system, which was developed using data from the Environmental Building.

sations (such as increased heights or yields) for agreeing to achieve certain ratings.

For designers, rating systems provide 'a methodology to ensure that an integrated approach is taken for the design of the project and that environmentally sustainable outcomes are aimed for. This maximizes the likelihood that the resulting project will have an enhanced environmental performance and reduced life cycle costs.'[3]

Building owners can use rating tools to demonstrate the environmental credentials of their buildings in operation. Tenants can use rating tools to assess their own tenancy fit-out, and to assess the performance of the base building prior to signing or re-signing a tenancy agreement. With the growth in ethical investment funds, rating tools can be used by investors to determine whether a building should be included in an ethical investment portfolio.

Types of systems

Rating systems are rapidly springing up around the world and the challenge is to pick the right one for a particular application in a given country. In Australia, for example, the current rating schemes are separated into two types, depending on whether the rating is done before or after occupation:

1   design phase systems; and
2   operational phase systems.

NatHERS (National House Energy Rating Scheme), FirstRate and BASIX (Building Sustainability Index),[1] cover residential buildings, while Green Star and ABGR (Australian Building Greenhouse Rating) cover commercial buildings. Furthermore, these systems measure either energy performance (NatHERS, FirstRate) or environmental performance (BASIX) for design. ABGR covers environmental performance. NABERS (National Australian Built Environment Rating System) is concerned with environmental performance for the operational phase. It can certainly get a little confusing specifying the right tool for the right job! In the UK and US, where BREEAM (Building Research Establishment Environmental Assessment Method) and LEED (Leadership in Energy and Environmental Design) are well established, there tends to be less variety, and consequently less confusion in the market.

Governments, research institutions, private firms and not-for-profit industry organizations have developed rating systems in various ways. There are no global standard assessment criteria or methods of measurement, so the schemes are generally not compatible across different countries.

Rating systems are designed for different building types and different stages in the property life cycle. The typical building types covered include commercial (typically offices), tenancy fit-out, residential, retail, hospitals, schools and industrial. While many environmental criteria are common to all building types, rating systems are usually best developed specifically to suit each type, because of the varying characteristics and operational functions of the different building types.

Rating systems can provide either design/construction stage ratings (predicting the potential environmental performance of the building) or operational stage ratings (measuring the actual environmental performance of the building). Again, while many environmental criteria are common to both, the differences in method of measurement and integration into the design process, design or operational phases, typically require different assessment systems. Rating systems for the design phase measure the *predicted* environmental performance, while operation phase assessment measures *actual* environmental performance.

Structure

Rating systems generally adhere to the same basic structure.

Environmental criteria

The environmental criteria are the fundamental component of any rating system and are usually developed by considering how the negative impacts of buildings on the environment can be reduced. These criteria are usually grouped under environmental categories such as energy, water and indoor environment quality.

The criteria in the rating system usually relate to a combination of the following depending on whether the rating is to be done during the design stage or for an existing building in operation:

• predicted performance (e.g. energy modelling during design stage);
• actual performance (e.g. actual energy consumption taken from meter readings in existing buildings);

- specification (e.g. selection of materials to meet specific criteria, such as off-gassing or recycled content);
- design process (e.g. appointment of qualified professionals);
- construction process (e.g. environmental management plans and waste targets);
- facility management (e.g. environmental management systems, green transport plans and occupant satisfaction monitoring);
- ability to influence or improve operation (e.g. commissioning, user manuals, energy policy and plans); and
- innovation (to encourage spread of new technologies and processes that reduce environmental impact).

Scores

A scoring system is used for assessing whether the environmental performance is improved. Credits or points are awarded for achieving various environmental criteria. The number of points or credits awarded for each criterion is usually scaled to the relative environmental impact of each issue within each environmental category.

Some rating schemes have mandatory requirements, which, if they are not achieved, mean that no rating is possible. For example, LEED has seven mandatory or prerequisite credit criteria, including minimum energy performance requirements and avoidance of building on land of high ecological value.

Weightings

This is the component where rating systems really start to diversify in their approach and structure. Some systems, such as BREEAM and Green Star, apply an environmental weighting factor to each environmental category, so that the relative impact of different issues such as energy and water can be consolidated into a single rating. For example, in Australia's Green Star system energy has the highest overall weighting (typically 25 per cent of the total score) because of concerns about greenhouse emissions and climate change.

The LEED system does not apply direct environmental weightings to environmental categories. Instead, points are simply added to give a total score. However, the categories have an inherent environmental weighting by virtue of the number of points awarded in each. With this approach there is less flexi-

bility in the application of environmental weightings. For example, it is not easy to vary the inherent weightings of the categories to account for changes in environmental impacts across large countries (e.g. water in desert regions may need a higher weighting than water in tropical regions).

Some argue that neither of these approaches to weightings is acceptable, and that you cannot compare or trade off environmental impacts such as energy, water and natural resource consumption – they are all important. However, rating systems typically need to do this to generate a single score, in order to provide clear and simple labels for the building industry to understand and embrace.

An alternative approach to weighting of the environmental criteria is to limit the final rating to the lowest score achieved in any of the environmental categories. This means that for a building to achieve a high rating it must score well in all environmental categories, and cannot trade off good performance in one area for poor performance in another.

Rating

For most rating systems an overall score is calculated, based on the scores achieved for the various environmental criteria and the application of the weighting factors. This score is then compared to a performance benchmark or set of benchmarks or levels. Assuming that all mandatory criteria are achieved, a rating is determined. The ratings, representing 'good practice' through to 'excellence', are described in different ways. Some schemes use star ratings, some use precious metals (silver, gold, platinum), while others use descriptions (good, very good and excellent).

Most rating systems do not allow a building rating to be publicly promoted until it has been independently certified and the necessary fees paid to the certifying organization.

BREEAM (UK)

The Building Research Establishment Environmental Assessment Method (BREEAM), launched in the UK in 1990, was the world's first rating system for buildings and is still going strong today. It was conceived as a tool to stimulate demand for green buildings in the UK market and to send signals to clients and occupiers who wish to do something for the environment. It seeks

6.4 The Environmental Building, BRE. **Left**. The use of daylighting in all areas where possible reduces energy consumption. In this case large southerly windows bring diffused light, reducing solar heat loads. Balancing the positive effects of natural light with the negative effects of external heat gains requires careful window-sizing and shading design. Rating systems reward the use of daylight but cannot necessarily include such subtlety in the assessment. **Right**. Use of the ceiling as a luminaire can enhance the synergy between electric lighting and daylighting systems.

to provide authoritative guidance on ways of minimizing the adverse effects of buildings on the global and local environments, while promoting a healthy and comfortable indoor environment. It aims to achieve this by addressing:

- environmental impacts, leading to protection and perhaps enhancement of the environment by reducing pollution of air, land and water;
- prudent use of natural resources by providing durable buildings able to survive changes of fashion and use; selection of materials and products with better environmental performance; encouraging appropriate recycling; encouraging the reuse of buildings; encouraging the reuse of land and water economy, as well as other environmental impacts; and
- quality of life, with competitive business providing high-quality built environments, buildings and indoor environments to satisfy human and business needs.

BREEAM approach

The basis of the scheme is a certificate awarded to individual buildings on the basis of credits for a set of performance criteria. The certificate provides a label for the building that enables the owners or occupants to gain recognition for the building's environmental performance. The certificate can be displayed in the building or used as part of an organization's overall envi-

ronmental statement. In the UK it has widely been accepted as representing best practice, with significant market penetration.

The first version of BREEAM developed by the Building Research Establishment (BRE) was for office buildings. It may be applied either at the design or the refurbishment stage, or for existing buildings in operation.

Since its launch in 1990 *BREEAM for Offices* has undergone numerous revisions and is now updated annually to take advantage of new research and data on environmental impacts, to build on experience gained and to reflect increasing legislative requirements. The aim is to ensure that BREEAM continues to represent current best practice, going beyond what is required by regulations.

BREEAM for Offices has formed the basis for rating schemes for other building types developed by BRE including:

- EcoHomes;
- Industrial BREEAM;
- NEAT (National Health Service Environmental Assessment Tool);
- BREEAM for Retail; and
- BREEAM for Schools (currently under development).

The framework for *BREEAM for Offices* is described below. The rating systems for other building types are generally consistent with this approach but will have different credit criteria.

Table 6.1 BREEAM rating scores

Rating	Points required
Pass	25
Good	40
Very good	55
Excellent	75

BREEAM framework

The framework for BREEAM is shown in Figure 6.2. It comprises assessment credits in nine environmental categories. The assessment credits are awarded when specific criteria or performance levels are achieved.

The credits achieved in a particular category are then added together and a category score, expressed as a percentage, is calculated, based on the credits achieved divided by the total credits available in that category. A weighting factor is then applied to each category score, and these weighted scores are then added together to give a single score out of 100.

Assessment credits

The philosophy of BREEAM is to reward positive steps taken to improve the environmental performance of buildings, rather than penalize for poor performance. If a building achieves the criteria for a particular credit issue then credits are awarded. If a building performs poorly against a particular issue then credits will simply not be awarded – there are no negative credits or credit deductions. Unlike LEED or Green Star, BREEAM does not have any mandatory or prerequisite credit requirements to achieve a rating.

The number of credits in each category does not reflect the relative importance of each category as this is defined by the weighting factors. Consequently a credit in one category is not equal to a credit in another category.

BREEAM for Offices covers both new and existing buildings. Some credits are common to both, while others are specific to either the design stage or the operation of the building. Consequently, *BREEAM for Offices* has three types of credits:

1. core buildings credits (C);
2. design and procurement credits (D); and
3. management and operation credits (M).

All assessments require core credits to be assessed. For new building assessments, design and procurement credits are assessed together with the core credits. For existing buildings, management and operation credits are assessed together with the core credits.

1. *Core (C).* The issues assessed allow a comparative assessment of a building's potential environmental impacts during operation. This enables buildings of any age to be compared across the range of issues covered to give a consistent index for the property market.
2. *Design and procurement (D),* These credits aim to optimize the outcome of the design/procurement stage and are carried out for all new build and refurbished designs. The credits address issues that are of relevance during the design process, such as issues of specification and process.
3. *Management and operation (M).* These credits are only applicable for existing buildings that are occupied, and essentially provide an independent audit of the way the building is being managed.

Environmental weightings

There are effectively two types of environmental weighting in BREEAM. First, there is an implicit weighting of credits within each category by virtue of how many credits are available for any particular issue. For example, Construction Site Impacts accounts for over half the credits available under the Management category for new buildings. Consequently, this issue has a higher inherent weighting than, for example, Commissioning.

The approach in BREEAM of consolidating the scores for each environmental category into a single score requires that weighting factors be applied to the different environmental categories (Table 6.2). Transport and energy are grouped together, since both categories are concerned with greenhouse emissions. BRE estimate that the emissions that result from commuting and business travel to and from a typical office building in the UK (pri-

Table 6.2 Weighting factors in BREEAM

Category	Weighting (%)
Management	15
Health and well-being	15
Energy Transport }	25
Water	5
Materials	10
Land use Ecology }	15
Pollution	5
	100

marily due to cars) are roughly equal to the greenhouse emissions that result from the building's consumption of energy. Consequently both have an equal weighting in BREEAM.

Environmental weightings are subject to much debate and opinion, and the determination of the weighting factors is therefore critical to the credibility and validity of a rating system. To determine the weighting factors, BRE sought expert opinion to create a consensus between government policy makers, construction professionals, local authorities, materials producers, developers, investors, environmental groups and lobbyists, and academics. There is debate as to whether this is effective, as it opens the rating system up to broader public policy, which may be conservative with regard to the move to sustainable development. However, rating systems are fluid, open to change and development over time, enabling them to adapt to reflect new research and changes in environmental concerns.

Certification process

BREEAM Accredited Assessors are trained and licensed by BRE to carry out formal assessment reviews and prepare assessment reports for submission to BRE for certification. Stringent quality management procedures have been adopted to ensure a consistent approach and level of service.

BRE review and certify all BREEAM assessments. A certificate is then issued on the basis of the report prepared by the BREEAM Accredited Assessor.

The green building market and BREEAM

The Building Research Establishment was previously a public sector organization. It was privatized in 1997 and is now run by the BRE Trust, a registered charity with a mission to champion excellence and innovation in the built environment. It has developed and administered BREEAM with support from the UK government. As its name suggests, it is primarily a research organization and has aims and funding streams different from those of not-for-profit advocacy organizations such as the US Green Building Council and the Green Building Council of Australia. Consequently, the way that BREEAM is promoted and administered in the UK differs from the more commercialized approach in the US and Australia.

In the UK, BREEAM tends to be a stand-alone rating system, rather than part of an integrated package of industry education, advocacy and product certification. Despite being less vigorous in its promotion than other rating systems overseas, BREEAM has had significant penetration in the UK market. The UK government have specified that BREEAM environmental assessments be undertaken on all new and refurbished government projects. The BREEAM rating required from 2003 onwards is 'excellent.'[4] Furthermore, since 1 April 2003, all new government-funded public housing schemes have to receive a minimum EcoHomes rating of 'pass' or they will not be funded. Financial incentives are in place to achieve higher ratings.[5] Finally, the track record for BREEAM shows that over 1,000 office buildings have been certified to the end of 2004.[6]

BREEAM has also had an impact worldwide and has formed the basis of rating tools in a variety of countries including Australia (Green Star), Hong Kong (HKBEAM), New Zealand (GreenHomes) and Canada (BREEAM Canada and BREEAM Green Leaf).

It should be realized that the development of this system has not been carried out purely as a theoretical exercise. The system has evolved, and continues to evolve with reference to built projects. The Wessex Water building is discussed in the case studies, and it provides one best-practice building from which the criteria for environmental performance have been developed.

Table 6.3   Credit summary for BREEAM for Offices 2003

Category	Type	Credits available	Category	Type	Credits available
Management			*Energy*		
Commissioning monitor	D	1	Fabric and form	C	5
Specialist commissioning agent	D	1	Electrical sub-metering	C	1
Commissioning clauses	D	1	Tenancy sub-metering	C	1
Building users' guide	D	1	CO_2 emissions	D	10
Construction site impacts	D	5	Energy policy	M	1
Environmental policy	M	1	Energy audits	M	1
Environmental purchasing policy	M	1	Energy information	M	1
Environmental management system	M	1	Energy CO_2 monitoring	M	1
Operating manuals	M	1	Energy CO_2 targeting	M	1
Health and well-being			Energy CO_2 reductions	M	1
Cooling towers	C	1	*Transport*		
Domestic hot water – legionellosis	C	1	Transport CO_2 and transport plan	C	10
Operable windows	C	1	Cyclist facilities	C	1
Failsafe humidification	C	1	Commuting public transport	C	1
Air intake location	C	1	Business public transport	C	1
Ventilation rates	C	1	Commuting transport initiatives	M	1
Daylighting	C	1	Business transport initiatives	M	1
Daylight glare control	C	1	*Materials*		
High-frequency lighting	C	1	Asbestos	C	1
Electric lighting design	C	1	Recyclable waste storage	C	1
Lighting zones	C	1	Reuse of façade	D	1
View out	C	1	Reuse of structure	D	1
Thermal zoning	C	1	Materials specification	D	4
Thermal modelling	D	1	Recycled aggregates	D	1
Internal noise levels	D	1	Sustainable timber	D	2
Maintenance schedules	M	4	Recycling policy	M	1
DHWS – maintenance	M	1	Hazardous materials	M	1
Smoking policy	M	1	*Pollution*		
Carpet and furniture cleaning	M	1	Refrigerant ODP	C	1
Occupant satisfaction feedback	M	1	Refrigerant leak detection	C	1
Occupant satisfaction survey	M	1	Refrigerant recovery	C	1
Ecology			NOX emissions	C	4
Ecological value	D	5	Water run-off	C	1
Change In ecological value	D	5	Watercourse pollution	C	1
Ecological enhancement	D	1	Refrigerant GWP	C	1
Protection of ecological features	D	1	Insulant ODP	D	1
Water			Boiler maintenance	M	1
Water consumption	C	3	Fire retardant ODP	M	1
Water meter	C	1	Energy benchmarking	M	1
Mains leak detection	C	1	Maintenance schedules	M	1
Sanitary supply shut off	C	1	Lighting maintenance	M	1
Maintenance schedules	M	1	*Land use*		
Consumption monitoring	M	1	Reuse of land	D	1
			Reclaimed contaminated land	D	1

An important tool that was used with the examination of this building is the BRE rating prediction checklist.[7]

The BREEAM system was also developed with regard to 'The Environmental Building' located on the BRE site. The building came about because of the need for a new office building and gave an ideal opportunity for a demonstration project.[8] BRE claim:

This building, opened in 1997, is a further icon in the move to sustainable buildings. What is often not recognised is that the focus is on both 'process' and 'product'. The design process involved using the BREEAM rating system to facilitate design, and it achieved an 'Excellent' rating.[9]

Notable features include the use of natural ventilation, maximum use of daylighting and maximum use of the building's mass to moderate temperatures. The building has control systems that balance the occupants' environmental needs. There are additional servicing strategies for on-site recycling and reuse of waste materials.[10]

Systems for housing

Another rating system has been developed by BRE for housing. Called EcoHomes, it is a system that tries to address the rating of environmentally friendly houses. Three case studies examine the use of this system: the first is the EcoHome designed by Dr Ken Yeang in Malaysia, the second an environmentally friendly low-cost housing in Melbourne, and the third the BedZED project in the UK.

These case studies raise issues of how to address the use of this type of rating system across different cultures and climates. Questions arise as to how these systems, which have been pioneered in specific countries, can be adapted and changed to be useful in the global context.

Acknowledgements

The information presented in this section is primarily based on information contained in the *BREEAM 98 for Offices* booklet (1998) and the *BREEAM for Offices 2003 Assessor Manual and Training Course* (2003). The contribution of Alan Yates of BRE is also acknowledged.

LEED™ (US)

The Leadership in Energy and Environmental Design rating system (LEED) is a voluntary, consensus-based, market-driven building rating system based on existing proven technologies and emerging concepts. It evaluates environmental performance from a whole building perspective over a building's life cycle, providing a definitive standard for what constitutes a 'green building'.

The genesis for LEED began soon after the formation of the US Green Building Council in 1993. The membership quickly realized that a priority for the sustainable building industry was to have a system to define and measure green buildings. After trialling a simple rating system from 1994 to 1997, the first formal version of LEED was released in 1998. The stated aims of LEED are to:

- define 'green building' by establishing a common standard of measurement;
- promote integrated, whole-building design practices;
- recognize environmental leadership in the building industry;
- stimulate green competition;
- raise consumer awareness of green building benefits; and
- transform the building market.

Through its use as a design guideline and third-party certification tool, it aims to improve occupant well-being, environmental performance and economic returns of buildings using established and innovative practices, standards and technologies.

When asked the question 'What is LEED?' in 2003, President of the World Green Building Council Rick Fedrizzi used an analogy that everyone could relate to, saying: 'LEED is like miles per gallon ... but for a building!'[11] Just as fuel efficiency is a primary performance and cost consideration in the operation of motor vehicles, so too should the concepts of energy and resource efficiency in building performance be during their design, construction and operation.

LEED approach

LEED is a performance-orientated system where points are earned for satisfying each credit criterion. Different levels of

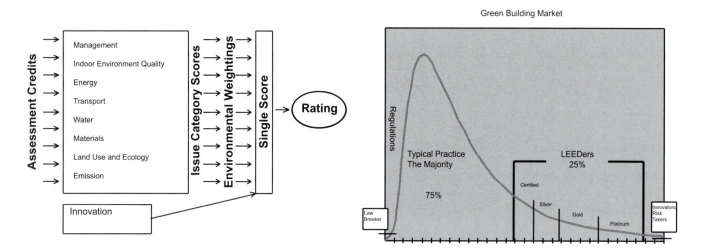

6.5 **Left**. LEED Framework. **Right**. Targets for projects in the green building market.

green building certification are awarded based on the total points achieved.

The following generalized synopsis by LEED director Nigel Howard[12] describes the system as:

- a third-party environmental assessment and rating tool for buildings;
- easy to criticize – difficult to replace;
- distinguishing the best from the rest in the market;
- working with the grain of the market; and
- easily used as a policy instrument – especially by state and local government.

While many of the aims and environmental issues are similar to those of BREEAM, LEED differs from the UK system in the following key areas:

1   There is no direct weighting factor applied to the environmental categories.

Table 6.4   Aspects of LEED with intended results

Aspects	Results
Checklist of standards	Challenges design thinking to select from a variety of sustainable strategies
Rating system	Offers suggestions about when, where and how users can strategically meet their choice of best practice standards
Training of LEED-accredited professionals	Educates professionals on how to use the system and conduct audits to certify buildings
Audits/certification	Enforces the implementation of required standards and recognizes developers for their efforts

2   Points are awarded for innovation and for employing sustainable buildings expertise during the design process, in addition to issues assessed under the environmental categories.

3   Formal certification is only achieved when construction of the new building is completed, whereas BREEAM allows certification to be achieved during the design stage.

4   LEED assesses a variety of commercial building types in a single version. This includes offices, retail, institutional buildings, hotels and high-rise residential. The BREEAM approach is to produce rating tools tailored for each building type.

5   LEED is more than a rating system and includes modular workshop programmes with multiple levels and marketing support for certified projects.

The original LEED rating system, covering new commercial construction and major renovations, is currently in its second edition and renamed *LEED-NC*. As LEED continues to improve and evolve, updates and addenda are made available to replace and augment current material. It is intended that major revisions should occur every three years.

New versions of LEED to cover houses, as well as other aspects of commercial building construction and life cycle stages, are currently being developed by the US Green Building Council. These include:

- existing building operations (LEED-EB);
- commercial interiors projects (LEED-CI);
- core and shell projects (LEED-CS; and
- homes (LEED-H).

The framework for *LEED-NC* is described below. The other LEED systems will follow a similar approach.

LEED framework

The framework for *LEED-NC* comprises the following six categories:

- sustainable sites;
- water efficiency;
- energy and atmosphere;
- materials and resources;
- indoor environmental quality; and
- innovation and design process.

Each of the categories is further divided into 'credits'. For each credit, the rating system identifies the intent, requirements, and technologies or strategies available to achieve the credit. One or more points are available within each credit, and points are achieved by meeting specified criteria or performance levels.

Most categories contain prerequisites, of which there are seven in total. All seven prerequisites must be met in order to qualify for certification at any level.

A total of 69 points is available. The total score used to calculate the rating is simply the sum of all the points achieved. There are no separate weighting factors. Ratings are then awarded based on the total number of points achieved.

Assessment credits

LEED-NC comprises both prerequisite and optional credits, as shown in Table 6.7. For example, in the category 'Sustainable sites', erosion and sedimentation control is a prerequisite. The prerequisites must be achieved, while enough of the optional credits must be achieved to score the number of points necessary to meet the required rating level. Some credits are divided into two or more measures, with points allocated for meeting each measure.

Environmental weightings

There are no weighting factors applied to environmental categories in *LEED-NC*, although weightings are implicit in the number of points available in each category. The distribution of points in each category, and the implicit weightings, are shown in the LEED points and implicit weightings table (see Table 6.6).

Table 6.5 LEED rating scores

Rating	Points required
Certified	26
Silver	33
Gold	39
Platinum	52

Table 6.6 LEED points and implicit weightings

Credit category	Points available	Implicit weightings (%)
Sustainable sites	14	20
Water efficiency	5	7
Energy and atmosphere	17	25
Materials and resources	13	19
Indoor environmental quality	15	22
Innovation and design process	5	6
Total	69	100

Certification process

The LEED certification process is administered by the US Green Building Council (USGBC) and involves the following stages:

1 *Registration.* Project teams interested in obtaining LEED certification must first register with the USGBC and pay a registration fee. Registration during the pre-design phase is recommended in order to get the most benefit out of the LEED system.

2 *Application.* The project team begins to collect information and perform calculations to meet LEED credit and prerequisite submittal requirements. This data is gathered throughout the procurement process, from pre-design through to building occupancy. Where project teams are not sure if credits are achieved, a Credit Interpretation Rulings procedure is in place to resolve the issues.

3   *Certification*. The project team submits a complete application to USGBC for review, together with the certification fees. Application reviews can take anywhere from six weeks to several months. There are several opportunities for response and appeal throughout the review stages (administrative, preliminary technical and final technical reviews). After acceptance of the USGBC's proposed LEED certification level by the project team, the project may be referred to as a 'LEED Certified Green Building'. The

USGBC presents the project with a plaque indicating the certification level and issues two press releases to acknowledge the project.

The green building market and LEED

The uptake of LEED in the US was initially slow because there was little evidence to support the economic incentives of using the system. However, *LEED-NC* is now enjoying significant

Table 6.7   Credit summary for LEED-NC (version 2.1)

Categories	Points available	Categories	Points available
Sustainable sites		*Water efficiency*	
Erosion and sedimentation control	Required	Water efficient landscaping	2
Site selection	1	Innovative wastewater technologies	1
Urban redevelopment	1	Water use reduction	2
Brownfield redevelopment	1	*Innovation and design process*	
Alternative transportation	4	Innovation in design	4
• public transportation access		LEED Accredited Professional	1
• bicycle storage and changing rooms		*Energy and atmosphere*	
• alternative fuel vehicles		Fundamental building commissioning	Required
• parking capacity		Minimum energy performance	Required
Reduced site disturbance	2	CFC reduction in HVAC&R equipment	Required
• protect or restore open space		Optimize energy performance	10
• development footprint		Renewable energy	3
Stormwater management	2	Additional commissioning	1
Landscape and exterior design to reduce heat island effect	2	Ozone depletion	1
Light pollution reduction	1	Measurement and verification	1
Indoor environmental quality		Green power	1
Minimum IAQ performance	Required	*Materials and resources*	
Environmental tobacco smoke control	Required	Storage and collection of recyclables	Required
CO_2 monitoring	1	Building reuse	3
Ventilation effectiveness	1	Construction waste management	2
Construction IAQ management plan	2	Resource reuse	2
Low-emitting materials	4	Recycled content	2
Indoor chemical and pollutant source control	1	Local/regional materials	2
Controllability of systems	2	Rapidly renewable materials	1
Thermal comfort	2	Certified wood	1
Daylight and views	2		

market penetration in the US. By October 2004, over 130 projects had achieved certification and 1,605 projects were registered with the US Green Building Council. This represents approximately 18 million square metres of building floor area spread across 50 states!

Membership of the US Green Building Council has expanded rapidly to over 4,000 companies. Over 10,000 people have attended LEED training courses and there are over 3,500 LEED Accredited Professionals in the US.

Both Howard, a Vice President of the US Green Building Council, and Fedrizzi, President of the World Green Building Council, stress that the secret behind the recent rapid uptake of the LEED system by the market is anchored in selling the business case for savings that LEED can deliver.

In recent years the monitoring of progress of building projects been developed using the LEED system. This has yielded the necessary research upon which the business cases can now be more successfully marketed. In other words, clients can now be shown, in an economic context, where the benefits can be found and when these can be expected in the life cycle of the building.

For example, evidence of savings versus costs from LEED projects is documented in a recent study of buildings in California. Survey data was collected from a ten-year performance period, from 1994 to 2004, on 28 office buildings and eight schools, which were LEED-certified silver, gold or platinum. Findings reveal 30 per cent energy savings, 30 to 50 per cent water savings and 50 to 97 per cent waste costs savings. The additional cost incurred to achieve these remarkable results was calculated as only 1.63 per cent.[13] The study also found, not surprisingly, that 'generally, the earlier green building gets incorporated into the design process, the lower the cost'.

Acknowledgements

The information presented in this section is primarily based on information contained in the LEED Reference Package Version 2 (2001) and on the US Green Building Council website (www.usgbc.org). The contribution of Nigel Howard, Vice President of the USGBC, is also acknowledged.

Green Star (Australia)

Green Star is an industry-owned national voluntary environmental rating system, which evaluates the environmental performance of buildings in Australia. It was launched in 2003 and its development has been the number one priority of the Green Building Council of Australia since its formation in 2002.

To get the rating system to market quickly, the Green Building Council of Australia adopted an Australian version of BREEAM that had been under development by Sinclair Knight Merz and the UK's Building Research Establishment since 2001. This system, originally called AusBREEAM, was then modified in conjunction with the GBCA Technical Committee to incorporate the best features of LEED, through the council's close relationship with the US Green Building Council, via the World Green Building Council.

The blending of BREEAM and LEED, the world's two leading rating systems, to suit the Australian property industry and environment, has resulted in a robust tool that was delivered to market in record time.

According to Huston Eubank of the US-based Rocky Mountain Institute, 'Green Star is "raising the bar" on green buildings beyond the other international rating tools . . . Green Star is a world-leading starting point to shift the market towards green development.'[14]

The stated aims of Green Star are to:

- define green building by establishing a common language and standard of measurement;
- promote integrated, whole-building design practices;
- recognize environmental leadership;
- raise awareness of green building benefits; and
- reduce the environmental impact of development.

Brendan Crotty, Chair of the Green Building Council and Managing Director of Australand Holdings Pty Ltd, says:

the benefit of an industry based rating tool is that it reflects the realities of the market. Not only will it reflect the realities of the market today but also the realities of the market tomorrow. What the Green Building Council members and particularly the Board – both government and industry representatives alike – understand is that, unless there is some economic benefit in environmentally sound design practices, they simply will not be implemented.[15]

Green Star approach

Like both BREEAM and LEED, the basis of the system is a certificate awarded to individual buildings based on credits for a set of performance criteria. The certificate provides a label for the building that enables the owners or occupants to gain recognition for the building's environmental performance.

The first version of Green Star – *Green Star – Office Design*, for the design of new or refurbished office buildings – was launched as a pilot in July 2003. Industry feedback on the tool was then sought, the tool modified, and version 1 released at the end of 2003. The key components of BREEAM and LEED that are incorporated in *Green Star – Office Design* are summarized as follows:

1 Both BREEAM and LEED assessment credits were used as a starting point for the credit criteria and methods of measurement used in Green Star.
2 The basic framework of BREEAM, with weightings applied to environmental categories, is used to calculate a single score.
3 The innovation approach in LEED is incorporated into the total score.
4 Conditional requirements for energy and ecology performance are necessary for certification, similarly to LEED prerequisites.
5 Individual rating tools are required for specific building types (e.g. schools, retail) as with BREEAM, rather than there being a general rating scheme for all commercial buildings (the LEED approach).
6 The certification process and accreditation/training of Green Star professionals is based heavily on the LEED system.
7 Certification can be awarded during design stage (as with BREEAM) rather than waiting until the building is completed (the LEED approach).

The Green Building Council of Australia is committed to developing a suite of rating tools to cover key building types and stages in the life cycle. The first priority has been the commercial office market and the suite of Green Star products is summarized as follows:

- Green Star – Office Design;
- Green Star – Office As-Built;
- Green Star – Office Interiors; and
- Green Star – Office Existing.

Green Star – Office As-Built uses the same criteria as *Green Star – Office Design* but is assessed after construction is completed. In other words, it confirms that the building was built as designed and that initiatives were not discarded or changed during construction. *LEED-NC* avoids this issue by not awarding any certification until after construction is complete.

Other versions of Green Star, for building types such as residential and retail, will be developed when funding becomes available, through industry sponsorship, government grants or revenue generated from the council's activities.

Green Star products will be reviewed and updated every year to ensure that the system continues to represent current best practice. This will take advantage of new research and data on environmental impacts to build on experience gained and feedback from stakeholders, and to stay ahead of changing legislative requirements.

The framework for *Green Star – Office Design* is described below. The rating systems for other building types are generally consistent with this approach.

Green Star framework

The framework for Green Star is shown in Figure 6.6 and is basically the same as that for BREEAM. It comprises assessment credits in eight environmental categories. The assessment credits are awarded when specific criteria or performance levels are achieved. The credits achieved in a particular category are then added together and a category score, expressed as a percentage, is calculated, by dividing the credits achieved by the total credits available in that category. A weighting factor is then applied to each category score, and these weighted scores are added together to give a single score out of 100.

The key difference between the frameworks for Green Star and BREEAM is the inclusion of an innovation category. Since innovation could apply to any environmental issue, weighting the

6.6 Left. Green Star Framework. **Right**. 60L Office building, Melbourne. Spowers Architects. This refurbishment of an existing building aimed at setting best practice for environmental performance. The development of rating tools such as Green Star has drawn from best practice to inform the criteria selection.

Table 6.8 Green Star rating scores

Rating	Points required
1 star	10
2 stars	20
3 stars	30
4 stars – Best Practice	45
5 stars – Australian Excellence	60
6 stars – World Leader	75

innovation category is not appropriate. Up to five points are available for innovation (awarded at the discretion of the Green Building Council of Australia) and these are added to the final score. The maximum score possible in Green Star is therefore 105.

Only projects or buildings that achieve a rating of four, five or six Green Stars are eligible for official certification from the Green Building Council of Australia.

Assessment credits

Like BREEAM and LEED, Green Star has the philosophy of rewarding positive steps taken to improve the environmental performance of buildings rather than penalizing for poor performance. If a building achieves the criteria for a particular credited issue then credits are awarded. The number of credits in each category does not reflect the relative importance of the category, since this is defined by the weighting factors.

Green Star has two conditional requirements, which must be achieved to obtain a certified rating. These are:

1   *Ecological value of site.* The building must not be on land of high ecological value.
2   *Maximum greenhouse emissions.* It must achieve a minimum of four stars using the Australian Building Greenhouse Rating system (ABGR).

Green Star has incorporated the ABGR rating system into the energy category to benchmark greenhouse emissions. ABGR is

THE ENVIRONMENTAL IMPACT MODEL

1 Approximately 20 per cent of water use in Australia is for urban and industrial purposes. The total volume of water used for these purposes increased by 50 per cent from 1985 to 1996.

2 About 26 per cent of Australia's surface water management areas are close to, or have exceeded, sustainable extraction limits.

3 Water use increased from 1985 to 1996/7 by 65 per cent and water is overused in some regions.

4 The rate of land clearance has accelerated, with as much cleared during the last 50 years as in the 150 years before 1945.

5 Australians have a high per capita level of greenhouse gas emissions by world standards.

6 Greenhouse gas emissions increased by 16.9 per cent between 1990 and 1998.

7 There is a high and increasing per capita energy usage in human settlements leading to increases in greenhouse gas emissions, particularly through electricity generation and transport usage.

8 The transport sector accounted for 16.1 per cent of Australia's greenhouse gas emissions in 1999.

9 The total vehicle kilometres travelled (VKT) by residents of Sydney increased by 24 per cent between 1991 and 1998.

10 Many of the warmest years on record have occurred in the 1980s and 1990s.

11 There has been no decline in four-hourly concentrations of ozone in urban areas, indicating that photochemical smog in those areas is still an issue.

12 Sewage treatment plants contribute significantly to nutrient levels in some river systems.

13 Over 95 per cent of solid waste is disposed to landfill, of which construction and demolition of buildings contributes between 40 and 50 per cent.

The environmental impact model for Green Star drawn from national policy provides the basis for criteria and weighting.

a well-established energy/greenhouse rating system for office buildings in Australia, administered nationally by the NSW government's Department of Energy, Utilities and Sustainability (previously SEDA – Sustainable Energy Development Authority). It benchmarks the actual energy consumption of buildings based on annual energy bills.

For the design stage, energy modelling is undertaken in accordance with ABGR validation protocols for computer simulation to predict the likely energy consumption in operation so that an ABGR rating can be estimated and used in Green Star. To reflect the differences between new buildings and refurbished buildings, a number of credits may be designated 'not applicable' and effectively removed from the scoring system.

For example, the asbestos credit is not considered in new buildings since it is not permitted by legislation and becomes 'not applicable'. However, asbestos is an issue in the refurbishment of existing buildings and consequently credits are available for its safe removal.

Environmental weightings

Applying a weighting to each category score ensures that each category is appropriately represented in Green Star and reflects both current knowledge and the opinion of the Green Building Council of Australia. This approach, similar to that of BREEAM, means that a credit in one category is not equal to a credit in

Table 6.9 Green Star average weighting factors

Category	Weighting (%)
Management	10
Indoor environment quality	20
Energy	25
Transport	10
Water	12
Materials	10
Land use and ecology	8
Emissions	5
	100

another category. This provides much greater flexibility in the tool compared to LEED, and allows credits to be added or deleted (e.g. the 'not applicable' credits discussed earlier) without affecting the overall importance of an environmental category.

A further advantage of the weighting system is that it allows Green Star to reflect the differing environmental concerns across the Australian continent by varying the weightings from state to state. The average weightings used in Green Star are shown in the Green Star average weighting factors table (Table 6.9). State by state, the weightings typically vary by +/– 5%, but the total always adds up to 100 per cent. As discussed earlier, innovation points are not weighted.

Management is not strictly an environmental issue. It addresses design process, commissioning and construction issues. Commissioning relates primarily to energy, and construction relates to pollution and waste. The effective weighting of energy in Green Star is therefore approximately 30 per cent, while emissions account for approximately 10 per cent.

The determination of weightings is critical to the credibility of a rating system. The approach adopted during the development of Green Star was to base the weightings on a variety of information sources:

- OECD report: *Environmentally Sustainable Buildings* (March 2003);
- Environment Australia report: *State of the Environment* (2001);
- industry-wide survey undertaken by Green Building Council of Australia in May/June 2003 (survey findings available at www.gbcaus.org); and
- comparison between BREEAM and LEED.

Certification process

The certification process for Green Star, administered by the Green Building Council of Australia (GBCA), is similar to that for LEED and comprises the following stages:

1 *Registration.* The project is registered with the GBCA who will then issue a Certification Contract to the project team. No fee is payable at this time.
2 *Application.* The project team prepares documentation and calculations to satisfy the conditional and credit submittal requirements defined in the Technical Manual.
3 *Certification.* The Certification Contract is signed and the certification fee paid to the GBCA. The required documentation is then submitted to the GBCA for review by the Green Star Certification Panel. If appropriate, the GBCA will then award a certified Green Star rating and work with the project team to promote the project's achievements.

Once Green Star becomes more established, Green Star Certified Assessors will undertake the technical review of applications on behalf of the GBCA. The GBCA Technical Committee will then award the Green Star certification, taking into consideration the recommendations and comments of the Certified Assessor.

Like both BREEAM and LEED, a project or building cannot publicly claim a Green Star rating unless the Green Building Council of Australia has certified the rating.

The green building market and Green Star

Green Star has generally been well received by the property industry in Australia. In the first 12 months after Green Star was launched in 2003, over 500 people attended Green Star training courses and over 100 have subsequently sat and passed the exam to become Green Star Accredited Professionals. The first

Table 6.10   Credit summary for *Green Star – Office Design*

Category	Credits available	Category	Credits available
Management	12	*Transport*	11
Green Star Accredited Professional	2	Provision of car parking	2
Commissioning – clauses	2	Small parking spaces	1
Commissioning – building tuning	1	Cyclist facilities	3
Commissioning – commissioning agent	1	Commuting public transport	5
Building users' guide	1	*Water*	12
Environmental management	3	Occupant amenity potable water efficiency	5
Waste management	2	Water meter	2
Indoor environment quality	27	Landscape irrigation water efficiency	1
Ventilation rates	3	Cooling tower water consumption	4
Ventilation effectiveness	2	*Materials*	20
Carbon dioxide monitoring and control	1	Recycling waste storage	2
Daylighting	3	Reuse of façade	2
Daylight glare control	1	Reuse of structure	4
High-frequency ballasts	1	Shell and core or integrated fit-out	3
Electric lighting levels	1	Recycled content of structural concrete	3
External views	2	Recycled content of structural steel	2
Individual thermal comfort control	2	PVC minimisation	2
Asbestos	1*	Sustainable timber	2
Thermal modelling	2	*Land use and ecology*	8
Internal noise levels	2	Ecological value of site	Conditional
Indoor air pollutants	6	Re-use of land	1
Emissions	13	Reclaimed contaminated land	2**
Refrigerant ODP	2	Change of ecological value	4
Refrigerant GWP	1	Topsoil and fill removal from site	1
Refrigerant leak	1	*Energy*	24
detection		Maximum greenhouse emissions	Conditional
Refrigerant recovery	1	Reduced greenhouse emissions	15
Watercourse pollution	1	Electrical sub-metering	1
Reduced flow to sewer	4	Tenancy sub-metering	1
Light pollution	1	Office lighting power density	4
Cooling towers	1	Office lighting zoning	1
Insulant ODP	1	Peak energy demand reduction	2

*   not applicable for new building unless it incorporates at least 25% of existing building
** not applicable for refurbished buildings

6.7   Office building. **Right**. Extending the thermal chimneys well above the atrium space improves draught though the system. **Left**. The spatial connection of office space and atrium provides view and amenity not found in the traditional 'milk crate' office building. This reminds us that the feeling of quality in an office building lasts long after the memory of the first cost. The absence of qualitative criteria in rating systems seems a problem when green design is a blend of both art and science.

Green Star building has now been certified: 8 Brindabella Circuit, a commercial office building in Canberra, achieved a five-star *Green Star – Office Design* rating in October 2004.

There are numerous projects currently either going through the certification process or aiming to achieve certification. At the launch of the Green Star pilot in July 2003, four buildings had preliminary assessments published, ranging from four to six stars.

Green Star has been embraced by federal, state and local government in Australia. The Department of Defence has the largest portfolio of government buildings in the country and intends to incorporate Green Star into a green building requirements policy for new projects. Similarly, many state and local government projects are specifying Green Star in their project briefs, usually requiring a minimum rating of four stars.

Local government planners have indicated a desire to incorporate Green Star into planning requirements, although this will turn Green Star into a legislative rather than a voluntary tool in these instances. Whether this causes legal problems remains to be seen.

Compared to BREEAM and LEED, Green Star faces unique challenges as a result of the plethora of rating tools recently emerging in the Australian market. Many of these use stars to define rating performance, which is creating confusion in the market (e.g. is a four-star Green Star the same as a four-star ABGR?).

How Green Star relates to the National Australian Built Environment Rating System (NABERS) – developed by the federal government's Department of Environment since 2001– will be of great interest.

NABERS assesses the performance of existing buildings. *Green Star – Office Existing*, when it is released next year, will do likewise. The Australian market is not large enough for two competing schemes and this competition may further confuse the property industry, already struggling to work out which star rating scheme applies to which project. Given government's investment in NABERS and its financial support for the Green Building Council of Australia, it may be that a compromise can be reached to avoid the continuation of 'star wars' in Australia.

Acknowledgements

The information presented in this section is primarily based on information contained in the *Green Star – Office Design* Technical Manual (2003), the Green Star Accredited Professional Training Course and the Green Building Council of Australia's website (www.gbcaus.org).

Rating system limitations and potentials

Two key main limitations of rating systems have been advanced: their simplification of the environmental impacts of buildings, and the cost of certification.

Environmental pragmatism

One of the major criticisms of rating systems, particularly from sectors outside of the property industry, is that in consolidating the assessment into a single score they oversimplify the environmental impacts of buildings. Also, a building can do poorly in one area yet still achieve a very good overall rating.

Some argue that rating systems need to be more rigorous. However, there is a danger that if rating systems become too involved in the fine print they will miss the big picture. Rating systems are a means to an end to facilitate environmental change in the property industry – an industry that is notoriously slow to change or to embrace new ideas.

If more rigorous environmental assessments of buildings are required, life cycle assessment (LCA) techniques can be used. LCA is a process that goes into significant detail to quantify environmental impacts. It is not commonly used in the design of buildings because it can be expensive and time-consuming, and ultimately it does not readily give designers ideas or guidance on how to improve their building designs. However, it is an important component of green building research as data and findings from LCA studies can feed back into the ongoing evolution of rating systems.

A pragmatic approach is required in the development and promotion of rating systems. If rating systems become too complex and expensive, they will not gain traction in the property industry. While being theoretically more accurate, ultimately they will have limited influence to reduce the environmental impact of the built environment since only a small percentage of buildings will ever use them. Rating systems need to influence the design and operation of all buildings, not just a handful of iconic green buildings.

Cost of certification

Some sectors of the property industry complain about the cost of obtaining a certified rating. The costs comprise:

- certification fees;
- consultants' fees to prepare documentation and calculations;
- the capital cost of improving the environmental performance of buildings.

Since most rating systems are voluntary, consumers will have a choice whether or not to use a rating system. After all, most systems are aimed at separating the best from the rest. Also, the costs for undertaking ratings are usually a small component of the overall cost of a construction project and may be offset through:[16]

- reduced running costs of the building;
- higher future valuation compared to poorly performing buildings (or environmental lemons);
- higher staff productivity as a result of healthier internal spaces;
- increased publicity and marketing through promotion of the rating to attract and retain tenants;
- planning dispensations to allow higher yield or higher buildings;
- speeding up of planning processes (time = money);
- potential tax incentives for green buildings.

Specific examples of the cost benefits of designing green buildings have been demonstrated in numerous studies from the UK and the US.

If a rating system is imposed on a project halfway through the design process it will be disruptive and expensive, in the same way that bolting on environmental initiatives costs more than integrating them into the design. If rating systems are used from the very beginning they can guide the project team to think smarter and challenge conventional solutions. Establishing a clear target from the start sets the tone for a project and focuses the whole team on the required sustainability outcomes.

And finally, most rating systems can be used at no cost to guide the design process. For example, the Green Star and LEED assessment tools can be downloaded for free from the relevant websites. Rating system payments are only required if a formal certification of a project is needed to publicly proclaim the environmental quality of the building.

Potentials for the rating systems in the design of buildings can be seen in the case studies. The projects are as follows:

- The Reservoir Centre, Melbourne, Australia; and
- CH_2, Melbourne City Council, Australia.

In both cases a pre-assessment was used during the design phase to assist in assessing the environmental impact of the building.

7.1 Multifamily residence. A Cepheus project in Wolfurt.

Chapter 7

Blueprinting

Introduction

The work of the IEA SHC (International Energy Agency, Solar Heating and Cooling Programme) Task 28 on Sustainable Solar Housing has developed the 'blueprinting' methodology to help feed information from innovative high-performance solar houses, developed by experts in the Task, to the broader housing delivery system in a large number of countries. This ambitious programme aims to significantly improve the market penetration of this type of building.

The research problem of Task 28 is broken into a number of sub-tasks that examine specific research issues, marketing, design, evaluation and construction. The work reported here on blueprinting[1] has evolved from examining how innovative construction approaches to sustainable solar houses are demonstrated.

This work focuses on technical matters, particularly in the case studies, but related issues forming the context of the projects are also discussed. Issues, for instance barriers to the mainstreaming of sustainable housing, need to be understood if designers are to work more innovatively to improve the performance of homes. Other useful concepts are introduced, such as marketing techniques, adding social or economic value, and understanding the legislative context.

Overview

The International Energy Agency (IEA) was established in 1974 as an autonomous agency within the framework of the Organization for Economic Cooperation and Development (OECD) to carry out a comprehensive programme of energy cooperation among its 25 member countries and the Commission of the European Communities.

An important part of the Agency's programme involves collaboration in the research, development and demonstration of new energy technologies to reduce excessive reliance on imported oil, to increase long-term energy security and to reduce greenhouse gas emissions. The IEA's activities are headed by the Committee on Energy Research and Technology (CERT) and supported by a small secretariat staff, headquartered in Paris. In addition, three working parties are charged with monitoring the various collaborative energy agreements, identifying new areas for cooperation and advising the CERT on policy matters.[2]

One of its purposes is to carry out research into specific issues concerning the way energy is used in buildings.

Collaborative programs in the various energy technology areas are conducted under Implementing Agreements, which are signed by contracting parties (government agencies or entities designated by them). There are currently 42 implementing Agreements covering fossil fuel technologies, renewable energy technologies, efficient energy end-use technologies, nuclear fusion science and technology, and energy technology information centers. The Solar Heating and Cooling Programme was one of the first IEA Implementing Agreements to be established. Since 1977, its 21 members have been collaborating to advance active solar, passive solar and photovoltaic technologies and their application in buildings.[3]

7.2 Hrach house. First air collector building with an energy use of 15 kWh/m^2. Heat from the atrium is distributed around the house.

7.3 Row houses, Batschuns, in 'passive house' standard.

PASSIVE HOUSE CHECKLIST (FOR COOL CLIMATES)[4]

SITE PLAN

1　Proximity to public transportation.
2　Equator orientation of the 'main' side (± 30°), and large equator-facing window areas.
3　Freedom from unwanted shade from building elements, to allow passive solar energy use.
4　Planting that will not cause unwanted shade in the future.
5　Is a compact form possible? Row and multi-storey buildings are advantageous.

CONCEPT DEVELOPMENT

1　Use a compact building shell, and take advantage of opportunities to combine buildings.
2　Glazed surfaces facing south are optimal; keep east, north and west windows small.
3　Minimize shaded areas (very little or no shade in winter from railings, parapets, building projections, balconies, roof overhangs, divider walls).
4　Use a simple shell form (if possible, without dormers, returns, etc.).
5　Use a building footprint that concentrates utility installation zones (e.g. bathrooms above or adjacent to kitchens and each other).
6　Leave room for ventilation ducts.
7　Separate basement (if any), airtight and free of heat bridges. Use the PHVP (passive house pre-planning package) (QCM).
8　Apply for passive house construction subsidies.

BUILDING PERMIT PLANS

1　Determine insulation thickness of building envelope.
2　Avoid heat bridges.
3　Determine size of utility room(s).
4　House footprint: short pipe runs (hot and cold water, sewage) and ventilation ducts. Cold air ducts outside; warm air ducts inside the insulated building envelope.

Legend (QCM): Quality control measures required.

The mode of operation used to develop a Task was to identify a current research problem, such as the 'Sustainable Solar Housing' project, called Task 28, and to form an international team of experts to work on this Task. The main aim of Task 28 is to examine ways to 'market housing for a better environment'.[5]

Precepts

The approach

There is a growing movement to build ecological housing with extremely low purchased energy consumption for heating and cooling, and minimal CO_2 emissions. Two examples are 'Factor-Four Plus Housing', requiring one-fourth or less of the purchased heating energy of houses built to current standards, and 'passive houses'. These houses typically require a maximum of 10 W per m^2 of space heating, amounting to an annual energy demand of 15 kWh/m^2 in temperate climates.[6]

Until now, these houses achieved this high performance primarily by *reducing heat losses*, that is, by using compact building forms, thick insulation and ventilation heat recovery. While the number of high-performance buildings is growing, market penetration could be further enhanced by a complementary approach, namely by *increasing energy gains* in very well insulated housing. This can be achieved by:

- passive solar design;
- active solar systems for domestic hot water and space heating;
- photovoltaic electric supply systems;
- improved daylighting (for better living quality); and
- natural cooling and solar/glare control.

Task 28 will address cost optimization of the *mix* of concepts: reducing energy losses, increasing useable solar gains and providing back-up efficiently in order to achieve high performance. This comprehensive approach has the potential to increase market penetration through greater architectural freedom, improved living quality, owner pride in using renewable energy and acceptable total costs.

Design thinking

The Task is structured around four sub-tasks, each having a distinct design and research character, aimed particularly at trans-forming the housing market by demonstrating improved performance. The outcomes of the subtasks are as follows.

SUBTASK A: MARKETING

Model solar sustainable housing will be reviewed; a website will show exemplary built marketable solar sustainable housing, with information on design, living quality, extreme low-energy demand and minimal environmental impact; definitions, criteria and benchmark values will be included. (Audience: builders and potential homebuyers.) Workshops and symposia will be developed after the conclusion of the Task; experts will hold regional workshops; exemplary projects, details and components will be presented;, analytical techniques to support cost optimization will be illustrated; and tips for marketing will be offered. (Audience: Builders and house designers.)

SUBTASK B: DESIGN AND ANALYSIS – A GUIDE TO COST-EFFECTIVE DESIGN

This identifies proven design concepts, and systems that reduce non-renewable energy consumption. Environmental impact and costs are presented in detail in a handbook. The facts, curves and graphs are the result of building monitoring, lab testing and computer modelling, and are aimed at optimizing costs of designs. Commonly used computer tools are reviewed for their applicability, and worked examples and data sets are provided. (Audience: specialists working for homebuilders.)

SUBTASK C: CONSTRUCTION AND DEMONSTRATION – DEMONSTRATION BUILDINGS.

Demonstrating built projects with proven performance is still one of the best means of convincing builders that the risks in building such housing are acceptable. To increase the multiplication effect beyond the local region, press kits will be produced and reworked into articles and brochures in local languages for builders.

SUBTASK D: EVALUATION – MARKETABLE SOLAR SUSTAINABLE HOUSING: PLANS, DETAILS AND PERFORMANCE.

Recently built housing is illustrated with plans, sections, details, performance data and reference costs. (Audience: builders, homebuyers, and teachers.)[7]

Background

Concept of IEA Tasks

The concept of the Task has developed with the ongoing succession of Tasks. Thirty Tasks have been initiated, and 21 of them have been completed. An operating agent from one of the participating countries manages each Task. Task 28 is managed by Switzerland.

Overall control of the programme rests with an executive committee comprising one representative from each contracting party to the implementing agreement. Some special ad hoc activities – working groups, conferences and workshops – have been organized.3 Typical current Tasks include Task 24: Active Solar Procurement, Task 27: Performance of Solar Facade Components and Task 31: Daylighting Buildings in the 21st Century

The development of Task 28 has followed a number of paths, one of which is aimed at the construction of innovative solar sustainable housing to establish whether they could act as demonstration projects for developers and builders in the mass housing market. It is suggested that the lessons learned from these projects can act as 'blueprints' for future projects (see Figure 7.1, the demonstration Cepheus project in Wolfurt).

Development

The development of the research work is centred on the term 'blueprint', for which there are two meanings in use. First, it can mean a 'photographic print of a technical drawing with white lines on blue background, usually used as a reference before or during the construction process'. The second meaning is more abstract, and relates to 'a plan of action or something already completed that can be a guide for future actions'.[8]

The notion of something that could be used at the beginning of the design process, as a guide for the designer, was taken from this second definition of 'blueprint'. Hence the work in sub-Task C: Demonstration and Construction involved extracting from existing projects a model or description of innovative buildings that could help transform the industry.

7.4 Casa Solar, Italy. Architect: Francesca Sotargo. Renovation of a worker's cottage for solar sustainable living. The use of solution sets that require sensitive integration of the new and old, and natural and manmade environments, is a lesson to be learned from this project.

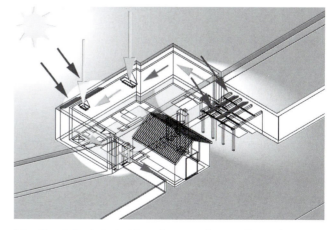

7.5 Casa Solar, Italy. Architect: Francesca Sotargo, The earth-integrated structure mitigates moisture movement thorough the envelope through a double-wall system. Roof systems include the use of solar thermal and solar electric systems. The approach minimizes the visual impact of the new building in the landscape. The solar technology is sensitively accommodated to reduce visual impact but also to create optimum performance. The solution set was included in the initial feasibility work to make this possible.

Research

Research questions

The main questions examined by the Task include:

- How can the information be used in the market to increase the uptake of solar housing?
- Can the design and construction of houses be improved with solar sustainable concepts and measures?

The task is conceived as a 'design research' exercise that is both theoretical and practical. The aim is to create a set of blueprints for this type of housing. In market transformation terms, this would be called a 'pull' mechanism. It addresses particular social barriers to the use of this type of housing, yet this approach is set in a problematic context.[9]

Barriers to mainstreaming sustainable housing

The barriers to mainstreaming sustainable housing have been researched in the UK through a project involving WWF. This ambitious programme is intended to promote one million sustainable homes in the UK. Wheeler (2003) reports:

> WWF initiated an independently facilitated dialogue process designed to identify the barriers to sustainable homes and ways to overcome them, to build on best practice and lessons learned to date, and to develop consensus among a wide range of stakeholders. A consultation questionnaire was sent to over 350 stakeholders, and a multi-stakeholder workshop was held with key organizations including representatives from government, house builders, a major developer, a major investor, the Housing Corporation, the Buildings Research Establishment (BRE) and the BioRegional Development Group.[10]

This process identified six key barriers to the development of sustainable homes.

1   current planning and building regulations that do not promote sustainable homes;
2   lack of fiscal incentives;
3   perceived lack of investor support;
4   perceived extra cost;
5   lack of consensus around the definition of a sustainable home; and
6   perceived lack of consumer demand.

Research within Task 28 has identified similar issues. The first three barriers are controlled by government and are outside the brief of Task 28. Barriers 4–6 concern definitions, cost-effective design strategies and methods of marketing sustainable solar housing. They are relevant to the housing delivery systems and could be investigated.

Perceived extra cost

The perceived extra cost of developing a sustainable home is not well understood. Edwards advises that the extra capital cost varies with design and specification but is usually about 5–15 per cent more than that of an unsustainable home. The Eco-Home by Professor Susan Roaf at Oxford cost approximately 11 per cent more than a comparable house.[11] The weakness in these arguments is that the whole-of-life cost benefits for these Eco-Homes have not been taken into account; nor have the subsidies provided to service the unsustainable homes been fully estimated.

Significant savings to the whole community would result if Eco-Home strategies were adopted more broadly. The Healthy Home Project on the Gold Coast in Australia uses 60 per cent less water than the normal house. If similar strategies existed in all Gold Coast homes, it is estimated that the water restrictions in 2004 could have been avoided and that new infrastructure in the form of dams and pipe-work could be deferred for 25 years. This would save A$85 million. If water were not taken from the watercourses, it would reduce the risk of the destruction of platypus habitats downstream.[12]

Studies by the Victoria state government in Australia have also indicated the cost benefit of improving house energy performance. Victoria has recently increased its energy code requirements from four to five stars and investigated the cost benefit of the change in legislation.

Overall, the standards would lead to a reduction in energy consumption. That is, private consumption falls relative to base, with the gap gradually widening over time,

7.6   Casa Solar, Italy. Architect: Francesca Sotargo. The solution set for photovoltaic integration demonstrates the innovative adaptations of existing solutions to create conceptually a multi-layered external space – that is, a space that integrates a range of ideas from the domains of function, experience and energy performance.

reflecting the accumulation of reductions in spending on energy. As well as the positive environmental impact of this, the standards would have many positive economic impacts for the State of Victoria in a range of areas. These areas would include Gross State Product (GSP), employment and economic welfare. The net present value of the estimated increase in GSP is over $500 million under the most favourable scenario and over $200 million under the worst-case assumptions. However, once expressed in proportional terms (that is, as a percentage of the NPV of 'base case' GSP), it is evident that these increases in GSP, while positive, are relatively small.[13]

The cost–benefit study found that the added cost of improved insulation and envelope design did not have a significant impact on mortgage payments. House owners were able to pay off the additional cost over a short period. Furthermore, the additional work for builders added to the growth of the economy, meaning more employment and better business. The rationale behind the legislation lay in a number of assumptions, as the authors of the report explain.

One question that is often raised by economists is why regulation is required to induce consumers to do something that would be in their interests anyway? A common response to this is to identify some market failure. What is the failure in this case?

There are a number of market imperfections in this area. First, consumers may not be aware that the additional costs of buying an energy-efficient house are more than outweighed by the benefits of reduced outlays on energy. Second, builders may not provide an energy-efficient product because, as with additional safety features built into motor vehicles, they fear that the 'sticker shock' will deter customers from purchasing it. Third, the main externality justifying measures of this kind is that they generate environmental benefits (less pollution and lower greenhouse gas emissions). Such benefits cannot be appropriated to any significant extent by individuals but provide benefits to the whole community. Without regulation, some individuals may 'free ride' on the back of action taken by the concerned.[14]

The thrust of this argument is threefold. First, it is in people's economic interest to adopt the standard, yet many do not. Why? The economists see this as a problem of 'market imperfections.'

While it is cheaper to operate a five-star building through energy savings, consumers do not see this as significant.

Second, there is a lack of information on the strategies and technologies needed to achieve a five-star home.

The third reason that legislation is needed in Victoria is the reduction in environmental impact: what is of small benefit to the individual has a significant cumulative benefit for the environment.

Evidence from the USA suggests that significant asset appreciation can result from adopting energy-efficient measures. A study by Rick Nevin and Gregory Watson in the USA found that the valuation of energy-efficient residential homes increased by US$10–US$25 for every US$1 reduction in annual energy consumption. This begins to show a trend that supports the market *value of adding* energy-saving features in the homes.[15]

Lack of definition

A problem exists with the lack of definition of what a 'sustainable home' comprises. There is a plethora of indicators and systems, but no agreed definition. There is not even an agreed set of key performance areas.

WWF made recommendations about using the British Research Establishment (BRE) EcoHomes standard as a starting point. It is a voluntary standard for the UK and cannot necessarily be generalized to other countries. Furthermore, this standard is more rigorous than most legislation in the UK, which is mainly aimed at mitigating energy consumption. Work is needed to develop a standard for EcoHomes.

Lack of consumer demand for sustainable housing

The WWF study in the UK identifies three factors that are responsible for the lack of demand by the market:

- lack of awareness;
- location; and
- demand for housing exceeds supply.

This reminds us that housing is essentially a social issue, centring on meeting peoples' social and cultural need for a home. The anthropological study by Amos Rapoport in the 1960s, called 'House Form and Culture',[13] identified the key proposition that the form of the home is dictated largely by the socio-cultural milieu. Concessions to the climate are largely modifications to that form, and are not first-order decisions but secondary ones. Furthermore, sustainable solar housing can be viewed as a technical problem of how to reduce environmental impacts of buildings by using effective renewable energy systems, and not a consumer concern.[16]

These two problems only partially overlap, as seen in an article by Nolan from a 'Blueprint for *Better Homes and Gardens* Home design for the year 2000'.[14] Nolan writes:

> Turn-of-the-millennium architecture doesn't have to (and shouldn't) look as if aliens just landed. With gabled roofs, dormers, wood-look lap siding, and mullioned windows and doors, the basic persona of our tomorrow home's exterior is reassuringly familiar – classic forms that look at home in just about any community.[17]

The popular image of the home is dramatically different from the standard solar sustainable design. Gone are the friendly gables and instead we see the large areas of glass, the solar collectors and the array of other systems. The modern sustainable house appears more like a scientific apparatus than a piece of architecture, when compared to the vernacular architecture that Nolan describes.

Nolan's blueprint for the millennium house is as follows.

1. *Neighbourly design*. The image should fit the context.
2. *Flexibility*. Adaptability of the interior to accommodate changes in life style.
3. *Cutting-edge technology*. Home-based electronic entertainment to foster the lifestyle. Computer-based central control for all electronic systems, including heating and cooling, security and support for home office work.
4. *Easy living*. The home and work environment is a refuge for its occupants. This means labour-saving devices and maintenance-free systems.
5. *Lifetime living*. People are living longer and so the home needs to accommodate inter-generational groups. This means 'barrier-free design'.
6. *Fun and function*. A house that plays as hard as it works. Spaces for home-based hobbies and recreation.
7. *People-friendly community*. Siting houses closer together to create a more compact neighbourhood.
8. *Easy on the environment too*.

The heating and cooling systems in our Blueprint 2000 home look well beyond the year 2000 – all the way to 2020, in fact. That's the year that federal regulations will entirely ban the manufacture of the ozone-depleting refrigerant R-22. All the air conditioners in Blueprint 2000 use a new, ozone-friendly refrigerant called Puron. Two high-efficiency central air conditioners cool the home's main level; heat pumps heat and cool the second floor, the over-the-garage studio apartment, and the separate workshop.[18]

The distinction between the vernacular and the solar sustainable house can be seen in the blueprint for a solar sustainable house. Examination of the Passive House Institute's checklist for energy-efficient design (passive house standard) produces a highly technical specification for designers to achieve high-efficiency housing. This is clearly not for the potential home builder or developer, as the language of the specification is alien to many home owners.

One of the key issues in the Task has been to identify ways of framing sustainable solar design in terms of the perception of the home owner. It is evident that the key issues concerning home owners that appear in Blueprint 2000 are image, comfort and lifestyle, with 'easy on the environment' almost as an afterthought. These may not be the priorities in all countries, but they do give some clues to strategies for marketing sustainable solar housing to the home owner.

Development of the Task 28 approach

Work on the sustainable demonstration projects involved developing case studies of projects, each designed to demonstrate a solution that improves environmental performance. At first, it was not certain what outcomes and lessons would result, but the analytical approach taken was based on four main questions:

1   What information can be derived from the project and how could this be marketed?
2   What is the legislative context and how much improvement in environmental performance do these buildings deliver over the normal house designed to the current legislation?

Table 7.1   The structure of 'Your Home', a success story in marketing sustainable solar housing

Your home: introducing good design
Your home, your future, your lifestyle
Achieving good home design
Getting started
Where to start
Budgeting for better design
Save energy and save money
Finding out about good design
Seeking professional advice
Where to live
Choosing the right place
Finding the right size home
Designing your home
Using passive design
Matching your home to the land
Cope with the slope
Planning and design
Insulating for comfort
Think about your windows
Buying good design
Buying a project home
Buying a villa or unit
Buying an existing home
Altering or renovating your home
Choosing your building materials
Inside the home
Choosing your furnishings
Choosing appliances
Choosing your hot water service
Staying warm and keeping cool
Helping the environment
Reducing your water use
Designing your garden
Renewable energy systems
Designing for the environment
Where to get help

7.7 IGS Project Prototype Solar House. NLCC Architects in collaboration with Frauhofer ISE, Germany. High-tech solution sets trailed to demonstrate feasibility. The use of steel substructure was necessary to provide sufficient structural stability for the photovoltaic system and to allow for ventilation.

3   What 'value' – social and/or economic – is added to the home by the use of sustainable solar strategies and techniques?

4   What is the underlying 'solution set' used in a project?

Marketing

Marketing is a business activity that presents products or services to the consumer in a way intended to make them eager to purchase. The Task has developed success stories of sustainable buildings that have been successfully marketed. One 'success story' from Australia is the Australian Greenhouse Office 'Your Home' project.[19]

The project reputedly cost A\$0.5 million Australian dollars. It consists of a booklet, a CD and a website. It is designed to popularize ideas of sustainable housing, with parts of the project addressing different issues. The booklet is primarily about marketing, and the CD and website show how to design and build a sustainable house.

Interestingly, the marketing booklet does not make any reference to sustainability (apart from the foreword for the Queensland version). Professor Roger Fay, who was on the technical committee, suggests that this was done to present sustainable solar housing to the public in terms of the *benefits* of sustainability to the home owner, rather than by trying to define it and explain the technical systems that underpin it.[20]

Analysis of the booklet reveals two main marketing strategies. First, the sustainable design principles are embedded into and implicit within the text. For example, the section on 'Finding the right size home' says: 'Building a more compact home to meet all your needs will save material and building costs.'[21] This is an attempt to counteract the Australian habit of building the largest size house for the block at the least cost.

The second strategy in the marketing booklet is the use of non-prescriptive language, which appeals to particular logical constructs within the schema of the home owner. For example, environmental strategies are linked to cost benefits, comfort benefits, and smart, clever, or sensible thinking.

In the booklet passive solar design is marketed by saying: 'Passive design simply makes the most of the local conditions to make your home more comfortable while reducing your bills.'[22] When choosing materials it is smart and clever to think long term. In the booklet, materials selection is marketed as: 'Do it once. Do it right. Build for life.'[23] Solar hot water is promoted with simple, self-evident advice: 'In Australia it makes good sense to get your hot water from the sun.'[24]

Interest in the project was indicated by the large number of people who attended the lecture series as it travelled around Australia. In Queensland some 400 people attended the 'Your Home' presentation. Unfortunately, there was no follow-up study to see how many participants then went on to construct sustainable houses. As the Victorian cost–benefit study suggests, the housing market is an 'imperfect market'.[25] Strategies that appear to lead logically to better comfort and savings in cost, and that result from making wise and informed decisions, are not necessarily carried through. This area of behavioural economics is worthy of further research.[26]

Legislation

A legislative (or 'pull') strategy for increasing the uptake of passive solar housing was considered for the demonstration case studies. It is generally understood that legislation leads to outcomes that avoid 'worst practice'. High-performance houses represent the other end of the spectrum; they aim to exemplify 'best practice'. To this end, further codes and assessment tools have been developed to enable the designers of high-performance buildings to get recognition for this work.

However, Wheeler favours legislation in the UK, so that this tool would become a new code to improve housing. He recommends that all new housing should achieve a 'very good' rating using the BRE EcoHomes rating tool.[24] This bold step is unlikely to succeed unless a cost–benefit analysis is carried out, so that the case studies will be examined and their performance gauged in terms of their improvement over local performance standards.

Adding value

Increasing the market value of the home is examined as an investment and a major source of income in later life. Asset management concepts are being used to inform home owners on how to obtain the best return on the investment made in their home. The media promote many home renovation programmes that help owners add value to their homes. Value adding for the home owner is explained by the BBC's Property and Lifestyle website:

Table 7.2 Free and inexpensive eco-efficiency strategies for residential construction in Australia[27]

Eco-efficiency categories
Shade east- and west-facing windows with an external blind in summer. In the tropics, shade all windows during summer.
Seal doors and windows to exclude draughts.
Fit efficient showerheads and taps. This saves money without changing your habits.
Gradually replace your old light globes with energy-efficient compact fluorescent globes.
Mulch garden areas to reduce water costs.
Install electric timers and movement sensors to automatically switch lights on and off.
Check energy ratings before buying appliances.
Plant a shade tree.
Recycle and make garden compost – improve the life of plants and the environment.
Reuse laundry water to water your garden.

If you want your property to sell for the maximum amount, it's essential that you spend time ensuring your property looks its best. This needn't cost a fortune. Simply cleaning and sprucing up the most tired parts of a house can often make a big difference. If you're lucky, investing £500 could add £5,000 to the resale value of your home. We've put together a room-by-room guide on how to maximise your property's saleability. Start by looking at our general tips for selling, then our advice on how to make each room look attractive.[28]

These guides show how a potential purchaser experiences a house, and how sustainable solar design can be exploited as a marketable feature. The work of Lisa Heschong underpins this approach. In her book *Thermal Delight in Architecture*, she examines how buildings can benefit users by providing both tangible and intangible experience.[29] She shows how user experience adds value to housing at the same time as other environmental and economic benefits are being realized.

7.8 Duplex units in Perth, Australia. The use of 'low-tech' solution sets provides a way of value adding through eco-efficient materials and passive systems.

Another concept that is useful for expressing how value is added to homes is the idea of 'eco-efficiency.' One source of this idea is the World Business Council for Sustainable Development. The term was coined by business to help develop principles for creating eco-friendly industrial processes. The approach aims to provide a framework for selecting strategies and techniques that show the greatest environmental benefit for the dollar.

Eco-efficiency is a management strategy that links financial and environmental performance to create more value with less ecological impact. We at the WBCSD have been pushing for eco-efficiency ever since we first coined the term in 1991.[30]

Eco-efficiency as an indicator

The object of eco-efficiency is to maximize value, while minimizing resource use and adverse environmental impacts. In simple terms, it is about 'doing more with less'. The World Business Council for Sustainable Development has identified seven components of eco-efficiency:

- reduce material intensity of goods and services;
- reduce energy intensity of goods and services;
- reduce toxic dispersion;
- enhance material recyclability;
- maximize sustainable use of renewable resources;

- extend product durability; and
- increase the service intensity of goods and services.

This can be expressed as: eco-efficiency = product or service value per environmental influence.[31]

Eco-efficiency in a project is achieved by the delivery of competitively priced goods and services that satisfy human needs and enhance quality of life, while progressively reducing ecological impacts and resource intensity throughout the life cycle. Eco-efficiency is established at a level compatible with the environmental capacity of the earth.

Table 7.3 Low-cost eco-efficiency strategies for residential construction in Australia[32]

Eco-efficiency strategies
Add insulation to save on heating and cooling bills and be more comfortable.
Add insulated skylights with sun control to save on lighting bills and allow indoor plants to flourish.
Use heavy drapes with pelmet boxes to reduce heating bills in winter, and cooling costs in summer.
Install a solar or gas hot-water service. They help the environment and can save you money.
Shade windows from the summer sun with a covered pergola.

Table 7.4 Medium-cost eco-efficiency strategies for residential construction in Australia[33]

Eco-efficiency strategies
Install new windows or doors when renovating, to improve light and ventilation. In most Australian climate zones you can use free heat from the sun.
Add an extension to collect winter sun and cool summer breezes and provide cross-ventilation.
Use high-performance windows to decrease energy bills and increase comfort.
Recycle your wastewater by installing your own treatment system to reduce excess water bills.
Capture free energy from the sun and wind.

The concept of eco-efficiency is found in the *Your Home* booklet under the section on 'Saving Energy Saving Money'. Solutions for 'green home design' are classified into three categories:

- free–inexpensive;
- low cost; and
- medium cost.

Good design can mean adding value by using these eco-efficient strategies. The case studies examine how eco-efficient strategies have been used to add value to the project.

The 'solution set'

The 'solution set' concept was invented by Professor Robert Hastings, leader of Task 28, with the intention of explaining the integration of all systems, passive and active, within the house form. This tool is useful to express the synergies that can be achieved between systems at the component level and over the whole house. The solution set can be applied to components or to houses; it involves the following structure:

1   Strategy description.
2   Concept: component description, special requirements for high-performance housing, discussion of the advantages and limitations.

7.9 Duplex units in Perth, Australia. The reconstituted limestone provides a self-finished material for the interior and exterior, reducing the need for ongoing maintenance. The spaces created provide for both thermal delight and high performance (internal temperatures are reduced by 10°C in summer, without air conditioning) making this house and its solution sets a blueprint that should be considered for this climate.

7.10 Lake Lagano, Italy, transformation of housing types has evolved from the use of different blueprints involving a range of 'solution sets'.

3   Comparison to other similar related components.
4   Design advice concerning the advantages and limitations of high-performance houses for different climates and energy, ecology and economic impacts.
5   Cross-comparison table.
6   Literature identification.

The 'solution set' analytical tool has been adapted to be used in housing.

The projects and experts

The projects identified are as follows.

Peterculter House, Scotland
Architect: Gorkay Deveci
A demonstration of a zero-energy detached house with passive house features (see Appendix 2).

Saline Housing, Italy
Architects: Francesca Sotargo and Valario Caldelaro
This comprises a theoretical study demonstrating a way of retrofitting existing buildings for low-income families to improve their environmental performance.

Lindås Housing, Sweden
Architect: Hans Eek
An award-winding row housing with passive house features, which provides a system of houses with no heating system.

Misawa House, Japan
Architects: Misawa Homes
This provides a demonstration of zero-energy houses powered only by solar electric systems. The detached house has a range of renewable energy systems and heat conservation strategies (see Appendix 2).

The documentation

Case study framework

Each case study provides information on a range of issues. First, there is an examination of the context to the demonstration home. This includes the country trends towards solar sustainable housing, the standards used and issues concerned with the quality and value adding to the building of the solar technologies. Second, the design brief is discussed in its climatic context. Third, the solution sets for the building are discussed, followed by the eco-efficiency strategies used. Finally, the lessons learnt are summarized, to assist with transferring the concepts to other projects.

Summary

Blueprints are case studies of demonstration projects that have integrated passive and active systems in a synergistic way. Lessons learned from this work are that the blueprinting concept can be a valuable tool for providing detailed information to all stakeholders. The case study approach yields in-depth information that can be simplified into basic 'solution sets' for particular locations and climates. It demonstrates a holistic interaction of systems that achieves a result with benefits greater than the sum of its parts.

Acknowledgements

The author wishes to acknowledge Professor Robert Hastings, Task 28 leader, for his invaluable guidance and patience in the work of the Task.

8.1　Kandalama Hotel, Dambula, Sri Lanka. Architect: Geoffrey Bawa. The use of the building transforms the tourism experience. This was also one of the first buildings to achieve international standards for environmental performance through the Green Globe programme. Industry can be transformed though the design and application of environmental standards.

Chapter 8

Transforming industry, reducing environmental impact and addressing the myths

Introduction

The previous chapters presented some of the opportunities for applying new methods and tools within the design phase. This chapter examines the ways in which they can transform the design and procurement of buildings to better meet the needs of ecological sustainable development. These could involve changes to processes, or the use of industry-based environmental standards or better solution sets in building design. Such initiatives will help dispel the myths surrounding green design and its applications.

Transforming building procurement through environmental briefing

The *environmental brief* is a methodology for pre-design in the form of a checklist tool; it has been developed and used in recent years to assist in the briefing phase and realization of projects. Prestructuring techniques are applied to thoroughly investigate the feasibility of a project, using activities such as clarifying design aims, then formulating environmental goals, strategies and techniques.

At the heart of this approach is the recognition that design problems are 'wicked problems' – the means and ends for realizing a project are not clearly identified at the outset. A large part of the designer's skill is vested in bringing some sense of vision to the project or building and in more clearly setting a direction to define the ends and means. It can be argued that

further complications exist when the designer is considering not just the building but also the environment – the problem becomes 'doubly or trebly wicked' as the factors to be considered increase exponentially.

The environmental brief attempts to define, at the outset of the project, the 'means' to achieve the design in both functional and environmental terms. This involves the activities of goal-setting and strategizing. The briefing document contains:

1 *Project details*: documentation of project information.
2 *Points of departure*: building designers have a large input into shaping the design parameters of the project (i.e. what is included or excluded). The point from which the design starts, and the initial concept used to shape the project, need input from environmental principles. Expressing the concept of the environment is an essential point of departure for any environmental project.
3 *Filters to be applied*: filters are the constraints and limitations placed on the brief that cannot be changed. The most common filters or constraints are to do with the climate and with legislation.
4 *Developing strategies*: environmental principles are addressed by previously developed strategies. In hot climates adequate solar defence is important; there are many strategies that can be used to achieve this (shading, insulation and so on). The brief is the appropriate place to start thinking about strategies arising from the basic goals, parameters and potentials of the project.
5 *Creating environmental concepts*: the environmental principles invariably become synthesized into a central concept for the building – the fundamental organization of the

8.2   Kandalama Hotel, Dambula, Sri Lanka. Architect: Geoffrey Bawa. A fusion of the natural and the built environment.

building, without which it would not exist. This environmental concept is best expressed as a section of the brief.

6   *Integrating standards and other environmental frameworks*: one way of improving the environmental brief is to adopt a defined environmental framework or standard. A summative statement is made according to how the brief addresses issues in the standard.

The case studies in Part 3 show some of the environmental briefs created using this approach. In the EPA fit-out brief for the interior of an office in a Cairns project, the environmental criteria from the Green Building Challenge tool were used to formulate the brief in another project, the Yeang EcoHome, the BREEAM EcoHomes rating checklist was used to create the brief (see Appendix 2).

Setting and adopting industry design and operational standards

On a broader scale, another approach has involved developing environmental standards for the international travel and tourism industry (see Chapter 5).[1] These standards are based on Agenda 21 issues supported through Green Globe (GG) a non-profit company for tourism operations around the world.[2] Two approaches can be used to transform industry:

- integration of principles for operational assessment;
- design phase assessment approach.

Green design and operational assessment

The tourism industry has standards already in place for assessing buildings during the operational phase (Company, Community and Eco-tourism standards). It was recognized that the integration of these standards into the building industry is crucial to achieving a building with minimal environmental impact. The reasons for this are fourfold:

1   The standards are based on a large body of building performance data used to construct benchmarks for environmental performance.
2   Building performance data is used to evaluate the performance of the tourism industry worldwide. This can be applied to different contexts: building types, climates and the level of service provided.
3   Environmental legislative methods vary globally so there is no common standard.
4   Self-assessment is not an acceptable means of validating the building's conformity to the standard. Third-party assessment is crucial. Data collection on the building's environmental performance must be confidential for reasons of privacy and intellectual property.

The example of the approach used can be seen in the Kandalama Hotel, Dambula, Sri Lanka. Located in an environmentally sensitive area, the building design involved the use of green design principles. This shows one way of applying the GG standard in the design phase, using green design principles and strategies, and then monitoring the performance through operational data using the GG Company standard and benchmarking systems.

SITING AND PROGRAMME

The building is located in the dry climatic zone of Sri Lanka. The site overlooks a local water basin called a tank, which attracts wildlife and provides a view to the horizon. The building is over 100 metres long and its form follows the shape of a rock outcrop to the south. The long thin building that results is ideally suited to its location. The circulation system snakes through the guest accommodation, giving glimpses of the rock outcrop and local flora and fauna.

LIFE SYSTEMS

The hotel rooms are connected to the circulation system so that the views of the tank are not compromised. The guest rooms are naturally ventilated; shading is provided by timber sun-breakers and vegetation. These strategies create a closeness to nature that is both physical and highly experiential.

MATERIAL SYSTEMS

The interconnected nature of the building comes from the material strategies. The earth roof and hard materials make it difficult to detect where the building ends and the site begins.

8.3   Kandalama Hotel, Dambula, Sri Lanka. A large rock outcrop forms the southerly backdrop to the building.[3]

Assessing the design phase

Another way is to apply a design-phase tool. The standard that relates particularly to this approach is called the *Green Globe 21 Design and Construct standard* (D&C standard). This provides developers with a design standard to brief the design team from the inception of the project. The advantage of this approach is that it avoids risk, clarifies objectives and ensures a best-practice design.

Data collection can be streamlined, and using information that is readily obtained in the design process can contain the cost of the assessment. Rating tools are notoriously data-hungry in the pursuit of scientific rigour, and so a trade-off is necessary between the accuracy of the model and the 'manageability' of the data collection process. Using data from the design process that is readily available from the designer's ISO 9000 quality assurance process means better access to data.

Reducing and simplifying the additional analytical activities required is another key strategy in containing the assessment cost. An example is green materials assessment, which is scientifically complex and draws on a range of data from such sources as life cycle and health impact studies. The Design and Construct standard brings together these studies and integrates them into a measure to help streamline the design and assessment process. This is a central element of the work of the standard.

In the past there was a wide range of guidelines and knowledge in the area of green design. Now the travel and tourism industry benefits from a voluntary standard, common to all, which has pulled together the sustainable design knowledge base into a readily available framework at the international level. The methodology has been developed for assessing the sketch design phase and is orientated for sustainable tourism projects. It uses design-phase assessment involving a benchmarking approach and eco-labelling.[4]

Examples of projects that have used this approach are found in Chapter 10. In some cases, buildings were assessed during or after the design phase was completed. The Novotel & Ibis Hotel in Sydney was assessed post construction, while the other projects were assessed during the design phase. Developers should carry out a feasibility study to identify which of these approaches suits the design process for their project.

Building environmental assessment tools

These methodologies use design assessment at all stages including post construction and are aimed at comprehensive assessment of a project. The tools used include checklists, scorecards and eco-labelling.

Assessment tools, such as LEED and BREEAM, place emphasis on evaluation of the output of design. These tools check the extent to which environmental goals, strategies and techniques have been integrated in a project, as well as any potential environmental loadings that may be created. LEED and BREEAM have checklists, which are intended to help with the pre-design step. These also have post construction evaluation for facility management. The tools provide an eco-label on completion of the assessment.

The Leadership in Energy and Environmental Design (LEED™) Green Building rating system represents the US Green Building Council's effort to provide a national standard to define what constitutes a green building. Through its use as a design guideline and third-party certification tool, it aims to improve occupant well-being, environmental performance and economic returns of buildings, using established and innovative practices, standards and technologies (LEED Version 2.1, p. 2).

The United States Green Building Council has a policy for the continuous improvement of LEED. The improvements expected from the new tool are:

- simplification of the documentation process for project teams;
- reduction in the costs of documenting LEED credits while retaining the stringency and integrity of the standard;
- use of new LEED letter template (seen as a 'dynamic tracking and documentation tool'); and
- a checklist for summarizing credit topics and point values.

Reducing environmental impact, saving money and improving quality of life

Implementing some of these methodologies in the design and procurement of buildings can lead to a nexus of benefits. First, what is the extent of reductions in negative environmental impact that can be expected from using these methodologies?

Experience has now been gained of the implementation of green design through the application of various standards. LEED has four standards, and the cost premium associated with the different standards has been calculated.[5] From this it can be seen that there is a significant difference in the cost premium between gold (1.82%) and platinum (6.5%).

There is clearly an issue of cost versus environmental performance; there is not a linear relationship between cost and environmental performance. If anything, the law of diminishing returns applies: the more improvement in environmental performance by way of reducing impacts, the greater the increase in the cost premium. Kats reports that 'the majority of this cost is due to the increased architectural and engineering (A&E) design time, modelling costs and time necessary to integrate sustainable building practices into projects'.[6]

Using 'solution sets' from exemplary green buildings

Developing new solution sets for green buildings is not an easy task. The work on high-rise buildings by architect Ken Yeang in Malaysia illustrates this problem. An example of the evolution of this type of building is seen in the design construction of the Umno (United Malays National Organisation) Headquarters in Penang, and proposals for Waterfront Place in Kuala Lumpur, Malaysia (see Appendix 2). Post occupancy studies of the earlier buildings and modelling work have led to the development of the Waterfront Place proposal.[7,8] Much of this work is piecemeal, identifying problems with the blueprinting approach, namely the need for more comprehensive summative studies across larger numbers of buildings.

Research work as part of International Energy Agency SHC Task 28 on Sustainable Solar Housing involved a 'blueprinting' approach, which addresses this problem and provides information for all phases of the design process. Emphasis is placed on the identification of environmental strategies and techniques, all of which can be optimized into archetypal solution sets for different contexts and building types characterized by Task 28.

The International Energy Agency (IEA) is a multinational organization that promotes research into the built environment. It was established in 1974 as an autonomous agency within the framework of the Organization for Economic Cooperation and Development (OECD). Its mission is to 'carry out a comprehen-

sive program of energy cooperation among its 25 member countries and the Commission of the European Communities' (www.iea-shc.org).

A central part of the programme involves collaboration in the research, development and demonstration of new energy technologies to reduce excessive reliance on imported oil, to increase long-term energy security, and to reduce greenhouse gas emissions.

The IEA research and development activities are headed by the Committee on Energy Research and Technology (CERT), with three working parties charged with monitoring the various collaborative energy agreements, identifying new areas for cooperation and advising the CERT on policy matters.

One research task is focused on Sustainable Solar Housing (Task 28). This project has a broader environmental model than energy alone. It recognizes that there are other aspects to sustainability than just energy, and that there is a growing movement to build ecological housing. It is suggested that the broad base to sustainability – social, economic and environmental considerations – may be useful for marketing this form of housing.

Task 28 has developed benchmarks for several types of houses involving low purchased-energy consumption for heating and cooling, and minimal CO_2 emissions. 'Factor-Four Plus Housing' requires one-fourth or less of the purchased heating energy of houses built to current standards to be used for heating (e.g. passive houses). It requires a maximum of 10 W per m^2 of space heating, amounting to an annual energy demand of 15 kWh/m^2 in temperate climates (central Europe). It is such benchmarks that form a useful basis for the brief for solar sustainable housing.

Until now, such housing achieved this high performance primarily by reducing heat losses, i.e. by having compact building form, thick insulation and ventilation heat recovery. While the number of such buildings is growing, market penetration would be enhanced by a complementary approach, namely increasing energy gains in very well insulated housing. This can be achieved by:

- passive solar design;
- active solar systems for domestic hot water and space heating;
- PV electric supply systems;
- improved daylighting (for improved living quality); and
- natural cooling and solar/glare control.

The aim of the Task 28 work is to provide blueprints that contain solution sets for typical solar sustainable houses in different climates. The solution sets are designs for a given building type, climate and strategy (conservation, or renewable energy focus). The designs are also the result of sensitivity analysis, being the best reasonable solution for the programmatic function and building type.

Information from the blueprint can be used as a whole or in parts and is integrated into the design process at many points. For example, the overall planning concepts can all be used or, if desired, only selective parts of the technologies. It should be noted, though, that the principle of the blueprint is that it is the combination of all the strategies that creates the most effective result.

A key construct used in the work is 'the solution set' (TSS). Task 28 is simply a good example of a typical (i.e. not extreme) residential building, like a concept or 'high performance catalogue house' which contains a description of the type of house (single-family, row or apartment building), including percentage of window areas, envelope constructions and the HVAC systems required, all designed in order to meet the Task 28 targets. The energy (and other) targets could be met using two strategies: conservation strategy (reducing losses) and use of solar and renewables (increasing gains).

For each strategy, examples can be found of good solutions for single-family detached houses, row houses, and apartment buildings. These building types are matched with climate types: cold (Stockholm), temperate (Zürich) and mild (Milan) climate. Each example of building concept (including HVAC systems) that shows how to reach the goals/targets is a TSS. The work will be described through examples in a handbook that will also show the energy performance, thermal comfort, plus LCA and economy when available.

As can be seen in Chapter 7, the value of blueprinting as a post construction activity is enhanced if a number of issues are addressed. Environmental performance data, such as energy use and thermal performance, is provided. Also cost data and occupancy feedback studies should be provided. As more experience is gained in the use of these systems, a more accurate picture of these issues will build up, although presently a number of myths have emerged. Chapter 7 provides information on the benefits of developing a blueprinting approach.

Addressing the myths

A major barrier to transforming industry is the number of myths that have developed around the design and procurement of green buildings. In many cases these are negative and are used as a reason for inaction. Research studies have shown that many of these myths are either a result of simplistic thinking, arrived at though poor building procurement (simply under-funding building projects to make more profit) or are unsubstantiated. Shailja Chandri suggests that four of the more important myths are as follows.[9]

Myth 1: Green buildings are expensive.
Myth 2: Developers have no incentive to build green.
Myth 3: Green buildings are based on fringe technologies.
Myth 4: The green design 'info glut' is both confusing and misleading.

Myth 1: Green buildings are expensive

This myth can be countered by two main arguments: first, by taking into account 'life cycle' costs rather than only capital expenses; and second, by appreciating the benefits to quality of life issues, such as better health and well-being, and the associated cost savings and financial benefits as a result of increased productivity. Research findings suggest that, even with a tight budget, many green building measures can be incorporated with minimal or zero increased up-front costs and can yield enormous savings.[10]

Kats reports on costs and financial benefit in a study of California buildings.[11] The report is thought to be the first of its kind to fully aggregate the costs and benefits of green buildings:

Specifically, the bulk of this report reviews and analyzes a large quantity of existing data about the costs and financial benefits of green buildings in California. Several dozen building representatives and architects were contacted to secure the cost of 33 green buildings compared to conventional designs for those buildings. The average premium for these green buildings is slightly less than 2% (or US$3–5 per ft2), substantially lower than is commonly perceived. The majority of this cost is due to the increased architectural and engineering (A&E) design time neces-

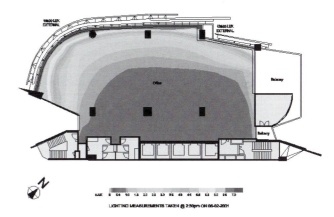

8.4 Umno Tower, Penang, Malaysia. Architects: T.R. Hamzam and Yeang Sdn Bhd. The floor plate of this building is fairly small, approximately 1,000 m², which allows the use of an operable façade and shading systems (top). The use of passive systems, such as shading and the core as a buffer device to the westerly sun (above), assists with reducing energy needs. There is access to local sea breezes, which are a useful cooling system in tropical areas. Centre lighting and shading assessment.

sary to integrate sustainable building practices into projects. Generally, the earlier green building gets incorporated into the design process, the lower the cost.[12]

The lessons learned from this are that there are multiple indicators of financial benefits. These include savings from efficient use of resources but also from other business measures such as improved productivity. The design costs of the project seem to improve if the decision to build green is taken early in the design process. This provides an important argument for the financial benefits of effective briefing in the project.

From this is can be concluded that it is possible to address this myth through better briefing to ensure that environmental performance is a key priority.

Myth 2: Developers have no incentive to build green

The development context is changing, and there are forces external to projects, within the environmental context, that are proving to be incentives for change. The building development process has been criticized, essentially for being largely dollar driven, with no incentive to build green.[13] A number of shifts are occurring to change this view.

First, the concept of adding value to the project by green design for marketing purposes is gaining ground. The concept of green buildings is catching on with buyers, particularly with respect to energy-efficiency measures and indoor air-quality benefits. Anecdotal evidence suggests there is a potential for increased property values of 10 per cent for green buildings on resale.[14]

SOLUTION SETS FOR BIOCLIMATIC HIGH-RISE BUILDINGS

High-rise buildings have usually ignored the use of passive strategies for climate control. Bioclimatic solution sets for this building type require careful study to evaluate the potential of the systems for improving environmental performance. The Umno Headquarters and Waterfront Place buildings provide examples of a number of buildings of this type that can be studied in order to evolve the solution sets.

SITE AND PROGRAMME

The plan form of each building is similar, comprising a distorted ellipse with its major axis north–south. In the tropical climate this exposes a large proportion of the façade to lower sun angles and higher intensity radiation. Mitigating these effects involved using the core of the buildings as a buffer to the west, together with shading systems on the east.

LIFE SYSTEMS

The plan form allows for the use of a passive zone – the use of natural ventilation and daylighting for a zone 8 metres deep from the exterior. The inner zone requires active systems. In the Umno building, which has a small floor plate of approximately 1000 m², this zone is small, but in Waterfront Place this zone is approximately half the area of the floor plate. The use of light pipes is proposed to increase daylighting to this area.[15]

MATERIAL SYSTEMS

Heavyweight materials are used in the structure to assist moderating the internal temperatures, through heat-sink effects.

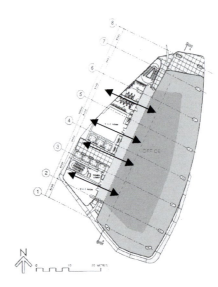

8.5 **Top**. Umno Headquarters Building, Penang, Malaysia.
Right. Waterfront Place. **Top right**. Proposed Waterfront Tower, Kuala Lumpur, Malaysia. The arrows show the proposed location of the light pipes in the design.

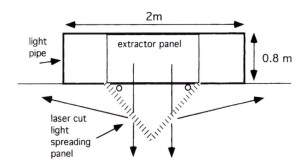

8.6 New solution sets for office design. Proposed Waterfront Tower Kuala Lumpur, Malaysia: Architects: T.R. Hamzam and Yeang Sdn Bhd. This building uses a similar floor plate design to Umno but is larger, at 2,000 m^2, creating the need for light piping to the interior. Research work into the use of light pipe technology provides opportunities to bring daylight into deep plan office buildings while reducing the need for electric lighting. The light pipe system utilizes prismatic diffusers to import light from the exterior to the interior space. The pipes are of similar size and construction to air conditioning ducts and can be double-functioning

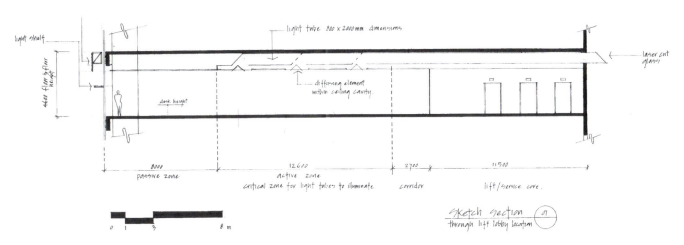

8.7 Proposed Waterfront Tower Kuala Lumpur, Malaysia: Architects T.R. Hamzam and Yeang Sdn Bhd. This uses a similar floor plate design as Umno but is larger, 2000 m^2 making the need for light piping to the interior.

159

Second, while reducing operating costs may not be the strongest incentive for a development company, the benefits can have a significant influence on rents and costs for tenants.

Third, the costs for building green can be offset by a variety of government-sponsored economic incentive programmes: for example, the subsidy on photovoltaic power generation systems and the rebate on solar hot water installations.

Fourth, there is a range of external issues that are driving green buildings to be more service-efficient and autonomous. Evidence from the Californian study suggests that one of the reasons for adopting environmental standards for buildings came from the risks and costs associated with variability in service provisions of water and energy, environmental quality, operations and maintenance. The details of the risks are:

- the high cost of electric power;
- worsening electric grid constraints, with associated power quality and availability problems;
- pending water shortage and waste disposal issues;
- continued state and federal pressure to cut pollutants;
- growing concern over the cost of global warming;
- the rising incidence of allergies and asthma, especially in children;
- the health and productivity of workers;
- the effects of the physical environment of schools on children's abilities to learn; and
- increasing expenses of maintaining and operating state facilities over time.[16]

Myth 3: Green buildings are based on fringe technologies

This myth concerns the risks of green technologies in terms of cost and performance. Interestingly, most of the case studies that have achieved green design have used conventional building systems more effectively through better integration and design. It seems the reason for the increased design costs of green buildings may be that the designers are trying to whittle out redundancy in the systems to achieve better efficiency in the building. The solution set research follows this model of pursuing sustainable outcomes through better synergies between active and passive systems in buildings. The use of such examples that can act as blueprints for future projects can be an efficient and effective design tool.

Existing systems can be better managed. The Novotel & Ibis Hotel, at Olympic Park, Homebush Bay, Sydney, has recently invested in a building management system. The hotel managers recognized the importance of energy efficiency, in keeping with the aim of making the 2000 Olympics the 'Green Games'. The existing energy system achieves a reported 30 per cent saving compared to a normal hotel. Further improvements are anticipated through using high-efficiency screw chillers to provide efficient air conditioning. The investment in a building management system of A$260,000 will achieve savings of A$100,000 per annum through better zoning control and accommodating small system loads over the life of the building.

Myth 4: The green design 'info glut', and the plethora of tools, is both confusing and misleading

Many observers of the move to green buildings note the surfeit of new guidelines, tools and standards that are emerging to assist designers with green buildings. Some have tried to compare the tools, and it is confusing to know which to use, and which should be applied to which building type.[17]

Nigel Howard, Vice President USGBC, Director of LEED and International Programs, suggests that the rating tools such as LEED are only part of the move to green design. He suggests that equally important is the range of expertise and information support behind the tools which helps to provide information to designers. The LEED[TM] certification process is a three-step process.

Step 1: Project registration
Welcome packet and on-line project listing
Step 2: Technical support
Reference package
Credit rulings
Step 3: Building certification.
Upon documentation submittal and USGBC review.[18]

The use of BEA tools such as LEED and the tran-professional groups that support the rating tools have the potential to bring 'structure' to the 'information glut' and assist developers in achieving improved performance.

Summary

Transforming industry by making more use of the design phase has potential to address the current myths concerning green buildings.

First, as regards the myth that green buildings are more expensive, research studies are showing that, while capital costs are marginally higher, there are life cycle benefits. Some of the added costs come from additional work by the building design team to demonstrate the economic and environmental benefits of the strategies proposed. The establishment of environmental criteria or the use of an environmental standard in the brief from the inception can reduce these costs.

Second, the myth that developers have little incentive to build green is addressed though the use of industry environmental standards such as that found in BEA rating and benchmarking tools. The Green Globe approach for the travel and tourism industry is an example. The use of these standards can reduce risks attached to development as well as demonstrate compliance with industry best practice. The eco-labels created have yet to gain currency with users but the top performers in the industry are positioning themselves for this purpose.

The third myth is that the technologies to create green buildings are developing but are high risk and on the fringe, not mainstream. Blueprinting studies are one way to counter this, if sufficient depth of information is provided.

Finally, there is the myth that the green 'info glut' creates confusion and lacks structure. Professional groups and trans-professional groups such as LEED are providing structure through the use of BEA.

Further evidence of the transformation of the design and procurement of buildings can be seen in Part 3. As many of the methods and tools are specific to particular building types, the chapters have been structured accordingly.

Acknowledgements

Illustrations, plans and sections: Richard Hyde, Joyce Law, Greg Evans. Light pipes illustrations: Veronica Hanson and Ian Edmunds.

Part THREE

Case studies

The aim of Part 3 is to study the application of the tools and methods described in Part 2. In particular it will look into their use in the briefing process and in the assessment of projects on environmental criteria. The buildings described provide case studies across a range of building types: housing, resorts, tourism and interpretation buildings and offices. These projects represent different ways of using the tools and methods within the design process.

The projects in the first section examine the use of these tools for houses and housing:

- BedZED project, UK. Post-construction assessment using the EcoHomes rating tool.
- IEA Task 28: the Ostia Antia proposal and the Lindås Housing from Sweden. These involve the use of blueprinting. The Ostia Antia project provides a theoretical model for retrofitting existing buildings in Italy; the Lindås Housing provides information from post-construction data.

In recent years the environmental performance of tourism facilities and related infrastructure buildings has become of increasing concern. Three examples are described in the second section:

- Novotel & Ibis hotel, Sydney, Australia. This involves the use of the Green Globe Design and Construct benchmarking tool for post-construction benchmarking of the design.
- Sundancer Resort, Lombok, Indonesia. The method used involves the Green Globe tool, this time for benchmarking during the design phase and construction.
- Lark Quarry Trackways building, Australia. Again, the Green Globe Design and Construct benchmarking tool is used for post-construction benchmarking of the design.

The third set of projects is related to office buildings:

- Environmental Protection Agency (EPA), William McCormack Place, Cairns, Australia. This demonstrates the environmental briefing approach.
- CH_2, Melbourne, Australia. The method of briefing and assessment is Green Star. (This is a pilot project, hence the rating is provisional.)
- Philip Merrill Center, Annapolis, USA. The method of briefing and assessment during the design phase involved the use of LEED. The *GBTool* was used for post-construction monitoring.
- Wessex Water, Bath, UK. BREEAM Offices 98 was used for briefing and design phase assessment.

Housing

Beddington Zero (Fossil) Energy Development: BedZED, London, UK

The development offers a coherent solution to the challenge of sustainable living within the urban environment. The ZED (Zero fossil-fuel Energy Development) system integrates environmental, social and economic needs, bringing together proven strategies to reduce energy, water and car use.

Architects: Bill Dunster Architects

Introduction

The project shows a systems approach to sustainability in the housing sector, using a demonstration to illustrate arguments for the system and to point out its likely benefits. BedZED is claimed as the UK's leading model of urban sustainability, and it is interesting to see how it performs against the BRE EcoHomes criteria. Also of interest is to investigate how it meets new criteria not yet included in the EcoHomes standard such as carbon storage, site car storage and the use of local materials and labour.

Pre-design and briefing

This section charts the pre-design activities that helped to capture sustainable goals and objectives in the project.

BedZED challenges the formal architectural and sustainability norms of housing in the UK. Setting aside the hype, it is the benefits of green design for the user that set this scheme apart from others.

Project organization

In order to resolve the challenge, the project uses a team of multidisciplinary groups. This includes the Peabody Trust, which is London's largest housing association, environmental specialists, the BioRegional Development Group and the design team of architects and engineers.

Application of EcoHomes rating and the BedZED approach

The design of the scheme addresses a wider set of issues than that found in the EcoHomes environmental rating scheme. EcoHomes is primarily concerned, and perhaps rightly so, with

BedZED project details

Characteristics	Details
Owner	Peabody Trust, Housing Association
Project team	Architects: Bill Dunster Architects
	Services engineer: Arups
	Structural and civil engineers: Ellis and Moore
	Quantity surveyors and project management: Gardner and Theobald
Completion date	2002
Cost	GB£1.7 million
Size	3,703 m²
Footprint ratio	1.7
Construction type	Domestic/commercial, three storey
Use group	Rented accommodation
Annual energy	Carbon neutral
Use	Mixed residential and offices
Lot size	0.64 hectares
City	London
Country	United Kingdom
Latitude	51°36′ N
Building type	Row housing and mixed use development
Occupancy	244 residents, 271 workers

environmental issues. BedZED, on the other hand, appears to take a broader, triple bottom line approach, which attempts to reconcile environmental, economic and social issues in the design project.

BedZED has developed a set of performance indicators that appear to match this triple bottom line approach to green design.[1] The main categories of the BedZED system are:

- site location;
- energy;
- travel and transport;
- materials;
- open space (shared green space);
- water saving; and
- cost and quality.

Design intent

Response to the brief

The reason behind the ZED system is, first, a need for over 600,000 homes in London by the year 2016. This will require construction of high-density developments located preferably on 'brownfield' sites – sites that have previously been developed.[2]

Housing design has traditionally been seen as a social design problem. Generally high-density housing schemes have been criticized for lack of amenity, such as access to natural light, ventilation and external space. These have now become powerful indicators of social sustainability in the design of higher-density schemes. Hence the system brief has explored the use of sunlight, roof garden terraces and conservatories.

Environmental issues the design team has addressed include a high level of energy conservation, particularly for heating and electric lighting. There is a strategy of substitution of renewable for non-renewable energy sources. A similar conservation approach is taken with water, materials and transportation; a 'green transport plan', aimed at reducing dependence on the car, involves a combination of economic incentives and location advantages, the most significant being that the development is within a kilometre of a main transport node. This gives the occupants a wide range of transportation options – car, train, bus, cycle or walking.[3]

Economic issues are addressed through mixed functional usage; both commercial and housing accommodation is included on the site, as well as a mix of shared social facilities, which results in reasonably priced homes. This mixed use, with a variety of ownership options, is seen to offset the higher cost of the green strategies and techniques.

Response to climate

The climate in the UK around London is characterized as a heating climate. Bioclimatically the external temperatures are below the comfort zone, with damp cold conditions in winter and warm wet summers. The months when passive strategies alone can be used are limited to about one-third of the year.

Passive strategies and techniques

The passive strategies suitable for this climate in winter are solar heat gain and thermal mass to extend the comfort zone.

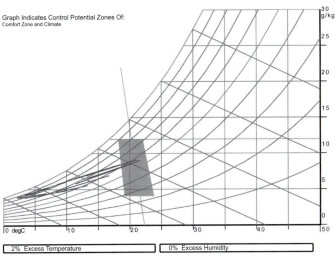

Graph Indicates Control Potential Zones Of:
Comfort Zone and Climate

2% Excess Temperature   0% Excess Humidity

Passive design strategies. **Top**. Atrium space is double-glazed, creating high-performance windows with low U value. Windows include the integration of photovoltaic cells. **Left**. Bioclimatic strategies of thermal mass and passive solar are only effective for about four months of the year to extend the comfort zone. For the remainder high levels of heat conservation and supplementary heating are needed.

THERMAL MASS AND INSULATION

In housing, the main problem is usually the environmental loads on the building. Thermal mass can be used to address these environmental loads in two ways: the use of insulation and the use of heat storage.

Using thermal mass for insulation is not recommended unless very thick walls are employed. This is because the high capacity materials used to provide thermal mass are not good insulators. In fact 400 mm of concrete has a U value equiva-lent to 10 mm of polystyrene insulation.[4] Resistive and reflec-tive insulation is usually used to isolate the thermal mass from environmental loads so that its heat storage effect can be ade-quately regulated. Thus, the wall construction of opaque ele-ments usually involves placing the thermal capacity materials towards the inside of the envelope. The interesting part of this scheme is the use of a 'super insulation' approach, comprising approximately three times the normal thickness of insulation.

SOLAR GAIN

Solar gain is needed to assist with providing natural heating to the thermal mass. This can be achieved through:

- direct gain –sunlit patches on the floor create a direct heat transfer to the storage; or
- indirect gain –the sun is used to heat the air inside the space, which is then circulated to heat the mass.

One of the inherent problems with designing for solar gain in this climate is the relationship between solar load and heating demand. A glance at the irradiation data for this climate reveals the problem –in winter when the solar heating is needed the irradiation levels are low. Care has to be taken that, with the heat losses through the glazing elements, there are in fact net gains to the building. Furthermore, the converse is true: when the heating is least needed in summer, radiation levels are high. So in this climate, it is not ideal to use solar gain for direct gain heating, as the strategy is working against the natural pattern.

Mitigating measures incorporated in the fabric of the building envelope are needed to maximize the benefits of the system. These are:

- creation of a sunspace –a semi-outdoor indoor space that can be isolated from the main building, the sunspace takes on a large range of temperatures and therefore needs to be separated from the habitable spaces to avoid transferring unwanted heat or cold to them;
- use of solar shading and ventilation to cool the sunspace in summer and prevent over-heating;
- use of double glazing to improve heat conservation in winter and reduce heat gain in summer.

In this building, solar gain through a sunspace has been used, with a number of mitigating measures. But there is a further benefit from solar input: the use of daylight can reduce the need for electric lighting, conserving energy and creating a greater sense of well-being in the home.

AIRFLOW

Airflow is needed for three purposes:

- providing fresh air;
- reducing over-heating of the structure; and
- providing cooling to the occupants.

Ventilation pathways designed to serve these three functions should be provided in the building.

In winter, with a heating climate such this, ventilation – both controlled, and uncontrolled through leaks in the envelope – causes discomfort in the form of draughts to the occupants and limits the degree to which the building can conserve energy. As will be seen, in the BedZED scheme the active systems and the envelope have been designed to control wanted and unwanted ventilation; considerable effort has been put into this, through the use of operable windows and also through ingenious design of the mechanical systems.

Active strategies and techniques

HEATING, VENTILATION AND COOLING

One of the striking features of the design of the scheme is the roof. In particular, the ventilation cowls on the roof are used for both visual appeal and functional purposes. These are the input and output air intakes of the heat recovery system used in the building, linked directly to the heating, ventilation and cooling systems. The features of the heating system are such that the waste heat from internal loads – occupants, cooking, and water heating – is sufficient to raise the internal temperatures to the comfort zone. No other heating is needed, apart from a small back-up system from the hot water unit, to stop the system winding down when occupants are not in residence. This approach is only possible if heat losses are negligible, so a highly thermally efficient envelope is essential. Heat losses were minimized by reducing infiltration of cold air from outside and by recovering waste heat from the ventilation system (heat is extracted from the outgoing air and used to warm the incoming air).[5]

RENEWABLE ENERGY SUPPLY

The goal of creating a housing development that uses no fossil fuel as an energy source required stepping beyond the boundary of the site and using the local community as its resource base. The architects, in conjunction with the local council, turned to biomass as an alternative fuel source.

Biomass is organic matter that can be converted into an energy source. In this case tree surgery waste is diverted from

Top left. The communal facilities provided for residents include a sport complex and playing fields. **Left.** The cooling and heating power plan is also included in this complex and provides the electricity and hot water heating for the housing. This cogeneration capability means that grid power is only used as a 'back-up system'. **Above.** Photovoltaic cells are used for electrical power generation and are connected to car-charging points. This provides an eco-efficient solution, considerably reducing the payback period of the PV system and also providing renewable energy for transport.[6]

landfill and converted to fuel. The main technical systems are as follows:

- 130 kW biomass-fuelled combination heat and power unit – provides heat for a district heating system as well as electrical power;
- 777 m² of photovoltaic panels, enough to power 40 electric vehicles;
- grid power as a back-up to accommodate peak loads.

HOT WATER

Hot water is provided from the renewable energy supply – the biomass-fuelled combined heating and cooling system.

ELECTRIC LIGHTING

Low-energy lighting is used throughout the scheme.

WATER AND WASTE CONSERVATION SYSTEMS

The development focuses on conserving the amount of water brought into the site and the amount of water-borne waste leaving the site, through the following techniques:

- rainwater is collected in storage tanks for toilet flushing;
- wastewater is treated on site in a biological sewage system, providing additional water for toilet flushing.

BRE EcoHomes criteria

This section examines the BedZED scheme from the point of view of the EcoHomes criteria.

Energy

Five main criteria are used:

Left. A home office is provided, which can influence transportation needs. **Top right**. Internal bike storage adjacent to the stairway. **Top middle**. Renewable energy car-charging point, part of the transport plan.

1   reduced predicted CO_2 emissions;
2   improve performance of the building envelope;
3   drying space provision;
4   eco-labelled appliances; and
5   energy-efficient external lighting.

PREDICTED CO_2 EMISSIONS

The use of predicted emissions allows energy from renewable sources to be set against that from non-renewable resources. This is a typical strategy in many environmental houses, but usually a large proportion of the power is still generated from fossil fuel energy. The situation here is different; in this case a balance is achieved with the extensive use of renewable energy for heating, cooling and power generation. The benefit of this approach is that the predicted net emissions for the development are zero. This creates a 'carbon neutral' development where the net carbon flux in the energy system is balanced.[7]

BUILDING ENVELOPE

The low predicted emissions are made possible by the use of renewable energy and energy conservation through efficiency measures: by doing more with less.

In the case of energy conservation this is achieved by a number of strategies but, since a significant proportion of the energy used is for space heating and cooling, one of the main ways of reducing energy use is to improve the thermal performance of the building envelope: walls, roof, floors and windows. The main techniques are:

*   insulation;
*   high-performance windows; and
*   reduced air infiltration and ventilation, since heat is lost through any air flows between inside and out (while there are energy benefits from a tightly sealed building, there are also health consequences for the occupants – see the section below on health and well-being).

All these factors are critical to reducing heat loss to an absolute minimum.

In the case of the BedZED project, the high U values for walls, roof and windows are well above current baseline standards found in building regulations and codes. The envelope design and the use of renewable energy reduce the need for heat to around 10 per cent of 1995 Building Regulations.[8]

DRYING SPACE

The scheme provides drying spaces within the dwellings. From observation, some occupants use the sunspace for drying, while others use the bathrooms. Sky gardens and external space are provided.[9]

ECO-LABELLED APPLIANCES

Triple A appliances contribute to the energy conservation approach.[10]

EXTERNAL LIGHTING

Energy-efficient external lighting is used.

Transport

Four criteria are used:

1 public transport accessibility;
2 cycle storage;
3 local amenity proximity; and
4 home office provision.

The importance of the transport criteria arises from the current patterns of use of transport in the UK, with car-based fossil fuel dominance amounting to approximately 30 per cent of household energy consumption. Improving energy conservation in buildings is therefore only a small part of the overall picture; strategies for reducing car-based transport place much more emphasis on the site location of a development, and on the calibre of the public transport infrastructure.

The BedZED team has been able to control the internal aspects of the transport problem through careful site selection and the development of an integrated transport provision (ITP). It has not been able to control the externalities, which depend on the quality of the public transport system.

PUBLIC TRANSPORT ACCESSIBILITY

The site is located within 1,000 metres of the local railway station of Hackbridge, which is approximately 30 minutes from the centre of London by train. The station is easily accessible by other forms of transport, such as foot, cycle and bus. The public transport accessibility indicators are as follows.[11]

1 pedestrian travel distance to the railway station 0.7 km – easy walking distance;
2 bus routes 100 m from the site.

The ITP also assists with reducing the environmental impact of car-based systems by promoting electric vehicles. This involves:

- 26 electric car charging points, free of charge; and
- parking rebates for LPG (gas) and electric cars on site.

CYCLE STORAGE

Cycle storage is needed to improve the options for people to consider forms of transport other than the car. Hence the ITP has also provided cycle storage of approximately 1.4 m² of covered space per home.[12]

LOCAL AMENITY PROXIMITY

In a similar way the close proximity of amenities cuts car dependence. The pedestrian travel distances are:

- bulk food shop 3 km, with local shops available;
- doctor (health centre) 100 m;
- nursery on site;
- café/pub proposed on site;
- schools 0.6–1 km; and
- vegetable garden adjacent.

HOME OFFICE PROVISION

Home units provide space for a home office as a separate room.

Pollution

The intent of this criterion is to avoid and/or reduce the amount of harmful substances emitted by the construction of the building. This applies to the fabric of the building, including the manufacturing process.

One important consideration is the emissions of ozone-depleting substances such as CFCs used in air conditioning cooling systems. Information from manufacturers in the form of building health data sheets and environmental profiling of products should assist with identifying compliance with pollution control. Two criteria are used:

- ozone-depleting materials not used in construction;
- nitrous oxide emissions low.

OZONE DEPLETING MATERIALS

The intent here is to ensure that no ozone-depleting substances are used in the construction of the building. Elements such as walls, roof, floors and hot water systems are considered separately.

Above. The selection of materials is based on a green supply chain. Case studies are provided for most materials to ensure minimal environmental impact and minimal impact on human health and well-being. Creating a supply chain allows the design and specification of products to be carried forward into the next project. **Right**. Recycled materials used in the bedrooms.

NITROUS OXIDE EMISSIONS

The heating boilers are based on a natural energy source that reduces nitrous oxide emissions (see section below on renewable energy supply).

Materials

SUSTAINABLE TIMBER MANAGEMENT

This criterion is to ensure that timber used in the development is sourced from sustainable developed forests. Forests are certified by tracking a 'chain of custody' that starts from the source of the material and continues to the finished product.

Approximately 200 m^3 of timber was sourced through the Forestry Stewardship Council (FSC).[13] This timber was used for:

- external studwork;
- weatherboards; and
- internal joists.

Over 3,000 m^2 of FSC plywood was used in the project.

STRUCTURAL TIMBERS

Over 50,000 m of recycled and reused timber studwork was used in the project, which resulted in cost savings.

FINISHING TIMBER ELEMENTS

MDF timber was replaced with birch-faced plywood, which was also used for the internal doors. Brazilian parana pine framing was used for the carcass of the kitchen cabinets.

RECYCLED WASTE STORAGE

There is provision for internal and external storage of waste from the homes and work units. This is located in the centre complex on site.

ELEMENT MATERIALS RATING

Generally this is a hard indicator to achieve since most construction systems use fossil fuel energy power for manufacture and transport.[14] To achieve this indicator local materials must be used, primarily organics and recycled materials.

In the BedZED project, LCA methodology was used to identify the selection of materials. This tool allows for monitoring of a wider range of environmental loadings, in addition to ozone depletion. The methodology enabled the production of a supply chain, the key features of which were:

- materials and products locally sourced within a 55-mile radius – this reduces transport emissions and encourages local industry;
- recycled materials included reclaimed pine doors, recycled steel beams for the work units; and
- locally sourced WWF FSC timber, oak, ash and local softwoods, and local aggregates.

Water

PREDICTED CONSUMPTION

The predicted water consumption is difficult to calculate in advance since it largely depends on user behaviour. The BedZED team used a range of strategies to conserve water and to use rainwater (see section below on active strategies). Water consumption figures will be derived from monitoring, and hence water meters are installed in the homes to enable occupants to easily check their water use. Predicted water consumption is 33 per cent less than for an average household.[15]

Land use and ecology

This section examines the strategies used for reducing the impact of the building on the site. Three criteria are used:

1 pre-existing ecological value of land should be low;
2 improvement in ecological value;
3 efficient building footprint.

ECOLOGICAL VALUE OF LAND

The aim of this indicator is to encourage the use of sites that have pre-existing low ecological value and to upgrade them. In this case, the site had low value and Sutton council had identified the area for 'ultra-low-environmental-impact housing'.[16]

CHANGE OF ECOLOGICAL VALUE

The aim is to improve the ecological value of the site and involves not only the site but also adjacent land, which is to be made into an ecological park. Strategies include mainly the development of a biodiversity plan, which includes a number of sustainability site features. These are:

- existing natural features retained, i.e. mature horse chestnut trees;
- existing ditches turned into water features;
- roof top gardens and green (sedum) roofs; and
- features to attract wildlife – for example, nesting sites for sparrows, bat roosts.[17]

BUILDING FOOTPRINT

The aim of this criterion is to encourage higher density –over two storeys –to reduce the building footprint on the site. The scheme follows this principle and comprises a medium density development with mainly three-storey units.

Health and well-being

Three criteria apply to health and well-being:

1 provision of daylight;
2 improvement in soundproofing;
3 private and semi-private outdoor spaces.

PROVISION OF DAYLIGHT

The use of solar gains as a heat source has allowed adequate daylight to all the habitable rooms. The kitchen shares light from the living room and also light from the stairwell, which acts as a light well to other rooms.

IMPROVEMENT IN SOUNDPROOFING

Soundproofing is provided between units through the use of concrete floors and party walls.

PRIVATE OR SEMI-PRIVATE OUTDOOR SPACES

Both public and private open space is well provided in this project and includes communal open space and private gardens reached by sky bridges.

The living room and the atrium with opportunities for planting, like this tree fern. The benefits of green design – a sense of air, light and space – are seen in this affordable development.

Lessons learned

The scheme uses a broader range of criteria for examining the issue of green design. In particular, a range of economic and social factors are considered in this design. The building cost includes the infrastructure cost of the cooling, heating and power facility. A feature of the project is that the council has assisted with the provision of these on-site facilities by way of land sale pricing; otherwise this approach would not have been feasible.

An important feature of the scheme is the liaison with Bioregional and the Building Research Establishment, which has produced useful supply chain information about the use of materials and systems in the scheme. This provides a model that can be transferred to other building types.[18]

Furthermore, the inclusion of other criteria within the cost and quality umbrella, such as durability and maintenance considerations, is central to the sustainability of the project.[19]

Acknowledgements

Bill Dunster, for his time explaining the scheme. Illustrations: Richard Hyde.

Main EcoHomes criteria addressed in the BedZED project

Criterion		Criterion	
Energy		*Pollution*	
Predicted CO_2 emissions	✓	Ozone-depleting materials not used in construction	✓
Building envelope	✓	Nitrous oxide emissions low	✓
Drying space	✓	*Land use and ecology*	
Eco-labelled appliances	✓	Pre-existing low ecological land value	✓
External lighting efficiency		Improvement in ecological value	✓
Transport		Efficient building footprint	✓
Public transport accessibility	✓	*Health and well-being*	
Cycle storage	✓	Provision of daylight	✓
Local amenity proximity	✓	Improvement in sound proofing	✓
Home office provision	✓	Private and semi-private outdoor spaces	✓
Water		*Materials*	
Water consumption will be monitored		Sustainable timber management – basic	✓
Water meters are installed	✓	Sustainable timber management – finishing	✓
Predicted water consumption	✓	Storage of recycled waste	✓
		Green specification: a rating of elements	✓

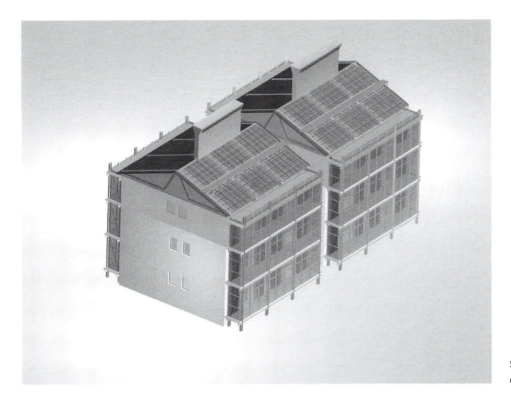

Saline Housing. View of the schematic design from the south-west.

CASE STUDY 2

Saline Housing, Ostia Antica, Italy: a typological model

Architects: Francesca Sartogo and Valerio Calderaro

Introduction

A general opinion that is gaining ground in Italy is that improved thermal and energy performance of buildings can be achieved by applying additional measures other than insulation to the vertical and horizontal opaque elements. The housing typological model project in Saline, a historic town west of Rome, investigates the use of a wide range of factors not restricted to just the opaque elements of building structure (i.e. not insulation only) that can contribute to a building's achieving a high thermal and energy performance.

Preference has been given to a holistic view of the design of sustainable buildings. This includes the operation and improvement of the buildings for the users and their thermal comfort and energy performance, while reinforcing a respect for the cultural and social aspects of sustainability, which are paramount in a country like Italy. The residents of Saline are burdened by problems because of the precariously austere conditions of their life and the high energy consumption needed to run their homes. Development of a new incentive and compensation pro-

gramme could make the costs to them and the environment more bearable. This research focused on providing affordable solutions at minimal running costs.

The antiquity of many buildings in Saline means that an understanding of the existing typology of the built form is paramount in order to provide new building design that reinforces the character of the area. The main problem with the existing building type is that its envelope responds poorly to climatic differences between summer and winter conditions. The proposal aims to recycle this envelope and make improvements through a bioclimatic approach, rather than to demolish the existing buildings, which have cultural significance to Saline.

It should be noted that the concept developed for renovating the existing building envelope could also be applied to new construction. Thus the typological model for housing applies to existing and new building design.

Saline Housing project details

Characteristics	Details
City	Rome
Country	Italy
Latitude	41° 54′ N
Building type	Row house and duplex
Year	1996

Traditional building typology in Rome.

Marketing

This section explains the market forces that helped to shape the selection of the general design principles used in the project. The reuse of the existing building typology as a marketing tool is envisaged in this prototype; hence it is important to analyse scale effects.

The main argument concerns the need to improve standards of building envelopes in many countries, particularly where occupants have low incomes and energy costs represent a significant part of their budget. This is an opportunity to promote passive solar design.

Country trends

An energy code was introduced in 1991 that is applicable to the building design research for typological housing for Saline. The code focuses on regulating 'the rational use of energy, energy-saving, and renewable energy development', and was integrated into local energy plans with economic incentives for renewable energies, energy consumption control and energy certification of buildings. The energy code applies to industries and farms, and renewable energy use is obligatory in new or restored public buildings.

The regulations aim to control the heating energy demand of buildings. This demand is regulated by code DPR 412/1993, which contains a variable value called FEN (normalized energy needs). FEN represents a unit value for the maximum allowable heating-energy losses and gains through the building envelope,

In 2003, 28 per cent of the cities in Italy have energy plans, but very few have codes to regulate building energy certificates and energy consumption based on building cooling.[20]

Standards

In Italy residential energy consumption in 2000 was over 25 per cent of total energy use, with a growth trend of 5.7 per cent in one year. The high energy growth rate has been attributed to the increased use of space cooling and electronic devices. Houses typically consume about 120 kWh/m^2 each year, which is high compared with the long-term goals of 15 kWh/m^2 set by energy experts and environmental associations. The same associations have set mid-term goals of 60 and 30 kWh/m^2 (Legambiente, Eurosolar Municipality of Bolzano, Faenza, Bologna, Carugate, in the year 2000/2003).

In 2000 the types of energy source were 60 per cent methane, followed by 21 per cent diesel and 18.5 per cent electric energy and biomass (wood). A high proportion of electric energy is used for space and water heating in housing, but a significant increase has been seen in the use of electricity for space cooling.

The local standard for this project is based on a volume dispersion coefficient, based on a surface to volume ratio. For proj-

Saline Housing: comparison of U values with local standards

Local standard		Project	
Roofs:	1.7 W/m² K	Roofs:	0.23 W/m² K
Walls:	0.85 W/m² K	Walls:	0.21 W/m² K
Floors:	1.54 W/m² K	Floor:	0.28 W/m² K
Windows:	4.6 W/m² K	Windows:	1.93 W/m² K

ects built before 1977 with the same surface to volume index as the typological housing project, the index is 0.97 W/m^3 per °C. This exceeds the present legal limit of 0.73 W/m^3 per °C. With the bioclimatic envelope system, the predicted index is 0.25 W/m^3 per °C.

Another important indicator of energy efficiency is the FEN (normalized energy need). For this project the FEN indicator is 57.5 KJ/m^3 per day per °C. This is approximately half the local standard of 100 KJ/m^3 per day per °C, while the Code limit is 75KJ/m^3 per day per °C.

BIOCLIMATIC CONTEXT

In the low Tiber valley, the principal winds come from the Northern quadrant during winter and from West-SouthWest in summer time.
During cold season the anemological regimes linked wich synoptic circulation are predominant, with winds from North, of medium intensity around 3 ÷ 5 mt/s.
In summer time the thermal discontinuity between land and sea origins the breezes.
The sea breeze, well-known in Rome as "ponentino", presents during evening hours in summer wedges in the hinterland until 50 Km from the coast.
The speed of the breeze front is reduced because of the attrition, and their direction is deflected by the presence of the heat island of the city.

climatic favour Tiber scenery

ecological agriculture with all year round continuos vegetation estate

dry/cold winds

landscape pocket/ cold air development

canal and plantation

as cooling fins

and prevention of dust

ventilation

energetic forest as windbreak

horticulture

cooling fin

bioclimatic zone and

permaculture garden

climate favour seawinds

plots as waterretension, green roofs road as rainwater storage = urban cooling strategy

windshelter energy forest

bioclimatic lanes

planting as „cooling fins"

Tiber - landscape park

urban microclimate countryyard / green roofs

Meso- and microclimatic analysis.

GENERAL TYPOLOGICAL PLAN

"A" tipology
single unit house
building case study

"B" typology
double unit house
building case study

"C" typology
triple unit house
building case study

"D" typology
multilple unit house
building case study

"A" 16%
"D" 5%
"B" 54%
"C" 25%
Typology recurrency

Typological analysis of buildings.

Quality

The proposed system aims to adapt existing building types.

TRADITIONAL BUILDING CHARACTERISTICS IN ROME

The traditional form of building in Rome, arrived at by successive typological phases of growth – such as the example shown for the 'Umbertine City at Rione Prati' (built after 1870 when Rome become capital of the Italian State) – comprises five- to seven-storey apartment buildings arranged around a central courtyard. The floor plates are two units deep (approximately 16 m) with apartments arranged back to back. The main circulation route is vertical, with hallways located centrally and adjacent to the main stairs. Cage elevators are placed in the stairwell so that air and light is provided, maintaining a level of transparency. Structural stability is achieved by the use of masonry bearing walls.

The low-tech bioclimatic principles used for the envelope design include:

- high thermal mass (to provide a heat sink that can modify internal temperatures) – 1 metre (30–50 cm) thick walls, concrete floors;

- integrated shading and security system;
- glazing ratios of 30 per cent of wall area;
- high-performance double-glazed windows that swing inwards;
- gas water-heating and space-heating;
- variable-speed ceiling fans for bedrooms; and
- balcony spaces.

TRADITIONAL BUILDING TYPOLOGY IN ROME

In winter, the operation of traditional types of buildings relies on a defensive approach to reduce heat loss through the envelope. In summer, air displacement from the interior to the exterior is needed to minimize heat gain in the thermal mass, and for the operation of the flywheel effect. Keeping the building closed and shaded on summer days will provide effective passive cooling, with the ceiling fans used as a back-up system.

MODERN BUILDING CONSTRUCTION IN ROME

With the development of reinforced concrete frame construction, the use of masonry load-bearing wall construction has become less popular. The new forms of construction consist of thin masonry breeze block systems, with typically a 60 mm cavity. It is clearly necessary to improve performance by increased thermal mass and/or insulation in these systems to obtain performance equal to that of the thick masonry systems found in traditional construction.

The urban design and planning of the traditional building typology comprises dense streetscapes. Buildings in close proximity shade one another as well as the street. The urban design of new areas of the city reflects a shift away from the traditional planning solutions to slab and point block. This creates typologies that provide few of the benefits of the traditional settlement pattern, making the need to consider the passive design of the envelope of great importance, since with these urban typologies the envelope is more exposed to solar gain.

General design principles

Climate response

The climate parameters for Rome show a Mediterranean climate with cool wet winters and warm dry summers. A key consideration is the low humidity and high solar radiation in summer. During winter, high humidity and temperatures below the comfort zone call for space heating for approximately six months of the year. A significant level of space heating can be achieved by passive solar strategies. However, there is a period of the year when the comfort levels might not be met by passive means; some sort of heating system is needed.

The passive strategies for winter are thermal mass and passive solar design. The passive strategies for summer are thermal mass, cross ventilation and evaporative cooling using indirect systems. Evaporative cooling is a form of air conditioning that makes use of the cooling effects of the phase change of evaporating water rather than the other phase change processes found in refrigerant systems. For three months of the year space cooling is required to maintain internal comfort.

Settlement analysis

CLIMATE ANALYSIS

The main design concepts focused on an examination of the climatic factors of the settlement and using this to inform the proposed improvements to the existing building type. Hence one of the initial tasks involved mesa- and micro-climatic analysis of the area. Saline is an area that is particularly affected by a summer sea breeze because of its close proximity to the Tirrenean sea. Forest areas to the west protect the area from cool breezes in winter.

BUILDING TYPOLOGY

Typological analysis of the area was carried out and revealed the following building types that were particularly suited to retrofitting passive elements for improved thermal performance. Two main types were identified.

Type A buildings are characterized as single detached buildings with one family unit. Buildings are located in the centre of the site with one floor raised above the ground level and one floor partially underground with a height of 3–4 metres. The total height over ground level is variable between 3 and 4.5 metres. This typology represents approximately 16 per cent of the number of housing units in the settlement.

Type B buildings are linked-detached buildings with two family units. Buildings are located in the centre of the lot with two floors raised above the ground level and one floor partially underground with a height of 3–4 metres. The total height over ground level is variable between 6 and 7.5 metres. This typology represents 54 per cent of the existing buildings and approximately 80 per cent of the number of housing units in the entire settlement.

Typological analysis

Site planning and landscaping

The proposed planning respects the existing site planning and building layout. Type B building typology is used in this study as it provides a useful example to demonstrate the application of bioclimatic principles; the type comprises approximately 54 per cent of house types in the settlement. Also many units have desirable south- (equator-) facing orientation of the living rooms. Furthermore, Type B buildings are located in the centre of the block so there is sufficient space between the building and its boundary for retrofit activity.

Form and fabric principles

The main architectural problems with the existing Type B houses are:

- small windows;
- single-skin construction;
- little shading to windows;
- water retention in basement level; and
- flat roof.

181

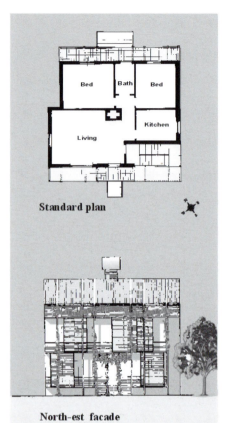

Standard plan

North-est facade

The new "B Typology" is the most widespread among the existing buildings as projection of the "A" Typology into the "B" Typology, **isolated two floor building for two residential units.**
This typology represents today 54%, and 80% in future of the total volume of the complex and respects the indication of the Detailed Plan regarding dimension and application instructions for the new residential and non residential buildings on private property free lots.

Taken as an **example of living trend** reproposable in such a situation, we have analyzed the present building and construction performances and characteristics.

TRIDIMENSIONAL MODULAR GRID STRUCTURE

As a demonstration, more or less the same existing typological layout has been reproposed, both in plan and facade, modified however with some project correction measures aimed at better energy performance among which are the following:
- The constitution of a new **energy polarity** for air accumulation and thermo-circulation, for heating and cooling of the internal spaces represented by a "**multifunctional chimney**" located in the center of the residence.
- The formation of a new **bioclimatic structure wrapping** the building vertically, along the bioclimatically significative facades as well as horizontally, on the roofcoverings and basement floors.
  Such **system** is composed by a **tridimensional modular grid structure** correlated to industrial energy technologies dimensions and ecological "aware" materials during their life cycle.

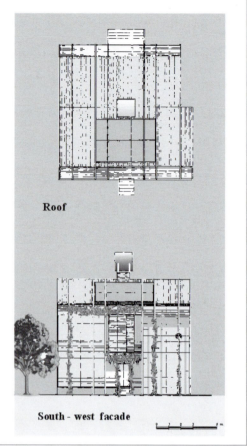

Roof

South - west facade

Top. Type B retrofit. **Below**. Existing Type B housing.

Existing housing Type B houses: room sizes

Spaces	Sizes(m²)
Living room	36
Kitchen/dining	27
Bathroom	8
Bedroom 1	21
Bedroom 2	14.8
Other spaces	3.2
Terrace	36
Total	142

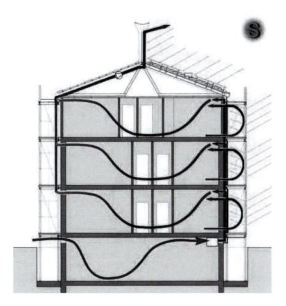
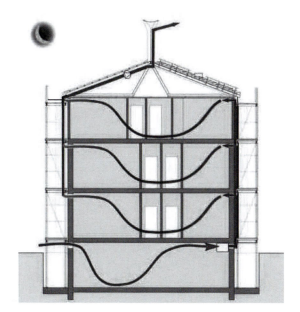

Winter day and night operation.

Design strategies

This section describes the priorities and strategies used in the project in response to the design principles with regard to energy.

Bioclimatic system

The proposed passive system for the project allows the building to provide heating, cooling, daylighting and ventilation in different seasonal conditions. The passive system integrates the following strategies:

- energy conservation techniques;
- solar heating;
- natural cooling and ventilation;
- daylighting; and
- photovoltaic panels and solar collectors.

SOUTH WALL

The passive system for the south face is composed of the following elements (inside to outside):

- the existing wall;
- an air gap and ventilation ducts (hollow space);
- an intermediate loggia space (about 1.5 m in width);
- the glass envelope; and
- a horizontal, seasonally movable element that can reflect heat and is used to pass the solar radiation to the internal capacitive system during the cold season, and to reflect solar radiation during the hot season.

NORTH WALL

The north wall system includes the following elements (inside to outside):

- the existing wall;
- an intermediate loggia space (about 1.5 m in width); and
- the glass envelope.

ROOF

A central ventilation chimney located on the roof serves as an exhaust for air and is connected to the internal ventilation system. On the south side, the chimney is composed of the following sections (outside to inside):

- single glass pane;
- hollow ventilation space;
- absorbent slab (roll-bond or similar); and
- layer of insulating material.

The north section is composed of two panels separated by a hollow ventilation space. The south face acts as a modified Trombe wall system with heating of the absorbent roll-bond panel and of the air within the cavity. The warm air will determine air movement towards the top of the chimney inside the ventilation duct. This is as a result of the stack effect, which in turn removes air from the interior spaces of the house (particularly during summer days). During the night, the chimney works only by stack effect (especially during winter nights). The north section draws in the air from the underlying rooms because of the stack effect during summer nights.

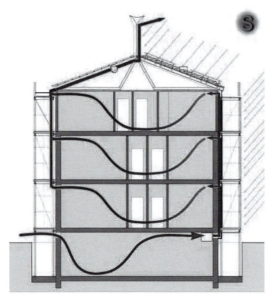
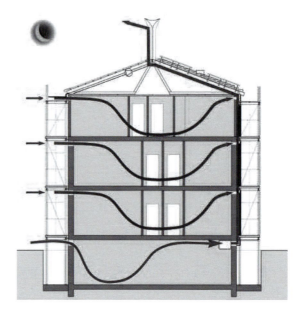

Summer day and night operation.

SEASONAL OPERATION

During a typical winter day, the horizontal solar reflecting element directs the solar radiation to be absorbed by the storage wall; the heat absorbed by the storage elements provides radiant heating to the interior rooms. Heated air from the outside passes through interior rooms and exits through the chimney located on the top of the building, and creates natural ventilation of the interior rooms.

The external reflecting elements on the south façade can be used to transfer solar radiation to the ceiling of the internal rooms. The solar radiation is divided into two parts: absorbed and reflected. The absorbed radiation will load the thermal storage in the ceiling, which produces direct passive solar heating. The reflected solar radiation will lead to uniform natural daylighting of the rooms.

During winter nights the heat storage provides heating, and natural convection of the air provides ventilation for the internal rooms.

On summer days the external air is drawn into the basement via vents, and crosses the 'cellar' structure, which acts as a thermal storage system. This has been cooled during the night, which means its mass is at a lower temperature than the incoming air. The air is cooled and is then transferred to the upper levels and expelled from the solar chimney placed on top of the roof. The storage cooled during the night produces a natural convection during the day, which cools the rooms and internal structures. An auxiliary fan below the roof comes into operation when the natural convective flow of the air drops below a certain velocity.

On summer nights, the storage elements heated during the day produce a natural convection, which cools the air and the internal structures. The cool night air coming from the north side descends as a result of the stack effect through the chimney placed on the roof and gradually cools the cellar storage area.

Saline Housing energy strategies

Strategies and tactics	Tick ✓	Comments
Reduction of energy demand		
Reduced transmission losses (insulation and thermal bridges)	✓	Double skin envelope
Airtightness		
Use of passive solar (heat and light)	✓	Double skin envelope
Recovery of heat		
Ventilation heat recovery and earth heat storage		
Optimization of energy supply		
Production of remaining energy (space and domestic hot water heating, electricity)	✓	Solar hot water heating, electricity
Optimization of controls		
Comfort control		
Envelope (shading and ventilation)	✓	Electronic controls
HVAC (innovative systems, automation)		
Combining systems	✓	Integrated system

Typical solution set (TSS)

This section describes the solution set used in the building for energy conservation technologies that promotes eco-efficiency. A diagrammatic section that identifies the heat flux and climate modification systems describes the solution set. The main solutions of this system are:

- solar thermal and solar electric photovoltaic systems;
- selected shading for summer, solar access for winter;

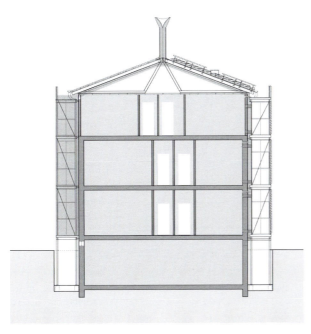

Solution set.

- solar chimney;
- thermal storage;
- solar collector in the form of a loggia;
- air diffusion system.

Technologies

The aim of this section is to describe the particular technologies that comprise the solution set.

Building envelope

STRUCTURE

The structural system forms a frame around the existing building, acting as an exoskeleton with new walling and roofing elements. The resulting structure has a pitched roof to form an attic space that assists with cooling. The materials used for this are lightweight materials (steel or timber). Lightweight materials can be braced from the existing concrete masonry structure to provide an acceptable level of structural stability.

The south wall comprises the following layers:

1 existing wall;
2 air gap and ventilation ducts (hollow space);
3 double glazing with low emissivity;
4 intermediate loggia space (1.5 m width);
5 glazing;
6 movable shading element;

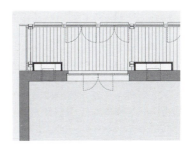

Top. Structural system placed outside the existing building.
Below. Details of the south wall and roof.

185

7 shunt system that assists air movement using an axial fan;

8 thermo-siphon that takes the air heat from the 'green house' to the interior; and

9 south wall.

ROOF

The roof system comprises the following layers:

1 photovoltaic panels;

2 steel grid steps (to allow inspection and maintenance);

3 steel grid transverse bridge (to allow inspection and maintenance);

4 security guides (to allow safety attachment during maintenance); and

5 roofing system.

The roof is tiled with photovoltaic panels and solar collectors. The solar collectors are arranged on the south face of the chimney and contribute to the expulsion of air. The photovoltaic panels contribute to the operation of a heating element through a single storage battery. The heating element heats the air, which is drawn into the ventilation ducts during the cold season. An auxiliary boiler produces the heat necessary to activate the heating battery during particularly cold days, when the active and passive solar systems cannot ensure the heating of the rooms.

Eco-efficiency indicators

The aim of this section is to rate the eco-efficiency of the project using eight main indicators.

Bibliography

Butera F., *Architettura e Ambiente*, Etaslibri, 1995.

Capra, F., *La rete della vita*, Santoni, 1998.

Prigogyne, L., *La nuova alleanza*, Einaudi, 1987.

Sartogo, F., *Integration of Renewable Energies in Historical City Center*, *Year book 1994*, James & James, 1995.

Scheer, H., *La strategia Solare*, Cuen, 1996.

Vitruvio, M. P., *De Architettura*.

Zaffagnini, M., *Rosso Mattone*, Edizioni, Bologna, 1987.

Saline Housing eco-efficiency indicators

Indicators	Tick ✓	Comments
Area efficiency	✓	
Service appliance efficiency		Not selected
Effective siting	✓	
Solar hot water	✓	
Green materials		Not selected
Passive design in place	✓	
Energy conservation	✓	
Sustainable building	✓	

Acknowledgements

Francesca Sartogo
Valerio Calderaro
Joachin Eble
Massimo Bastiani
Carlos Brizioli
Angela Violo
Illustrations, plans and sections: Richard Hyde and Francesca Sartogo and Valerio Claderaro.

Lindås Housing, Sweden. Demonstration housing that requires no heating at latitude 57° 30′ N.

Lindås Housing, Sweden

Architect: Hans Eek, EFEM Arkitektkontor

Introduction

The housing in this case study demonstrates the principles of Task 28 – that is, the integrated use of effective passive and active systems to create a solution set – which the architect describes as 'houses without heating systems'. Actually this is not strictly true; the houses are heated, but not in a conventional manner. The traditional heating system has been replaced by a heat exchanger in combination with an exceptionally effective building envelope that conserves heat and also admits solar gain when it is available. This ability to conserve heat and also collect available solar heat gain creates a building that needs very little heat input from non-renewable energy sources. In addition, solar collectors on the roof provide half the energy needed for the supply of hot water. The project is situated in an area of great natural beauty at Lindås, 20 kilometres south of Göteborg; the houses were built by a city-owned building company, Egnahemsbolaget.

Lindås Housing project details

Characteristics	Details
City	Göteborg
Country	Sweden
Latitude	57°30′ north
Building type	Attached row-houses
Year of construction	2001

The row houses were designed by the architectural practice EFEM arkitektkontor, and are the result of a research project extending over many years, carried out in cooperation with Chalmers University of Technology, Lund University and the Swedish National Testing and Research Institute. The Swedish Council for Building Research (Formas) and the EU have financed the research and evaluation.

Marketing

Country trends

The trend set by this design seems to follow a strategy described by Edwards and the Building Research Establishment in the United Kingdom as 'the changing relationship between heating and passive gains through insulation'.[21] They observe that the trend in house design since the 1900s has been to progressively increase insulation; this has reduced environmental impact and the cost of space heating. Insulation is a fabric strategy that improves the envelope performance significantly, while in a conventional home active strategies for heating, such as furnaces and boilers that support ducted warm air systems, typically consume non-renewable energy. The last century shows the following trend:

- 1900 – active heating 75 per cent, passive gains 25 per cent.
- 1950 – active heating 60 per cent, passive gains 40 per cent.
- 2000 – heating 40 per cent, passive gains 60 per cent.

A consequence of this change in approach is that the cost of heating hot water for the home can now exceed the cost of space heating. However, simply increasing insulation is not the complete solution to indoor warmth.

The Lindås houses demonstrate ways that passive gains can be increased to 100 per cent, making dedicated active heating sys-

Left. South- (equator-) facing façade design for passive heating. **Right**. North- (polar-) facing façade.

tems unnecessary, despite the very cold climate. How is this done and how can the trend to passive house systems be accelerated?

The answer is not simply to keep adding insulation. Beyond an optimum level, the thermodynamic performance of insulation decreases with thickness; that is, doubling the thickness of insulation does not double the performance. Instead, an integrated 'solution set' approach is indicated, such as that espoused by the Task 28 model. The solution is to combine a number of strategies, each of which seems small but that together add up to significant benefits greater than the sum of the parts.

Standards

The building improves on the existing local standards. The improvement can be seen by examination of the R values of the elements used in the building envelope, which achieve values of between two and three times those of the local standard (see tables below). The better performance comes from improvements to three elements in the design:

- super insulation;
- high performance windows; and
- heat exchanger.

These elements cost some €4–5,000 (40–50,000 SEK), the same as a very basic heating system. The passive building is eco-efficient and the passive system is comparable in cost to the standard approach of normal insulation and window performance with a ventilation system (opening vents in the exterior wall and a central fan).

Overall, passive building costs are estimated to be close to normal. Significant savings in the operating cost of the building pays for extra measures such as greater airtightness and insulation, adaptation to 'passive solar heating' and heat recovery in the ventilation. There is no need to install, use and maintain an active heating system. The success of this passive design solution set makes a good argument for upgrading the local building standard.

The usual argument against changing building standards relates to increases in building costs or perceived bias in the

Lindås Housing: comparison of U values with local standards

Local standard		Project	
Roofs:	0.2 W/m² K	Roofs:	0.08 W/m² K
Walls:	0.3 W/m² K	Walls:	0.1 W/m² K
Floors:	0.2 W/m² K	Floor:	0.09 W/m² K
Windows:	1.8 W/m² K	Windows:	0.85 W/m² K

Lindås Housing – R values of the elements of construction

Element	U value	R value
Roof		
Lindås	0.08	12.50
Local standard	0.2	5.00
Walls		
Lindås	0.1	10.00
Local standard	0.3	3.33
Floors		
Lindås	0.09	11.11
Local standard	0.2	5.00
Windows		
Lindås	0.85	1.18
Local standard	1.8	0.56

Elements of the system include roof-integrated skylights and the vent for the ventilation heat-recovery system, high-performance windows with retractable shading to reduce summer heat gain, and glass balcony rails.

direction of the standard. In terms of the life cycle, the capital cost of the building with a passive solar solution is cost-effective. The higher capital cost of the passive solar design for the building envelope is offset by reduced costs for active systems, such as boilers, and by reduced ongoing operating costs.

Value adding

Internal environment quality is important to any solar housing design. Does the house deliver good acoustic performance, air quality and daylight?

All rooms need access to daylight, to avoid the need for permanent artificial lighting of habitable spaces. Control systems are required in an energy-efficient house; these must fit in with the occupants' (comfort) needs.[22] Hans Eek explains:

> The houses are neither more nor less complicated than living in ordinary houses. Obviously a house without a heating system demands that those who live in it modify their behaviour, but mostly it's a matter of common sense.[23]

The occupants control the thermal performance of the envelope as they would with a normal building; windows are opened in summer and closed in winter.

Design principles

Climate response

The climate of Copenhagen is used for project design as it is reasonably similar to that of the project location. It has most of the characteristics of a cold climate with temperatures generally below the comfort zone. The main parameters are as follows:

- *Temperatures*. January temperatures are around freezing with a range of –2 to +2°C. In summer the temperatures range from 22 to 14°C. These temperatures are below the human comfort zone.
- *Irradiation*. In winter, when it is most needed, solar radiation is low: 530 Wh/m^2 in January compared with 5700 Wh/m^2 in July.
- *Humidity*. Humidity is high, particularly in winter.

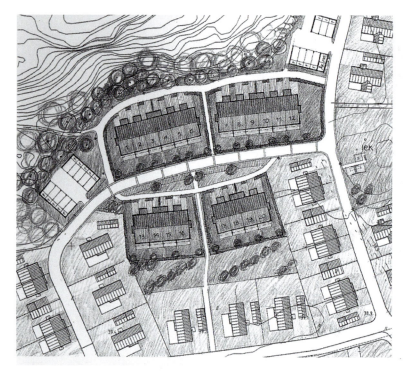

Site plan (north is to the top of the page).

The bioclimatic chart shows a significant need for heating for the coldest three months of the year. Very little solar radiation is available at that time. Spring and autumn are the seasons when solar heating is used the most. In summer it is likely that some heat rejection through natural ventilation will be needed. The low external temperatures in summer make the use of stack ventilation an option; external temperatures are below the comfort zone and this temperature difference can be used to drive the stack system effectively.

Design concepts

The design concept is focused on two main ideas: providing a pleasant indoor environment and minimizing energy use. The harsh external climate and long hours of darkness in the winter make it essential to maximize light levels in the building. Adequate lighting gives a sense of connection to the external environment and limits the sense of claustrophobia and 'cabin fever' common to people living in cold-climate houses. The second idea, minimizing energy use, is largely technical; combining appropriate site planning and layout and form and fabric of the building achieve it with innovative active systems involving a range of service plant and equipment.

Site planning and landscaping

The house plan follows solar orientation principles, a basic strategy of passive housing design. The row house is good for heat conservation, as all units except the end ones share two walls per house (party walls) with neighbours. If the buildings are all occupied this reduces heat losses, as the temperature differences across the party wall are small. The disadvantage is that a row

Mahoney passive design recommendations for the climate

	Strategies
Layout	Orientation: north-south (long axis east–west)
Spacing	Compact estate layout
Air movement	Double banked rooms, with facility for cross ventilation
Opening sizes	Medium: 30-50 per cent of wall surface
Opening position	In N and S walls, at body level on windward side, openings in internal walls
Opening protection	N/A
Walls and floors	Lightweight, of low thermal capacity
Roof construction	Lightweight, well insulated
External features	N/A

house has only two walls available for access to the outside for daylight and ventilation, unlike a detached house, which has four (as well as the roof).

The design challenge in the row house typology is to optimize orientation and avoid overshadowing the equator-facing wall. The sun in January is low, with an inclination of 15 degrees, so distances between the houses should be sufficient to allow solar access.

In this case the buildings are aligned on an east–west axis to maximize solar access, and are laid out in two parallel rows, separated into four clusters. The clusters to the north have four units; the clusters to the south have six. The rows are separated by some 30 metres to give sufficient solar access in winter. At this distance the buildings nearer the equator do not cast a shadow on those further away.

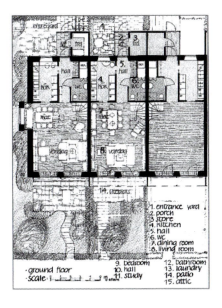 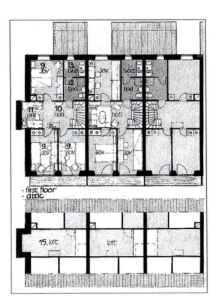

Lindås House plans.

Lindås Housing: energy efficiency and conservation strategies

Strategies	Tick ✓	Comments
Reduction of energy demand		
Reduced transmission losses (insulation and thermal bridges)	✓	Timber internal window frames. No heating system is installed.
Airtightness	✓	The tightest houses in Sweden. It is very important to build airtight in every climate and to prove it during the building process.
Use of passive solar (heat and light)	✓	Passive solar heating is used when available. The building shell has high insulation levels, which retain heat on cloudy days.
Recovery of heat.	✓	Heat recovery of the ventilation air is very important – 85 per cent (or more) is needed.
Ventilation heat recovery and earth heat recovery		Earth heat recovery was calculated at 1200 kWh/year (due to the inefficiency of the heat exchanger, it resulted in too little savings).
Production of remaining energy (space and domestic hot water heating, electricity)	✓	Remaining energy for domestic hot water is wind-powered electricity (from the grid).
Optimization of controls		
Comfort control	✓	Manual. Opening of windows (roof window) when it is too warm.
Envelope (shading and ventilation)		Roof edges and a balcony shade nearly 100 per cent of the solar radiation in summer.
HVAC (innovative systems, automation)		Heat recovery system can be turned off and natural ventilation used.

Even with a distance of 30 metres between rows for winter solar access, the row house design makes for a compact layout when compared to the surrounding detached housing development. Buildings in the surrounding estate generally face the street and are not orientated for solar passive design (see table above).

Landscaping consists of shelterbelt trees to the north (the polar-facing edge of the site). This creates a micro-climate that reduces the intensity of cold winds from the north. The layout is consistent with the recommendations of the Mahoney analysis for creating a compact layout.

Form and fabric principles
The form and fabric of the building incorporate the following principles:

- *Orientation:* the one long façade faces south towards the equator and has large windows to make full use of solar heat.
- *Selective shading:* balconies and projecting eaves provide protection against excessive solar radiation during the summer.

Lindås Housing: spaces and sizes

Input spaces	Sizes (m²)
Living/dining area	40
Kitchen	12
Bathrooms	14
Bedrooms	39
Gallery space	15
Total size	120

- *Appropriate plan depth:* the row house form lends itself to an 11-metre plan depth.
- *Reduced external surface area.*
- *As few external walls as possible.*
- *The envelope is super-insulated and airtight.*
- *Mixed mode ventilation:* the skylight above the staircase brings light to the middle of the house and gives effective ventilation in the summer. High performance houses such as these are designed to operate at low external temperature. The airtightness and insulation allow little cooling through the skin in summer, hence the need to allow for stack ventilation through the operable skylights in summer.

These strategies conform to those in the Mahoney analysis (see table on page 191). The result of these strategies is an energy consumption of approximately 5,400 kWh per year, which results in 45 kWh per m² per year. This includes:

- household electricity 2,900 kWh;
- hot water 1,500 kWh (3,000 kWh from solar collection);
- service power, fan pumps and heat exchanger 1,000 kWh.

Design strategies

The design strategies for energy efficiency in this building use a combination of passive and active systems. Energy efficiency and conservation of the buildings is measured in terms of relative energy use: the reduction in kilowatts used when compared to other houses (see table above). It is also measured by the substitution of energy generated from renewable sources to replace that from non-renewable sources.

Designers need to develop passive systems (particularly the envelope) that conserve energy and use renewable solar energy. They need to select active systems that deliver a high level of service while consuming less non-renewable energy. A combination of active and passive strategies is indicated for the best result.

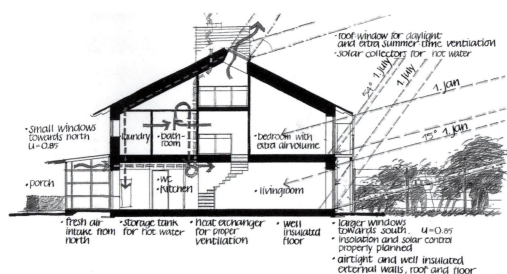

Illustrations: Hans Grönlund, EFEM

Solution set.

Interior views. **Left**. Living dining area. **Right**. Bedroom, research instruments and the skirting ventilation system.

Typical solution set (TSS)

The section illustrates the building solution set, showing both the passive and active strategies (see figures above). The building is planned on three levels.

- *Level 1 – ground floor:* living and dining room, kitchen/storage and bathroom/laundry.
- *Level 2 – first floor:* three bedrooms and a bathroom.
- *Level 3 – second floor:* loft space for study and storage

In section, the striking feature is the envelope thickness. The thickness results from the use of up to 450 mm of insulation to significantly reduce heat losses. There is no uninsulated attic space; the raked ceilings in the first-floor bedrooms make use of this volume. Winding stairs are used, which link into an atrium space at the first and second levels. It is through this atrium that light and air can pass. Windows are sized to respect their orientation:

- small windows polar-facing to reduce heat loss;
- large windows equator facing for solar gain.

The windows are not used for ventilation (fresh air supply) in winter for two reasons: if the windows are opened, the incoming air is so cold, and heat is lost so rapidly, that occupants would soon need to turn up an active heating system to be warm enough for comfort. A more manageable method is to duct fresh air from the outside, preheat it using a heat exchanger and distribute the warm air to the various rooms. The air is brought into each room and distributed through a register at the skirting level, below the windows. Exhaust air is passed into the heat exchanger, the heat is extracted, and the air is vented from the chimney on the roof. In this way a constant supply of fresh air is provided with good energy efficiency. In summer mode, the ventilation system can be turned off and the windows opened for fresh air and for cooling. The atrium is ideal for this purpose, as the skylight can be opened to vent hot air.

An important feature of the ventilation system is that air intakes are located on the polar-facing side of the building (the colder side); air is taken from this side to avoid overheating in summer.

Technologies

The aim of this section is to describe the particular technologies that comprise the solution set.

Building envelope

STRUCTURE

The structure consists of a concrete slab on the ground. Local plantation timber is used for framing the external and internal walls. The walls are 500 mm thick to allow space for the insulation; plasterboard is used on the inside surface, with wood panels on the outside. The roof is clad with clay tiles on a wood panel substrate. It is supported by engineered timber beams and is 500 mm thick to allow for insulation.

INSULATION

Under the concrete slab 250 mm of styrene insulation is used to insulate the floor from the ground.

External walls have 430 mm insulation of mineral wool and styrene. Layers of polyethylene are added during construction to ensure that the walls are airtight.

WINDOWS

Low 'E' triple glazing with krypton gas is used for the glazing system. An aluminium frame is used on the outside and a wooden frame on the inside to reduce thermal bridging.

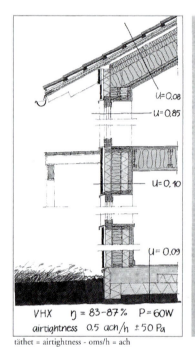

External wall:
U value: 0.10 W/m²K
Framed construction with 43 cm insulation.

Roof:
U value: 0.08 W/m²K
Masonite beams with 48 cm insulation.

Floor:
U value: 0.09 W/m²K
Concrete slab laid on 25 cm insulation.

Windows:
U value: 0.85 W/m²K
Three pane windows with two metallic coats and krypton fill.
Energy transmittance 43%.
Light transmittance 63%.

External door:
U value: 0.80 W/m²k

U=0.08
U=0.85
U=0.10
U=0.09

VHX   η = 83–87%   P = 60W
airtightness 0.5 ach/h ±50 Pa

täthet = airtightness - oms/h = ach

Left. Envelope construction. **Right**. Entrance provides storage and acts as a draught lobby to reduce infiltration of cold air in winter.

Sustainable materials

The calculated lifetime of the building is 50 years. The Swedish experience of wood-framed buildings is very good; the realistic lifetime of the buildings should be hundreds of years.

Ventilation and counter-flow heat exchanger

The ventilation system is a supply and exhaust air unit with a counter-flow heat exchanger, which provides 85 per cent heat recovery, mainly in winter. In the summer the heat exchanger can be turned off and the house ventilated with open windows. The houses are neither more nor less complicated to live in than ordinary houses.

Heat delivery

HEATING SYSTEM

The exhaust air in the heat exchanger heats the supply air. The rest of the heat requirement is supplied by heat from the occupants' appliances and lighting. The heat from occupants is equal to an energy input of 1,200 kWh/year. Heat gains from lighting, the fridge-freezer, the cooker and other appliances produce about 2,900 kWh/year if the most energy efficient appliances available on the market are used; part of this is useful to heat the building.

The houses have been designed for normal climatic conditions. Low outdoor temperatures over extended periods are rare and are regarded as extreme, and can result in a drop in indoor temperature of a degree or two.

Lindås Housing: service efficiency

Specification and description	Environmental reasons	Application benefits and disbenefits
Garage	Non-heated garage, including storage room	Store room in the garage
Utility	Cable-TV, telephone, broadband.	
Kitchen	Swedish standard kitchen, low-energy appliances, cooler	Cooler, refrigerator, washing machine
Bathrooms	Swedish standard WC, bath or shower	All fittings installed are the best on the market

Eco-efficiency of the Lindås house

Indicators	Tick ✓	Comments
Area efficiency	✓	A place for everything and everything in place, no surplus space
Service efficiency	✓	Excellent no-heating system and passive cooling
Effective siting	✓	Passive design used for unit layout
Solar hot water	✓	Maximum performance for Swedish latitude
Green materials	✓	Good
Passive design in place	✓	Excellent
Energy conservation	✓	Excellent
Sustainable building	✓	Very good

Heat production

HOT WATER SUPPLY

Solar collectors of 5 m^2 are estimated to provide enough energy for half the household hot water requirement. The storage tank has an electric immersion heater as back-up.

Services

BATHROOM APPLIANCES

There are two bathrooms with shower and space for a bath. The bathroom on the upper floor houses the washing and drying equipment. Reducing and reusing service elements achieves service efficiency (see table above).

Eco-efficiency indicators

The eco-efficiency aspects of this house result from the trade-off between active and passive systems. Improved envelope performance requires less service equipment (see table above right).

With regard to area efficiency, the houses appear neither under- nor oversized for the functions provided. The size of 120 m^2 for a three-bedroom house is a reasonable standard for space. The ample provision of storage space within the envelope of the house is a good marketing feature. There is no surplus space; in the words of the *Australian Good Residential Design Guide*, there is 'a place for everything and everything is in place'.[24]

Service efficiency is achieved by rationalizing the services. The ground-floor toilet is combined with the laundry. Effective siting of the building follows passive design principles and sup-

ports the high performance of the envelope. Solar hot water achieves the maximum performance for the latitude. Paints and finishes used reduce off-gassing and are a good example of green materials.

Sustainable building practices were used. During construction, care was taken to ensure the envelope was made airtight as this is essential for energy efficiency measures to be effective.

Postscript

Hans Eek, together with Wolfgang Feist of Germany, received the Göteborg International Environmental prize (the Nobel Prize for the Environment). The Prime Minister of Sweden, Göran Persson, presented the prize and will visit the houses in Lindås.

The 'Houses without Heating Systems' will set a new building standard for Sweden. Hans Eek is working intensively to change the Swedish building code to adopt these new standards. The Swedish government's goal is to achieve at least 50 per cent energy savings in new and existing buildings within five or ten years.[25]

Lessons learned

The demonstration building is the result of the evolution of a set of ideas, from concern for the environment to the successful design

Ongoing monitoring of the houses is continuing after the project is completed to learn further about the strategies used in this system.

and engineering of passive solar houses. Wolfgang Feist, the engineer, describes the evolution of the project as a continual improvement process from theoretical ideas to practical realization.

With the first passive houses built in 1990 using Hans Eek's concepts, we have proof from measured data. The con-

sumption was as low as 1,600 kWh (or 160 litres of oil, four full tanks in your car) for the whole house over a whole year. But our opinion was, that the project was purely academic: Prof. Bo Adamson and myself tried to find out how far one could go on with efficiency. Again it was Amory Lovins who spontaneously declared during his 1995 visit, 'This solution should be economically feasible. You just have to think once more through it.'[26]

Acknowledgements

The Swedish National Testing and Research Institute SP drew up the specifications for the functions and properties of the building, and were responsible for measurements and evaluation. Its staff took part in the research into heat exchangers.

The Department of Building Technology and Building Physics at Chalmers University of Technology (CTH) studied the feasibility of preheating air in a buried pipe, and took part in designing the foundation insulation. Energy and Building Design (EBD) at Lund University (LTH) performed computer simulations of indoor climate and researched issues such as thermal bridges, properties of windows and the need for solar control, and into ventilation systems, heat exchangers and energy-efficient electrical appliances. This is an extension of the report 'Houses without Heating Systems'. The design and construction team is as follows:

Client: Egnahemsbolaget
Contractor: PEAB
Architect: EFEM arkitektkontor, Göteborg
Constructional engineer: WSP, Göteborg
HVAC consultant: Bengt Dahlgren AB, Göteborg
Electrical services consultant: Probeko, Göteborg
Site works consultants: Landskapsgruppen, Göteborg

Those in charge of the different areas of the research project:
EFEM arkitektkontor Göteborg, project management: Hans Eek.
Lunds University, Energy and Building Design: Maria Wall
Chalmers University of Technology, Department of Building Physics: Carl-Erik Hagentoft and Fredrik Ståhl.
Swedish Testing Institute (SP) SP: Svein Ruud and Leif Lundin.

Illustrations, plans and sections: Richard Hyde and Hans Eek.

Hotels, resorts and interpretation centres

The Novotel & Ibis Hotel, Homebush Bay, Sydney, Australia

Architects: Architectus, Sydney

Introduction

The Novotel Hotel is part of the Novotel & Ibis complex, which is located at Olympic Park, Homebush Bay Sydney. The building was built as part of the infrastructure for the 2000 Olympic Games by the Olympic Coordination Authority (OCA). After the Games the Sydney Olympic Park Authority was established on 1 July 2001.

> The Authority is constituted by the Sydney Olympic Park Authority Act No. 57 (available by searching in the NSW Legislation site under S for the Act), which established the Sydney Olympic Park Authority (SOPA) as a statutory authority, with responsibility to manage the public assets of Sydney Olympic Park – open space, venues, parklands and development areas. The legislation focuses on ensuring the best use and management of a large and unique area right in the geographical centre of Sydney, an area which is a world renowned destination.[1]

A key objective of SOPA was:

> To ensure that the principle of sustainability [environmental, social and economic] is a driving element of SOPA's

The Novotel & Ibis Hotel.

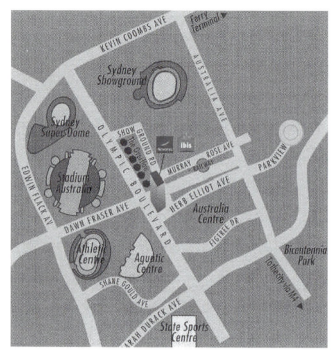
Location of the Novotel/ Ibis hotel, commonly called the Green Hotel.

Novotel & Ibis Hotel project details

Characteristics	Details
Building type	Hotel, 4-star
Building area	23,353m²
Number of visitors	10,000 per annum
Nature of occupancy (hours per week, days per week)	60–70% average/year, 100% on special event days
Activities carried out within building	Range of accommodations, conferences, restaurants
Number of storeys	17
Building address	Sydney Olympic Park, Homebush Bay, Sydney
Owner occupied or tenanted	Owner occupied
New or refurbished building	New building
Total building cost	A$61.8 million
Completion date	February 2000

place-leadership activities and the international recognition of Sydney Olympic Park as an outstanding example of intelligent place-making.[2]

This case study presents the environmental work carried out on this building. It is interesting to note the role played by SOPA as an organization in assisting at the planning and infrastructure level of sustainable design. Decisions at this scale of precinct design greatly assist in making the buildings at the micro level more sustainable, particularly with service-intensive buildings such as the Novotel & Ibis hotel.

The brief

Novotel has come to be called the 'Green Hotel' in Sydney, a reputation that has come about because of its location at Olympic Park, Homebush Bay, Sydney, the home of the Olympic Games 2000. This was the first Olympic Games to promote sustainable buildings as one of the criteria for infrastructure design and construction. The facilities at Olympic Park set a new benchmark for Olympic facilities in terms of 'green design', a tradition that is now continuing in subsequent Olympic Games. It is this commitment to sustainability in the wider context that has given the project a strong green focus.

The aim in the brief was to deliver a new standard in more than one area. First, in terms of green design, the Olympic Coordinating Authority, in liaison with the Accord Group of hotels, demanded a green approach. Second, the hotel has a key role on the site in servicing the needs of sporting groups, families and guests coming to Olympic Park. Third, there is a met-

ropolitan function: the infrastructure that services Olympic Park – the trains and buses – makes it an ideal location for conference attendees and business travellers.

The Olympic Coordinating Authority's commitment to a 'Green Games' had a direct impact on the design and projected operations of the hotel, but a challenge still remains in coupling resource efficiency with superior environmental performance, while providing the four-star level of customer service needed to compete in the metropolitan hotel market – 'When caring for environment is also caring for guests.'

The aim of this case study is to report the assessment of the building, according to the Green Globe Design standard. This assessment is retrospective and took place in 2002.

Location, climate and design

Location
The hotel is part of the master plan for Homebush Bay, now known as Sydney Olympic Park, a 760-hectare site located south of the Paramatta River, about 14 kilometres west of the Sydney CBD.

Situated next to the Olympic Boulevard, at the centre of the Homebush Bay master plan, the Novotel site has an area of 5,184.1m². With a history of industries, including an abattoir, brickworks and armaments depot, occupying the site, an extensive remediation plan was developed to reclaim the value of the site; the Novotel site itself, however, did not have such critical characteristics.

Ecological studies revealed that Homebush Bay's terrestrial and wetland ecosystems had considerable ecological value, supporting a number of valuable species of plants and animals. This broadened the site's appeal as a place for conservation, recreation and environmental education, and enhanced its value as a showcase for ecological sustainable development for the Olympic games.

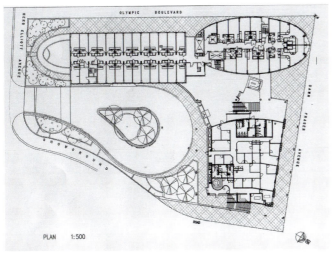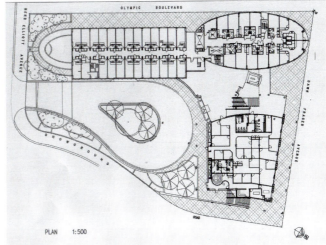

Building plans.

Climate

The climate of Sydney is categorized as coastal temperate, consisting of warm/hot summers and cool/cold winters.

CLIMATIC DATA

Climatic data for the site was assumed to be that for Sydney. The average daily maximum temperature in summer is 25.5°C, while the average daily minimum temperature in winter is 8.6°C, with an average annual rainfall of 1,315 mm. Average daily sunshine is 7.4 hours.[3]

- January and February are the only months that are not close to the comfort zone (20–25°C).
- For other months, the average temperature levels are well within the comfort zone.
- Heating will be required from May through to September. Also, these months have quite high humidity (above 60 per cent).

Bioclimatic strategies are:

- for winter – solar gain and thermal mass; and
- for summer – thermal mass and air effect.

Layout and envelope recommendation

The envelope recommendations from the Mahoney analysis are that the climate is not classified as a warm climate, although periods of the year do have temperatures above the comfort zone:

- *layout:* orientation: north–south (long axis east––west);
- *spacing:* compact estate layout;
- *air movement:* no cross ventilation is required;
- *opening sizes:* medium: 30–50 per cent of wall surface;
- *opening position:* n/a;
- *opening protection:* summer shading;
- *walls and floors:* insulated or heavyweight construction;
- *roof construction:* lightweight, well insulated; and
- *external features:* n/a.

Building planning

The building has been planned as a tower and podium complex on a sloping site. The complex contains two hotels: the Novotel occupies the elliptical tower while the Ibis is accommodated in the connecting building to the south. The hotels share a foyer and reception, restaurants, conference facilities to the west, and back-of-house facilities. In summary:

1   The key to stabilizing the temperature for the users is the use of thermal mass and insulation.

2   Heating and cooling is required to provide comfortable indoor conditions for hotel guests. However, the temperature levels also permit a mixed mode heating/cooling system, provided by operable windows in the guest rooms and natural ventilation through angled louvres in the foyer and public areas.

3   Sun control devices are required.

4   Thermal mass and insulation should be included.

5   The sunshine hours are good for solar energy.

6   Large glazing areas should be provided for natural lighting in public spaces, with external shading and awnings.

The massing and the building form respond to the context of the surrounding site. It is adjacent to a number of heritage buildings, so the building was planned as a two- and three-storey podium to relate to the mass of these buildings, with an elegant tower of 14 storeys at the intersection of the boulevard. It was required to be of a high design standard as it is one of the most visible buildings on the Olympic Plaza. The brief for the project called for the procurement of a hotel with a minimum of 250 rooms and ancillary functions to enliven the building edge.

The building defines the intersection of Olympic Boulevard and Station Square in a manner that is in scale with adjacent buildings and complements them, while being consistent with the overall design of the Olympic venue:

1   It is a building of the highest quality, in keeping with the surrounding stadia and showground buildings and its prominent location on the Olympic site.

2   It creates a strong Olympic and sporting theme in its design and interior fit-out.

3   It provides an orientation point within Olympic Park as a whole.

This resulted in the hotel accommodating the following functional areas:

- 10 rooms plus 2 suites per floor for 14 floors – 168 rooms in total;
- hotel administration and service;
- restaurants, bars and a bistro;
- functions/conferences (a 400 m^2 ballroom);
- education facilities on level 17;
- OCA observation area/event management on level 18;
- retail and coffee shops;
- car parking – 150 spaces, with provision for valet parking up to 190 spaces for special functions.

The architects succeeded in creating a visual emphasis, at the corner of Olympic Boulevard and Dawn Fraser Avenue, through the height and shape of the tower. Furthermore, through providing entertainment and retail opportunities at the podium level, they have created a high level of human activity at the building edges, helping to scale the building in relation to the adjacent historical buildings.

The building has a mixed-use concept involving three buildings: the Novotel, the Ibis hotel that is connected to the tower, and a brewery and bar to the south. These buildings have been conceptualized as three separate buildings with three separate functions connected by a transparent glass link.

The appearance of the Novotel comes from its plan and from its high-tech metal and concrete façades. The Novotel tower shape is elliptical, giving a sculptured and curved appearance that articulates the corner. The curving form has consistency with the neighbouring buildings, reflecting the character of Stadium Australia while having a clear and simple style that enables the building to stand alone in the Olympic Precinct.

Finally, the building was developed as part of the Homebush Bay master plan. This took into consideration the urban design priorities, which overshadowed the building design to a certain extent in terms of the positioning of the tower and the orientation of the building, while nevertheless offering infrastructure benefits at the same time.

Another factor influencing the design was its proximity to Olympic Boulevard; wherever possible public areas were orientated towards it. As a result, the east and west façades have quite large areas of glass facing Stadium Australia.

Furthermore, because of the existence of railway lines below the site, there were some additional structural considerations and costs associated with the foundation design to cope with vibration, which placed further constraint on the planning of the project.

Left. The hotel acts as a landmark on the Olympic site, and is adjacent to most of the main buildings, Telstra Stadium and the railways station. **Above**. Passive design involves extensive use of daylight. In the conference centre, daylight through skylights assists with reducing energy needs.

Meeting the Green Globe Design standard

This section includes the indicators for the Green Globe Design standard. The indicators, which make up the Green Globe benchmarking system,[4] evolved by relating Green Design to the Agenda 21 issues for reduction of environmental impacts.

The Green Globe Design standard comprises eight indicators and further sub-indicators. The eight indicators are:

Indicator 1: Design approach and sustainable policy
Indicator 2: Energy efficiency and conservation
Indicator 3: Potable water consumption
Indicator 4: Solid waste production
Indicator 5. Social issues
Indicator 6: Selection of building materials and process
Indicator 7: Siting
Indicator 8: Wastewater management.

Indicator 1: Design approach

The design and procurement approach facilitated sustainability initiatives. Three main strategies emerged:

1   The design brief stipulated 'green design', using OCA guidelines.
2   The hotel lease stipulated environmental management systems based on the use of ISO 14000.
3   The architects, Architectus, a Sydney-based firm, used a multidisciplinary team.

There were three levels of commitment to green design. First, the design was developed in conformity to the Olympic

Sustainable policy for improvement in building design

Indicator 1: Design approach and sustainable policy	Design targets	Benchmarked indicators (✓)
1.1 Sustainability goals and vision in the design brief and undertaking of effective environmental management system	Policy in place	✓
1.2 An interdisciplinary and coordinated approach between all design professionals	Policy in place	✓
1.3 An operational statement for post construction project assessment, operational control and where appropriate, continual improvement of environmental and local impact	Policy in place	✓
1.4 Cost plan to include budget for sustainable strategies and measures as non-negotiable measures	Measure in place	✓
1.5 Contractual agreement with builder to include the Green Globe Construction standard	Measure in place	✓

Coordination Authority's Environment Strategy for the Olympic Park venues and facilities. In support of that, Accor Asia Pacific also had a commitment to integrate the most stringent environmental initiatives into the operation of the hotel complex.

The second level of commitment was arranged by the builder/project manager through their environmentally responsive project management plan.

Third, ISO 14000 certification was awarded to the hotel for its environmental management, making the Novotel hotel the first in Australia to achieve this certification. An operational environmental management plan was also developed as an ongoing commitment to the environment.

Sustainability goals and vision in the design brief, and undertaking of an effective environmental management system, followed OCA's Environment Strategy that includes environmental sustainable development (ESD) principles and an environmental management plan (EMP). The construction group, Bovis Lendlease, deployed a project management system.

An operational statement for post construction project assessment, operational control and, where appropriate, continual improvement of environmental and local impacts was carried out and continues. An operational environmental management plan is in place, as well as staff induction training for disseminating environmental information. An operational environmental management plan was developed that included ten sections.[5] The hotel was the first in Australia to achieve ISO14000 certification, in June 2000, for its environmental management system; this is renewed annually after environmental auditing of the hotel.

An integrated design approach between designers, engineers and environmental managers was part of the regular project management practices of Lendlease. Monthly project meetings and workshops were held to discuss and to decide on a breadth of issues, environment being one of them. Workshops were held to take decisions in an integrated manner among all involved professionals. To ensure that environmental targets would be met, frequent audits of the building's energy use were proposed.[6]

Construction involved builders Bovis Lendlease, who were assigned to deliver the building to the OCA's guidelines. At that time Bovis Lendlease had developed a wide experience and a history of successful implementation of green building practices through work on Newington Village.

Bovis Lendlease added to and supported the OCA's commitment to the environment, and, as one of the members of the Accor/Lendlease consortium, they brought a number of initiatives to the Novotel & Ibis Hotel project. These included *an environmentally responsible project management plan* involving a detailed waste management plan, strategic procurement for responsible material inventories and an integrated design and construction process. The builder was therefore integrated with the team at an early stage. Key aspects of the process helped deliver the 'green building':

- Regular meetings and workshop sessions facilitated an integrated design approach.
- The Accor/Lendlease consortium was formed to deliver the project by way of a Design and Construct contract, with construction by Lendlease and operation of the hotel post construction by Accor. This consortium approach provided the best environmental benefits for the dollar, with minimum risk to the OCA. Furthermore, linking design and operational considerations avoided problems normally found with hotel construction, where the capital cost and operations budgets are seen as separate items. This often results in selection of systems based on up-front costs, rather than on life cycle and operational criteria.
- Moreover, this allowed consideration of the impact of sustainable construction. A notable strategy was the use of precast concrete panels, which enabled off-site prefabrication and reduction of on-site waste.
- An environmental construction management process was used to create a responsible construction schedule. Lendlease followed the project management plan that underpinned OCA's strategy and commitments. This involved a detailed environmental health and safety management system.

Sustainable construction

A model of sustainable construction evolved during this project, which can be utilized in other projects. It is a refinement of previous work with the Newington housing project. Three key components are found in this model.

OCA made it a contractual pre-requisite that *contractors have experience in environment management* as part of the tender requirement. Once it appointed Accor and Lendlease, OCA specified that training and education in sustainable construction was to be provided for the workers.

A *strategic procurement alliance* was put in place that involved a coordinated approach to supervision of sub-contractors and communication with them. In addition, a specification for building systems and methods was created that will reduce energy consumption and waste during construction in the future. This created what could be called a *green specification* for building systems and methods. Specifications for materials included the maximum use of recycled steel formwork, within the constraints of safety and availability. Also, careful control was kept

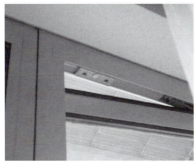

The bedrooms can operate on a mixed-mode principle whereby guests can open windows to receive natural ventilation or close the windows and receive air conditioning. Sensors monitor which mode is selected for energy-efficiency purpose so that air conditioning is not operational when the windows are open.

up over the materials inventory, to limit over-ordering and related wastage.

A *waste management system* was introduced, involving the use of waste depots, recycling plans and hiring of recycling contractors in conformity with the OCA guidelines.

Strategic procurement was adopted with an efficient materials inventory, designed by staff from the alliance to help maximize efficiency and minimize waste of building elements, with the approval of structural designers.

Indicator 2: Energy efficiency and conservation

Passive design

The *orientation* of the podium follows the street edge, while the hotel accommodation forms a spine with its axis north–south. This form of orientation is not ideal for passive design, as it exposes both east and west façades to solar gain. In summer this happens from sunrise to 11 a.m. on the east façade and from 1 p.m. to sunset on the west façade. This heat load requires mitigation through envelope design, with respect to shading and insulation.

A major strategy is to provide natural *ventilation* as an alternative to air conditioning. First, cross-flow ventilation is provided in public areas by the inclusion of louvres and openings on the lower ground and ground floors, combined with mechanical extraction systems to reduce the load on the air conditioning system.

Second, cross ventilation is achieved by having operable windows in guest rooms, which allow the hotel to operate for over 100 days per year with little or no air conditioning.

Shading is provided to the east and west façades, but not to the north. External horizontal raked shading is used for the accommodation. Shading to the large glazing areas of the public spaces was deliberately omitted to preserve the spectacular views of Stadium Australia from the hotel

Daylighting is provided to most areas; the public areas have light shelves to allow natural lighting. Strategies include the use of skylights to admit sunlight to functional areas, such as conference meeting rooms. These skylights have controls for opening and closing them according to the season.

Insulation is provided for the external walls, and pre-cast concrete panels are used for thermal mass efficiency. Insulation also maximizes the benefits of the concrete thermal mass and there-

Energy consumption for energy efficiency, conservation and reduction in emissions

Indicator 2: Energy efficiency and conservation	Design targets	Benchmarked indicators (✓)
2.1 Total predicted gross energy consumption per guest night per year (GJ)	30% reduction in energy consumption	✓
2.2 Total predicted energy consumption (GJ) for the main function area, per guest night per year	Target: 30% reduction in CO_2 emissions	✓
2.3 Use of passive design	Strategies in place	✓
2.4 Use of efficient active design	Strategies in place	✓
2.5 Total predicted renewable energy use/total energy use	10% use of renewable energy	✓

fore the energy efficiency and comfort levels. A pale external colour is used to reduce heat loading. External precast concrete walls have their insulation and thermal efficiency improved by internal lining with plasterboard to give an R value of 2.0.

In summary, active systems include the energy-efficient lighting in public areas and guest rooms that reduces energy consumption as well as air conditioning loads. High efficiency electrical chillers are installed to produce chilled water at lower energy consumption. REED switches automatically disable air conditioning in guest rooms once windows are opened. CO_2 sensors in the parking area allow exhaust fans to run only when necessary. High-efficiency filters on air conditioning units allow for the reduction of supply air intake quantities, hence using less energy. Hotel vehicles run on a renewable energy source.

Finally, water flow controllers are installed in hot/cold water outlets to reduce consumption and reduce hot water demand.[7] There are reduced dependencies on high-emission fuels, in favour of low-emission fuels. The hotel is designed to use 40 per cent less energy compared to a traditionally built hotel, as a cumulative result of all the passive and active energy-efficient initiatives. It also reduces CO_2 emissions significantly as a result of the purchase of all electricity through the green power tariff offered. This policy of the hotel makes a saving of 1,200 tonnes of CO_2 per annum,[8] reducing significantly the dependency of the hotel on high-emission fuels with their associated environmental impacts.

Indicators 3, 4 and 8: Protection of air, earth and water

The protection of air and water is assessed for compliance through a number of indicators: potable water consumption, solid waste and wastewater management.

First, the protection of air is achieved by avoiding waste from *non-biodegradable chemicals,* including polluting chemicals that affect the composition of the atmosphere, such as HCFCs and HFCs used as refrigerants or in air conditioning systems, and including chemicals likely to be used by the hotel and its guests. An example of avoiding these is that mini-bar refrigerators in Novotel & Ibis guest rooms use ammonia and isobutane refrigerants.

Second, *potable water-use* is minimized through a number of strategies.

- OCA provided a grey water main across Olympic Park for use by the buildings. Hence a dual water system is installed in the hotel that uses reclaimed water from the stormwater run-off from the Olympic site. This water is used in toilets and for landscaping and contributes to 50 per cent of total water consumption.
- Low-water-using fixtures are used, such as low flow taps and AAA showerheads.[9]
- Rainwater from the hotel roof is captured and stored in a 10,000-litre on-site tank for the irrigation of the hotel's landscaped areas. Landscaping was designed using locally occurring native Australian plants that are drought tolerant.
- The number of bathtubs is reduced by around 50 per cent.[10]

Potable water consumption and solid waste production for protection of air, earth and water.

Indicator 3: Potable water consumption	Design targets	Benchmarked indicators (✓)
3.1 Total predicted potable water consumption per area	Target: 60% reduction	✓
3.2 Total predicted potable water breakdown per area	Target: 60% reduction	
3.3 Use of water conservation and efficient appliances	Strategies in place	✓

Solid waste production for protection of air, earth and water

Indicator 4: Solid waste production	Design targets	Benchmarked indicators (✓)
4.1 Predicted volume of solid waste to landfill per area	Target: 30% reduction	
4.2 Use of onsite waste disposal and efficient appliances	Strategies in place	✓
4.3 Predicted non-biodegradable chemical use per area under roof	Target: 0%	✓

Solar hot water heating saves 22 per cent of electrical energy.

Overall, precise figures for water consumption were not available, but annual potable water consumption is reduced by 40 per cent.

Third, the protection of earth is achieved through the reduction of waste, particularly to landfill. A number of strategies in this area were used.

- An operational plan to reduce waste involves soap dispensers in toilets. The high-quality toiletry dispensing system saves 100,000 small plastic shampoo bottles and soap cases each year.
- A worm farm is used for food waste; 50 kg of bio-waste is converted to nutrients by the hotel worm farm each day and used as fertilizer by a local nursery garden.[11]
- Recycle bins are provided in guest rooms.
- Increased electronic communication: guest compendiums are accessed through the television rather than printed. Use of email and voicemail technology in each guest room minimizes the use of paper. Reduction of paper waste is achieved by encouraging and promoting electronic communication among staff. Staff induction programs include information about resource efficiency and the hotel's commitment to the environment.[12]
- Stormwater run-off is treated before reaching the wetlands.

Overall, the annual volume of solid waste sent to landfill by the hotel is not available, but about 80 per cent is recycled and does not go to landfill.[13]

Social issues

The building displays a number of measures that respect and are *integrated with the local contextual parameters*. These are:

- The hotel acts as a focal point for the site.
- There is an observation centre at level 17.
- The building acts as an airport beacon.
- There is a partnership with the leading conservation organization, WWF, which organizes events for community awareness.

First, the building acts as a focal point on a number of levels. From the visual point of view, the tower acts as a marker; at the contextual level, it provides a hub for the social and community events in the Olympic Park – indeed, during the Olympic Games, OCA used the reception area as the centre for media and other events. The design therefore fulfils its aim of creating an environment, and a social and physical node, to promote social and community interaction through bars, restaurants, and outdoor recreation spaces. This makes a major contribution to creating a lively edge to the public domain, particularly during the 2000 Olympics and the Paralympic Games. The observation level, and the use of the building for aircraft navigation, reinforce the contextual role played by the building.

Second, the partnership with WWF makes a further important connection to broader concerns with the environment. The

Social commitment

Indicator 5: Social commitment	Design targets	Benchmarked indicators (✓)
5.1 Design measures to integrate contextual parameters	Strategies in place	✓
5.2 Minimal impacts on native land and population	Strategies in place	
5.3 Enhancement of the users' understanding and integration with the natural and social environments	Strategies in place	✓

hotel has been designed to be sensitive to local community issues and *seeks to enhance users' understanding of the environment.* The hotel has a partnership with the leading conservation organization, the World Wide Fund for Nature, and donates $1 to WWF from every room-night sold. This arrangement, where a major hotel developer, Accor, is in association with a leading world organization for saving the environment, is believed to be unique,. This significant factor is attributed to Accor winning the management contract for the hotel of the 'Green Games'; the WWF is now actively promoted through the hotel. In col-

Waste management is a key policy in the hotel. Reducing the volume of waste to landfill is achieved through recycling and reuse. Space for this activity is needed in the back of house facility. **Left**. A compaction machine, which compresses paper waste and reduces the number of skips (**top**) needed per week, saving operational costs. **Right**. The worm farm digests organic waste, which gives very rich compost.

laboration with WWF, the hotel launched a booklet in 1999 aimed at hotel guests and educational institutions: *A Practical Guide: A Few Simple Actions to Conserve the Environment.* The hotel obtained feedback on this approach in 2000, and published the results of an internally conducted survey concerning environmentally friendly practices that hotel guests indicated they were ready to adopt:

- 95 per cent are in favour of using waste-sorting bins;
- 83 per cent approve of the idea of replacing individual soap bars with a soap dispenser;
- 57 per cent would agree to use their towels more than once;
- 35 per cent would agree to sleep in the same sheets as the previous night;
- 90 per cent prefer staying in a hotel that is concerned about the environment.[14]

Third, on community issues the hotel organizes a series of events and programmes to promote community awareness. Initiatives such as fact sheets, website and integration with local initiatives are also developed, including events such as 'Breakfast with the Birds'. This event is linked to WWF, and is used to introduce the community to the 140 species of birds that can be found in the Millennium Parklands and their living environments.[15]

Events such as tree-plantings are organized as an initiative for community awareness. The hotel aims at replacing the equivalent of twice number of trees used in paper each year by growing native seedlings to be replanted in local areas. The chef's rooftop herb garden, managed by the hotel, contributes to the kitchen's herb requirements.

Indicator 6: Resource conservation through selection of building materials and processes

Bovis Lendlease undertook life cycle assessments. However, no document recording this evidence could be obtained.

Materials rating
The designers and builders made a commitment to OCA's environment strategy. There were preferences given to the use of the following materials:

Resource conservation through selection of building materials and process

Indicator 6: Selection of building materials and processes	Design targets	Benchmarked indicators (✓)
6.1 Selection of green materials and processes for low environmental impacts	Rating achieved	✓
6.2 Eco-label products purchased	Strategies in place	✓

- Precast concrete panels allowed a great deal of standardization and on-site waste reduction.
- Recycled timber was used for flooring and furniture.
- Natural wools and fibres were used for carpets.
- 'Breathe-Easy' paints were used on wall and ceilings.
- There was minimal use of solvent glues with VOCs.
- There was minimal use of PVC for flooring, electrical wiring and water pipes.

Biodegradable chemicals as used in the building to reduce impacts during operations. The use of soap dispensers reduces waste from packaging.

Eco-label products purchased

Lendlease used an eco-labelling programme through the Strategic Procurement Alliance policy that was developed, involving green material inventories during the construction. This is a regular practice of Lendlease; the strategy involves monitoring and assessment of alliance companies and their processes. Accor certified and approved suppliers who were then used for on-going operational purchases.

The outcomes of this process are to maximize the health, safety and comfort of building users. In particular, the design specifications such as 'Breathe-Easy' paint and natural fibres and carpets are combined with other strategies such as operable windows. These materials reduce risks concerning toxicity and off-gassing and improve indoor environmental quality.

Finally, in service-intensive buildings such as this, planning for maintenance is crucial. In this case, carpets with 80 per cent wool and 20 per cent nylon increase durability and recyclability.[16]

DESCRIPTION OF SITING ISSUES

Prior to European settlement, extensive tidal wetlands and thick woodlands covered Homebush Bay. From the early 1800s, large areas of wetlands were gradually reclaimed and the forests cleared for farming and industrial use. From the mid 1800s up to the 1960s, Homebush Bay was used as a racecourse, brickworks, armaments depot and abattoir. During the 1960s and 1970s, some parts of the area became contaminated through uncontrolled dumping of household and industrial waste.

Despite the impact of past activities, Sydney Olympic Park, and the Parklands in particular, contain a number of important habitats and different types of vegetation including a eucalypt forest and casuarina woodland and the nearby wetlands, which are rare in the Sydney region. These habitats support a broad range of fauna, in particular water and woodland birds, some of which are listed on international treaties dealing with migratory birds.

In 1993 it was discovered that the disused brick pit was a breeding habitat for the endangered green and golden bell frog. OCA has worked to secure the future of this colony, establishing new habitats and building fences and tunnels along roads to protect frogs migrating between these habitats.

Environmental performance has been and continues to be an important element of all works undertaken at Sydney Olympic Park, with a commitment to energy and water conservation, waste minimization, air, water and soil quality and the protection of significant natural and cultural environments. The work undertaken there has been recognized by major environmental awards.

In 1997, as construction was proceeding, OCA undertook a further review of the public spaces between the venues, the Parklands, gathering spaces and the role and function of Olympic Boulevard. As a result of this review, additional features were added to the master plan, including water features at the Fig Grove between the Aquatic Centre and Olympic Stadium, the Northern Water Feature and its distinctive 'sharp-edged' landscaped mound from which thousands of people photographed the Olympic Village during the Games, and the creation of a more unified public space called Olympic Plaza. A feature of this plan was the planting of a canopy of large native fig trees along Olympic Boulevard.

A major feature that emerged at around the same time was the blue lighting towers along Olympic Boulevard, which provided light, shade and amenities for spectators and visitors while generating solar power during the day to offset energy use at night. Subsequently the permanent features of the Park were overlaid with a wide range of temporary facilities for the Games.[17]

(Source: SOPA)

Indicator 7: Siting

The site of the building is bound up with the development of the Olympic Park site.[18] During September 1995 a blueprint planning document, the master plan, was established, which divided the site into four major zones:

1   an urban core containing sporting venues and entertainment facilities, the showground and exhibition area, and commercial sites;
2   the Newington Urban District, which was the Olympic Village for athletes and team officials;
3   a major metropolitan park, Millennium Parklands, providing several ecologically distinct areas, nature corridors, habitat and active recreational opportunities for Sydneysiders;
4   the waterfront development and Parklands, providing public access to the shoreline.

From this description, it can be seen that the building site can be classified as a 'brownfield' site, i.e. one where there has been considerable previous redevelopment. In this case the Novotel & Ibis was part of the overall remediation work for the area.

The building attempts to reduce its *building footprint* through the tower concept. Areas of the site have been designed for landscaping, and have been planted with local indigenous drought-resistant flora. This approach is consistent with the *siting attributes* for sustainable sites.

Siting suitability has been accommodated through the OCA's environment strategy of promoting public transport, a newly designed railway station being a part of the strategy. In support of this strategy, less than the prescribed car parking area was

Siting to reduce impacts through land management

Indicator 7: Siting	Design targets	Benchmarked indicators (✓)
7.1 Area of habitat conserved/ total site area		38%
7.2 Siting suitability	Rating achieved	✓
7.3 Building footprint/site area	Rating achieved	✓
7.4 Environmental siting attributes	Rating achieved	✓

Wastewater management

Indicator 8: Wastewater management	Design targets	Benchmarked indicators (✓)
8.1 Predicted wastewater treatment on site/total wastewater generated	Target: 30% reduction	✓

provided for the hotel. Pedestrian connection to the railway station and other public means of transport were highlighted. Awnings and/or other appropriate weather protection were provided on the footpath to make pedestrian walks protected and comfortable.

Design lessons

Two main lessons were learnt from this project.

1   The importance of thorough environmental planning and infrastructure requirements. The master planning of the precinct at Olympic Park played a central role in facilitating good environmental performance of the hotel. This involved the 'green lease arrangements' that included sustainable goals in the brief and in the post construction EMS (environmental management strategy). This 'green' design process was supported by a number of environmentally appropriate infrastructure decisions such as the Olympic Park grey water main, which provided a 50 per cent reduction in potable water use in the building.
2   A large number of small (eco-efficient) environmental strategies in the building created a significant reduction in the environmental footprint.

The design team started with a large shopping list of strategies to use and these were rationalized to a number of small but cost-effective measures, e.g. solar hot water, daylighting, effective envelope including operable windows. With the purchase of 'green power', the hotel is effectively net carbon neutral.

The approach taken in this project can be mirrored in other buildings, with a greater focus on the operational savings that can be achieved through green design. The Australian government initiative through the Department of Industry, Tourism and

Resources and the Australian Hotels Association has carried out a benchmarking study to identify strategies and benefits.[19]

Within the commercial building sector, the hospitality industry is one of the largest and fastest-growing energy users. Hundreds of hotels, from boutique operations to large resorts, rely on a daily basis on significant amounts of electricity and natural gas.

Through the Energy and Environment Best Practice (EEBP), the Australian Hotels Association has developed a benchmarking report and a series of case studies demonstrating how the hotel industry can maximize profits, minimize energy costs, and show leadership by reducing energy use and greenhouse gas emissions – without negatively impacting on the comfort or satisfaction of guests and customers. The benchmarking study included 50 hotels.

These benchmarking case studies demonstrate real and proven results. They report on ways to improve energy efficiency – ranging from simple changes that involve little or no capital investment, to longer-term improvements that may require some funding.

Many initiatives have quick payback periods. Examples include:

- installing efficient ice makers at a capital cost of $6,000, which deliver estimated annual cost savings of $23,000;
- installing water-efficient shower roses and a temperature setback system at a capital cost of $3,600, which deliver annual costs savings of around $14,500.

Benchmarked resource use and waste reductions

Indicators	Novotel and Ibis	Comments regarding the targets
Predicted energy consumption	40% reduction in energy	Effective active design and passive design
Predicted CO_2 emissions	Net carbon neutral	Reducing consumption and then purchasing the surplus energy with 'green power'
Predicted potable water consumption	40% reduction	Use of water-saving appliances and on-site grey water system
Predicted volume of solid waste to landfill		

Yet the danger of this kind of example is that it suggests a piecemeal approach to refurbishment and, in terms of the overall running costs of a hotel, a more holistic approach is preferred. The Novotel & Ibis Hotel is presently undergoing refurbishment. This tends to occur every four to seven years and it is an opportunity to revisit the vision of the hotel and its direction towards its guests.

Refurbishment goals

One major question arises when considering refurbishment. What do the occupants want from their hotel environment?

The refurbishment of hotels takes place approximately every seven years. This is an opportunity to review the environment issues. In this case the shading to the west-facing lobby, which was omitted for visual reason during the Olympics, is being applied to improve thermal performance in the space.

1 security – physical and psychological sense of safety;
2 healthy environment – materials and air quality – comfort;
3 good-quality interior – spaciousness, daylight, comfort;
4 low noise intrusion – reduction of unwanted noise from outside and inside;
5 personal control of their environment – thermostats, operable windows;
6 good electric lighting, suited to visual tasks;
7 mixed mode of climate control – use of mechanical, as well as natural, heating and cooling.

A second question concerns what the environment needs from the hotel.

HUMAN SYSTEMS
1 Policy shift to consider/reflect a balance of social, economic and environmental issues.
2 Process control – 'if you can't measure it you can't manage it' – hence engage ISO 14000 or GG standards for operational efficiency. Obtain third-party certificates to demonstrate due diligence.

PHYSICAL SYSTEMS

1 Reduce CO_2 emissions through energy intensity reduction.

2 Reduce water consumption through conservation and recycling.

3 Reduce waste by on-site processing and materials selection.

4 Take a life cycle approach:

(a) biodiversity – review landscape plan, audit species, rework plan to increase biodiversity, and maintain or reduce hard surfaces;

(b) transport efficiency – develop transport plan for guests and workers to mitigate energy emissions;

(c) social responsibility for environmental issues – establish greater links with community to promote environmental issues;

(d) review construction and ongoing maintenance impacts – environment-maintaining construction policy and measures.

The refurbishment of hotels takes place approximately every seven years. This is an opportunity to review the environmental issues. In this case the shading to the west-facing lobby, which was omitted for visual reason during the Olympics, is being applied to improve thermal performance in the space.

The Novotel & Ibis refurbishment

The hotel is seeking to improve performance in many area but acknowledges that without large capital cost this is difficult. Presently the strategies involve first, the front of house activities, and second, those environmental management issues concerning energy, water and waste.

A focus on front of house – that is, those strategies for refurbishment that directly affect the quality of service for the guests – should be given priority. The Novotel has developed a loyalty programme to encourage guests to return to the Novotel on a recurring basis. This is encouraged presently through discounts on rates, but is augmented by better service and facilities. Promoting this can be achieved by selecting 'green strategies'.

NEW LIFTS

Installation of new lifts will reduce energy consumption, and also provide better service support for staff and service to the guests.

REFITTING THE ENVELOPE TO THE LOUNGE AND ENTRANCE AREA

The envelope has operable windows, which means the building can operate without air conditioning and heating. This dynamic façade reduces the need for permanent mechanical ventilation, further mitigating energy use. Consideration is being given to an improved façade design. This is a critical issue for refurbishment and should be given high priority in new as well as refurbished buildings.

Re-design and refurbishment of the envelope to the lounge and entrance area is an important strategy, with the aim of improving ventilation and reducing western sun penetration in the evening. The existing design prioritized views out to the Stadium, but in recent years the large number of visitors using this area on 'match days' has necessitated a re-think of the façade to improve thermal and visual comfort for the visitors, which will avoid high peak loads on the air conditioning and hence reduce energy use.

FIXTURES AND FITTINGS

Part of refurbishment is renovation of fixtures and fittings. During the present renovation, there are priorities for the selection of carpet adhesives that are water-based and non-toxic and have limited off-gassing.

Furthermore, the use of 'green paint' systems that are water-based and non-toxic has been, and still is, a priority. This not only provides a healthy environment for the guests but also for the construction workers applying the systems.

Back of house activities

ENERGY MANAGEMENT

There is a need for improved operational energy performance through management of energy systems. Presently, this achieves 30 per cent savings compared with a normal hotel, but further improvements are anticipated through using high-efficiency screw chillers to provide efficient air conditioning.

Investment in a building management system of $260,000 will achieve savings of $100,000 p.a. through better zoning control and accommodating small system loads. Essentially, this is achieved by matching the supply of energy with the demand more effectively through a 'stepped lag' approach. This approach involves anticipating the need for power and is managed through the use of the building management system.

In addition to energy management, consideration of the fuel source is an important issue. The use of renewable energy, such as solar power, has been implemented. Using solar-heated water as a pre-heat system again saves a considerable amount of non-renewable energy and also reduces ongoing costs. Water is preheated from 12°C to 45°C and then boosted to 65°C using gas (a relatively less problematic fuel source than electricity in terms of greenhouse emissions).

WASTE

Waste management has been an integral part of the hotel from its inception. The refurbishment has provided an opportunity to re-examine these systems. New strategies of dealing with organic waste are proposed: 30 tonnes of organic waste will be sold to Earth Power in the form of methane. Earth Power, a generation company in Sydney converts this into 'Green Power'; this is Australia's first regional food waste to energy facility. Earth Power accepts source-segregated food wastes from the industrial, commercial and domestic sectors and converts them to green energy and nutrient-rich fertilizers using state-of-the-art technology. (www.earthpower.com.au).

Furthermore, on-site solid waste is managed through a sorting process. To control the volume of solid waste such as cardboard, compaction equipment has been purchased. This reduces the need for skips from six per week to one, and considerably reduces the volume of waste going to land fill.

WATER

Water savings can be achieved by controlling demand and by substituting recycled water (i.e. grey water) for activities such as cleaning, toilet flushing and irrigation. The availability of a grey water main supply on the site of Olympic Park provides a reduction of 40 per cent in the use of potable water. During refurbishment, better use of this facility for external cleaning will improve savings.

Acknowledgements

CRC – Sustainable Tourism
Green Globe International Ltd
Jakki Goven, Sales and Marketing Manager, Novotel
Peter Hunt, Building Manager, Novotel
Gabrielle Vanwilligen, previous Environmental Manager, Novotel
Micheal Mangos, Sales and Marketing Coordinator, Novotel
David Martin, Project Manager, Lendlease
Paul Jerogin, Environment and Strategic Planning Manager, Lendlease
Ray Brown, Architect, Architectus, Sydney
Greg McTaggart, Sydney Olympic Park Authority, NSW

Contributing authors: Shailja Chandra and Deo Prasad, The Centre for the Sustainable Built Environment, University of New South Wales.

Illustrations, plans and sections: Richard Hyde and Architectus.

Project team
Client: Accor Group of hotels and OCA
Project Manager: Lendlease
Architect/designer: Architectus (Travis McEwen Group Pty Ltd)
Structural Engineer: Connell Mott McDonald
Hydraulic consultants: Donnelly Simpson Cleary & Partners Pty Ltd
Passive thermal/daylight modelling: Donnelly Simpson Cleary & Partners Pty Ltd
Electrical engineer (lighting): Donnelly Simpson Cleary & Partners Pty Ltd
Builder: Lendlease
Landscape design: Belt Collins
Insulation design: Donnelly Simpson Cleary & Partners Pty Ltd
Indoor air quality advice: N/A
Environment consultant: Mandis Roberts

The Sundancer Resort, Lombock, Indonesia.

CASE STUDY 5

The Sundancer Resort, Lombok, Indonesia

Architects: Pt Wisata Bahagia, Indonesia

Introduction

The construction of Balinese architecture is steeped in the past as much as is in the present. Whenever a new house is built it receives a blessing from the priest, and a figure of Sanghyang Widi is hung above the doorway to signify 'God be with us'. The symbolic male figure of Sanghyang Widi, the Supreme Being, has flares emanating from his body.

While some could draw a parallel between the custom of blessing the building on completion and the modern performance assessment, the connection is tenuous. In this case the resort design is aimed to address both the Balinese tradition in architecture and the present need to address issues of area with the attendant reductions in environmental impact.

Kerry Hill, designer of many hotels, describes the transformation of Balinese design in the hotel sector. This has seen a coalescence of two models of design: the western with its roots in modern architecture, and the Balinese with its traditions and culture. The resolution of this duality has produced hotel architecture that is open to criticism, debate and discussion. It certainly engenders some strong feeling – the feeling of place.

Hill's commentary on the evolution of the hotel style revolves around two dominant themes – scale and luxury. The Bali Hyatt by Palmer and Turner, built no higher than the palm trees, has guided a style of hotel development that ensures privacy, by proximity of the natural environment, and visual amenity.

The second theme, complementary to the first, is that of luxury, celebration and indulgence. The modern hotel has redefined tropical resort architecture from 'grass roots and swimming pools' to a quality integrated 'tourism experience'. The celebration of climate, form, fabric and service transport the hotel client to a 'mythical place far away'. Environment is a key element in new formula, and the Sundancer Resort takes the tradition of tropical resort design to a new dimension.[20] The attention given to improving the environmental footprint of the

Left. The site is located in a coconut plantation. **Right**. The building follows the Balinese tradition of building. Whenever a new house is built it receives a blessing from the priest, and a figure of Sanghyang Widi is hung above the doorway to signify 'God be with us'. The symbolic male figure of Sanghyang Widi, the Supreme Being, has flares emanating from his body.

Sundancer project details

Characteristics	Details
Building type	Interpretation centre for Dinosaur Trackways
Building area (m²)	Total: 1090m² (plus 37m of walkway to lookout track; 78m of bridge from entry display building). Trackways building: 850m² with veranda: 155m². Trackways entry shelter and display building: 85m²
Number of visitors	10,000 per annum with continual occupancy
Number of storeys	One
Building address	Lark Quarry Conservation Park via Winton
Owner occupied or tenanted	Owner occupied
New or refurbished building	New building
Building cost	$1,208/m² (estimated unit cost)
Total building cost	$2 million estimated
Completion date	June 2002

building, through the Green Globe process, has set a new standard for the future.

The brief

The functional brief for the resort is for provision of a spa and beach resort, comprising 40 one-bedroom apartment suites and 26 two-bedroom suites. The centre complex contains restaurants and recreational facilities such as sports, gymnasium, beach club and swimming pool. A coastal road services the resort. Subsequent stages to the resort include villas situated above and around the resort. The resort forms the centre of an emerging residential development in the area.

Project description

The initial environmental feasibility work for the project comprised an environmental impact study, following the standard procedure for a study of this type. The aim of the design was to achieve low environmental impact. The existing land use was agricultural, comprising a coconut plantation on the coastal strip with mixed crops and grazing on the steep hillsides that rise from the coastal area. Hence the topography of the site provided a significant challenge to the design and construction of the project.

Other key issues in this project are the availability of electrical power and water. With limited electrical grid, diesel generators serve the site. Also no mains water is available so there is a reliance on subsurface supplies of potable water. Rainwater harvesting and wastewater recycling is proposed.

The adoption of the Green Globe Design and Construct standards for design and construction has assisted with addressing these resource issues through proving alternate strategies, and also facilitated demonstrating the environmental, social and economic benefits of the design. This involves two-stage benchmarking and certification. Benchmarking usually occurs during the

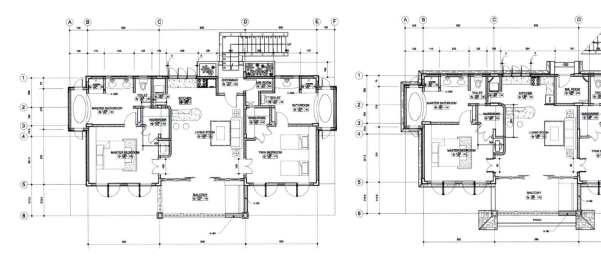

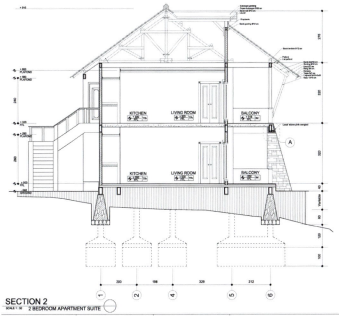

Top left. Ground floor plan of the two bedroom units.
Top right. First floor of the units. **Bottom right**. Section through two bedroom units.

design process, preferably at the sketch design. The second stage is certification, which occurs after construction is completed. Benchmarking was finished in 2004, and as the project is still under construction certification has not been completed.

Construction assessment requires measures to be initiated to obtain data on the environmental impact of the construction process. The intention is to use a further Green Globe operational standard post construction.

Location, climate and design

Location

The resort is located in an area of spectacular natural beauty. The area of west Lombok and the nearby town of Sekatong are serviced by an airport at Matran and local ferries from Bali. The resort is reached by road or boat.

Site and site response

The site of the resort is in a coconut plantation, which has been retained. The coastal plain at this point is small, necessitating efficient planning of the layout of the villas and centre complex.

From the coastal plain the topography changes rapidly to steep rock hillsides. The gradient of these hills has necessitated the traditional practice of 'terracing' to make the site useable.

Climate

Lombok is located east of the Wallace line, sharing much of its climate and flora and fauna with Australia. The region of 'west Lombok' is particularly hot and dry, making it ideal for a beach resort but posing significant infrastructure problems of water provision and climate control for adequate thermal comfort. As with Australia, the climate has distinct wet and dry seasons. The tropical climate is ocean-influenced with moderate temperatures in the range of 25°C–30°C. There is a wider range of humidity, from 100 per cent relative humidity in the wet season to 40 per cent relative humidity.

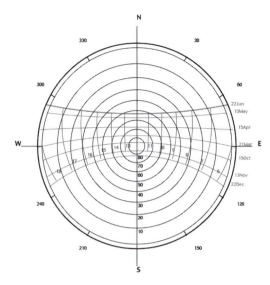

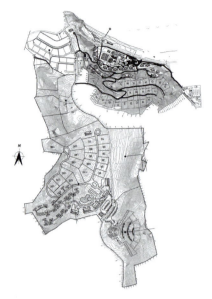

Top. Master planning of the site responds to sun path information. **Left**. The beach house and the villas have a rectangular plan with short sides facing east and west to minimize heat gain from the setting and rising sun.

Design response

The master planning of the resort involves a concentric approach, using the pool and centre complex as the focus. Around the centre is the beach resort and terracing up the hillside. The dispersed nature of the apartments allows access to views and the breeze.

Meeting the Green Globe Design standard

This section includes the indicators for the Green Globe Design standard. These indicators have evolved from relating Green Design and the Agenda 21 issues for reduction of environmental impacts using the Green Globe benchmarking system.[21]

Eight indicators and further sub-indicators make up the Green Globe standard. The eight indicators are as follows.

Indicator 1: Design approach and sustainable policy
Indicator 2: Energy efficiency and conservation
Indicator 3: Potable water consumption
Indicator 4: Solid waste production
Indicator 5. Social issues
Indicator 6: Selection of building materials and process
Indicator 7: Siting
Indicator 8: Wastewater management.

The project is examined first with regard to design approach.

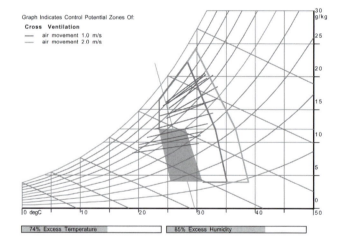

Graph Indicates Control Potential Zones Of:
Cross Ventilation
—— air movement 1.0 m/s
······ air movement 2.0 m/s

74% Excess Temperature   85% Excess Humidity

Top. Typical psychometric chart for the area demonstrates the need for ventilation as a method to extend the comfort zone. **Left**. Local traditions of building design are integrated into the design, such as shading windows to reduce solar gain and including external spaces to utilize the sea breeze for comfort.

Passive and active design with mixed-mode operation ensure energy efficiency. Insulation for the roof spaces reduces internal temperatures by 8°C. **Right**. The site layout has achieved an optimum orientation for most units, reducing solar gain and providing natural ventilation.

Design approach and sustainable policy

The sub-indicators are:

- sustainability goals and vision in the design brief and undertaking of effective environmental management system;
- an interdisciplinary and coordinated approach between all design professionals;
- an operational statement for post construction project assessment, operational control and, where appropriate, continual improvement of environmental and local impact;
- cost plan to include budget for sustainable strategies and measures as non-negotiable elements; and
- contractual agreement with builder to include the Green Globe Construction standard.

The sustainability issues focused mainly on saving operational energy and water-efficient strategies. A target of 40 per cent reduction in energy use was established with 100 per cent of waterborne waste treated on site. The building footprint was reduced and saving on potable water use was a priority.

The post construction environmental management system nominated was the Green Globe Company standard that was established for assessing the operational efficiency of hotels of this nature. Eco-efficiency measures were integrated in the design process and yielded significant operational and capital cost savings. Operational savings of US$480,000 are predicted through energy savings alone. Capital expenditure was incurred in some areas with the use of an improved envelope design and energy-efficient plan as follows:

1 lighting design improvements US$20,000 (saving);
2 hot water (use of solar) US$13,000 (increase); and
3 air conditioning and envelope US$33,000 (saving).

The aim was to use an integrated design and costing approach. This involved a life costing approach where savings in the cost of one aspect would offset costs in other systems if

Green Materials Rating

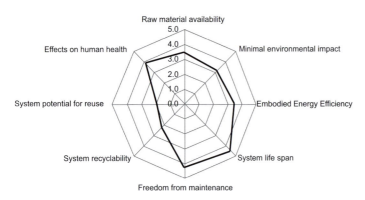

operational gains were found. A total saving on capital cost of US$39,000 per unit was made with an operational cost saving of US$40,000 per month.

The construction process was integrated with the standard. Construction was carried out through a process of training the builder in the Construction standard. In this case the builder is part of the project team so no contractual agreement was necessary.

Energy efficiency and conservation

The sub-indicators are as follows:

- total predicted gross energy consumption per guest night per year;
- total predicted energy consumption (GJ) breakdown per guest night per year;
- use of passive design;
- use of efficient active design; and
- total predicted renewable energy use/total energy use.

Energy consumption
The design of the project focused on improving the standard of the building envelope and selecting energy-efficient appliances and systems. The primary energy source for the project is diesel generators, which will provide power directly to the project. Minimizing power demand in the completed hotel is achieved primarily through reducing demand for HVAC and lighting

Passive design
The orientation of the apartments and centre complex is largely dictated by the topography and the view. The building was aligned along the contours predominantly east–west, partly to achieve a level of efficiency in construction, and because this affords the optimum orientation to most of the apartments. Strategies for passive design include the following:

- appropriate plan form for climate;
- high specification of insulation (15 cm styrofoam with vapour barrier for the roof);
- appropriate light colour to walls;
- use of micro-climate control for shading;
- cross ventilation to all rooms;
- appropriate glazing ratio;
- shading to windows;
- ventilation to attic space to reduce heat sink effects;
- improved acoustic separation between rooms; and
- daylight to all habitable rooms.

Efficiency of active system
The design of the HVAC system was carried out to integrate the performance efficiencies in the envelope. The signing of systems took into consideration the reduced heat load through the envelope. In addition, the operation of the HVAC system allowed flexibility in its operation. A mixed mode control system was used to allow guests to select either natural ventilation with ceiling fan assistance or air conditioning. The control system was designed to avoid waste of energy, i.e. running on active mode when the windows are open (sensors are used to avoid this type

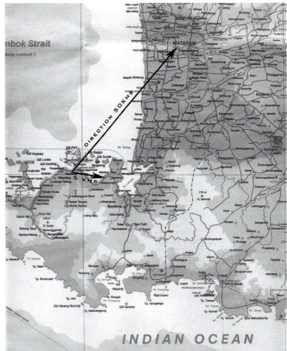

Studies of the transportation distances of materials were used to assist with design decision-making.

of waste). High coefficient of performance (COP) systems were selected with pollution control (i.e. HFC refrigeration).

Efficient lighting systems, such as low-mercury fittings with photo sensors to external lights, were specified. Solar hot-water systems were used, which created a renewable energy fraction of 3 per cent of total energy used.

Overall, energy efficiency measures and conservation are predicted to reduce gross energy consumption by 30 per cent with an operational cost saving of US$100,000 per annum. The predicted CO_2 reduction is estimated to save 4.3 tonnes of CO_2 per guest per night every year. With an estimated 40,000 guests per year visiting the hotel, this is a significant reduction in CO_2.

Potable water consumption

The sub-indicators are as follows:

- total predicted potable water consumption per area under roof;
- total predicted potable water breakdown per area under roof; and
- use of water conservation and efficient appliances.

Water is provided to the project through a spear pump from an underground well. The intention is to use this water primarily for drinking and washing. A reduction in the demand for water is achieved through the use of water-efficient appliances and using recycled water for irrigation. A 20 per cent reduction in predicted water use is anticipated from these strategies.

Solid waste production

The solid waste sub-indicators are as follows.

- predicted volume of solid waste to landfill per area;
- use of on-site waste disposal and efficient appliances; and
- predicted non-biodegradable chemical use per area under roof.

A waste management plan has been established for the sorting, separation and on-site disposal of solid waste. Organic waste is to be treated through a worm farm. Biodegradable chemicals are specified for cleaning and laundry operations.

Social commitment

The social sub-indicators are as follows:

- design measures to integrate contextual parameters;
- minimal impacts on native land and population; and
- enhancement of the users' understanding of and integration with the natural and social environments.

The design of the project has attempted to reflect the local context with regard to scale, materials and texture. The design, construction and operation of the project have involved local inhabitants, many of whom have worked on the project. The project acts as a provider of much-needed community support to the local villagers through medical and employment opportunities. On completion, measures are in place to use the building to foster a better understanding of the environment. This is important not only for guests but also for the education of the

Construction work is currently in progress. The Green Globe Standard includes mentoring construction impacts through an additional nine indicators. On completion of the project, this is taken into consideration for final certification.

local inhabitants, many of whom are subsistence farmers and fishermen.

Resource conservation
The resource conservation sub-indicators are as follows:

- selection of green materials and processes for low environmental impacts; and
- eco-label products purchased.

The project uses primary materials and local source materials. Timber is locally grown and dried hardwood is used for roofing timbers and windows. Clay bricks are made from local clay with a timber fuel source. Concrete is made with local aggregates and cement.

Siting
The siting sub-indicators are as follows:

- area of habitat conserved/total site area;
- siting suitability;
- building footprint/site area; and
- environmental siting attributes.

The site has designated areas for biodiversity protection. This includes areas of landscaping and areas retained in their natural state. Approximately 22 per cent of the site will be retained for biodiversity protection. The built area as compared to the site area represents a building footprint ratio of 25 per cent.

Environmental siting attributes examines issues area around the buildings in terms of site scape and landscape issues. The area around the building is designed to enhance the environmental qualities of an external space. This includes a number of strategies. Landscaping for micro-climate control will be used to reduce solar gain to the buildings. The landscape includes the selection of native species and reintroduction of natural species to help in maintaining the existing gene pool. Rainwater irrigation will be used, and planting will be zoned for efficient maintenance (i.e. higher-maintenance plants are closer to the building).

Finally, the site suitability indicator is a composite of environmental site selection issues, such as reducing transport energy, and neighbourhood and community issues as well as ecological impact. The project is weakest with regard to pedestrian and bicycle infrastructure and strongest with regard to recreational value. The development of housing areas adjacent to the site is taken into consideration.

Wastewater recycling

The wastewater management sub-indicators are as follows:

- redirected wastewater treatment on site/total wastewater generated.

The project utilizes on-site collection of rainwater and also recycles water from the biosystem. It is intended that this water will be used for irrigation and for cleaning when practicable.

Benchmarks achieved

The predicted benchmarks for the scheme are summarized in the table above. These were generated from calculations developed by the design team. The benchmarking system developed for the Green Globe Design and Construct benchmarking system contains two calculation spreadsheets, which assist with the benchmarking process. One spreadsheet assists with the assessment of the design and one with the construction. The percentage improvements were generated from comparing a base case 'business-as-usual' unsustainable design[22] and an improved Green Globe design. The improved performance was evaluated from the economical standpoint to understand fully the life cycle cost benefits. Green Globe has qualified assessors who help with this kind of process.

Construction assessment

Construction assessment involves establishing an environmen-

Sundancer predicted quantitative performance benchmarks achieved by the design

Indicators	Novotel and Ibis	Comments regarding the targets
Predicted energy consumption	30 per cent reduction in energy	Effective active design and passive design
Predicted CO_2 emissions	4.3 tonnes per guest night per year	Reducing consumption Grid not used
Predicted potable water consumption	20 per cent reduction	Use of water-saving appliances and water-recycling system for irrigation
Predicted volume of solid waste to landfill	100 per cent organic waste recycled	Worm farm and waste sorting and compaction

tal management approach to construction. Rather than use an ISO 14000 system, which can be expensive, a series of indicators have been developed and are being applied to the construction. The main indicators are described below.

Sustainability construction policy

The indicators are as follows:

- builders experienced in sustainable construction; and
- appropriate sustainable construction management.

Measures were used to upgrade the construction team, which included attendance at a Green Globe training course. Appropriate construction management was agreed, which included establishing a waste management plan. This included an on-site recycling area.

Resource consumption and waste production

The indicators for resource consumption are as follows:

- total energy consumption on the building site (MJ) per day/area of building site (m^2);
- total water consumed on building site (kl) per day/area of building site (m^2); and
- total volume of construction waste to landfill (m^3) per day/area of building site (m^2).

A site-monitoring programme was set up to examine measures concerning resource consumption. Electric meters and water meters were installed on incoming mains. The waste to landfill was also calculated from waste skips leaving the site.

Social commitment

Indicators for social commitment include:

- management plan for accommodating social and cultural issues in place; and
- workers living within 20 km of building site/total number of workers.

The social commitment management plan for construction was included in the main management plan for the project. Most of the villagers worked on the project; an estimate 90 per cent of the workforce were local.

Construction resource conservation

Finally, the indicators for resource conservation include:

- appropriate building construction process and systems selection for location and site conditions;
- construction containment area/total site area m^2;
- documented storage and use of environmentally harmful substances;
- total wastewater collected for disposal per day/water used m^2/litres per day; and
- number of noise and air pollution complaints/violations per week.

A low-technology construction system was used, which focused on traditional methods. The steeply sloping site meant that terracing was needed. To avoid the energy and CO_2 emission consequences, the traditional construction system for terracing was used. A containment area around the site was established and the storage of harmful substances managed within a site waste recycling area. Wastewater collection from then main 'wet' process, which was concreting, proved to be difficult. Wastewater was simply emptied on to the site, and leached into the subsoil,. Settlement ponds were established, and water evaporated; the dry solid waste could then be used as road base.

Lessons learned

The main points that can be taken from this project are as follows:

1. The integration of the Green Globe Design and Construct criteria with the project brief at the outset of the project.
2. Problems with sourcing the supply chain with regard to 'green systems' and equipment in Indonesia. The location of remote communities in islands such as Lombok requires companies that can service these projects. Difficulties have been found in selecting appropriate energy-efficient appliances and equipment, photovoltaic equipment and water recycling systems.
3. The adoption of the Green Globe Design and Construct standards for design and construction has assisted with addressing these resource issues through proving alternative strategies. Also it facilitated demonstrating the environmental, social and economic benefits of the design.
4. Overall, energy efficiency measures and conservation are predicted to reduce gross energy consumption by 30 per cent, with an operational cost saving of US$480,000 per annum. The predicted CO_2 reduction is estimated to save 4.3 tonnes of CO_2 per guest per night every year. With an estimated 40,000 guests per year visiting the hotel, this is a significant reduction in CO_2.

Acknowledgements

Project team
Client: Dwayne Hill
Project Management: Jerry Cardinale, Ni Nyomah Aut Astuti
Architect and designers: Thomas Suwito, Chris Diono
Structural engineer: Ir Rendon, Hanna Tanome
Hydraulic consultants: Ir Rendon, Hanna Tanome
Passive thermal/daylight modelling: Llianna Hidayat
Electrical engineer: Budhi Yadmaika
Builder: Hap Kuy, I B G D Suberati
Quantity surveying: Ni Made Ambarawati
Materials: Beatrix Mugirato
Illustrations, plans and sections: Richard Hyde, Pt Wisata Bahagia, Indonesia.

Trackways building. Entry.

Lark Quarry Trackways Building and Shelter, Lark Quarry Conservation Park, Winton, Australia

Architects: Gall Medek Architects

Introduction

The Lark Quarry Trackways building is located in a remote desert area of Queensland and accommodates a set of dinosaur footprints that are unique to the area and have been recognized to be of significant archaeological value.

The Lark Quarry Conservation Park protects these excavated dinosaur footprints, which are 93 million years old and provide Australia's and the worlds best known record of a dinosaur stampede. The isolation and fragility of this natural resource require special consideration with regard to access, conservation and presentation.[23] The tourism aspect of this project made it an ideal case study of sustainable tourism as well as appropriate architecture in a remote and highly fragile desert ecology.

This case study examines how the building met the Green Globe Design standard. The project became an exercise in 'seeking to explore opportunities for the development of a conservation and visitor facility, of world's best practice standard'. The Green Globe Building Design and Construct standard for tourism infrastructure contains specific environmental targets that can be used for the briefing process.

Project details

The project details explain the scope of this project, but because of the tourism nature of this project the ecologically sustainable design of the building was envisaged as part of the visitor's experience and complemented the archaeological experience.

The project was at the sketch design stage when this assessment was started. A number of issues were instrumental in making this project work within a 'green building' framework.

First, Queensland Tourism prepared a pre-feasibility study of the project, which set up its main thrust and direction. This involved setting up a working group with a wide range of stakeholders, and the architects and Winton Council. Second, this document paved the way for a business plan and communication plan, aimed at marketing the facility from a commercial and sustainability perspective.[24]

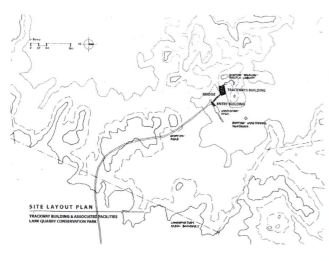

Left. Site plan. **Right**. Entry building with bridge to the Trackways building.

Lark Quarry Trackways building project details

Characteristics	Details
Building type	Interpretation centre for Dinosaur Trackways
Building area (m²)	Total: 1090m² (plus 37m of walkway to lookout track; 78m of bridge from entry display building). Trackways building: 850m² with veranda: 155m². Trackways entry shelter and display building: 85m²
Number of visitors	10,000 per annum with continual occupancy
Number of storeys	One
Building address	Lark Quarry Conservation Park via Winton
Owner occupied or tenanted	Owner occupied
New or refurbished building	New building
Building cost	$1,208/m² (estimated unit cost)
Total building cost	$2 million estimated
Completion date	June 2002

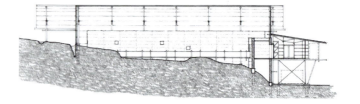

The brief

A working group, with representatives from Tourism Queensland, Queensland Parks and Wildlife Service, Department of the Premier and Cabinet, Queensland Heritage Trails Network and a number of consulting organizations, was established to produce a concept design and pre-feasibility study in order to progress development funding for this project. The major issues considered by the working group in the formulation of this report were:

- preservation of the trackway surface;
- ongoing funding of site facilities; requirements created by increased site visitation; the interpretation focus for the facility;

Top. Long section. **Bottom**. East elevation. Low-maintenance materials comprising steel roofing and shading with steel sandwich panel construction to provide insulation.

- promotion of the trackway facility; accommodation at the facility; and
- incorporating ecologically sustainable design and technology appropriate for the environment and the experience.

The Queensland Museum advised that the trackways could potentially extend further into the hill on which they are situated, and that other as yet undiscovered palaeontological resources could be found in any or all of the surrounding ridges. This information resulted in the decision to locate the primary visitor facility, together with any camping accommodation, away from the trackway conservation building.

In order to differentiate this facility from others in the region, and provide an interactive authentic visitor experience, which would appeal to the current and potential Outback travellers and generate income for the facility, it was decided to include within the development:

- a supervised participatory dig activity;
- a significant interpretive experience focusing on the formation of the trackways and the current natural environment;
- a camping area and walking tracks; and
- a conservation building with minimum interpretation to facilitate the viewing experience.

The design objectives for the project encompassed mainly conserving the dinosaur tracks. Central to this process on an ongoing basis was to utilize the eco-tourism potential by providing accommodation and access for visitors. To support the visitors, building needed to provide interpretation of the meanings of the tracks and the surrounding landscape. The interpretation component can be further divided into examination of the existing landscape and its history and theories, and information behind the dinosaur trackways. An important component also included the role the build could play in educating 'best practice' ESD (ecological sustainable development).

The experience for the visitors and the method of explanation and 'interpretation' is set around three themes.

The first theme concerns the dinosaur story, the international scientific significance of this site, the age of dinosaurs and the trackways event – the stampede. This involves the visitor stepping back in time to understand what actually happened here, what the footprints tell us about the event itself, the animals that lived here and how these footprints were preserved and then discovered by local graziers and opal gougers. The subsequent involvement of Queensland Museums and Queensland Parks and Wildlife has conserved and preserved the site.

The second theme is about the local environment, called 'The Jump Up Country'. The biodiversity and ecological features included landforms; escarpment, mesas and gullies, Mitchell grass downs to the east; vegetation; spinifex, Normanton box, lancewood, herbs after rains; wildlife, bird life, mammals – wallaroos, echidnas, impact of foxes (local extinction of rock wallabies), reptiles.

The climate and its connection to landscape formation included important features such as landscape formation – a water-carved land; stratification of past waterborne sediments – links to past landscapes of the trackways event; impacts of rain events – erosion, mineral leaching of substrates creating hard-topped mesas; climate – after rains/floods, the dry, long-term drought, and the impact of bushfires.

Human history and impact on the landscape also feature as a theme, in particular European settlement – grazing, mining, scientific discovery and conservation – and the Aboriginal use/ownership of the land.

The final theme is 'The ESD story', involving the ESD design principles of the trackways building and its construction, and individual aspects of the design – solar electricity, rammed earth walls, passive temperature and humidity control, water collection, waste management and materials selection, and also site impact and conservation.

The design of the project allows these three themes to be presented at different points in the path around the building, creating an integrated experience for visitors.

Location, climate and design

Location

The Trackways building and Trackways shelter are located in the Lark Quarry Conservation Park, which is 111 km south-west of Winton (180 km north-west of Longreach) in an isolated arid region of central western Queensland on the edge of the Tully Range. Winton (originally known as Pelican Waterhole) was first settled in 1875, although land was taken up as early as 1866.

Winton is regarded as one of the most significant Outback Australian townships. During the Great Shearers' Strike in the 1890s, 500 shearers camped on the common just south of

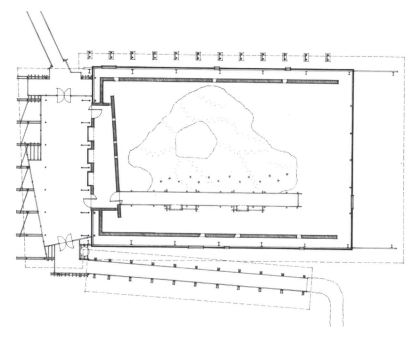

Top right. Water conservation strategies are used and the technology integrated under the building.
Top left. Display area provides an opportunity to show information concerning the users' understanding of the environmental qualities of the building.
Left. Plan of the Trackways building. The dinosaur tracks are found in the large space, with the display space forming the entrance.

Winton and the township was placed under marshal law. This was the beginning of the foundation of the Australian Labour Party. Winton is home to Australia's national song 'Waltzing Matilda', which was written by 'Banjo' Paterson at the nearby Dagworth Station and first performed at the North Gregory Hotel in Winton in 1895. Finally, Australia's national airline, Qantas, was formed in Winton in November 1920, with the first Board meeting held at the Winton Club in February 1921. Winton is recognized as the 'home' of Australian bush poetry and hosts the annual Bronze Swagman Award, which is regarded as one of the country's most prestigious literary prizes.

The 374-hectare Conservation Park encompasses a stark landscape of dissected low hills and tablelands, mesas, buttes, rolling stony plains and undulating plains. The vegetation community is diverse.[25]

Climate
The building was designed to replace an existing building that provided some protection. Holgar Wilrath, the energy consultant, reported:

The footprints are being damaged by contraction and expansion of the ground due to the large diurnal temperature variation. Skies are generally clear at night, so heat is radiated, cooling the ground. Clear skies during the day produce high temperatures due to solar radiation. Temperatures are even higher near the footprints due to the glazing in the roof of the surrounding structure producing heat and trapping it like a large solar collector. The current level of thermal comfort for visitors is poor. The current structure enclosing the footprints is to be replaced.

The temperature near the footprints is to be stabilized and thermal comfort; particularly in summer is to be increased. The illumination for viewing the footprints is to be provided by natural daylight, with possibility of some oblique task lighting.[26]

Climatic data

Climate data for the site was taken for Longreach as there was no recording on the site and this is the nearest weather station. Situated at latitude: 23° 27′ S, longitude: 144° 15′, this gives a hot dry climates. The key features of the climate are as follows:

- The average temperature levels are mostly within the vicinity of the comfort zone (22–27°C) throughout the year.
- From May to August, the average temperature levels are below the comfort zone. Thus, heating might be required for these months. Passive solar heating can be used.
- For other months, the temperature levels are mostly higher than the comfort zone.
- For ventilation, stack effect (cold air entering the bottom of the building during the night and displacing the lighter, hotter air exiting the top) is considered, but air will need to be filtered to keep out dust from the vast landscape surrounding the building.
- The key to stabilizing the temperature for users is by thermal mass for this building.
- In addition to thermal mass, insulation and limiting the glazing area are also important for comfort issues and to preserve the dinosaur footprints.
- Humidity ranges from around 20 per cent to 50 per cent.

In summary, with low humidity and a high diurnal range of temperatures, three bio-climatic strategies can be used to cool and heat the building naturally: mass effect, which involves the use of the thermal flywheel effect of heavyweight materials; air effect, using the cooling effect of lower night temperatures; and evaporative effect, using the cooling from water.

Envelope recommendation

The envelope recommendations from the Mahoney analysis are as follows:

- *air movement*: no cross ventilation is required;

- *opening sizes*: very small: 10–20 per cent of wall surface;
- *opening position*: not critical;
- *opening protection*: full permanent shading;
- *walls and floors*: heavy, over eight hours' time lag;
- *roof construction*: heavy, over eight hours' time lag;
- *shading*: to exclude western sun; and
- *building's orientation*: 8° west of north, with its longitudinal side facing north and south, thus minimizing exposure to west and east.

Overall, a defensive building is recommended for the dry, hot climate. A defensive building is defined as one that is primarily using the envelope to mitigate heat gains from or losses to the exterior environment through envelope design. The opposite of this is an interactive building where the envelope works to accept favourable heat flux and reject unfavourable climate events. This building can be both. In winter, it is primarily closed to conserve heat. In summer, it can be closed during the heat of the day and opened during the night to ventilate the building and keep temperatures constant inside.

The main objective of this project is not only to provide thermal comfort for visitors but also to avoid damage to the footprints through excessive expansion and contraction. This strategy of combining defensive with interactive capability in the envelope is appropriate.

Building planning

The building comprises three elements:

- the Trackways building, which consists of the dinosaur tracks;
- the entry building, which includes an entrance lobby, collection point, toilets and display;
- a bridge linking the two buildings.

The planning of the Trackways complex is based on a number of factors. A key influence on the position and the form of the Trackways building and its geometry is the nature of the dinosaur tracks. The excavation is approximately 22 metres by 22 metres, and roughly triangular.

The result is a 'big shed' comprising a steel superstructure (6-metre grid), which spans across the tracks providing the enclosure. The form has additional bays added to the roof structure,

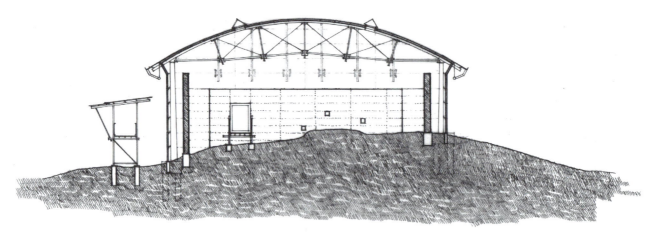

Cross section showing the use of thermal mass made from rammed earth with cladding of sandwich panel construction. Left. Entrance bridge. Centre. Walkway above the dinosaur tracks.

which 'carry' the building into the hill to provide good shading and keep ground water away from the building. Cladding is lightweight, with insulated external walls and heavyweight pise internal walls The Trackways building is linked to the entrance building by a walkway, which forms a bridge over the landscape.

The entrance building, which is based on a 3-metre grid, has seating and an information area. The building is heavy in weight, with timber batten screens and a louvre system to control ventilation.

Meeting the Green Globe Design standard

This section includes the indicators for the Green Globe Design standard. These indicators have evolved from relating Green Design and the Agenda 21 issues for reduction of environmental impacts using the Green Globe Earthcheck benchmarking system. There are eight indicators and further sub indicators that comprise the standard.

Indicator 1: Design approach and sustainable policy
Indicator 2: Energy efficiency and conservation
Indicator 3: Potable water consumption
Indicator 4: Solid waste production
Indicator 5: Social issues
Indicator 6: Selection of building materials and processes
Indicator 7: Siting
Indicator 8: Wastewater management.

The project is examined first with regard to design approach.

Design approach

The first set of indicators are concerned with environmental policy as contained in the brief and the pre-feasibility study carried out by Tourism Queensland. The *sustainability goals and objectives* were included in the pre-feasibility study carried out by Tourism Queensland. This is a comprehensive document, which includes sketch design concepts. Sustainability objectives, although not in the brief, were integrated through this study.

An *integrated design approach* between designers, engineers and environmental managers occurred in this project. The complete team, with multidisciplinary team members, has joint analytical work and testing. This is an interdisciplinary and coordinated approach, using design charrettes.

Evidence of the use of energy audits, benchmarks, targets or thermal modelling is found where energy concepts were shown in the energy consultant's report, and this included studies of daylighting.

Top left. Interior view showing the rammed earth from local sources which acts as the thermal mass system. A bridge is used to take visitors over the tracks. **Top right** and **right**. Rammed earth was used to provide thermal mass in the building.

The team also worked within an *environment management system*, which is in operation for the Conservation Park. This included statements of the energy concept, energy ratings and thermal modelling. An operational manual for energy standards and energy audits shows an operational statement for post construction project assessment, operational control and, where appropriate, continual improvement of environmental and local impacts through Queensland Parks and Wildlife Service.

The ESD initiatives were included in the *cost planning stage*, at an early stage of this project. Information is found in the pre-feasibility study cost planning. The architects developed a policy to integrate the builders at an early sketch design stage of the project to better mesh the environmental, construction and economic issues in the design. A valuable strategy in the exercise was to use a bill of rates for work for the project so there was a level of transparency in the project costing process, allowing variations during design development to be easily costed.

An added benefit was that the builder was selected and engaged early in the process and provided input into the construction documentation of the building. This means *the builder* *became a critical part* of the design team for documentation. The builder's advice on suitable construction methods was critical. Also, the builder became involved directly with QPWS (Queensland Parks and Wildlife Society) in relation to minimizing impacts on the site through the Conservation Park EMS (environmental management system).

Energy efficiency and conservation

Energy efficiency is gauged by the extent to which passive and active systems have been designed.

Passive systems design

The form of the building follows this geometry, meaning that its form is optimized not necessarily for climate considerations – that is, optimum orientation – but by function. Both the Trackways building and the Trackways entry and display facilities building are orientated along an east–west axis with orientation 8° west of north. The optimum orientation would have been to align the building east–west. This is a common situation with this type of building, where function is of primary importance. As a consequence it is necessary to rely on manipulating the envelope to achieve energy efficiency, occupant comfort and preservation of the site:

- shading to exclude western sun;
- building orientated 80 west of north, with its longitudinal sides facing north and south, thus minimizing exposure to west and east;
- building designed with minimum window area to suit the preservation/interpretation function and to minimize heat gain in the building; and
- heavyweight wall construction, with rammed earth set well clear of the footprints and an external veneer of sandwich panel construction to act as insulation and for night purging.

Using the passive design checklist, the Trackways building scores 80 per cent and the room assessment meets all the criteria. The buildings are designed to exclude breezes during the day in summer when the maximum external temperature is around 40°C. The cooling for visitor comfort is derived from the mass effect and removal of dust from the environment.

Thermal mass and insulation

The main strategy for energy efficiency and conservation is use of passive strategies such as thermal mass and passive solar energy. Internal walls are made of rammed earth 450–300 mm thick that provides thermal mass for the building. The envelope and line of enclosure comprises a lightweight cladding system of 100 mm thick composite steel sheets with polystyrene core. This gives an R value of 1.5 in the walls.

The roof is a lightweight galvanized iron cladding with rigid plastic insulation and sisalation felt (radiant barrier), providing an R value of 2.5. The rammed earth walls and floor are the main elements of thermal mass. The question that arose was whether the insulated skin was necessary or whether the 450 mm thick pise walls would be sufficient, given that it has an R value of only 0.5.

From the modelling, a number of conclusions were reached:

- With the pise walls only, the energy required to maintain comfort between 23 and 28°C was:
  - 154 MJ/m cooling;
  - 46 MJ/m heating.

- If externally insulating the walls with R1.5, the requirement was:
  - 33 MJ/m cooling;
  - 23 MJ/m heating.

The performance improvement with external wall insulation reduced cooling energy by 80 per cent and heating energy by 50 per cent. The positive effects on thermal comfort were also found with the insulated walls. The building was simulated under free- running mode in summer (assuming a small degree of night-time ventilation) to assess comfort and the effects of insulation. Uninsulated walls kept the annual temperature range in the building to 14°C or between 18 and 33°C for the whole year. Insulating the walls reduced the annual temperature range to 11°C (19–30°C). This reduction of temperature range is crucial for the preservation of the Trackways building, and modelling has shown the indicative range of temperatures that can be maintained. Further parametric studies were done to check the range of temperatures on hot days in summer and in winter, and these demonstrated similar results.

Night purging

Theoretically, buildings of this type with thermal mass should perform better if the thermal mass can be cooled from the external night air. Desert locations such as this have a high diurnal temperature range and the heat sink effect of the thermal mass can be utilized.

The simulations were carried out with night purging. The comfort conditions inside the building are much better but the diurnal temperature variation is also greater. This system is better for human comfort but worse for preservation of the Trackways.

- *Winter.* On a cold winter day in July, the external temperature variation was between 4.0 and 21.9°C. In the building with externally insulated walls this produced a temperature range between 19.4 and 21.5°C.
- *Annual temperature variation.* Throughout the year, every 6–7°C variation in external temperature produced about 1° variation inside the building when the walls are externally insulated.[27]

Daylighting

Daylighting is delivered into the building by ten angular selective 1.2 m^2 Skydome skylights.[28] Modelling of daylighting in the Trackways building revealed that these provide adequate daylight all of the year and for differing sky conditions.[29] Light is admitted through the roof, and a diffusing panel is placed at the ceiling to reduce glare.

Active systems design

Ceiling fans were recommended above the walkway and in the air lock. This would give an additional 3° of physiological cooling without changing the air temperature, which would maintain comfort conditions even during hot spells in summer, provided the walls are externally insulated.

Mechanical ventilation was considered for the night purging in view of the need to filter dust and improve air quality (the issues of dust and moisture control were considered because of the monsoon influences).[30]

Renewable energy

With the 4 kW grid-connected photovoltaic system installed for the Trackways building, reliable power supply is ensured. There is a total saving of around $2,000 using the PV system rather than the local SWIR line. The single wire (SWIR) line has limited capacity to deliver power to the site, so rather than upgrade this system it was cost effective to provide the photovoltaic system, which sends excess power into the grid. The SWIR line was also reportedly unreliable.

Protection of air, earth and water

The protection of air and water is accommodated through a number of indicators: potable water consumption, solid waste and wastewater management.

Conservation and collection of water

This building does not need complicated water services. It has no kitchens or residential accommodation and water use is only for drinking, hand-washing and toilet-flushing. Because of the hot arid climate and the nutrient-sensitive environment, particular water conservation and waste disposal systems have been adopted.

Water conserving appliances

A key water conservation strategy in this building is to use a low-flush toilet linked to an evaporation system. A commercial version of this toilet is used.[31] The dry hot arid climate has many advantages for this type of system, increasing the rate of evaporation and aerobic digestion. In addition, the liquid waste from the digester can be removed and the water evaporated, leaving a crust that can be disposed of in a similar way to the humus from the bins. The advantage of this system is that there is no waterwaste to pollute the dry ecosystem in which the building is located. Water conservation appliances such as water-saving tap fixtures are provided.

Water collection

Rainwater is collected from the roofs of the two buildings. Four rainwater tanks have been installed on the site, giving a total rainwater capacity from the tanks of 60,000 litres. Two rainwater tanks are under the entrance veranda and two are in the entrance display building.

Water harvested from the roof provides some 13 litres per person per year, assuming 35,000 visitors. This gives a water consumption of 32 litres per m^2 per year. The water use is primarily for hand washing. Indicator 8 – predicted wastewater treatment – is linked to other issues and is therefore described in this section.

Wastewater treatment

A storage system is used for wastewater with an evaporation system for waste liquid. This can achieve both economic and environmental benefits. The system works as follows:

1   wastewater taken from the toilet;
2   delivery to the evaporation chamber;
3   evaporation of water by the sun;
4   residual collected every 12 months.

The effectiveness of this system means that the predicted wastewater treatment on site ratio is 1: that is, 100 per cent of all wastewater is treated on site.

Social issues

The design of the building has been sensitive to local community issues. In response to and in support of the local social context and local economy, a number of strategies were put in place. Local labour was used to achieve cost efficiency. Ongoing community work with different social groups will help *contribute to the user's understanding of the environment*. Local economic benefits may accrue from the use of locally based tour operators, the employment of local knowledge, the purchase of provisions and services, and the use of local facilities.

A participatory design process, including discussion of the desired 'building image' with the community, was carried out at the briefing stage. This has enabled the building to address the Green Global criteria of responding to *contextual parameters*. This approach was carried out using workshops, *the local Aboriginal community* and Queensland Parks and Wildlife. Involvement of the Aboriginal community facilitated a better understanding of and integration with the natural and social environments. Placing environmental and social sustainability at the core of professional practices and responsibilities maximizes the health, safety and comfort of building users.

Resource conservation

The selection of materials and eco-labelling of products used in the buildings assist with reducing environmental impacts. The rating of materials follows these criteria:

1 raw material availability;
2 minimal environmental impact;
3 embodied energy efficient;
4 system lifespan;
5 freedom from maintenance;
6 system recyclability;
7 system potential for reuse; and
8 effects on human health.

Green materials rating

Green materials and processes are selected for the project, for their low environmental impacts. A rating system has been devised, based on the work of Bill Lawson.[32] A score of 3.6 was reached using the system (the higher the score, the lower the impact).

Lark Quarry Trackways building materials rating

Elements	Specification
Substructure	Reinforced concrete strip footings, pad footings to columns and walls
Rating	3.00
Primary structure	Steel SHS sections
Rating	3.25
Roof/columns	Steel roof framing, truss with CHS purlins, bracing and metal deck
Rating	3.25
Ground floor	100 mm reinforced ground slab
Rating	3.63
Ramp	Steel access ramp
Rating	3.25
External walls	100 mm insulated wall panels with fibre cement
Rating	3.63
Internal walls	300–450 mm thick rammed earth
Rating	3.63
Windows	Aluminium frame with single-glazed window panes 6 mm
Rating	3.63
Doors	Fully toughened clear glass
Rating	4.00
Shading	Steel and aluminium vertical shades
Rating	3.25
Floors finishes	Plywood floor, with sealer
Rating	3.75
Ceiling finish	Insulated ceiling panels, fibre cement
Rating	4.13
Wall finish	Fibre cement, paint finish
Rating	4.13
Average rating	3.60 (maximum 5)

Materials with low volatile emissions were selected wherever possible. The internal walls of the Trackways building are pise or rammed earth. A demountable recyclable steel structure supports the truss roof. The steel roofing structure has cantilevered eaves. It is not necessary to galvanize the steel in this low-humidity environment.

Particular strategies help with making decisions about materials. These include:

• local materials content and reduced transportation requirement;

- LCA and embodied energy;
- resource efficiency – minimum material for maximum effect;
- reused and recycled components and content;
- future recyclability of materials;
- durability and ongoing maintenance requirements.

Life cycle assessment of selected materials and processes (including embodied energy and maintenance)
A life cycle costing study was carried out comparing the use of a steel portal frame structure prefabricated in Brisbane and transported to the site with a steel column and truss system made from locally available steel components. The local design used available components and local skilled labour. The result of using the local system rather than the non-local portal frame system was a saving of $80,000, and local employment was gained as well. The system selected as a result of the study involved the use of a hybrid system, with larger components manufactured from sources outside the local community and smaller sources within the community.

Use of local materials
The earth pit for the pise walls is only 2 km from the building site. This has saved transportation costs, which also reduced the embodied energy.

Further reduction in embodied energy came from the minimization of member sizes for transportation purposes and using prefabricated small pieces. Structural optimization was achieved through prefabrication, which reduces on-site waste. Sandwich panels were used. Low-impact products were purchased whenever possible and the use of non-renewable resources has been minimized. Local labour was employed, which brings income to local communities.

Maximization of use of renewable and/or recyclable materials and components
The use of concrete is minimized. The soil type required the use of concrete for footings/piers. Rammed earth is sourced from a local supply. Therefore, appropriate materials are selected with respect to their source and type for minimum environmental costs. Site works are minimized; recycled and local materials are used where possible; low-maintenance, long-life materials

and finishes are selected; building structure is designed for flexible planning and reuse, and materials and construction methods that facilitate reuse are employed – for example, the insulated panel wall can be dismantled and relocated if required. A prefabricated, site-assembled steel structure was designed for the roof.

Considerations regarding toxicity, off-gassing and indoor air quality
Self-finished materials with no off-gassing were used. Natural oil-based stain was used for floors. The existing building is demolished and components will be treated and reused.

Planning for maintenance
The elements in the envelope are designed as long-life elements with minimum maintenance. The low humidity environment with high levels of solar radiation (and ultraviolet light) creates issues for maintenance. Corrective maintenance involves painting the fibre cement cladding every five years with acrylic water-based solar-resistant paints.

Siting Issues

The objective of the siting issues is to reduce negative impacts and/or create positive interactions with the natural environment.

The first sub-indicator is the area of *habitat conserved*. This could comprise the whole 300 acres of the Conservation Park. In this case the area of the building site is used as a more meaningful measure. The building area is 1,090 m^2 and the site area is 3,920 m^2; The area for conservation is 2,832 m^2. This gives a ratio of 0.72, which is within the range of 0.5–1.

The next criterion is *site suitability*. This concerns the suitability of the site in terms of its proximity to local neighbourhoods and the availability of public transport systems. Also ecological value and recreational value are considered.

The size and siting of the building was determined by the location of the tracks. This project does not score particularly highly against siting criteria – at 38 per cent – because of the remote location (in terms of transport availability). This is balanced by good performance in terms of the extent to which the project retains the existing ecological value of the site. This is the case with most remote area projects, while urban projects tend to have good transport availability and poor retention of ecological value.

Building footprint is a measure of the total building area in relation to site. In this case the new building retained the footprint of the existing building and achieved a footprint ratio of 0.27. This means the site coverage by the buildings is 27 per cent.

The final sub-criterion is the use of *environmental siting attributes*. This includes factors concerned with the relationship between the landscaping and the building, as follows:

1 landscaping for micro-climate control;
2 site-specific species selection;
3 re-introducing planting native to the specific site;
4 maintaining existing gene pool and existing natural vegetation protection;
5 encouraging retention of adolescent planting and saplings;
6 ensuring that group plantings are diverse species;
7 grouping plantings from similar habitats;
8 ensuring appropriate rainwater irrigation strategies (soakage pits, contour terracing and swales);
9 minimizing area of grass planting or eliminating totally;
10 zoning areas of planting.

In the case of this building the main strategy was to conserve existing trees and to replace them where necessary.

Design lessons

The project is an example of a remote tourism facility designed to work within the ecosystems that form its context. This includes the natural and man-made environments. Lessons learned from this project are as follows:

1 Coordinated supervision of and communication with sub-contractors is important in order to influence the sub-contractors to use environmentally responsible construction processes. Because of the fragile nature of the Trackways, everything needs to be done either from above or outside during construction.
2 Building systems and methods are specified to reduce energy consumption and waste during construction.
3 Transportation energy is a key component of remote projects. Using locally sourced materials and labour minimizes this demand for energy.

4 Minimization of waste during construction is achieved through extensive prefabrication to avoid on-site cutting and minimize waste from off-cuts.
5 A key factor in this building is the level of building services used. Highly serviced buildings can attribute about 30–40 per cent of their costs and resources to servicing. A low service-intensive building has been achieved by reducing the amount of mechanical systems, and this in turn reduces resources intensity. Air conditioning has been avoided, so it is possible to achieve a high degree of autonomy with the building. Service needs for energy and water are met from on-site harvesting.
6 The most important design lesson for the Lark Quarry project is to understand the interaction between all issues, which include land impact, energy-related issues, resources, construction methods, local economy, local approval, expertise and intervention and social issues. As everything is interconnected, decisions need to be well thought out. Certain difficulties emerged at different times for the various parties involved, especially as the site has great historical importance and complex programming, budgeting and monitoring issues. Thus, conservation and minimal site disturbance during construction, and good communication among all parties, are vital for the Lark Quarry project.

Lark Quarry: use of resources

Indicators	Lark Quarry	Comments regarding the targets
Predicted energy consumption per person per day or m²	2.5 W per person per day	Lark Quarry has a renewable energy system using photovoltaic systems.
Predicted potable water consumption per m² per year	13 litres per person per year; assuming 35,000 visitors, 32 litres per m² per year	Water consumption cannot exceed the water catchments. This is estimated as a function of the roof area available and the rainfall.
Predicted volume of solid waste to landfill per m² per year	Follows the Park environmental management plan	

7   Cooperation with the builder was a key strategy in achieving the level of sustainable development in this project.

In conclusion, the Lark Quarry project has offered valuable design lessons for architects and designers. It is the preservation, accommodation and interpretation that make the project instructive and worth documenting for future reference.

Acknowledgements

Australian Research Council
BERS, Energy Consulting Service
Centre for Integrated Resource Management, UQ
CRC – Sustainable Tourism
Green Globe Asia Pacific
Jim Gall, Gall & Medek Architects
Melinda Watt, Sustainable Travel & Tourism
Queensland Water Recycling Strategy, EPA
Tourism Queensland
Photographs: Lin Martin
Illustrations: Lin Martin
Plans and sections: Gall Medik

Project team
Client: Winton Shire Council
Project Manager: Lorelle Schluter (Tourism Advisor), Niall Mackin (QLD Heritage Trails Network), Project Steering Committee (Local Representatives), Gall and Medek Architects.
Architect/designer: Gall & Medek Architects
Monitoring and assessment: The University of Queensland
Structural engineer: McWilliam Structural Engineers
Hydraulic consultants: Hamilton Design Group
Passive thermaldaylight modelling: Holger Willrath
Electrical engineer (lighting): Integrated Energy Services
Electrical engineer (lighting, PV, glazing and shading design): Integrated Energy Services
Builder: Hutchinson Builders
Insulation design: Holger Willrath – Solar Logic

Bibliography

ATS Group Pty Ltd, Lark Quarry – Business Planning Issues Paper prepared for Winton Shire Council, August 2001.
ATS Group Pty Ltd, Lark Quarry – Dinosaur Trackways, Business Plan (Draft) prepared for Winton Shire Council, November 2001.
ECONNECT, Lark Quarry Heritage Trails Network Project – Communication Plan (Revised), June 2001.
Holger Willrath, Solar Logic Report, BERS, Energy Consulting Service – service for an energy efficient future, 2001.
Lark Quarry – Preserving and Presenting the Trackways, Document prepared by Tourism Queensland, July 1999.
D.A.Sketch PAD, Longreach climatic data and graphs, Lark Quarry, LQ Conservation Park, Australia.

Chapter 11

Offices

CASE STUDY 7
CH$_2$, Melbourne, Australia

Architects: DesignInc

> CH$_2$ will add enormous vibrancy to this significant section of Little Collins Street, with new shops, cafés and pedestrian connections and, as it does so, it will strive to set a new standard in how buildings can deliver financial, social and environmental rewards.
>
> Lord Mayor John So

Introduction

Council House 2, affectionately known as CH$_2$, has sustainable technologies that 'break the mould' incorporated into its ten-storey structure. Innovation has driven the design, with features such as phase change materials for cooling, automatic night-purge windows, wavy concrete ceilings, a façade of louvres (powered by photovoltaic cells) that track the sun, and even a sewer-mining plant in the basement.

Although most of the principles followed in the building are not new – using thermal mass for cooling, using plants to filter the light – the innovations and comprehensive integrated process make the building notable. This case study introduces the CH$_2$ building, discusses its use of an innovative brief and collaborative project structure, and reflects on the experiences of applying the Australian Green Star rating to the design phase of the project.

CH$_2$ uses a range of conceptual ideas (left) and performance measures in design to assist with achieving green design.

Pre-design and briefing

The client's vision
Known as CH$_2$, the striking building will set a new international standard in ecological sustainable design. It also offers a financially responsible way of meeting the Council's long-term need to house staff and breathe life into an under-used part of the central city.

Construction of CH$_2$ commenced early in 2004, but already the design stage of the building has been given a six-star rating – world leader status – by the Green Building Council of Australia, under the new method of comparing the environmental performance of commercial properties. The building will bring vibrancy to a significant section of Little Collins Street, with new shops,

CH$_2$ project details

Characteristics	Details
Owner	Melbourne City Council
Project team	City of Melbourne in association with DesignInc Architects
Engineer	Lincolne Scott
Services	Advanced Environmental Concepts (AEC) ESD consultant Bonnaci Group structural engineers
Construction	Hansen Yunken
Cost consultant	Donald Cant Watts Corke
Completion date	End 2005
Cost	$51M excluding fit-out
Size	12,800 m² GFA
Footprint	1,113 m²
Construction type	Precast concrete ten-storey office
User group	MCC staff
Annual energy use	Expected to be 50–60kWh/m²/yr
Site area	1,316 m²
Country	Australia
Occupancy	540 Staff
Latitude	37.81°S
Longitude	144.91°
Elevation	18 metres

cafés and pedestrian connections. CH$_2$ will make an unmistakable statement that Melbourne is a city that understands, values and excels when it comes to the environment, technology, leadership, teamwork, design, liveability, health and culture.

Brief for CH$_2$

The brief was developed by the City of Melbourne in August 2002, and the concepts were refined during a highly intensive workshop comprising the whole team of consultants from 6 to 17 January 2003. The aims for the building are:

- to be a lighthouse for future City developments;
- to provide a comfortable, adaptable and stimulating working environment for its users, the staff of Melbourne City Council;
- to be seen and understood to respond to its natural and social environment and to make use of resources, bearing in mind the efficient use of embodied energy both in the choice of materials and in the process of their use;
- to maximize the use of renewable energy within the bounds of present technology by harvesting sunlight, wind and rainwater alongside the complexities of the Melbourne climate; by following these principles the building should reduce CO$_2$ emissions to almost zero;
- to provide at least the same area of green cover as its footprint, bearing in mind that this area can be measured vertically as well as horizontally; and

- as a work of art, to inspire a new relationship between the City and nature.

Considerations involved in achieving these objectives were discussed, and the list that was developed included considering the most efficient floor plans for human use, the cost efficiencies of perimeter walls and the structure for the distribution of air and light. The process of the workshop and these considerations evolved into a concept that is owned by all parties.

The team

To make this building a success, the City of Melbourne assembled experts from around Australia and beyond who have pooled their expertise in a collaborative process devised to re-think the way buildings operate. From its inception, the process of designing CH$_2$ has been a highly collaborative effort.

The design process began with the project team attending a two-week workshop, followed by weekly design meetings that ran for eight months. The principal consultants are the City of Melbourne

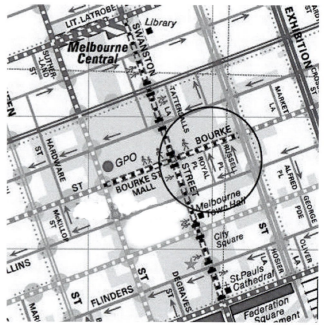

Tivoli site

240

(design and project management), DesignInc (architectural design and documentation), Lincolne Scott (services engineering), AEC (Advanced Environmental Concepts) as ESD consultant, the Bonacci Group (structural and civil engineering), Marshall Day (acoustics) and Donald Cant Watts Corke (quantity surveying).

In December, the City of Melbourne announced Hansen Yuncken as the company to build CH_2 in a contract valued at $51.045 million, not including fit-out. Work began in January 2004 and was due to be completed late in 2005.

Design process

From interviews with those working on the project, one clear theme emerges: the innovative approach to the design process that supported a multidisciplinary collaboration. All consultants appointed to the project to work on the design set aside a two-week period of time. Weekly design meetings that ran for eight months followed this. This project team included all consultants, artists, the CSIRO and the Sustainable Energy Authority of Victoria.

The design team's goal was to produce a building that led the way to ecological sustainability in office development, supported workplace cultural change, was economically responsible to the city and its ratepayers and could be used as a model for future development. The design process was distinguished by its interactive exchange of information and ideas between the consultant teams. Through this process, all parties involved were able to have a strong input into the design and to achieve professional 'ownership' not just of their particular discipline but also of the project as a whole.

The City's position on the charrette process that they put to the consultant group was a philosophy of 'let's put all our knowledge on the table now. Don't let me hear in November that there was a better way of doing it.' The charrette was facilitated and consisted of a series of presentations, discussions and working parties. 'The process was supported by a relatively simple but clear brief: the building needed to be greenhouse neutral, a lighthouse project to improve employee well-being, analogous to industry transfer.'[1]

In the first week there was team-building, developing the project goals and building attributes and establishing a process of logistics for team collaboration and communication. The whole team developed target outcomes and then objectives associated with each were developed in a standard format.

Two-week design charrette.

Through the process, most of the issues related to the concept design were both refined and resolved. For example, the building façade and use of natural lighting were refined to a square format, away from the 'Swiss cheese' design and atrium to the square building design with external stacks and windows increasing in size from top to bottom. This was facilitated by a discussion with a climatologist. Up until this point the main focus had been on how to get natural light into the building; he pointed out that for Melbourne the main issue was not this but was in fact cooling the building. This change in focus also catalysed the discussion on the use of thermal mass, passive cooling and innovative phase change and chiller technology.

During the workshop stage, detailed computer modelling was conducted to quantify and develop the system's broad outcomes. This was an extremely important part of the process as it allowed the building form to be developed to maximize natural light, thermal comfort and energy efficiency. For example, façade performance was tested and evaluated using both natural lighting modelling (Radiance) and thermal modelling (TAS). This led to the windows increasing in size at the bottom and becoming smaller at the top.

The modelling process meant that most of the problems were resolved and, more importantly, all the consultants had a concept of the design and its components in context. As the project manager, Robert Lewis, said: 'through this process we were not only able to lock down the design and discuss its innovative elements as a team, we were able to do so in record time and for less cost than the normal procedure'.

The best way to illustrate how the two-week design intensive facilitated the innovative leading-edge qualities of the building is to tell a story that is often repeated by all the participants. By being given the freedom to explore innovative ideas and propose solutions without recrimination, the consultants felt empowered to support the solution process. One such problem was the proposed innovative high-mass ceiling and flooring system. In a whirlwind of ideas, a concept of a wavy form with integrated ducting as a precast element was suggested. Being such an integral element of the building, this untried and innovative idea caused several problems. For example, the quantity surveyor could not give an accurate estimate of the cost, as this was a unique system. Questions had to be resolved, such as: 'Is it possible to precast a system of this nature and deal with all the associated issues with cost of transportation delivery, storage and actually lifting the systems?'

The structural engineers took on this challenge and contacted precast concrete manufacturers, and within the week had a solution and a budget for the project. This provided the confidence for the team to decide on this as the flooring/ceiling system.

Design outcomes

CH$_2$ has been designed to reflect the planet's ecology, which is an immensely complex system of interrelated components. It is impossible to assess the role of any part of this ecology without reference to the whole. Similarly, CH$_2$ will comprise many parts that work together to heat and cool the building as well as to provide power and water with minimal environmental impact.

For example, in nature dark colours absorb heat and hot air rises. Accordingly, the north façade will comprise ten dark-coloured air-extraction ducts that will absorb heat from the sun to help the stale air inside rise up and pass out of the building. Light colours reflect heat and cool air sinks, so the south façade will comprise light-coloured ducts that will draw in fresh air from the roof and distribute it down through the building. Staff will be able to control the flow of this 100 per cent fresh air to their individual workspaces by vents in the floor.

Recycled timber louvres will shade the west façade. Energy from photovoltaic panels on the roof will power the louvres, which will move according to the position of the sun.

About 100,000 litres of black (toilet) water a day will be extracted from the main sewer in Little Collins Street. A city's sewer usually contains 95 per cent water, which is a burden on the system and a waste of water. The sewage, along with any generated on site, will be put through a multi-water treatment plant that will filter out the water and send the solids back to the sewer.

The water recovered will supply all of CH$_2$'s water cooling, plant watering and toilet flushing needs. More water will be saved through recycling water from the fire safety sprinkler system and from rainwater collection on the roof.

Some of the water recycled from the sewer mining plant will be used in the vertical gardens that will run the full height of the northern façade. The plants will be grown from special planter boxes built into the balconies on every storey. The role of these boxes is to grow 3–4 metre vines up the façade of the building via stainless steel mesh stretching from the ground to the roof. As one vine trails out, the vine on the next level takes over.

The boxes are filled with fytogen flakes, a soil additive that looks like polystyrene flakes but acts like large water crystals, storing an enormous amount of water and air until the soil needs it. Within each planter box is a sub-irrigation system that functions not unlike a toilet cistern; when the crystals dry out and the water is used up, a float triggers the device to re-fill with water, which is stored in the planter box until required. The combination of this device and the crystals provides the ideal wet-and-dry cycle required for the plants to thrive, and the system works without any water wastage or any need for manual watering.

Much effort has been invested in ways to cool as well as warm the building. This is because human activity and electronic equipment give off vast amounts of heat, which means that if the building and its air conditioning system are designed to capture and use that heat, the major source of energy consumption in this climate is in cooling.

Additional passive strategies, such as the shower towers, phase change tanks and use of night purging of thermal mass, are discussed in the next section.

Applying Green Star to the CH$_2$

This section describes how the building addresses the issues in Green Star. In applying the rating to this project several things need to be noted.

1 This rating is a design rating.
2 A second rating will be carried out on the fit-out.
3 A third rating will be carried out on completion of the building.

An accredited professional was employed at the start of the project as an integral member of the design team; this professional was responsible for managing and evaluating the environmental outcomes for the project and also the Green Star process, including the initial rating of the building. It should be noted that Green Star did not exist at the beginning of the project; it was launched on 31 July 2003, when the project was already in the design development and documentation stages. Ideally one would introduce Green Star at the concept design stage.

Overview of Green Star

The Australian Green Building Council (GBC), combining the best of the US LEED and UK BREEAM approaches, has developed the Green Star programme. It aims to give industry a language with which to integrate ecological sustainable development into the built environment. CH_2 has in many ways helped to test this new rating scheme, feeding directly into the GBC review of the scheme; from observation of the design and construction teams at work, it is clear that the rating scheme has achieved its aim. The clients and other team members now have a clear mutually understood way to communicate with the quantity surveyors, the builders, the other project members and external stakeholders. The text below briefly describes how CH_2 achieved its six-star rating.

The scheme has categories for various areas of the process and the building; these are listed below and expanded upon over the remainder of the case study:

1 building input
2 management
3 indoor environmental quality (IEQ)
4 energy
5 transport
6 water
7 materials
8 land use and ecology
9 emissions
10 innovation.

It is relevant to go through the rating process and explain how it was achieved, but the most interesting stories concern how the process was managed. Every point in the rating scheme was verified and the documentation required was filed to show the validity of each of the claims. Responsibility for the provision of documentation was explicitly passed on to the consultants working on the project from the beginning. As in all aspects of the project, everyone was well informed and encouraged to provide as much input as possible to make this a leading-edge project.

A lesson learned from this process was that it would have been helpful for the consultants to have, from the beginning of the project, an outline of the elements so that their involvement could be matched with the requirements of the rating system. As the rating system supports improved 'green' performance, an additional advantage was found to be that the availability of this information before design and planning encouraged the integration of green practices from the beginning. This created motivation and innovation, and contributed to the development of a world-leading green building. The Green Star information also helped the consultants create the required documentation as the project progressed.

Building input

This entry applies to standard information on the building: what its main construction is, who designed and built it, managed it, designed the services, and so on. It is fairly straightforward, with sections to describe the building type and services. It is important that the person entering the data has access to information on all those areas, and to all personnel involved in the project, in order to complete this section.

Management

The management section of the rating focuses on making sure the systems are in place to give the building the maximum chance of performing as designed, and continuing to perform at that level or better. For this reason there is an emphasis on commissioning and management systems. This highlights the importance of using this as a pre-design assessment and verification tool, as well as for use post occupancy.

GREEN STAR ACCREDITED PROFESSIONAL

The first mechanism Green Star uses for optimizing the chance of success of the building is giving points for the employment of an accredited Green Star Professional throughout the project. The role of the Green Star Professional is to manage and coordinate the environmental agenda on the project and to ensure that the most appropriate environmental outcome is achieved. The Green Star Professional is also responsible for managing the Green Star process and the coordination of inputs from the client and the design team.

COMMISSIONING CLAUSES, BUILDING TUNING AND AGENT

The next questions explore the extent of planning for commissioning. This is vital since good commissioning ensures that the building is fine-tuned for the first period of operation.

CH$_2$ has not only included commissioning clauses as part of the relevant contracts but it is also employing a separate firm to audit the commissioning process, to ensure that all the requirements are met.

The importance of adequate commissioning has been recognized by the client and the design team; including relevant commissioning clauses in the tender documents and appropriate specifications has reflected this. Project programmes issued with the tender documents allowed for a sufficient time period prior to practical completion for a dedicated commissioning and building tuning phase.

COMMISSIONING – BUILDING TUNING

Melbourne City Council has committed to a 12-month building tuning period, during which all building services and passive systems are monitored and fine-tuned. The tender documents ensured that the contractor is also involved in this process.

COMMISSIONING – COMMISSIONING AGENT

Melbourne City Council has committed to employ an independent commissioning agent to manage the commissioning process and to ensure that the building and its services are commissioned to the client's satisfaction. A brief was produced by AEC to detail the role of the commissioning agent, and tenders were sought for suitably qualified and experienced agents.

BUILDING USERS' GUIDE

A building users' guide will be produced, which will include relevant information for the building users, occupants and tenants. As required by Green Star, the guide will address the following aspects:

- energy and environmental strategy;
- monitoring and targeting;
- building services overview;
- transport facilities;
- materials and waste policy; and
- expansion, tenancy and refurbishment requirements.

Although Melbourne City Council has committed to produce the guide, it will be produced while the building is under construction.

ENVIRONMENTAL MANAGEMENT

The tender documents ensure that the contractor provides and implements a comprehensive environmental management plan (EMP) in accordance with section 4 of the *NSW Environmental Management System Guidelines* (1998). As part of each tender return, contractors were also required to submit a draft of their environmental management plan (EMP). Further, the tender documents required the contractor to have ISO 14001 accreditation. In order to comply with this requirement, the contractor obtained certification prior to commencing the project.

WASTE MANAGEMENT

The contract documents require the contractor to reuse or recycle 80 per cent of construction waste during the construction process, and to record and demonstrate that this is achieved on a quarterly basis. During the tender period each contractor was to confirm that this requirement was to be achieved.

Indoor environment quality

Next in the Green Star rating is a set of questions on indoor environment quality. These are questions aimed at ensuring that the building's users, and those constructing it, receive a minimal impact from materials and benefit from all the advantages of sensitive design.

Top. Daylighting simulation studies. (Source: AEC) **Top right**. Initial plan form of concepts to maximize daylighting. **Bottom right**. Precast concrete ceiling creates the vaulted roof.

VENTILATION RATES

Up to three points are awarded for providing outside air rates greater than the minimum requirements of Australian Standard AS1668.2–2002. For an office building this is 7.5 litres/second/person. Following the large amount of research on the improvement in health and productivity obtained by increasing outside air rates in the workplace, the need to increase outside air provision has always been a high priority for CH_2. However, it is important that any increase in the outside air rate is balanced against the increase in energy consumption associated with the heating and cooling of this air.

The final design of the air conditioning and ventilation system for CH_2 ensures that 22.5 litres/second/person is delivered to the building occupants. This level of outside air provides the benefits associated with an increased outside air provision without too great an increase in the building's energy consumption.

AIR CHANGE EFFECTIVENESS

The ventilation system for CH_2 is a displacement ventilation system that delivers air into the office space via a raised floor void and evenly spaced floor grilles. Such a system typically has an air change effectiveness (ACE) of about 1.2 when measured in accordance with ASHRAE F25–1997. Green Star awards two credits where the ACE is greater than 0.95.

CARBON DIOXIDE MONITORING AND MANAGEMENT

The ventilation systems designed for CH_2 deliver outside air into the space without mixing or recirculating air at the central air handling plant. In addition, carbon monoxide (CO) monitoring and control is provided to each of the office spaces. CO sensors monitor the level of CO within each of the occupied zones and adjust the amount of air entering the space accordingly.

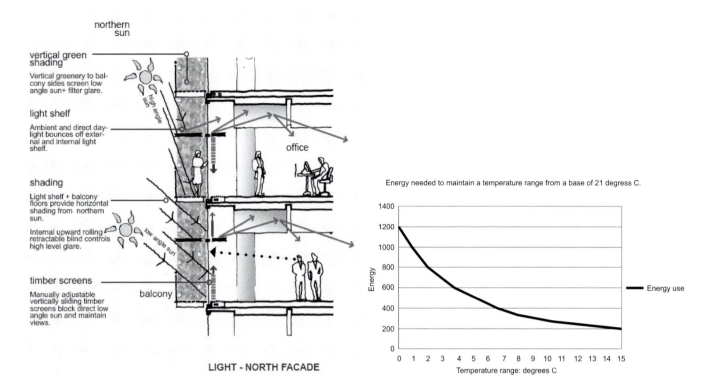

vertical green shading
Vertical greenery to balcony sides screen low angle sun+ filter glare.

light shelf
Ambient and direct daylight bounces off external and internal light shelf.

shading
Light shelf + balcony floors provide horizontal shading from northern sun.

Internal upward rolling retractable blind controls high level glare.

timber screens
Manually adjustable vertically sliding timber screens block direct low angle sun and maintain views.

office

balcony

LIGHT - NORTH FACADE

Energy needed to maintain a temperature range from a base of 21 degress C.

Energy use

Energy

Temperature range: degrees C

Left. Section through the proposed building envelope to show use of daylight.
Right. Studies of energy use by widening the temperature parameters.

DAYLIGHTING

Because of the constrained nature of the site and the commercial requirement for a deep plan office space, the provision of adequate daylighting has always been a challenge for CH_2. However, daylight design and analysis has driven much of the decision-making with regard to building form and façade systems, from day one.

During the initial two-week workshop process, daylight modelling using radiance software was conducted to assess the most appropriate form of the building. As the design developed, further analysis was undertaken to look at the design of the façade and technologies to enhance the provision of daylighting into the building. This modelling influenced the design of the façade in providing larger windows at the lower levels and smaller windows at the upper levels, and the provision of light shelves on the northern façade. However, because of the physical constraints of the building, no more than 25 per cent of the building floor area has a daylight factor greater than 2 per cent, as measured at the working plane under a standard overcast design sky.

Initial concepts considered buildings with staggered walls and atria. Lower floors generally receive less daylight than upper floors, so windows on the north and south façades will be larger on the lower floors than on the upper ones. This allows the total amount of glass to be minimized, thus reducing energy loss while maintaining desirable natural light levels. Sensors will monitor the amount of daylight coming in and adjust the artificial light required accordingly.

Light shelves on the north façade will reflect sunlight onto ceilings and produce a soft indirect light, reducing artificial lighting requirements. The light shelves are internal and external and made of perforated steel. Sensors will increase and decrease the artificial lighting according to the amount of sunlight being reflected into the building; thus a balance of natural and artificial light will be achieved.

DAYLIGHT GLARE CONTROL

Although external shading is provided to the north and west façades and internal adjustable glare screens are provided to all façades, no credits are available under the Green Star scheme, since Green Star specifically requires the glare control devices to be external only. Shading to control sun and glare will be used on the north, east and west façades. The north façade uses vertical gardens for shading, the east uses perforated metal, and the west uses recycled timber louvres that move with the sun.

The north-facing façade will comprise steel trellises and balconies supporting a series of vertical gardens nine storeys high. The foliage will help protect the building from the sun and filter sunlight to reduce glare indoors. The entire west façade of CH_2 is protected by a system of timber louvres that pivot with the sun to be fully open in the morning and closed against the full sun in the afternoon. The louvres will be made from recycled timber and will be controlled by a hydraulic system that moves the panels through a six-hour open and close cycle.

HIGH-FREQUENCY BALLASTS

T5 lighting incorporating high-frequency ballasts will be provided to all office areas. The T5 fittings are linked to sensors that will reduce the light when sufficient daylight is available. This will be supplemented with individually controlled task lamps at workstations, to give occupants more control over their environment. Thus the level of lighting on a floor or in an area will reflect the level of activity.

ELECTRIC LIGHTING LEVELS

Artificial lighting systems are designed as a two-component lighting system, with a background lighting system provided as part of the base building design, and a separate task lighting component provided as part of the fit-out works. The background component provides an average of 150 lux to the office space, and the task lighting component provides 320 lux on each desk. No illuminance greater than 400 lux will be provided anywhere on the office floor.

EXTERNAL VIEWS

Because of the constraints of the site and the commercial need to build a deep plan office space, approximately 75 per cent of the office floor plate will be less than 8 metres from a façade, to have access to external views. This will achieve one credit out of two available under the Green Star scheme.

INDIVIDUAL THERMAL CONTROL

Each of the floor grilles can be relocated on the raised floor to be adjacent to each desk and each of the occupants. In addition, each floor grille is constructed so that the occupants can adjust it. This initiative achieves the credit available under the Green Star scheme. Although not recognized by Green Star, a further initiative provided is to allow each user to control their lighting environment through the provision of task lighting at each desk.

THERMAL MODELLING

Thermal modelling using TAS software has been used extensively throughout the design of CH_2 to influence decision-making on those aspects that affect thermal comfort. In addition, computational fluid dynamic modelling (CFD), using Phoenics discrete element software, was used to quantify and optimize their performance.

Through the use of TAS and the international thermal comfort standard ISO 7730, all building and services elements that affect thermal comfort have been designed to achieve a predicted mean vote (PMV) level between –0.5 and 0.5. This was achieved by addressing all of the factors that affect thermal comfort, such as radiation, convection and conduction. This has been further validated by detailed calculation.

COOLING WITH SHOWER TOWERS AND PHASE CHANGE MATERIAL

Outside air is drawn in from 17 metres or more above street level and channelled into the shower towers on the south side of CH_2. The towers are made from tubes of lightweight fabric 1.4 metres in diameter. As the air falls within the shower tower it is cooled by evaporation from the shower of water. The cool air is supplied to the retail spaces and the cool water is supplied to the phase change material, which acts as a heat sink.

CH_2's phase change material (PCM) tank comprises a series of tanks filled with 20 mm stainless steel balls containing the PCM. Phase change refers to the process of a material changing from a liquid to a solid or vice versa. Water is a PCM that freezes at 0°C. The PCM in the CH_2 system will freeze at 15°C. Water cooled by the shower towers will travel through the tank and freeze the PCM. A separate stream of water will pass through the tank to be chilled, travel through the chilled ceiling panels and chilled beams to cool the building, then run back into the tank to begin again. During short periods in summer the system may have insufficient capacity and will be supplemented by a chiller.

COOLING WITH CHILLED CEILINGS

Cool water running through chilled panels fixed to the ceiling – and chilled beams in front of the windows – creates gentle radiant cooling that descends into the workspace at around 18°C. This replaces traditional variable air volume (VAV) systems that use fans to blow 13°C air directly at occupants.

COOLING WITH NATURAL VENTILATION (NIGHT PURGE) AND THERMAL MASS (SEE ABOVE)

Natural ventilation cools the building late at night. Windows on the north and south façades will open to allow fresh cool air to enter the offices, flush out warm air and cool the building. This

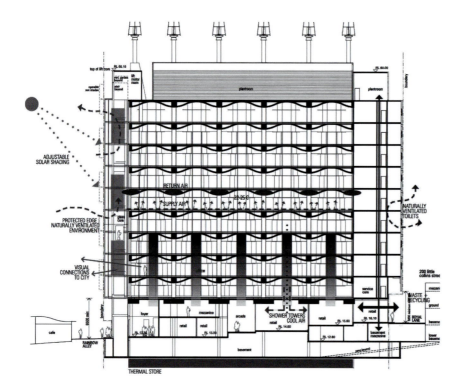

bioclimatic section east west

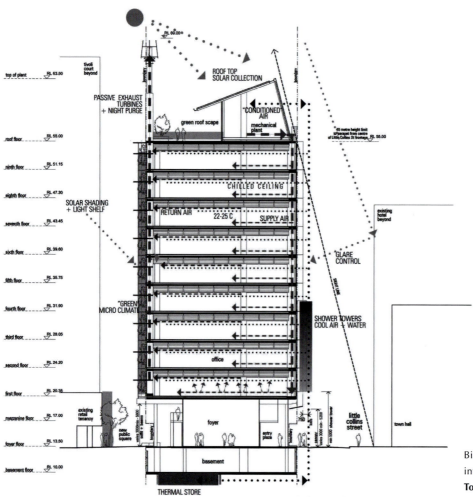

bioclimatic section north south

Bioclimatic strategies involve the integration of active and passive systems. **Top**: Section east–west. **Left**. Section north–south.

process is referred to as night purging. Sensors will close the windows when they detect high winds and rain or higher temperatures. Outside air that enters the building during the night, cools the 180 mm-thick precast concrete ceilings, which then act as heat sinks during the day. The high diurnal range of temperature at certain times of the year in Melbourne makes this an attractive passive strategy.

HEATING

Convection heaters are set into the floor near the windows. Warm air rises from the heaters, creating a barrier of warmth around the external walls to prevent the cold air coming in. Heat rises into the space naturally, using buoyancy rather than fans.

INTERNAL NOISE LEVELS

Acoustic consultants were employed to ensure that the internal noise levels are within suitable limits for an office space. This has been achieved through the installation of acoustic insulation above the perforated chilled ceiling panel. In addition, the acoustic consultants have ensured that the noise generated from the building services systems are within suitable limits. These limits have been validated through detailed calculations.

INDOOR AIR POLLUTANTS

The detailed selection and specification of internal materials and finishes has ensured that indoor air pollutants are kept to minimum. In addition, to prevent mould growth the ventilation and air conditioning systems ensure that relative humidity is no more than 60 per cent in the office space and no more than 80 per cent within the ductwork and distribution system.

The materials credits claimed are claimed for low VOC paints, low VOC carpets, and low VOC adhesives and sealants; all composite wood products have low formaldehyde emissions.

Energy

Through many of the design elements described above, it is aimed to reduce energy consumption of the CH_2 building to a minimum and to achieve zero greenhouse gas emissions from energy use.

ENERGY

It is a conditional requirement of Green Star that the building achieves four stars under the ABGR greenhouse gas rating scheme. This has been demonstrated through the use of detailed energy modelling conducted in accordance with the ABGR validation protocol.

ENERGY IMPROVEMENT

Further credits are available for improvement to a five-star ABGR greenhouse gas rating. It has been predicted that the building will achieve a five-star rating plus a 40 per cent reduction in CO_2 emissions. This low level of greenhouse gas emissions has been achieved by a combination of the following elements:

- selection of low-energy plant and equipment;
- selection of efficient lighting;
- effective shading and façade systems;
- natural night purge ventilation and exposed thermal mass;
- free cooling via phase change material thermal storage; and
- co-generation via gas micro-turbines and absorption chillers.

ELECTRICAL SUB-METERING

Sub-metering has been provided for all substantive energy uses greater than 100 kVA and for the computer rooms. All metering is logged and recorded by the building automation system (BAS).

TENANCY SUB-METERING

Sub-metering is provided to the lighting and power for each floor. This is logged and recorded by the BAS.

OFFICE LIGHTING POWER DENSITY

The lighting design utilizes low-energy T5 luminaires, which achieve a lighting power density of less than 2.5 W/m^2 per 100 lux.

OFFICE LIGHTING ZONING

The lighting system has been designed to provide a number of separately switched zones for each office floor. The design of the lighting system is fully addressable, which means that each luminaire can be separately programmed to adjust zoning requirements to suit the future fit-out requirements. As a minimum the office floor is zoned so that each lighting zone is no greater than 100 m².

PEAK ENERGY DEMAND REDUCTION

Peak energy demand reduction has been achieved by the micro-turbine co-generation system and the use of phase change material for thermal storage.

Transport

Next in the rating system is a series of credit points earned if the building facilitates the use of public transport and reduction in use of and dependence on cars.

REDUCTION IN CAR PARKING SPACES

Twenty-one car parking spaces have been provided to the basement car park area. This is over 50 per cent fewer than the local planning allowances.

SMALL CAR SPACES

This has not been claimed, but one point can be awarded for the provision of 25 per cent or more of the car parks to small cars only. This encourages only those with small cars to drive into the car park, and hopefully encourages those with larger cars to think about buying smaller cars in the future.

CYCLIST FACILITIES

Cyclist facilities, including secure bicycle spaces, lockers, showers and changing facilities, have been provided for 10 per cent of building staff. An additional point has not been awarded for visitor bicycle parking near the front entrance, as this was not part of the pilot Green Star scheme.

PUBLIC TRANSPORT

The city centre location means that there are numerous tram and train services in the vicinity of the building. Maximum credits are achieved using the Green Star transport calculator.

Water

CH_2 estimates that it can halve its consumption of water from the public water main. It treats black water and grey water on site via a multi-water treatment plant (providing 72 per cent of non-potable water). It collects rainwater, reuses water from the sprinkler system (providing 25 per cent of potable water) and uses AAA-rated water saving fittings.

OCCUPANT AMENITY AND POTABLE WATER EFFICIENCY

The Green Star system requires information be entered into a potable water calculator. This determines which toilets will be used for water purposes – i.e. how many times the waterless urinal will be used or the half flush (3-litre) or full flush (6-litre) cisterns on the toilets, the showers, taps, etc. This resulted in a calculated figure of 8 litres used per person per day.

The calculator then requests information on any rainwater collection and waste treatment on site, and to which level this water is treated. Two systems are used: one avoids waste and the other recycles wastewater.

The figures on page 218 show the two systems. The first collects the potable water that is usually wasted in Australia when fire system testing is done; for an average ten-storey office building this is 10,000 litres per week. This water will not be treated and will be used in conjunction with mains water for potable, drinkable use. The second system involves sewer mining of a neighbouring pipeline. This water will be filtered and treated to class A standard, not recommended for drinking (though sev-

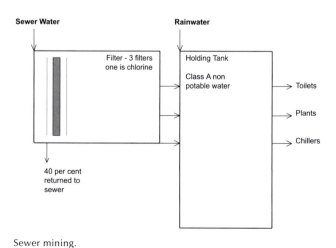

Sewer mining.

eral of the design team are rumoured to have done so from the Flemington prototype plant). This water will be reinvigorated with the addition of rainwater collected from the roof of the building.

WATER METERS

Linked to the building management system, water meters will be installed for all major water uses in the building including the cooling systems, hot water systems, irrigation and other services.

LANDSCAPE IRRIGATION WATER EFFICIENCY

For watering the plants on the façade and the roof garden, 100 per cent of the water will be sourced from the sewer-mined water enriched with rainwater. The landscape strategy is an interesting story: one of the innovative concepts that CH_2 represents is the provision of the same number of leaves on the building as would have been present on the site if it had been a green field with bush on it. This is depicted in the iconic image of the building shown at the beginning of this case study (see page 239). The roof gardens, together with the planter boxes on the northern façade, meet this aim and provide a lovely microclimate for various building spaces.

The northern green façade is made up of planter boxes situated to the east and west of each northern balcony. The interesting challenge for these planter boxes was how to get water to the plants. The landscape architect involved in the project developed innovative solutions in collaboration with the architects and hydraulic and structural engineers.

COOLING TOWERS

Water from the sewer mining plant has been approved for use in the cooling towers. As such, four points are available under Green Star for the use of non-potable water by the cooling towers.

Materials

An environmentally preferable material is a commercially available product that has a relatively low environmental impact throughout its life cycle. The CSIRO, with the cooperation of DesignInc, the architects for CH_2, has conducted a comprehensive audit of all materials to be used in the construction and operation of the building. The audit covers all aspects of the manufacture and transportation of materials in relation to their effect on the environment and the occupants of the building. Each material is evaluated and rated according to the following criteria.

EMBODIED ENERGY

This is the non-renewable energy used by a material from cradle to cradle, i.e. by the collection of its raw material, its manufacture, transportation, maintenance and, ultimately, recycling. The less embodied energy used, the better the rating.

EMBODIED WATER

This is the water used in all the activities associated with the production and delivery of a material. The less embodied water used, the better the rating.

WASTE AND RECYCLING

Producing no waste is the preferred option; recycling and reuse of materials are the next preference; treatment to reduce the volume and toxicity of the waste is the next.

AIR, LAND AND WATER EMISSIONS

Producing no waste and by-products is the ideal; minimizing and disposing of waste properly is the next preferred option. Emissions to air, land and water are all considered, and the worst performer determines the rating. Many products emit toxic gases for months or years after construction and significantly reduce indoor air quality. The relationship between gases from volatile organic compounds and reduction in employee health and productivity has been clearly established.

OTHER ENVIRONMENTAL IMPACTS

A further aspect investigated was the presence of other environmental impacts associated with maintenance, recycling and reuse. Criteria for selecting products were developed, based on evaluation of their impact on ozone depletion, emission of greenhouse gases and effect on biodiversity.

The service life criterion (without maintenance) evaluates the expected lifetime of a product without maintenance, and rates it in relation to a standard expectation of that type of product. The maintenance criterion evaluates the maintenance activities required to ensure a product can perform its specified tasks until the end of its service life.

RECYCLING WASTE STORAGE

Recycling facilities have been provided on each floor and within the basement. Each storage area has been sized to accommodate the storage of paper, glass, plastics, metals and organic waste.

SHELL AND CORE OR INTEGRATED FIT-OUT

An integrated fit-out ensures that maximum points are achieved for this credit.

RECYCLED CONTENT OF STRUCTURAL CONCRETE

This score needs verification, and thus at this time has not been allocated any points. Interviews with the project participants revealed that all efforts were made to maximize the use of recycled content in the structural concrete elements. The concrete being mainly pre-cast, the challenge was to work with the suppliers to achieve the aim of 30 per cent recycled aggregate and 30 per cent replacement of cement with industrial waste such as fly ash and slag.

On interviewing the structural engineers, the comment was made that such a target was useful but they needed to work with manufacturers to ensure the other requirements such as appearance and strength were met. Their comment was that they would achieve the overall target, but that some elements would have more recycled content while others would have less, depending on their functional requirements.

RECYCLED CONTENT OF STRUCTURAL STEEL

Another interesting story was that in trying to meet this target the team had to go outside Australia to source steel with a guaranteed recycled content of 60 per cent. Manufacturers in Australia have recycled content but could not give the guarantee needed to achieve the rating. The steel is now being sourced from Thailand.

PVC MINIMIZATION

All effort has been made to minimize PVC. This has been achieved for all hydraulics and for the electrical component, though the latter is proving to be expensive because of the volume that needs to be ordered. It is not a mainstream product in Australia.

SUSTAINABLE TIMBER SELECTION

It is aimed to source over 90 per cent of the timber used on the project from recycled or certified sources. The main issue that confronted the design team when trying to achieve this rating was the transparency and validity of the certification processes. Some certification schemes, because of their recent introduction to the market, are not being as well received or supported by stakeholders as others.

Land use and ecology

This section of the ratings system looks at the impacts on the ecology in terms of land use – what the land was used for previously, and whether improvements and regeneration are planned for in the development.

ECOLOGICAL/SOCIAL VALUE OF THE SITE

It is a conditional requirement that the site is not on land of high ecological/social value.

REUSE OF LAND

The building is being built on an existing car park.

RECLAIMED CONTAMINATED LAND

The land is not contaminated, therefore the two credits available for cleaning up the land could not be awarded.

CHANGE OF ECOLOGICAL VALUE

The change of use has been from an impermeable concreted surface to a building incorporating both horizontal and vertical gardens. Credit points are awarded for the garden areas.

TOPSOIL AND FILL REMOVAL FROM THE SITE

Because of the constrained nature of the site, this credit cannot be achieved.

Emissions

There are nine emissions sub-categories with a total of 13 credits.

REFRIGERANT OZONE DEPLETION POTENTIAL

All refrigerants have been selected with an ozone depletion potential of zero.

REFRIGERANT GLOBAL WARMING POTENTIAL

Because of the lack of products available that can utilize refrigerants with a GWP below ten, this credit cannot be achieved.

REFRIGERANT LEAK DETECTION

Because of the requirement to ventilate the chiller plant room, this credit cannot be achieved.

REFRIGERANT RECOVERY

This has not been specified.

WATERCOURSE POLLUTION

All rain- and stormwater falling on the site is collected and reused for non-potable water purposes.

REDUCED FLOW TO SEWER

Using the calculator, maximum points are achieved for this credit as a result of the use of efficient fittings and the black water treatment plant.

LIGHT POLLUTION

All lighting has been designed so that no beam of light is directed beyond the site boundaries or upwards without falling directly on the surface that it is illuminating.

COOLING TOWERS

Cooling towers are important to the building services systems achieving such a low energy consumption, so no credits are available for this.

INSULANT OZONE DEPLETING POTENTIAL

All thermal insulants specified avoid the use of ozone-depleting substances in their manufacture or composition.

Innovation

Because of the innovative nature of the building and its services, maximum credits are claimed under this category. Some innovative aspects are that it is the pioneer of the application of chilled ceiling technology in Victoria and Australia; of sewer mining technology and multi-water reuse technology in an Australian building; of cooling via phase change storage batteries in the world; and of the use of shower tower technology for cooling of air and water.

Evaluation and result

A pre-assessment rating was carried out on the project, in conjunction with the Green Building Council of Australia, through the Green Star Professional, who was trained through GBCA. The results are shown in the table overleaf.

Although this does not constitute certification under the GBCA system, it indicates that the building could receive a high score under the rating scheme. This could be equivalent to the 'international best practice' level. It should be recognized that if the developers wish to use this label on their building they will have to follow the GBCA certification process.

Lessons learned

While it is commendable that CH2 achieved the six stars that define it as being a world leader in sustainable building design, some interesting repercussions could be observed because of the focus on getting the rating. For example, at one of the design meetings water issues were discussed, and new options were put forward to save additional water. One of the team commented: 'But we already have all the points in that category.' There was agreement around the table, and the decision was made not to look into that area.

This is a very interesting story to dwell on. The Green Star is a highly needed tool, which the building and construction industry can use to communicate their level of green commitment. It is an auditable quantitative tool, which as much as possible looks to verify any claims made by a building. Yet in being so prescriptive, opportunities outside of the scope of the Green Star could be missed. The innovation section of the star rating does provide some scope for addressing this issue, yet in a building achieving all its innovation points there was no further scope for the inclusion of anything else over and above that, in some areas.

Pre-assessment of CH_2 during the design process

Category	Credits available	Credits achieved	Category	Credits available	Credits achieved
Management			*Energy*		
Green Star Accredited Professional	2	2	Energy (ABGR rating 4 or more)	✓	yes
Commissioning – clauses	2	2	Energy improvement	15	9
Commissioning – building tuning	1	1	Electrical sub-metering	1	1
Commissioning – commissioning agent	1	1	Tenancy sub-metering	1	1
Building users guide	1	1	Office lighting power density	4	2
Environmental management	3	3	Office lighting zoning	1	1
Waste management	2	2	Peak energy demand reduction	2	2
Total	12	12	Total	24	16
Water			*Indoor environment quality*		
Occupant amenity potable water efficiency	5	5	Ventilation rates	3	2
Water meter	2	2	Air change effectiveness	2	2
Landscape irrigation water efficiency	1	1	Carbon dioxide monitoring and control	1	1
Cooling tower water consumption	4	4	Daylighting	3	0
Total	12	12	Daylight glare control	1	0
Land use and ecology			High-frequency ballasts	1	1
Ecological/social value of site (conditional)	✓	yes	Electric lighting levels	1	1
Reuse of land	1	1	External views	2	1
Reclaimed contaminated land	2	0	Individual thermal comfort control	2	2
Change of ecological value	4	1	Asbestos	0	na
Topsoil and fill removal from site	1	0	Thermal modelling	2	2
Total	8	2	Internal noise levels	2	2
Emissions			Indoor air pollutants	6	5
Refrigerant ODP	2	2	Total	26	19
Refrigerant GWP	1	0	*Materials*	2	2
Refrigerant leak detection	1	0	Recycling waste storage	2	2
Refrigerant recovery	1	0	Reuse of façade	0	na
Watercourse pollution	1	1	Reuse of structure	0	na
Reduced flow to sewer	4	4	Shell and core or integrated fit-out	3	3
Light pollution	1	1	Recycled content of structural concrete	3	1
Cooling towers	1	0	Recycled content of structural steel	2	0
Insulant ODP	1	0	PVC minimisation	2	2
Total	13	8	Sustainable timber	2	2
Transport			Total	14	10
Provision of car parking	2	0	*Innovation*		
Small parking spaces	1	1	Innovation	5	5
Cyclist facilities	3	3			
Commuting public transport	5	5			
Total	11	9	**Total credits**	**120**	**88**

Notwithstanding this small criticism of an otherwise impressive initiative, observing the implementation of the CH_2 design highlighted how useful the Green Star tool is to the design team. In particular, the Green Star tool provides tangible measures for creating a green building by setting specific targets. This assists the design team in its management of the project, in parallel with cost control

The strengths of the process are that the design team were aware of the six stars target and understood the role certain decisions had in the 'greenness' of the project. The performance basis to the process allows the discussion of various options: 'well, this will give us extra points, and at this stage of the process we should have some extra points up our sleeve in case anything falls off'; 'we are aiming to get the 20 per cent recycled content in the concrete – some elements because of their properties cannot have 20 per cent but others can have more so we should just aim to get an across-the-board 20 per cent'; 'we need the lighting to achieve x w/m^2 to get our star rating'.

Again, to link back to the first point, what this can take away is the understanding of why things are designed or planned the way they are. Getting the six-star rating becomes more important than remembering that the natural ventilation and light has been designed primarily to provide extra comfort to the occupants, and that recycled content in the concrete is specified to reduce the impact of that concrete on the environment. Most of the project team were part of the initial workshops, which discussed all the reasons why various decisions were made and why they are more sustainable. The difficulties occur when new people join the team who have not gone through the whole design process. The star rating then can become just an accounting tool, rather than a reflection of the building's green design.

Acknowledgements

We would like to thank and acknowledge all those in the CH_2 team who worked on this project and had input into reviewing this case study. Also sincere thanks to DesignInc and Melbourne City Council for the use of many of the images in this report.

For further information on this project, you can visit the project website at http://www.melbourne.vic.gov.au. Mark Cummins from Advanced Environmental Concepts (AEC) has been working with the design team since the initial workshops and will maintain an involvement through construction and into post occupation. His role has been as the Green Star Professional.

CASE STUDY 8

The Philip Merrill Environmental Center, Annapolis, Maryland, USA

Architects: Greg Mella, Smith Group

The Merrill Center is a wonderful example of the importance of client/architect working together to establish environmental goals before the design phases of a project begin. This early visioning allows the architect's design to be shaped by those goals rather than retrofitting sustainable strategies into a pre-defined form. The Merrill Center's initial goal-setting was primarily based on the LEED rating system created by the US Green Building Council. At the time, LEED was in its infancy and the client and team were happy to embrace this programme as a benchmarking tool.

Introduction

The Philip Merrill Center accommodates the headquarters of the Chesapeake Bay Foundation, which is an organization dedicated to ecological preservation and restoration of the Bay and its environs. The Chesapeake Bay Foundation (CBF) is a 35-year-old organization, whose aims include resource restoration as well as environmental protection, advocacy and education. CBF works to reduce pollution, restore habitat, and replenish fish stocks in North America's largest estuary.

The estuary is a seriously threatened ecosystem. CBF research has estimated losses to the ecosystem of approximately 98 per cent of its oysters, 90 per cent of its underwater grasses, 60 per cent of its wetlands, and 50 per cent of its forests. CBF has turned the 31 acres of shoreline into a restoration project focused around the Philip Merrill Center.

The building is used as a facility to connect CBF with the Bay in both a functional and a visual sense, yet at the same time minimize its environmental impact. Sustainability is an intrinsic value of this organization and hence it creates the simple logic of extending the vision of sustainability for the Bay to the design of this new building. The vision fuses logic of purpose and ideology to the building's fabric and seems to have created an underlying ethos in the design team and its working activities.

The Philip Merrill Environmental Center. Architect: Smith Group, Inc., 2000. The front entrance is on the first floor, with car parking and service entry below.

The Philip Merrill Center is home to the Chesapeake Bay Foundation (CBF). Headquarters is dedicated to ecological preservation and restoration of the Bay.

Chesapeake Bay Foundation project details

Characteristics	Details
Owner	Chesapeake Bay Foundation
Project team	Architect: SmithGroup, Inc.
	Engineer: SmithGroup, Inc.
	Project Manager: Synthesis, Inc.
	Contractor: Clark Construction Group
	Consultant: Janet Harrison, Architect
Completion date:	November 2000
Cost	$US6.36 million
Size	30,600 gross square feet
Footprint	12,000 square feet
Construction type	3B, two storeys over open parking
Use group	Business(B), assembly (A-3), storage (S-2)
Annual energy use	23 kBtu/sf/year
Lot size	33 acres
City	Annapolis
Country	United States of America
Latitude	Approximately 39°0′ N
Building type	Interpretation
Occupancy	90 staff

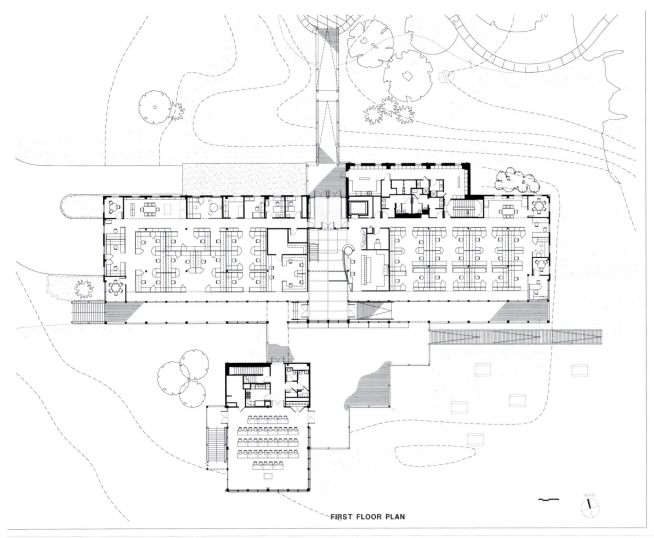

FIRST FLOOR PLAN

First floor plan.

LEED was instrumental in conveying the importance of the sustainable elements of the design to the client. This case study initially examines the relationship between the pre-design stage and characteristics of the design. It describes the environmental strategies used and the benchmarks achieved thorough the LEED and GBC assessment and evaluation.

Pre-design and briefing

This section charts the pre-design activities that helped to capture sustainable goals and objectives in the project. Two important decisions were made by the architects at the outset.

Project organization
An important part of the organization of this project related to the skills and activities used pre-design.

First the project architect had particular skills in sustainable design and was able to become involved with goal-setting of the project. Second, this led to several 'green charrettes' – long meetings with representatives from the owner, design team and user, where appropriate environmental goals for the project were established at the outset. The form of the building was developed by the team, which also identified the sustainable strategies that would be a goal for the new design, such as rainwater collection and natural ventilation. Also, in the pre-design phase the team analysed the site for micro-climate characteristics, habitat survey and terrain analysis.

First Floor Plan
As a result, the design that followed in the schematic design phase was responsive to the site's views, climate, prevalent breezes, habitats and so forth; and its design facilitated incorporation of the sustainable strategies identified for the project. It should be noted that full team involvement (client, architect, ecologist and all engineers) was critical during this stage.

257

Application of LEED and GBC

The LEED system was used as a starting point for design and the design team then expanded from there. The tool (see section 2) is a scorecard system, which identifies a number of environmental criteria and gives credits where these are met. This creates the design standard, which can be applied across building types with some modifications. There is a sliding scale of performance that allows projects to be rated from best practice to baseline. To help designers build a methodology within the design process, the tool has other features:

- a checklist that describes the criteria;
- description of the strategies and technologies that can be used to meet the criteria; and

- a certification process whereby LEED assessors validate the work of the design team.

Generally the project team favoured using the tool at the programming step, which allows the data from LEED to be integrated into the building programme. LEED was used as a checklist and then used as a pre-rating advisor. This gave an indication of the likely rating for the building. Indeed, this provides a performance-base design process where clear goals and levels of sustainability can be defined, strategies discussed and costed, and techniques selected.

The project was one of 12 LEED pilot projects that aimed at trialling the tool in practice. Mella explains that the tool favours ease of use above the accuracy of its environmental model. As

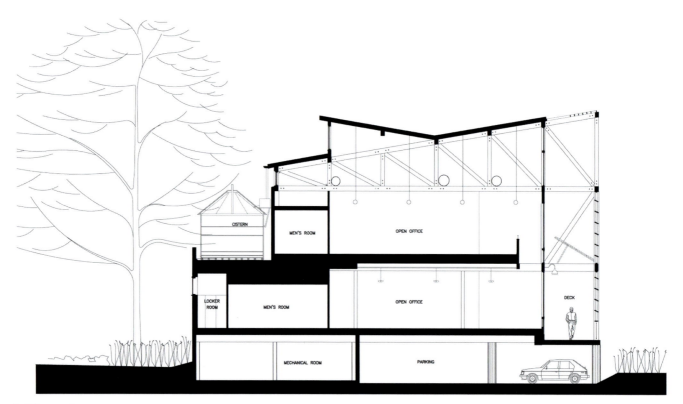

Building section.

Left. South façade showing the shading system and expressed rapidly renewable materials comprising engineered timber that forms the frame of the building. **Right**. Operable windows to provide natural ventilation. Mella argues that this method was most favourable for this project because of the client's concern with the environmental performance of the building. As a result, using LEED to assist with the realization of the project made sense but there was also a need to go back and monitor the building. This is where the use of the GBC database tool did a great job of closing the design loop for pre-design, sketch, design development and evaluation. Few projects follow this methodology, but it is increasingly common for projects to do so.

a consequence the team used the GBC post construction to obtain more detailed information of the building's environmental performance. The building has been monitored subsequent to its construction and the data produced was used to input into the GBC system.

GBC is a database tool that is driven through an Excel spreadsheet. The spreadsheet covers a range of issues from economic through to environmental performance. It provides a method of calculating the rating and is a handy way of storing project information. Hence the design team can self-assess the building using this tool.

At one level, therefore, the tool can be applied to any build in any location. It is, however, generally applied to most building types such as multi-residential and commercial buildings but is too complex for small housing units.

The standard is designed with respect to the performance of a reference building, so unlike LEED, which has an absolute standard, the GBC standard is relative to the baseline perform-

ance in the area in which the building is located. Furthermore, the tool has a set of weightings that can be adjusted to calibrate the environmental model so that it fits the context in which the building is located. The power of the GBC therefore lies in the rigour of its environmental modelling, but this is at the cost of additional complexity and its extreme hunger for data.

Hence we see involved in this project the methodology of two tools – one more attuned to the design phase and the other more to the post construction. This begs the question: Why two tools, which involves twice the work?

Design intent

Response to the brief

The building is approached from the north, with the entrance located in a central position. Cellular offices are placed at the north and open plan offices to the south (equatorially aligned),

allowing a view to the Bay. In addition, the green features – such as an open floor plan – help the staff work together collaboratively.

Car parking is placed on the ground floor underneath the building, and is a relatively small area designed to meet occupancy needs. An area of outside car parking, covered by a permeable surface, is used for visitors. A service core containing water tanks and other service facilities is placed to the east of the entrance. A lecture theatre is placed to the south in counterpoint to the main building. The section shows synthesis between function and passive design. Single-storey car parking is placed on the ground floor with two floors of offices above. The service core is placed to the north with horizontal servicing though roof and intermediate floors.

The deep envelope provides a range of bioclimatic functions for passive design. The resulting language of the building expresses this link between climate and human occupancy. The shed roof form is used for water catchment purposes and pro-

vides symmetry to the sense of space in the main office hall. A void between the office floors creates a small atrium linking the two floors, for visual and thermal purposes.

Response to climate

The area shows a cool continental climate with overheating possibilities in June, July and August. Low humidity and high irradiation are found in the summer, with the opposite in winter.

PASSIVE STRATEGIES AND TECHNIQUES

The passive strategies that can be used for this climate in winter comprise solar and thermal mass as a way of extending the comfort zone. In summer, high humidity means that effective use can be made of both cross ventilation and thermal mass.

ENVELOPE

A simple, natural approach to the building envelope has been taken. The aim is to provide the healthiest and most effective climate control and efficient operational processes.

SHED ROOF

This has visual consequence in the form of the shed roof of the Center – a traditional indigenous form of architecture, historically visible along the shoreline of Chesapeake Bay. The shed roof is particularly efficient for this building because it allows for easy collection of rainwater and encourages an open interior design, which are both important components of this office space.

WINDOWS

Natural light, views, and fresh Bay air are never far from any desk or meeting room. Building occupants use operable windows for natural ventilation. Sensors keep track of outdoor temperatures and humidity and automatically shut down air conditioning and open motor-operated windows. Sensors also switch on indicator signs throughout the building when conditions favour open windows. As the Bay's breezes cool the building, it relies less on air conditioning. High-performance windows with high thermal performance are used.

WALLS

Structural insulated panels (SIPs) form the building envelope, using less wood than conventional framing and resulting in a higher R value. A SIP consists of foam core 4 to 8 inches (10–20

cm) thick with faces consisting of orientated strand board (OSB). The structural insulated panels (SIPs) provide an insulation value of R 20 walls and R 30 roof.

Active strategies and techniques

HEATING, VENTILATION AND AIR CONDITIONING

The environmental design of the HVAC system was aimed at reducing energy through conservation and by optimization of passive systems.

An interpretation of the climate data reveals that there is a need for cooling in the summer months but that there are periods when natural ventilation use is possible to minimize the operational time of air conditioning systems. Hence a hybrid system of air conditioning and natural ventilation for cooling, as well as solar heating and auxiliary heat production, is feasible. This gives the option of a mixed operational mode.

'Free running' mode is where passive systems deliver thermal comfort; then there is an alternative active system, which provides heating or cooling mode. This hybrid approach requires an appropriate control system to run the bimodal operation at optimal performance. As will be seen, this led to a significantly low energy use for this sector of the energy budget.

Three types of system are used:

- *Open plan office:* ducted central air system provided for extreme summertime temperature conditions and winter heating; services are exposed; a desiccant dehumidifier and a heat recovery wheel on the heat pump's ventilation system also save energy; ground water heat pumps.
- *Auditorium and meeting rooms:* ducted central air conditioning through exposed services with partly acoustic ceilings.
- *Mix mode:* operated in conjunction with natural ventilation system, i.e. when natural ventilation is used, the active system is automatically shut off.

In naturally ventilated mode the fresh air ventilation is brought in through large openings at level one and exhausted through high-level windows in the roof of level two. The high-level windows are operated by actuators, which mechanically open and close the windows when necessary. Signage alerts the occupants when the external conditions are suitable for natural ventilation. In this way the air conditioning system can be turned off at the crossover periods between summer cooling and

Chesapeake Bay Foundation: comparison of R values[2] for insulation with local standards

Base case/standard		Project	
Roofs:	15	Roofs:	30
Walls:	13	Walls:	23.5
Floors:	19	Floors:	20
Windows: solar heat gain coefficient:	0.39	Windows: solar heat gain coefficient:	0.49
U values:	0.57	U values:	0.32

winter heating when the climate is benign. Using natural ventilation and passive heating in this way saves energy and contributes to reducing the building's running costs.

Monitoring of the building has revealed that it can run on 'free running mode' for between 10 and 30 per cent of the year, which is higher than expected. A 'green light' building energy management system notifies staff to open windows when outside conditions comply.

Electric lighting

The building is designed to use supplementary electric lighting in conjunction with daylight. Within the open plan units, lux is provided on the work plane utilizing the suspended uplight system on level one and down lights on level two.

Luminaries are automatically regulated with dimming control gear that are sensitive to daylight. To regulate the use of electrical lighting outside working hours, a time-clock control is used for the lighting. In this way, when there is ample daylight the electric lights are switched off or dimmed, and when the building is not occupied the lights are extinguished automatically.

Other main systems

The other main systems are:

- Roof-mounted solar thermal panels are used to heat the hot water.
- Façade-mounted photovoltaic systems deliver about 2 per cent of the building's energy use (but were installed mainly for education purposes).
- Rainwater collection and recycling system rainwater is collected from the roof.
- A heat pump is connected to a geo-exchange closed loop heat exchange system that comprises approximately 30 wells drilled into the ground to a depth of 300 ft (100 m) to take advantage of the earth's natural temperature of 55°F. This acts as a heat sink in summer whereby waste heat is transferred to the ground and additional heat drawn back from the ground in winter. This greatly improves the efficiency of the heat pump compared to a heat pump that uses air–air heat transfer. Thus the electrical energy used to drive the heat pump is balanced with the energy sourced from the environment;

- A building management system monitors and automates some of the environmental control system.
- A lift for disabled access and goods is provided.

LEED criteria

The aim of this section is to examine the building design in terms of the LEED criteria. The criteria are listed and then the main strategies are discussed with regard to these criteria.

Sustainable sites

The aim of this section is to explain the strategies used for reducing the impact of the building on the site.

Sustainable siting criteria are organized around three main issues. The first concerns the ecological value of the site and how the building development enhances or reduces the ecological value of the site. The second set of issues is concerned with the site location, its accessibility and the influence of transport energy. The final set relates to the impact of the building on the site and how it changes the natural pattern of drainage and erosion. The criteria are as follows.

- *Site and its ecological value impacts*:
  - site selection;
  - urban redevelopment;
  - brownfield redevelopment.
- *Transportation impacts*:
  - alternative transportation;
  - public transportation access;
  - bicycle storage and changing rooms;
  - alternative fuel vehicles;
  - parking capacity.
- *Building impacts on the site and its neighbours*:
  - reduce site disturbance;
  - protect or restore open space;
  - disturbance and development footprint;
  - stormwater management – rate and quantity;
  - stormwater management – treatment;
  - landscape and exterior design to reduce heat islands, for non-roof and roof areas;
  - light pollution reduction;
  - erosion and sedimentation control.

The building response is as follows.

Left. Retention pond and landscaping to avoid water runoff.
Top. Water catchment cisterns and water recycling systems.

SITE SELECTION

One of the key issues in site selection and planning is to try to avoid building on virgin land to help maintain biodiversity. The Center is built in a Smart Growth Funding area.[3]

CBF came to the site through invitation from the local community. Prior to CBF interest the site was home to an inn, but when the site came up it was earmarked for residential development. The community had some reservations concerning the residential proposal since the site is one of natural beauty, and it preferred a group who could maintain the quality of the natural environment to take ownership of the 30-acre site. A coincidence of interest emerged between the landowner, the community and CBF, which resulted in CBF purchasing the site. Resources were raised from the sale of the development rights to the state of Maryland and through low-interest loans the project was born.[4] Hence site selection not only achieved the preservation of biodiversity but also allowed the adoption of mit-

igation strategies for the development of a brownfield site – a site previously occupied by an existing building.

ALTERNATIVE TRANSPORT

The building infrastructure and management supports a reduction in fossil-fuel-powered transport to reduce emissions from travel by staff. These strategies are:

- For cyclists, storage space and wash facilities are provided in the building.
- Charge points are provided for electric cars to take advantage of the federal subsidies for the ownership of electric cars or hybrids (fossil- and electric-fuelled cars), which make them price-comparable with fossil-fuel cars.
- A canteen service is provided on site to avoid staff having to drive off site at lunchtime. The amenity provided by the location and design of the lunchroom reinforces this strat-

egy. It is located on the beach side of the building in the auditorium building along with the staff room and provides internal and external space.

EROSION CONTROL

First the design took specific steps to accommodate erosion control. The area surrounding the building respects the site flora and the topography with regard to water runoff. There are a number of strategies that address this criterion:

- Careful consideration of water flow and connection to a bio-retention system – a collection pond is provided for water runoff, which collects debris and sediment before discharge.
- Porous surfaces were selected for the car park, which allows water to drain into the soil and feed the underground water table.

REDUCING SITE DISTURBANCE

In order to reduce site disturbance there is a woodland, wetland and tidal water restoration plan in place to maintain the biodiversity within the site. A further issue concerns the extent of the building floor plate. In particular, considerable attention was placed on the area occupied by the building in relation to the size of the site as well as to the area occupied by existing buildings or those replaced.

A desirable goal is to keep the area of new building the same as that of the buildings being replaced, or less if possible. In this way the amount of biodiversity lost is minimized and/or more land is made available for regenerating flora and fauna. The term building 'footprint' has been used to encompass this concept. In this case the footprint of the new building is similar to that of the building it replaces, leaving approximately 26 acres of Trust land undisturbed.

A final issue was the interface between the building and the ground plane. Excessive benching though excavation creates waste, which has to be disposed of either on or off the site. The designers chose a construction system that did not touch previously undisturbed portions of the site containing mature hardwoods. Placing the building on piers allowed for under-building parking, which also helped keep the building footprint small and minimized excavation.

STORMWATER MANAGEMENT

A bio-retention system is used as part of the erosion control system. Stormwater passes through a bio-retention stormwater treatment system in the form of manmade wetlands to filter water and treat oils before the water enters the Bay or the adjacent Black Walnut Creek. Water from the building is also collected and recycled, helping to avoid problems of off-site disposal.

LANDSCAPE TO REDUCE HEAT ISLAND EFFECTS

Heat island effects are increases in the ambient temperatures of cities and built areas because of the effects of buildings and the hard surfaces in the streetscape. These can result in temperatures 2–4°C above those found on rural sites.

The implication for design is to use sustainable features in the building and on the landscape, which mitigates the reflection of heat into the atmosphere and dissipates the energy in a natural way – i.e. natural systems absorb energy for growth and produce water that evaporates, absorbing heat. The natural landscaping strategies used to reduce effects include:

- local flora is used for landscaping;
- 30 mm gravel is used for driveways and external car parking – gravel stone of approximately 20–30 mm in diameter has a high surface area and works best for dissipating heat;
- timber decking is used for external spaces and reduces the reflection of heat; and
- undercroft – the building is placed on concrete columns, which provides a service area under the building for staff car parking, reducing the external hard surfaces.

LIGHT POLLUTION

A conventional lighting system is used but luminaries have been selected to provide a downlight system, which shields the light source and minimizes horizontal spread of light.

Water efficiency

The criteria for water efficiency are aimed at reducing the demand for water resources within the building. The main criteria are as follows:

- water-efficient landscaping, including reduction of water use for irrigation;
- innovative wastewater technologies; and
- water-use reduction.

The building response addresses these criteria very well.

WATER-EFFICIENT LANDSCAPE

Water for irrigation is reduced through drought-tolerant native plants and assisted by restricting mowing of the meadow and grasslands to only once per year. This policy also reduces fuel use and pollution on site.

INNOVATIVE WATER TECHNOLOGIES

Using water as a material for discharging waste from buildings poses issues concerning the complexity of reuse and recycling of the materials. In this case the use of composting toilets, which use very little water, has been chosen. The toilets, of Swedish design, reduce water use in the building to less than 90 per cent of that of a typical office building of a similar size.

WATER USE REDUCTION

A rainwater system captures water, also reducing the need to draw from wells. The shed roof, covered in galvanized metal, allows for a single rain gutter, which drains the water through filters and into cisterns. Since only residential taps were available for the area's water system, installing cisterns avoided a massive city infrastructure upgrade. A sand filter treats the rainwater and CBF employees use it for washing their gear and hands and for mop sinks, laundry, irrigation and fire suppression.

Water storage is provided on-site, which creates a strong visual impact on the building form. In the design, water cisterns are used to collect water from the roof, which is then stored. The rainwater is reused for hand-washing and irrigation.

Energy and atmosphere

The issues dealt with in this section concern the selection and management of the energy resources in the building with the objective of reducing impacts on the atmosphere. A building's performance can be affected by up to one star through the effectiveness of management systems, so this is an important issue. The second issue is the impacts from the chemicals used in the energy systems. CFC and chemical emissions from the energy systems can have twice the impact on the atmosphere of the CO_2 from the power generation.

The main criteria are as follows.

- *Management*:
  - fundamental building systems commissioning required;
  - minimum energy performance required;
  - measurement and verification; and
  - additional commissioning.
- *Chemical pollution avoidance*:
  - chlorofluorocarbon[5] (CFC) reduction in servicing and refrigeration equipment required; and
  - ozone depletion substances.
- *Energy demand reduction*:
  - optimize energy performance.
- *Renewable energy sources*:
  - renewable energy;
  - Green Power.

The building design addresses most of these criteria.

MANAGEMENT

The design team was involved in the commissioning of the building and a facility manager is now in place to provide ongoing support for the building operation and maintenance. The building energy performance is optimized through the use of the facility manager.

ADDITIONAL COMMISSIONING

The building should be verified to ensure that the entire building is designed, constructed and calibrated to operate as intended. A commissioning agent is usually involved in this process. The facility manager is using the Bonneville Standard for Building Performance, set by Bonneville California – one of the strictest in the nation.

MONITORING AND EVALUATION

The building has undergone monitoring and evaluation through the GBC tool. This has been carried out with the US Department of Energy. This tool has been used as a post construction assessment tool considering the operational conditions of the building.

Left. Electric hybrid cars form part of the alternative transport plan. **Top left**. Recharging point provided in car park. **Top right**. Façade-integrated renewable energy systems.

ENERGY DEMAND REDUCTION

The building is designed to improve on existing baseline standards (ASHRAE/IES Standard 90.1–1989) by 50 per cent. This is achieved through a number of strategies, such as use of passive and active modes – the building can be cooled and heated naturally, which reduces the demand on active systems.

RENEWABLE ENERGY

Renewable energy is used for electrical energy production and hot water heating. Renewable energy sources provide approximately 30 per cent of the building's energy load. Solar hot water heating provides all the domestic hot water for the building, saving approximately 120 kilowatt-hours (kWh) of electricity per day. A 4 kWh photovoltaic system helps generate a portion of the building's electrical load.

Photovoltaic panels and solar hot water heating meet 10.7 per cent of the energy needs. This is called the renewable frac-tion and, given the present eco-efficiency of these systems, this fraction is high.

CHEMICAL POLLUTION AVOIDANCE

CFC reduction in the heating, ventilation and air conditioning systems is in place.

Materials and resources

The criteria in this section are organised around three main issues. The materials and resources criteria are as follows:

*   *Management of materials*:
    -   storage and collection of recyclables.
*   *Reuse of materials*:
    -   building reuse – there are three categories: maintaining 75 per cent of the existing shell of the building; maintaining 100 per cent; maintaining 100 per cent of

the shell and 50 per cent of other elements of the building (non-shell);

- construction waste management – this involves diverting material from landfill so that it can be used for other purposes.[6]
- *Reduction of material transport impacts supporting local industries*:
  - local/regional materials.[7]
- *The use of renewable materials*:
  - rapidly renewable materials;
  - certified wood.

The building has developed a number of strategies to address these criteria. Some issues could not be addressed because of the design break. For example, the criterion of building reuse is intended to foster the reuse of existing buildings through renovation. This was not possible in this case, but the building uses materials from local existing buildings and this has been included in the specification.

MANAGEMENT OF WASTE
Provision of space for on-site waste management is ignored in the brief of many buildings. In this case the brief called for adequate storage space for the collection of recyclables. There is space for storage in the service area of the building. A waste management plan is in place.

CONSTRUCTION WASTE MANAGEMENT
A management policy was enforced in the construction of the project. It led to the diversion of 75 per cent of waste from landfill.

REUSE AND RECYCLED MATERIALS
Recycled materials in the building include galvanized steel siding, galvanized roofing, and medium-density fibreboard (MDF). Parallel strand lumber, made from scrap wood that is normally wasted, was used for posts, beams and trusses. The sun louvres are made of salvaged pickle barrel staves. Reused broken concrete from the previous structure covers the roadbeds.

LOCALLY SOURCED MATERIALS
The majority of materials used for construction were produced within 300 miles of the site, reducing the transport energy used

Locally sourced and non-toxic materials were a priority.

to bring materials to the construction site. Timber framing and structural insulated panels (SIPs) were the main structural materials used. SIPs decrease wood use by forming a strong bracing system for the roof, adding increased efficiency to the other benefits of using local materials.

RENEWABLE MATERIALS
Rapidly renewable materials such as Paralam (engineered timber made from wood chips) posts, beams and truss system and bamboo, cork and linoleum floorings were specified.

Indoor environmental quality
Indoor environmental quality criteria are focused on the following issues:

- *Air quality*
  - minimum indoor air quality (IAQ) performance required;
  - environmental tobacco smoke control required;
  - carbon dioxide (CO_2) monitoring;
  - ventilation effectiveness;

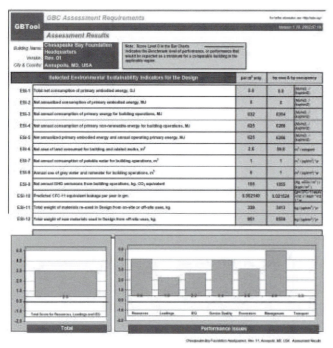

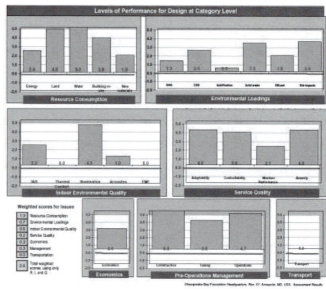

Green Building Challenge Assessment was used post construction. This shows the level of environmental performance through rating each indicator, rather than giving a total score as is found with LEED.

- construction indoor air quality management plan during construction and before occupancy;
- low-emitting materials, adhesives and sealants, including paints, carpets and composite wood; and
- indoor chemical and pollutant source control.
- *Occupant comfort*
  - controllability of systems to the perimeter and interior (non-perimeter);
  - thermal comfort;
  - permanent monitoring system;
  - daylight and views – daylight 75 per cent of spaces; and
  - views for 90 per cent of spaces.

The fundamental design aspects of the building are aimed at addressing these criteria.

The building has a thin plan configuration with is longest façade facing the equator, allowing an effective synergy between passive and active systems. The benefits in terns of environmental quality are seen.

AIR QUALITY

The building meets the minimum requirements of voluntary consensus standard ASHRAE 62-1999, Ventilation for Acceptable Indoor Air Quality, and the management of the building has established an agenda[8] for operations that includes the control of smoking in designated areas.

Ventilation effectiveness has been established through the development of a mixed mode building system, which uses both active and passive systems. This allows fresh air to be brought into the building through operable windows when conditions are favourable.

A construction IAQ management plan was in place to monitor the air quality during construction and before occupancy. This ensures that occupants are not subjected to effects of construction pollution that may be retained in the building, particularly in the air conditioning system

Low-emitting materials, adhesives and sealants were used in the building in addition to control of indoor chemical and pollutant sources. There is permanent monitoring of CO_2 and VOC used in the building to maintain ongoing air quality.

OCCUPANT COMFORT

Thermal comfort has been considered in the design, and the building complies with ASHRAE 55-1992. The building can run on free-running mode when external comfort conditions are appropriate. Daylight and views are provided to all habitable rooms. Occupant control of the indoor thermal comfort environment is provided.

Innovation in design

THE CBF AWARENESS MISSION

The Trust land and the new building on site have been used to form the basis of an education system aimed at creating awareness in visitors of the issues concerning the CBF mission.

LEARNING FROM THE CENTER DESIGN

CBF uses the Center and its environmental features as a teaching tool, giving public tours of the building and opening it up to use by outside groups. As visitors enter from the north they can see high-performance sustainable features, such as solar water heaters, operable and clerestory windows, and rainwater cisterns. The building's south wall, mostly glass, faces the Bay. The remaining site contains interpretive trails and demonstrations for the public.

LEED assessment

The building was assessed under Version 1 of the LEED rating tool and rated at the platinum level, which is the highest rating under this system.

Lessons learned

The Center used the Leadership in Energy and Environmental Design (LEED) rating system of the US Green Building Council as a guiding framework for design. The council awarded the building a platinum rating, their highest rating. The National Renewable Energy Laboratory is monitoring the energy flows and performance of the building's components to assess the effectiveness of the design and the design framework. The research will be helpful for planning future high-performing commercial building designs.

Acknowledgements

The case study is an adaptation of a paper produced for presentation to the GBC at the Sustainable Buildings Conference, Oslo, 2002. Thanks to Greg Mellor for his time and help with this case study. Plans and illustrations: Smith Group and Richard Hyde

Contacts

Chesapeake Bay Foundation, Inc.
Philip Merrill Environmental Center
+1(410) 268-8816
www.savethebay.cbf.org

US Department of Energy
Energy Efficiency and Renewable Energy
Clearinghouse (EREC)
1-800-DOE-3732
www.eren.doe.gov

US Department of Energy
Office of Building Technology, State and
Community Programs
www.eren.doe.gov/buildings/highperformance

National Renewable Energy Laboratory
Center for Buildings and Thermal Systems
www.nrel.gov/buildings/highperformance

US Green Building Council
Leadership in Energy and Environmental Design
(LEED)
www.usgbc.org/programs/leed.htm

William McCormack Place, Cairns, Australia.

CASE STUDY 9

Environmental Protection Agency (EPA) Fit-out for William McCormack Place, Cairns, Australia

Architects: Queensland Department of Public Works – interiors

A brief comes about through, essentially, an ongoing relationship between what is possible in architecture and what you want to do. And everything you do modifies your idea of what is possible … you can't start with a brief and [then] design, you have to start designing and briefing simultaneously…'.[9]

Introduction

The environmental briefing approach in this case came about for three reasons. First, the new tenant for the building was to be the Environmental Protection Agency of Queensland (EPA) who needed new office premises in Cairns. The existing available office buildings for rental in Cairns did not match their needs, which were for a wide range of office functions but also with the need for a 'green fit-out' contained within a green building.

Second, a new Cairns State Government Office Building was commissioned to include EPA Queensland, with a vision for ecological sustainable design (ESD).

Third, there was a stated aim on behalf of the building owners, the Queensland Department of Public Works (QDPW), to distinguish this project from other state government office buildings and provide the EPA with a demonstration of the practical implementation of environmental criteria in the workplace, and to send a signal to the community concerning the importance of green design.

The approach was further complicated because the Government Office had at that time a standard procurement brief, which did not comprehensively address ESD issues. Issues such as energy standards were called up in the form of the SEDA energy rating tool but other ESD issues were not fully addressed.[10]

Public Access Area (central)

Public/Staff Interaction Area (internal)

Multi-purpose Rooms/Storage (internal)

Open Plan Work Area (adjacent to windows)

**Cairns Government Office Building
Sheridan Street**
Flexible Office Design Concept
Level 3 (one of four floors designed)

William McCormack Place. Plan.

William McCormack Place: key priorities from the standard building brief

Design intent	Design strategies
Key priorities	Horizontal expansion and flexibility High-quality finish Energy efficiency Long-term life cycle costs Minimum life 50 years
Equitable building design[11]	Adopt project brief requirements
Ramps	Equal opportunity for access
Standards	Adopt standards in project brief
General	Provide 'state of the art office building' Provide flexibility of use
Site	Use climatic potential of site to harvest natural resources, wind, water, sunlight
Social objectives	Provision of openness between government and the public Develop interactive educational displays in public areas
Energy efficiency	4-star SEDA[11] energy-efficiency rating

Environmental briefing process

To achieve ESD initiatives in the proposed fit-out for the building, an 'inside out' design concept was envisaged whereby ESD initiatives are integrated into the office fit-out design and reinforced in the base building shell. Too often, office fit-out is not considered at the same time as the base building design criteria. The building owners stated that:

This project provided DPW with the ideal opportunity to develop a building that realized the State Government's objectives for sustainable office accommodation. A key goal was to prove that an office building could be constructed to meet strict environmental sustainability targets while remaining economically and commercially viable.[12]

To give an idea of the intentions for the project, the key design strategies were listed in the standard building brief. The resulting building, William McCormack Place, is a four-storey commercial office building of 4,568 m^2 (net lettable area) located in Sheridan Street, Cairns. The building was constructed by a private sector construction manager under a two-stage, design and construct contract with an overall budget of A$17.5 million including the fit-out and public art. This project demonstrates how an environmental briefing approach can be used to facilitate the implementation of ESD practices in the fit-out of a large office building.

Issues of ownership and tenure complicate this type of project. For example, in many office buildings the owner is not necessarily the user or tenant so different objectives with regard to the use of the facility and its environmental performance come into play. In this case, the building owner and manager, QDPW, and the tenants, the EPA, were both from the public sector. It was the EPA as tenants who wished to strongly promote green design. The EPA established a brief for the fit-out of its space with the intention of helping to inform the other aspects in the building design.

This type of building can be considered as having four layers to its construction. These layers are:

- envelope;
- structure;
- services; and
- fit-out.

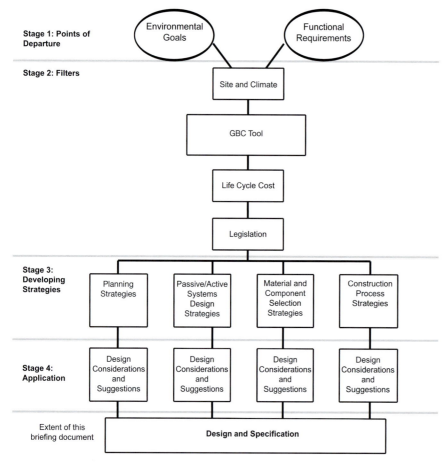

Stage 1: Points of Departure

Environmental Goals

Functional Requirements

Stage 2: Filters

Site and Climate

GBC Tool

Life Cycle Cost

Legislation

Stage 3: Developing Strategies

| Planning Strategies | Passive/Active Systems Design Strategies | Material and Component Selection Strategies | Construction Process Strategies |

Stage 4: Application

| Design Considerations and Suggestions | Design Considerations and Suggestions | Design Considerations and Suggestions | Design Considerations and Suggestions |

Extent of this briefing document

Design and Specification

Flow chart of the environmental briefing process.

The case study provides information on the *environmental brief* for the fit-out, which was established to complement the *standard project brief* developed for the base building, the envelope, structure and services. This important departure from normal practice was to help the tenant achieve sustainability goals without being reliant solely on the building owners and the standard project briefing process.

As has been seen in other projects, the environmental briefing approach is essentially a 'reporting tool' to assist documentation of key decisions that take place in the early stages of the design of large complex buildings such as this. The fit-out brief was intended to achieve the following:

1   identify ESD objectives for the project;
2   provide a context for these objectives within the international scene to ensure 'best practice' issues are addressed;
3   link the functional objectives with the environmental objectives of the office fit-out;
4   provide the EPA with a framework to advance the project towards meeting its functional and environmental objectives within a broader project context.

William McCormack Place EPA office fit-out project details

Characteristics	Details
Client	Environmental Protection Agency, Queensland
Street address	Sheridan Street
City	Cairns
Country	Australia
Latitude	16°53' S
Building type	Office fit-out
Year of construction	2002

The intent was to use the 'fit-out brief', though it was only one part of the project, as a way of influencing the design of the whole project. Several key documents were used to inform the fit-out brief. These included:

1   Building Code of Australia;
2   relevant SAA standards;
3   local government bylaws and regulations;
4   Ecologically Sustainable Office Fit-out Guidelines, prepared by Queensland Department of Works Building Division, the TVS Partnership Pty Ltd and Lincolne Scott Australia;
5   GOAU Guidelines for Government Office Accommodation;
6   Project Brief (Volume 4) State Government Office Building Cairns, September 2000;
7   GBTool;[13]
8   ESD Briefing System.[14]

Outcomes from the design process in terms of the extent to which the fit-out brief was realized are provided. The final form of the building is described, illustrating the extent to which the synergies between the fit-out and the other building systems, envelope, structure and services have been achieved to improve the environmental performance. The table above shows the project details for the EPA Fit-out.

The environmental brief

The structure of the environmental briefing process for the EPA Fit-out was altered from the residential projects that had pre-ceded it to reflect the commercial context. The original vision for the environmental brief has three distinct phases.

- Phase 1: *The point of departure*, or goal-setting for functional and environmental purposes.
- Phase 2: *Applying filters*, or constraints within the context of the building.
- Phase 3: *Developing strategies*, or potential solution sets to meet the goals while working within the scope of the applied filters.

In the case of the EPA Fit-out the goal-setting that formed the point of departure became more complex and additional activities and studies were carried out to help establish the goals and objectives. These are described in the following section.

Phase 1: The point of departure

DIAGNOSTIC STUDY

Information was compiled from a two-day interview process with key EPA personnel. This group represented existing sections and department programmes within the organization. Records of the interviews were made and returned to the interviewees to confirm their acceptance of the views and factual information collected. This is called 'participant confirmation' and is an important part of the diagnostic process. It minimizes the chance of misrepresentation of the reported opinions and facts concerning the building.

Initial feedback from the interview process raised a number of ESD issues and objectives. The emphasis from occupants, as might be expected, was largely centred around indoor environmental quality issues, the single most commonly raised issue being that of occupant control over environmental conditions within the individual workspace. The two primary parameters for control are those of lighting and ventilation. The occupant objectives have been grouped into useful issue categories.

ECOLOGICAL SUSTAINABLE DEVELOPMENT (ESD)

The aim was to achieve 'world's best practice' ecological sustainable development (ESD) through a holistic environmental approach that integrated both architecture and engineering to improve environmental performance. This involved education of staff and users in ESD issues and avoiding technical domina-

Usage matrix F = Frequent O = Occasional R = Rarely	Env Ops	Coast Wet & Waterways	Cultural Heritage	Dev, Assess, Biodiversity & Planning	Directorate	Corporate Development	Wildlife	Indigenous Cultural Serv	Public Contact	DM Wet Tropics	DM CYDT	DM Marine - North	Env Impact Mgmt	Conssvn Planning	Compliance	Ecosys Mgmt
Environmental Ops					R	F	R	R		O	O	O	R	O		R
Coast Wetlands & Waterways	F		F	F	R	F	R	R		O	O	O	R	O		R
Cultural Heritage	O	F		F	R	F	O	F	O	O	O	O	R	F	O	O
Dev, Assess, Biodiversity & Planning	F	F	F		R	F	O	O	F	O	O	O	R	F	O	O
Directorate	R	R	O	F		F	F	F	R	F	F	O	O	O	F	F
Corporate Development	O	O	O	F	F		F	F	O	F	F	F	O	O		F
Wildlife	R	R	R	F	F	F		F	F	O	O	F	R	R	F	F
Indigenous Cultural Services	O	R	F	O	F	F	F		R	F	F	F	F	F	F	F
Public Contact	R	R	O	O	F	F	F	O		F	F	F	R	O	F	O
DM Wet Tropics	O	O	O	F	F	F	F	O	F		O	O	O	F	F	F
DM CYDT		R	O	F	F	F	O	F	F	O		O	O	F	F	F
DM Marine - North	O	F	O	F	F	F	R	F	F	O	O		F	F	F	F
Env Impact Management		O	O	F	F	F	O	F	O	F	F	F		F		O
Conservation Plannng	O	F	O	F	F	F	R	F	O	F	F	F	F		O	F
Compliance	R	R	R	R	F	F	F	F	R	F	F	F	O	R		R
Ecosystem Management		R	R	O	F	F	F	F	F	F	F	F	O	F		

A usage matrix enabled examination of organizational and adjacency issues for space planning purposes.

tion from the building systems – returning environmental control to the occupants.

- *Image of the building.* Create a demonstration building of the ESD initiatives addressing the EPA departmental vision. Communicate a 'green' perception to building users and the greater public.
- *Ventilation and fresh air.* Provide occupant control of mechanical and natural systems, with operable windows and a high level of outside fresh air.
- *Lighting.* Occupant control of active lighting, maximizing the use of natural daylighting especially for ambient lighting levels. The use of active task lighting, controllable by occupants. The prevention of glare and the provision of adequate lighting in areas with special requirements, for example office document filing systems such as compactus units.
- *Thermal comfort.* Occupant control of thermal environment through prevention of overheating.
- *Acoustic performance.* Acoustic control within and between the various office environments.
- *Psychological issues.* Visual access to the outside of the building. Interior colour schemes that improve environmental quality.
- *Building form.* A courtyard-style building (for increased lighting, ventilation and visual amenity). Promotion of the use of stairs as an alternative to lifts.
- *Materials.* Sustainable material selection; recycling during building operation. Durability of materials.

- *Energy.* Energy efficiency of lighting and mechanical systems. Solar energy and hot water production on site. Energy management initiatives.
- *Transport.* Ample on-site bicycle storage
- *Functional requirements:* The functional requirements for the fit-out were defined and the nine main function issues were as follows:
    1 client and user objectives
    2 workplace culture
    3 access and circulation
    4 work-point types
    5 work-point amenity
    6 work-point floors
    7 work-point enclosure
    8 services
    9 signage, path finding and security.

An important task in developing the environmental brief for the fit-out was to sift out key priorities in the standard building brief and assess how these met the needs of the fit-out, and to try to ensure that the two documents were as consistent with each other as possible.

ENVIRONMENTAL GOALS

For the EPA Fit-out environmental brief, the environmental performance criteria were developed with reference to the international Green Building Challenge (GBC) assessment tool.[15] This tool is used extensively worldwide to assess a range of buildings types including offices, schools and housing. Using such an internationally recognized tool was seen as important when assessing the design in terms of world's best practice, which was desired by the clients.

The primary aim of the GBC tool is to assess buildings post construction, but for this project the intention was to front-load the design in terms of environmental issues. To this end a set of environmental criteria was obtained from the GBC tool. The criteria were regrouped to better facilitate brief development and continued assessment of environmental performance throughout design development. The range of criteria was altered to tailor them to a fit-out project, and some specific criteria were altered to the same end.

In summary, the setting of environmental goals for the EPA Fit-out was a two-stage process. The first stage was to obtain desired environmental objectives and issues from the client and occupant user groups as described above. These objectives and issues were used to place emphasis on the more objective, comprehensive set of environmental criteria from the GBC tool.

Together the occupant objectives and the comprehensive set of environmental criteria determine the range of issues for consideration. A benchmark level of performance relating to each of these issues must be assigned as goals for the project. These benchmark levels of performance are used to direct the environmental design response, that is, the strategies chosen in the design of the building.

Phase 2: Filters applied

Filters are the constraints within which the project is placed. In designing a fit-out one of the main constraints is the base building. The first set of filters applied was from the standard building brief for the envelope structure and services. That was followed by three other sets of filters, examined here in turn.

THE STANDARD BUILDING BRIEF

A key goal of the project was to prove that an office building could be designed and constructed to meet environmental sustainability targets while remaining economically and commercially viable in a normal commercial market. The goals of Queensland Government, Department of Public Works (QDPW) for the whole building as contained within the standard building brief included:

- a minimum four-star energy rating;
- a design that minimizes the environmental impact throughout the building's life cycle;
- commercial viability without the use of federal or state government environmental incentives;
- a design suited to the Queensland Government as owner, manager and occupier in the longer term;
- a design that provides flexibility and manageability in recognition of the comparatively high churn rate in government buildings;
- a design that minimizes life cycle costs; and
- employment of local consultants, contractors and suppliers in order to provide local jobs and improve the local knowledge base.[16]

ENVIRONMENTAL ISSUES

The integration of the GBC tool was undertaken at the conceptual and practical level. First, the environmental criteria were established and then, using the tool, a set of benchmark levels of performance for those criteria.

A holistic approach to the environmental design of a building includes consideration of the whole of the building's life cycle and the materials and components from which it is constructed. Conceptually, the building life cycle is represented as an input-output-model. At each stage of the life cycle there are inputs, or resources that enter the life cycle, and outputs, or resources that leave the life cycle. Resources that do not leave the life cycle at a given stage are maintained within the cycle and transferred to the next stage. A theoretically achievable position of sustainability would be attained if there were no resources entering or leaving the life cycle, or if all of the resources entering and leaving were of an ecologically sustainable nature.

When considering an approach to designing a building with this building life cycle in mind, it is beneficial to have a breakdown of issues into categories that are conceptually easy to comprehend. For the EPA Fit-out there were five such groups used to achieve this. The first two of these, relating directly to interaction between the building life cycle and the environment, were *resources entering* and *resources leaving*. An example of criteria relating to resources entering would be the consumption of water during the operation of a building. An example of criteria relating to resources leaving would be the CO_2 emissions from energy used during the operation of a building.

There are other important environmental issues, not easily conceptualized as resource inputs or outputs, that must also be considered. These fall into two other issue categories, *human health* and *context*. An example of a human health criterion would be the measure of physiological comfort of occupants during the operation of a building. An example of a contextual criterion would be the proximity of a building to services or transport.

The fifth category of criteria added for the EPA Fit-out was *process*. Process criteria are included in recognition of the fact that there are certain processes that, if undertaken, are likely to improve the chances of achieving environmental goals. An example of process criteria would be the provision of a multi-disciplinary design team.

It was under this structure of five categories that the GBC criteria were organized for the EPA Fit-out brief. The designation

for individual criteria has been rearranged from that of GBC tool to fit in with the life-cycle structure as follows:

- resources entering;
- resources leaving;
- indoor environment;
- context; and
- process.

Note that the human health category has changed into *indoor environment* in the transition from a generic environmental concern to the specific concerns for the EPA Fit-out project. This reflects the nature of the project as a fit-out and the users' focus of concern on issues of human health relating to their own use of the building during its operation.

ENVIRONMENTAL PERFORMANCE LEVELS

The GBC tool provides a scoring system and suggested benchmark levels of performance for each criterion. The international recognition of the tool was embraced to allow a level of comparison with other buildings assessed under the tool, and to a level of international acceptance of claims made about the environmental performance of the EPA Fit-out.

The benchmark levels of performance contained in the fit-out brief were derived from the GBC tool. The scoring system used in GBC tool ranges from –2 to 5 for each assessment criterion. Zero represents a benchmark level of performance that is the typical current performance level for criteria. Therefore –1 and –2 represent performance levels poorer than the current standard and level 5 represents a level significantly in advance of current performance, but a level that is nonetheless achievable given currently available technologies and practices. Driven by the client desire to achieve a world's best practice office building, almost all of the benchmark levels of performance for the office fit-out were set at the top level – that is, to achieve a score of 5.

Also borrowed from the GBC tool was an additional designation of 'critical' that could be used for specific criteria. This was used in the EPA Fit-out to give recognition to the emphasis given by user objectives to certain issues, as well as to current environmental imperatives, such as greenhouse gas emissions. Reflecting the user objectives, many of the criteria designated as critical appear in the indoor environment category.

LEGISLATION: ENERGY CODE REQUIREMENTS

At the time of the project there were no legislative standards for sustainability in Queensland, although some energy legislation has since been introduced into the Building Code of Australia (BCA). Standards for achieving sustainable buildings are largely voluntary, hence the use of the GBC tool to assist with the briefing process and provide a reasonably objective set of assessment criteria.

In Australia the Australian Building Greenhouse Rating Scheme (ABGRS) has become the de facto standard for energy assessment of commercial buildings. After one year of monitoring the building was found to have achieved a rating of five stars under the ABGRS, the first new building in Australia to achieve such a rating.[17]

ECONOMIC COSTS

A *business case* for this project was established, which placed priority not only on environmental issues but also on economic goals. The economic objective was that the project be financed in a similar way to a normal commercial project. The equity structure and financing was made through the commercial banking system without government subsidy. The following description of the business case is from the Department of Public Works.

One of the objectives in the development of William McCormack Place was to demonstrate that a commercially viable office building could be built in the wet tropics region of Queensland that met a number of environmental requirements including specific energy targets. An overall project budget of A$17.5 million, including fit-out and a 2 per cent allowance for art work, was established. Feasibility studies were carried out using a number of assumptions:

- the entire project cost was to be borrowed and interest payments factored into the running costs;
- no federal or state government environmental subsidies were to be used;
- a commercial rate of return was required; and
- market rents were to be achieved.

The business case for including ecologically sustainable design in the project was based on a number of principles. These held that:

- Increased up-front capital costs can result in reduced operating and life cycle costs.
- Ecologically sustainable designs do not necessarily cost more to build.
- An environmentally friendly building is more attractive to current and future tenants and can therefore attract higher rents.

Internal and external quantity surveyor's reports indicated that the cost of addressing the environmental issues was generally no greater than would be expected for a 'normal' building of the same quality. Savings in other areas where less complex designs were used offset the additional cost of plant such as the thermal wheel. It was discovered that it was not a case of the development of complex or costly new technologies but one of effectively using a combination of existing, proven technologies.

A significant financial impact of the environmental initiatives at William McCormack Place is the reduction in energy costs compared to similar buildings in Cairns. This is a true life cycle saving that is apparent from day one and results in savings for both the owner and the tenant. It is estimated that the energy savings will provide a recurrent net reduction of A$5 per square metre per annum in the building operating costs, which, if capitalized, gives an increased property value of around A$300,000. In addition, the lower tenant energy cost represents a recurrent saving in occupancy cost to the tenant that will assist in the building maintaining its market rent position.

An example of how slightly increasing capital costs can both reduce life cycle costs and address environmental issues was in the choice of carpet. Carpet is a major capital outlay and becomes a major and non-recoverable cost to the owner many times during the life of a building when replaced because of wear and damage. The carpet used in William McCormack Place has a number of economic and environmental advantages arising from its ability to be 'remanufactured' to provide an extended life. The carpet has an expected 'first life' of 15 years, after which time in can be lifted, 'remanufactured' and re-laid with a further warranty at a cost that is approximately 50 per cent of that of new carpet. It is believed that the carpet life can be extended to 30–35 years in this manner. A comparison of costs (in 2002 dollars) over a 35-year life cycle shows a life cycle saving of A$613,000.

Many ecologically sustainable design initiatives included in William McCormack Place have resulted in reductions in energy use, waste minimization and reduced refurbishment costs. Examples include:

- Provision of additional fresh air and self-balancing air supplies as well as ready access to chilled water and condenser water simplifies the design and installation of air conditioning when fit-out changes or office refurbishments occur.
- Retention of original air conditioning and lighting layouts reduces the cost of refurbishment or make-good. It also prevents the slow deterioration of the systems over time (as a result of incremental changes to ducts, for example) as is often seen in older buildings where costly refurbishment of duct work and rewiring is eventually required simply to return building services to their original design condition.

The business case for determining the benefit of environmental initiatives in any project is not just a case of establishing simple payback. In the case of the air conditioning, a comprehensive whole of life cycle cost equation must be considered including additional factors such as maintenance costs and future fit-out design and construction costs. It must also take into account future capital costs when replacing plant at the building half-life stage. The project team for William McCormack Place focused not only on the direct short-term payback but also on the future costs.[18]

Phase 3: Strategies developed

The development of design strategies for the fit-out was complicated as the issues relating to the fit-out were intrinsically connected with the issues of the base building, its envelope, structure and services. In this respect the methodology used was to develop the fit-out strategies within the context of the standard brief. In this way it would be clear how the fit-out strategies related to issues in the standard design brief. The strategies for the fit-out were presented in the environmental brief as a number of tables. Within the tables the strategies were cross-referenced to the standard brief as well as being cross-referenced to other sources upon which they were based such as GOAU, and the ESD Fit-out Guidelines. The intention was that designers could use the tables created in the brief as a checklist.

PLANNING AND ENVIRONMENTAL POLICIES

The first set of issues examined as part of the planning process related to the policy context set by the owner and manager, DPW. In particular, issues concerning quality management of the project were investigated and included in the brief. Another issue of policy examined in the brief was that of government procurement policies.

Standardized procurement policies can be a barrier to the selection of environmental materials and systems. The development of further policies by the owners and tenants was encour-

Design brief objectives and strategies

Standard design brief objectives	Fit-out design strategies
Use of effective quality assurance methodologies	Use design-phase assessment to meet ESD standards. Adopt internationally recognized ESD assessment tool. Adopt user satisfaction survey, pre and post occupancy.
QSG environmental purchasing policy[19]	Adopt policy for procurement of 'green' components.
Staff and user education	Prepare guidelines for the use of the building to assist with operational performance of the building, i.e. building user manual.
Waste management	Prepare guidelines for the use of the building to assist with operational performance with regard to waste management.
Conservation of resources and heritage	Prepare guidelines for the use of the building to assist with the conserving of resources.
Environmental health assessment	Manufacturers to provide product health data sheets on all products and materials in fit-out.
Prohibited and preferred environmental products	Adopt the list of prohibited products. Develop a list of preferred environmental materials and systems for fit-out.

External planning issues

Building address and security line

Adopt entrance planning principles in standard brief.

Plan to use the address point as a display area of tenants' educational material.

Plan to provide a meeting area for visitors to tenants outside the security line.

Image and character of entrance should 'bring outside in' to facilitate tenant identification.

Facilitate frequent public access to building.

Locate service reception point close to public entry point of building.

Facilitate 24-hour access to incident control room; ensure security of building while admitting users to control room.

Permit flexibility of use of mechanical services for after-hours usage.

aged in the brief. These centred on improving indoor environmental quality and appropriate waste management post construction.

FIT-OUT PLANNING GUIDELINES

The second set of issues concerned internal planning needs of spaces. Issues relating to climate, plan and depth have a direct

effect on the internal environmental quality. These are examined under passive systems. This set up the performance requirements for the envelope structure and services of the building. The fit-out planning principles were organized into categories responding to external and internal issues.

FIT-OUT FORM

A number of issues influenced the form of the fit-out. A key issue was the need for appropriate levels of visual and acoustic privacy in individual workplaces. Recommendations were made to use appropriate products in partitions to achieve sound attenuation and for partitions to be of appropriate height to achieve visual privacy.

To allow future organizational change, the recommendation was made to utilize modular and/or standardized partitioning and furniture systems, and a modular and removable flooring system was recommended.

Another critical requirement identified in the survey of users was the need for common areas for the viewing of large reference items such as maps and charts. The recommendation was made that these areas be close to the individual workpoints.

A key role of the fit-out form is to allow maximum opportunity for natural lighting throughout the building. Several related

Interior issues

Internal issues	Strategies
Lifts and stairs	Plan to avoid the need for lifts or use of lifts. Enhance pleasantness of stairs to promote their use. Make stairs a focal point of building – promote interaction through associated foyer spaces.
Facility management	Prepare activity space data sheets for all workplace areas to facilitate audits and future planning.
Facilitate frequent public access to building	Locate service reception point close to public entry point of building.
Facilitate frequent service deliveries	Locate service delivery points in close proximity to areas that require the service.
Facilitate 24-hour access to incident control room	Ensure security of building while admitting users to control room. Permit flexibility of mechanical services for after-hours usage.
Facilitate staff removing themselves from work spaces for short breaks	Locate covered external spaces adjacent to internal workplaces.
Allow access to reference materials (maps, charts, etc.)	Optimize space used for reference material storage. Allow for space for viewing of large items such as maps through office areas.
Allow access to significant reference materials. (maps, charts etc.)	Optimize space used for reference material storage. Allow for space for viewing of large items such as maps.
Modular coordination	Adopt space-planning principles for modular coordination.

The office fit-out, design using the environmental briefing process.

strategies were recommended in the fit-out brief. These strategies were:

- Place enclosed offices to the middle of the building.
- Select appropriate partitions so as not to obstruct natural light entering work areas.
- Colour of materials (walls, ceiling, furniture) should be light so as to optimize the penetration of natural lighting deeper into the building plan.

At the level of the individual workpoint there were also a number of strategies suggested relating to the form of the fit-out:

- Provide adequate space at individual workplaces.
- Provide desk mountings for desktop equipment in addition to desktop space for tasks.
- Provide ergonomic comfort for occupants, in particular provide properly designed and functional chairs and adjustable desktops.
- Implement a standard workspace allocation module.
- Provide adequate storage for users, including storage at individual workpoints and storage in immediate areas for less commonly used items.
- Allow flexibility of spatial arrangement within individual workplaces.
- Utilize standardized furniture systems.

Strategies for indoor environmental quality

Standard design brief objectives	Fit-out design strategies
Indoor air quality	Institute a user satisfaction survey of existing building and another study of the proposed building. Adopt air quality guidelines in SFB.
Infestation control	Develop guidelines for infestation control and non-toxic pest control.
Noise and vibration control	Adopt provisions in SFB.
Personal safety	Adopt provisions in SFB. Provide safety for disadvantaged groups (see project brief).
Thermal comfort	Provision of fresh air. Uniform temperatures. Remove extremes of temperature by passive means rather than active systems.
Visual environment	Welcoming and comfortable ambiance. Provide a visual connection to outside or to internal landscaping. Interior should integrate and reinforce the connection with external environment. Provision of minimum lighting levels. Provide task illumination through daylight. Avoid excessive contrast between low and highly lit areas.

PASSIVE DESIGN

The main aim for fit-out, in terms of thermal comfort, is to provide high levels of environmental quality inside the space. The problem is primarily one of tempering the tropical external conditions. The building is located in a warm tropical climate where cooling is the main requirement. The critical issues of plan depth, envelope design and ceiling height, which were all determined in the building brief, had a significant impact on what could be achieved by the fit-out design. These factors from the building brief therefore also guided the strategies delivered in the fit-out brief:

- Provide comfortable, attractive accommodation that is sensitive to climate.
- Reconcile the envelope prescriptive requirements from the standard brief and the needs of fit-out ESD requirements.
- Use performance standards rather than prescriptive standards.
- Optimize orientation, glazing area and sun shading to reduce thermal loads and increase natural daylighting.
- Revise maximum plan depth from 12.6 metres to 8 metres to make the building envelope sensitive and reduce environmental impact.

The first issues in developing the environmental brief were to examine the criteria for passive design to achieve indoor environmental quality. This included finding out from the users of the fit-out, before and after occupation, their opinions of the environmental quality of the fit-out.

ACTIVE SYSTEMS

The active system design objectives centred on meshing the thermal comfort of the occupants with energy consumption reduction. The active systems are essentially a function of the building services covered in the standard brief. However, the fit-out acts as the interface between the building and the user.

THERMAL ZONING

A recommendation in the environmental brief was to balance thermal comfort with the tasks being undertaken in various spaces. With the warm climate, the opportunity was seen for some of the spaces to operate as free-running (naturally ventilated) spaces. This would provide more variation in the thermal zoning of the internal spaces and also allow a reduction in air conditioning and energy loads. Therefore a recommendation was made to provide thermal zoning in the base building and fit-out so that the zones can operate independently of each other in one of three modes:

- free-running (natural ventilation);
- air conditioned; and
- hybrid.

Providing thermal zoning for different activities in the tenancy areas and matching the load profile to ensure operational efficiency of 80–100 per cent would lead to greater energy efficiency. This can be demonstrated by carrying out life cycle assessment of plant and equipment to justify system selection.

Active strategies

Standard design brief objectives	Fit-out design strategies
Alternate energy sources	Employ co-generation for electric lighting of fit-out space.
Building envelope, OTTV	Complement OTTV transfer assessment with optimization study of thermal performance of the envelope in relation to daylighting and electric lighting loads. Carry out energy conservation assessment to reduce energy demand through building form and fabric.
Building management environmental control systems	Provide automatic and user-controlled air conditioning. Sector and zoning measuring of resource consumption (follow Energy Audit Guidelines). Identify operational schedule for plant and equipment. Educate users throughout building life on building use and management systems.
HVAC installation	Set points for air conditioning should relate to thermal comfort criteria for Cairns and vary seasonally.
Landscape	Provide internal landscape for visual amenity and better perception of comfort.

In addition to these strategies, thermal mass is used to attenuate the cooling system by exposing the thermal mass of the building structure (ceiling and floors) to encourage a thermal flywheel effect. Thermal insulating materials for ceilings and walls should be minimized. Surface area of exposed ceilings should be maximized and the use of night purging using HVAC will improve the efficiency of the flywheel effect.

ELECTRIC LIGHTING AND DAYLIGHTING

The main recommendation in the environmental brief regarding lighting was to attempt to optimize the use of natural daylight. This is important from the point of view of energy consumption and from the psychological perspective of the users. The detailed strategies included:

- clear differentiation between ambient and task lighting;
- use daylighting for ambient lighting during daytime;
- luminaire selection should be based on LCA assessment;
- automatic switching of ambient lighting;
- convenient switching of task lighting for individual users;
- colour rendition of electric lighting;
- ultraviolet radiation control;
- lamp flicker control;
- minimal impact, low energy, fluorescent lights;
- high-efficiency lighting fixtures; and
- motion sensors in low-occupancy areas.

Other recommendations included improving the visual environment for the user by attempting to minimize glare at workplaces and VDU screens; also specialized work in the offices requires adequate lighting levels to all specialized work areas in the building. The techniques recommended were the use of external or internal shading devices that may be controlled by the occupant, utilizing appropriate diffusers on artificial lighting and task-based lighting for specialized work.

OTHER ACTIVE STRATEGIES

Other active strategies relating to the operation of the building were recommended.

MATERIAL AND COMPONENT SELECTION

The recommendations in the environmental brief specifically called up the selection of 'green materials' for the fit-out. It was realized that to specify those materials in the fit-out and not the base building would be inconsistent. A policy recommendation was made in the brief that materials and finishes for areas other than tenancy fit-out should be 'green'. This brought about a revision of materials and finishes in the standard project brief.

The main issues of concern relating to materials selection were air quality, acoustics, and visual amenity. Main building elements considered were wall, floor and ceiling finishes and the furniture and fittings.

Interior materials and finishes

Strategy	Techniques
Maximize indoor air quality	Select materials that will not produce pollutants in the indoor environment. Minimize the use of soft furnishings to reduce 'sinks' for indoor pollution. Minimize the use of materials that would produce toxic gases in the event of a fire, particularly PVC. Utilize solid timbers or structural grade plywood in furniture in preference to MDF. Utilize linoleum or other non-toxic alternatives in preference to vinyl.
Cleaning services and office waste	Design for and implement recycling of office waste by planning recycling receptacles throughout the office.
Services	Specify alternative insulation products to fibreglass to services installations.
Floor finishes	Avoid composite tiles bonded with synthetic resins and specify recyclable products.
Wall and ceiling finishes	Reduce the need for applied coatings and finishes. Where required, select environmentally friendly, low VOC finishes.
Acoustics	Adopt internal noise control as defined in standard brief.

CONSTRUCTION PROCESS

Though construction strategies were not included as part of the environmental brief for the fit-out, the Department of Public Works, as building owners, reported that the integration of the fit-out with the main building was achieved to save cost and to keep the construction period to a minimum.

The construction of the fit-out was incorporated seamlessly into the main construction programme and was completed shortly after the building itself. The hard fit-out, including partition walls, air conditioning duct work, and electrical and communication cabling was carried out by the managing contractor as a main contract variation. This was to ensure that the fit-out work was incorporated into the original construction work and that no wastage occurred as a result of removal of or changes to work already completed. To ensure that the construction of the fit-out did not compromise the project programme, a fit-out design freeze was implemented in September 2001.[20]

OPERATIONAL MANAGEMENT

It was recommended that the processes started during the environmental brief development should continue through the life of the building by undertaking the following measures.

An in-house action group was used to develop management solutions to specific issues that will impact on the office layout. Research was also carried out to support the use of various environmental initiatives based on post occupancy information. Some practical methods were developed to integrate the Green

Response to life cycle issues

Issues	Strategies	Environmental benefits
Design life	50 years	Long life
Capital cost per m²	Medium	Higher capital cost offset by life cycle cost benefits through operational savings
Internal flexibility	Open plan	Ease of reuse
Fabric quality	High	Low maintenance
Corrective maintenance schedule	Low	Low energy
Minimize running costs	Low	Low energy
Other		

Building Challenge criteria into a workable and usable project reference document. Additional strategies were recommended regarding the life of the fit-out, its maintenance and life cycle costing.

Design response

This section describes some of the more prominent ESD strategies that were actually put in place in the design of the fit-out and building at William McCormack Place, as a result of the environmental brief and/or the standard brief. The significant advances towards sustainable design were made in the areas of energy efficiency, and materials use and indoor environmental quality in the fit-out design.

Energy efficiency

The main theme of this project was to achieve energy efficiency chiefly through operational energy. The reason for this is that approximately 75 per cent of C02 emissions in commercial office buildings are generated by this phase of the building's life cycle. The dominance of fossil-fuel-produced electricity in Queensland makes this a major area for improvement. Other issues such as waste heat from electric lighting and office equipment contribute to the problem, making up 33 per cent of office CO_2 emissions and adding to the load for cooling the building.[21]

As mentioned earlier, the building actually achieved a five-star rating under the ABGR. There were three main initiatives that contributed significantly to the energy efficiency achieved in this project. The first key initiative was the act of target setting. Targets for energy performance were set as follows:

- air-conditioning 77.8 kWh/m²/year;
- ventilation 19.2 kWh/m²/year;
- lighting 24 kWh/m²/year;
- hot water4 kWh/m²/year; and
- office equipment15 kWh/m²/year.[22]

The second set of initiatives centred on the selection of energy-efficient plant and equipment. As can be seen above, air conditioning is the highest energy consumer in the building. Two key objectives were to be achieved in the design of the air conditioning system for William McCormack Place. These were that the system must be highly efficient, given that the hot, humid conditions in Cairns require air conditioning all year round; and, given the semi-remote location, the system was to be simple and reliable with a level of redundancy to compensate for the occasional difficulty in obtaining spare parts in Cairns. These objectives have been achieved through incorporating several strategies into the design, summarized as follows:

- A common pre-conditioning unit, incorporating a thermal (heat recovery) wheel, recovers approximately 61 per cent of otherwise lost energy from used air as it is exhausted from the building.
- A high-efficiency chilled water plant incorporating rotary screw chillers runs in a duty/standby configuration. Each of the two chillers will carry 105 per cent of the building load.
- A 15,000 litre chilled water thermal storage tank eliminates prolonged periods of low load (and poor efficiency) operation of the chiller.
- Variable speed drives (VSDs) have been fitted to all pumps and fans in the air conditioning system and zoned variable air volume boxes have been used throughout.
- The building management system (BMS) controls and monitors air conditioning and ventilation and ensures efficient operation of the air conditioning after hours.[23]

The third set of initiatives contributing to the energy efficiency of the building is based around the integration of strategies across the building envelope, structure, services and fit-out. The integration of building elements, in particular the shading elements, and openings as part of the envelope design, the thermal mass of the structure and the layout and form of the fit-out design, have worked together to optimize internal environmental conditions and reduce the demand for air conditioning.

Similarly, the integration of the overall building dimensions, openings, fit-out form and material selection has maximized the potential for natural daylighting.

Fit-out concept

The office accommodation in the building was designed using the principles in the Ecologically Sustainable Office Fit-out Guidelines developed by the Queensland Department of Public Works and launched at the FMA National Conference in 2001. The guidelines provide designers, contractors and end-users (ten-

ants) of office accommodation with practical advice on ecologically sustainable design considerations to ensure a healthier, ecologically sustainable fit-out that would reduce risks associated with hazards and liaise with industry to improve sustainable trade and employment aspects.

The fit-out was designed by QDPW's interior designers following extensive consultation with the end-users and has many features that address environmental issues:

- Open plan workstations are adjacent to perimeter windows to maximize natural light and views, with offices and meeting rooms arranged towards the centre of the floor. The workspace is highly flexible and open, with minimal built zones.
- All demountable partitions and furniture are of modular design and doors are of uniform size to allow for future reuse. Where possible, mechanical connectors rather than glues are used in the assembly of workstations and screens to promote reuse.
- Materials with very low off-gassing of volatile organic compounds (VOCs) were used throughout.
- Wide use is made of recycled materials in the construction of furniture. Mobile units, partition screens and shelves are made of high-density polyethylene (HDPE) and polypropylene (PE) sourced from recycled residential and commercial waste. Screens are upholstered with fabric made from recycled PET bottles. The use of PVC was minimized.
- No timber products derived from non-sustainable sources have been used.

The carpet used throughout the building was chosen on the basis of its environmental and life cycle cost benefits (see p 277 for cost benefits). It is a carpet tile that can be 'remanufactured' to provide an extended life. The environmental benefits include an expected 'first life' of 15 years, at which time in can be lifted, 'remanufactured' with minimal energy or materials used, and re-laid. The manufacturer expects a useful life of at least 30 years from the carpet whereas a conventional broadloom carpet may be replaced (and discarded as landfill) up to four times during that period. Health impacts could be reduced by installation using water-based solvents, with low off-gassing of VOCs from either the carpet or solvents. The carpet backing can be recycled when the carpet is finally discarded.

A carpet tile system allows small sections (down to a single tile) to be replaced, thereby minimizing the effect of damage, and allows the carpet to be easily accommodated around partition walls and storage units (many broadloom carpets are replaced early because they have been damaged as a result of being cut around walls during fit-out works). Small quantities of replacement carpet can be supplied to the original print design, negating the need to store large quantities of spare carpet (often up to 5 per cent of the gross floor area).[24]

Lessons learned

One of the main lessons learned from this project was to the use of the environmental brief and its relation to the on-going design and project management:

> Significant consultation with the Environmental Protection Agency (EPA). EPA was particularly interested in the project, as it was to be a major tenant in the completed building and needed to be sure that environmental targets were met. EPA produced an 'Environmental Brief' for the project that contributed greatly to the environmental initiatives incorporated into the design.[25]

The building project management philosophy by QDPW involved considerable dialogue between the project team, external consultants and contractors. This discursive approach resulted in numerous improvements to processes that contributed to the success of the project. The importance of this is the impact on the process of design. The process changes included:

- A clear and concise project brief was developed, which clearly articulated environmental requirements and targets.
- Architects and consultants were selected on their experience and ability, not just on competitive price.
- The building was delivered as a two-stage design and construct project, thereby reducing its risk and, at the same time, ensuring that the design met all the requirements of the project brief.
- An extensive value management workshop was conducted as part of the design development stage.[26]

The way the value management worked is contingent on the successful application of the brief. The project team reported that the workshop was used

to ensure that the proposed designs met the project brief and could be constructed within the budget. At this stage calculations showed that the project cost would exceed the budget by $1 million and it was necessary to make changes to control the potential over-run. To this end, changes were considered to both the building itself and its services. As is often the case, the services were considered an easy target for cost reductions that would not affect the appearance of the building; however, the project team insisted that any changes must not affect the energy or environmental targets or the flexibility and manageability of the building. Ultimately the necessary savings were mainly realized through changes in the requirements for some back-of-house areas, the deletion of one lift and architectural changes to the roof and façade treatment. The value of effective communication and processes, particularly during the planning and design stages, has been proven by the fact that there were very few trade package variations during the construction of the project and the building was delivered on time and on budget while achieving the project objectives.[27]

Other lessons learned

Collaboration between tenants, users and owners is very important to the success of the project. It is easier to achieve on this sort of government project. It would be more difficult, but should nonetheless be an aim, on standard commercial projects in which there is no relationship between owners and users or tenants.

Having the input at the earlier stage of the design process – when the building brief was being developed – would have been better still. It would have saved some effort, prevented some duplication and reduced the potential for conflicting recommendations or strategies between the two briefing documents.

Acknowledgments

Consultants for the fit-out brief: Mark Thomson of the TVS Partnership
Richard Hyde and Stephen Watson of the Centre for Sustainable Design, UQ
Plans and illustrations: Queensland Department of Public Works

Wessex Water Operational Centre. The northern courtyard provides an external space, which creates additional amenity for the staff.

CASE STUDY 10

Wessex Water Operational Centre, Bath, UK

Architects: Bennetts Associates

The new building was a central part of the Wessex Water's long-term business plan, which placed sustainability at the centre of its operations. In consequence, the project not only considered environmental issues but also a wide range of social and economic factors...[28]

Introduction

Dean Hawkes, reviewing this project for *Architecture Today*, commented:

Natural selection is nature's way of ensuring through the process of evolution that species survive in the ever changing environment. The idea of evolutionary change is also an appropriate analogy for the way in which architecture responds to changes in its environment.[29]

In the case of Wessex Water, the office typology for green buildings has evolved as the result of the design of a number of buildings, creating 'an excellent example of how a commercial building can be environmentally sustainable'.[30]

As well as the architects, with their track record, the client was a notable catalyst in the realization of this building, playing the role of primary initiator and setting a firm direction towards integrating sustainability into the project. These factors were coupled with a site of great natural beauty occupied by an existing building, and the involvement of the Building Research Establishment (BRE.) The alliance with BRE enabled the building to be a pilot project for the BREEAM environmen-

Wessex Water Regional Operations Centre project details[31]

Characteristic	Detail
Owner	Wessex Water Services Ltd
Project team	Architects: Bennetts Associates
	Engineer services: Buro Happold Landscape architect: Grant Associates and Bernard Ede Construction management: Mace Ltd Cost consultant: Davis Langdon and Everest
Completion date	July 2000
Construction cost	GB£22.5 million
Size	9,921 m²
Footprint	Site area divided by 2[32]
Annual energy use	100 kWh/m² per year[33]
Site area	28,000 m²
City	Bath
Country	United Kingdom
Latitude	50°18′ N
Building type	Office and control centre
Occupancy	530 people

tal assessment system; versions 1993 and 1998 were used in the design process to achieve an 'excellent' rating.

Since that time the BREEAM system has advanced, and a new checklist has been developed to indicate performance, which is helpful in mapping the strategies used.

Pre-design and briefing

This section charts the pre-design activities that helped to capture sustainable goals and objectives in the project.

Project organization
THE CLIENT'S VISION

The vision for this project had two sources: the need for cultural change in the organization and the company's commitment to sustainability. Ann Bodkin explains:

Wessex Water's headquarters was intended to consolidate several dispersed buildings into a much more efficient Operations Centre that would first bring about a culture change through improved working conditions, and second demonstrate the company's deep-seated commitment to social, economic and environmental sustainability.[34]

These two main concepts formed the basis of a strategic brief, developed by the architects and their team.

THE STRATEGIC BRIEF

The design period for the project ran parallel with the development of a more systematic approach to the environmental impact of construction in the UK. Wessex Water issued a strategic brief that identified the main issues to be addressed in the design process. This brief set demanding energy targets and encouraged whole-of-life performance and costing studies.

Appointment of consultants involved the architects and client in selecting those with experience in sustainability issues raised by the strategic brief. A multidisciplinary design team was formed.

TESTING THE STRATEGIC BRIEF

The client selected a management team of key personnel from the office organization. The strategic brief was tested through analysis, feedback from staff sessions and one-to-one sessions to fully understand user needs and aspirations. Further activities helped test the brief for feasibility purposes:

- building visits by the design team and client;
- liaison with the planning authority;
- open meetings with the local community, continued throughout the construction process; and
- BREEAM Office 98 environmental assessment methodology for office buildings;

- ENVEST, BRE's computer analysis program for assessing design options for the environmental impact of construction materials;
- benchmarking cost studies of office buildings; and
- meetings with key contractors at an early stage to investigate systems, with regard to cost, programme, materials and environmental performance.[35]

Right. Site planning created a number of external spaces and courtyards, which have different landscape themes, providing added social and environmental purposes. **Left**. The nature pond creates a natural landscape while other courtyards have planting for species that are tolerant of dry conditions

'FLESHING OUT' THE BRIEF

Project organization involved a multidisciplinary design team and a construction management team. The construction management approach enabled the use of a wide range of consultants in the delivery of the project. The construction manager took a key role in responding to sustainability issues, using various strategies to facilitate sustainability in the procurement process:

- engaging in scheme design and providing ongoing expertise during the entire design process;
- providing workshops for trade contractors and performance reviews on sustainability issues;
- developing a site waste and recycling scheme to save costs;
- involving the facility manager, who would eventually be responsible for the operation of the building in the pre-commissioning and commissioning process;
- commencing trade packages early, to ensure timely completion of project; and
- ensuring snagging was done before practical completion.

The environmental impact of construction impact was also considered. Trade contractors were required to consider environmental issues in their work, such as having 100 per cent health and safety track record, pride in their work and a clean site.[36]

Application of BREEAM Office Rating

The use of the BREEAM approach is linked to a number of other analysis tools to make the assessment possible.

First, the environmental strategies proposed by the design team can be examined for inclusiveness, by using the Design and Procurement Assessment Prediction checklist provided by BREEAM. This gives an estimate of the number of sustainable issues the design team has included in the design to reduce environmental impacts. In this case study, a simple strategy mapping exercise was used to qualitatively assess the extent of strategies used in the design. The strategies used by the design team are compared with the indicators to establish the extent to which the indicators can be met.

Second, it is of interest to note how the tools such as BREEAM were used, and for what purpose, and where in the design stages

Left. Integration of the building with the landscape involves the use of roof terraces, which contain local species. **Right**. The degree of transparency of the envelope balances the need for view and thermal performance issues. High-performance glazing systems are an integral part of the design of the façade to control heat flux.

they were most effective. Discussions with the project designer revealed some interesting observations.

BREEAM IN PRACTICE

Discussions with the project designer revealed that the BREEAM assessment tool is not just an assessment system. It does more than just provide an eco-label, like a star rating on a refrigerator. The designers of the Wessex Water project seem to have used it for three purposes:

1   a framework for performance issues;
2   a decision-making tool;
3   an information base for the brief.

First, the framework. Sustainable development is an oxymoron and the field has been made overly complex; a practical framework is needed if it is to be put into practice. The designers found the best use of the tool was as a framework around which to build creative ideas about the project. Being performance based, it avoids prescriptive design and allows a wide range of strategies to be used to solve problems.

To carry out the assessment, further analytical work is needed to demonstrate that the building meets the standard. In this respect, some of the criteria require basic calculations and measurements while others simply check that the strategies are in place. Some of this analysis suits the skill base of the architect, and some that of the engineer.

The design team used the tool for design decision-making for the best outcome. During the design of the project, two evaluations were made to estimate the environmental impacts of the building. This matched the iterative process of the design work, which involved an initial check to see how things were going, modifications to the design and re-evaluation. This used the tool to help inform decision-making and can continue throughout the design process.

The time-consuming part of this is supplying the information to support the evaluation. In this case, two important additional tools and methodologies were used. The first was ENVEST, which provides environmental impact assessment of materials and systems; however, simple material preference lists can be used. A whole-of-life costing methodology was used as well, to examine the cost benefits of the materials and systems proposed.

The normal quantity surveying process of cost auditing was modified to assist with both these additional analytical exercises. This led to a supply chain report, which provided a materials and systems preference list for the team and the client.

How did the design team integrate the BREEAM tool with their design processes?

The Royal Institute of British Architects has established 11 stages for the design and procurement of a project. Each stage comprises certain tasks, activities and personnel. In the case of the Wessex Water project, the main work with the BREEAM tool took place at Stage C: Outline proposal. This stage involves:

- brief development;
- planning; and
- outline design and cost options.

The main actors are project client, construction manager, design team, quantity surveyor and CDM planning supervisor. From this it can be concluded that using BREEAM has two advantages. First, the criteria contained within the BREEAM tool can be incorporated into the design brief. Second, the tool can be used as a framework for design decision-making. While it is commonly thought that assessment tools should be used after design is complete, this approach emphasized the use of the checklist at the early stage of the design process, particularly at Stage C: Outline proposal stage in the RIBA Plan of Work. The project engineer for the building concludes:

The building and systems design incorporate the objectives of the BREEAM assessment method and the goals of M4I, the Movement for Innovation, for which this is a demonstration project.[37]

Response to the brief

Site

Wessex Water bought the site, located on the corner of Brassknocker Hill and Claverton Down Road, in October 1997. Located approximately 3 km from Bath, the site overlooks the Limpley Stoke Valley in the Cotswolds Area of Outstanding Natural Beauty.

The topography comprises rolling limestone escarpments with lush vegetation; the site is on one of the southerly (equator-facing) slopes of the valley, providing good solar access. Prevailing winds are from the south-west, providing cooling breezes in summer and warm winds in winter.

Building form and fabric

The building form responds to the site through a cascade of two-storey modules down the slope of the site. The module on the top of the ridge comprises the entrance, and the operations facility is on the second floor; this is the 'nerve centre' of the facility, which dictates its location in relation to other modules of the building.

The design sensitivity for the natural and building environment in this area is an indication of the approach taken with the building planning as a whole. Notable strategies concerning the planning of the form of the building are:

- thin-finger planning to provide solar access and ventilation;
- air-conditioned meeting rooms placed to the west, to buffer naturally ventilated spaces from the western sun;
- courtyards to provide external sheltered spaces;
- two-storey height to minimize the visual impact of building massing;
- visual axis to link views from inside to external features of natural beauty; and
- open-plan offices connected by way of a central circulation spine (forming a 'street'), which links communal spaces such as restaurant, community centre and meeting rooms.

The fabric of the building is primarily designed to be interactive with the natural environment. This involves rejecting unwanted heat and accessing cooling breezes for ventilation in summer, while conserving heat in winter. With office buildings of this kind, internal heat gains from the occupants and the equipment, rather than environmental loads from outside, are normally the dominant loads on the internal climate control system. These loads are normally addressed by air conditioning. In this case, a primarily passive approach was taken to avoid the use of active systems and increased energy consumption. Response to climate in this case is crucial.

Response to climate

Bath, in the Vale of Evesham in the west of England, has a climate influenced by the Gulf Stream. The area where the site is located has temperatures that are noticeably more moderate than the London climate, which is influenced to a greater extent by the European continent. Nevertheless, the climate in the region of Bath is still characterized as a heating climate; bioclimatically, the external temperatures are below the comfort zone, with damp cold conditions in winter and warm wet summers; the number of months where bioclimatic strategies alone can be used is limited to about one-third of the year.

Passive strategies and techniques

The passive strategies that can be used for this climate in winter comprise solar gain and use of thermal mass as a way of extending the comfort zone. In summer, the strategies used depend on airflow and thermal mass. The details of the passive strategies are as follows.

THERMAL MASS

Thermal mass uses high-capacity materials such as concrete and masonry to store heat and create a thermal flywheel or inertia in the building. This has the effect of evening out the temperature swings in the building, giving a more balanced thermal environment and improved thermal comfort for the occupants. This implies reducing peak temperatures in summer and raising low temperatures, such as the early morning chill, in winter.

Thermal mass is often claimed to be 'free heat', but this is a myth. It is really a heat distribution system, which takes in heat at one point in time and redistributes it at another. Using thermal mass for indoor climate control still requires a method of charging it. The availability of sufficient thermal mass is a prerequisite.

In this case, concrete walls, floors and roofs are used to provide mass. Charging is by way of indirect air effects. In summer, ventilation brings in cool air at night to reduce the temperature of the mass; the cool 'stored' in the mass is then used during the day to reduce air temperatures. In winter, the mass is charged during the day by the heating system and this heat is retained overnight so that the building requires minimal start-up heating the next day.

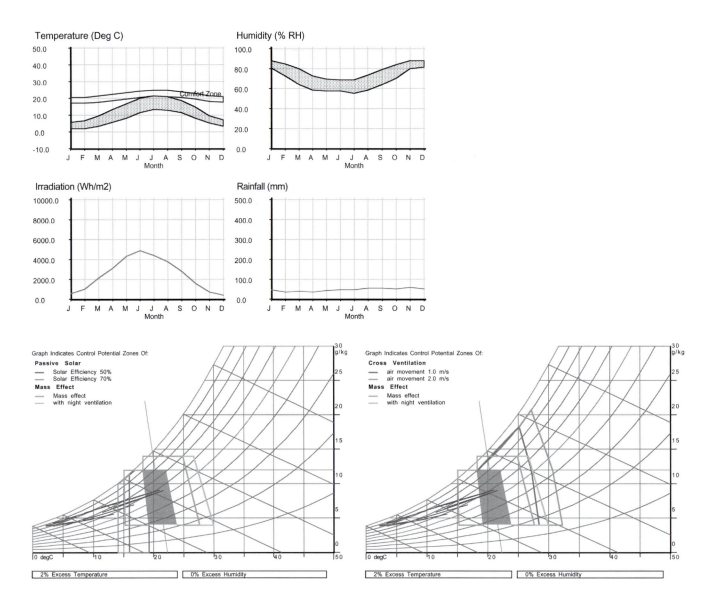

Left. Macroclimate for the site. **Right**. Bioclimatic strategies of thermal mass and passive solar are only effective for about four months of the year to extend the comfort zone. For the remainder, high levels of heat conservation and supplementary heating are needed. In summer the internal heat loads from the office function combine with the environmental loads to create a potential for overheating, hence the need to consider air flow as a means of cooling in summer.

SOLAR GAIN

Solar gain is minimized in summer by shading devices and solar glass, preventing the thermal mass from overheating.

In winter, solar gain is accepted, but because of low external air temperatures heat must be conserved by means of an airtight façade, insulation of opaque elements and double-glazing of transparent elements.

AIRFLOW

Airflow is provided by the use of pressure-driven cross ventilation through operable windows. Pop-up roof lights assist stack

ventilation, that is, airflow driven by the temperature difference between inside and outside.

Active strategies and techniques

HEATING, VENTILATION AND AIR CONDITIONING (HVAC)

The environmental design of the HVAC system was aimed at reducing energy through conservation. With respect to cooling, by using predominantly natural ventilation it was possible to minimize the running time of the air conditioning systems. The air conditioning became a back-up system, rather than a mainstream climate control system. This led to signifi-

Left. Open plan office environment. **Right**. Ambient light provided to space via direct light to coffer ceiling. Shading is used to create diffused light.

cantly lower energy usage for this component of the energy budget.

Three types of system are used:

1 For open plan offices, a peak lopping displacement system is provided for extreme summer-time temperature conditions.
2 For meeting rooms, control centre and communications/ server rooms, mixed mode air conditioning systems are operated in conjunction with natural ventilation systems, so that when natural ventilation is in use the active system is automatically shut off.
3 To provide thermal comfort, particularly in the open plan offices, the building energy management system was programmed to operate the windows in the façade to optimize performance.

Typical cycles for the HVAC systems utilize three modes. When temperatures are higher outside than in – such as during the day in summer – the windows are closed and the thermal mass is used to cool the internal air. When temperatures are higher inside than out – such as at night time in summer – the windows are open and heat is taken from the internal air and from the thermal mass. When temperatures are continuously below the comfort zone in winter, convection-heating systems located at the main points of heat loss are used. These are set around the perimeter in a floor trench, and under the roof lights, to prevent draughts and radiant cooling effects from the glass.

ELECTRIC LIGHTING

The building is designed to use supplementary electric lighting in conjunction with daylight. Within the open plan units, 400 lux is provided on the work plane, using a suspended up and down light system with diffusers incorporating T5 indirect and direct luminaires that direct light to the coffer ceiling and back to the space, providing ambient light. Direct down-lighting with egg-crate diffusers to control glare is used to provide task lighting. Individual task lighting is avoided.

The luminaires have no user controls, but are automatically regulated by high-frequency dimming control gear that is sensitive to motion and daylight. This gives a predicted lighting load of 11.5 W/m^2.

OTHER MAIN SYSTEMS

- roof-mounted solar thermal panels to heat the hot water;
- grey and rainwater collection and recycling system;
- building management system to monitor and automate some of the environmental control systems;
- small power capacity for electronic equipment, 20 W/m^2;
- standby generator and UPS (uninterrupted power supply);
- two-person lift for disabled access and goods;
- CCTV and security system; and
- telecommunications system.

BREEAM 98 criteria

The building addresses the BREEAM criteria by adopting some specific strategies. The link between design and the management of the building is an important element in these strategies.

Management

The management assessment checklist has the following criteria.

1 Commissioning audits:
   - monitoring by design team;
   - monitoring of active systems by agent;
   - pre-commissioning and quality management; and
   - operational guidelines for non-experts.
2 Construction process audits:
   - contractor certification – 'considerate contractors scheme'; and
   - site impact monitoring – energy, fuel, waste, pollution.

Addressing the monitoring process is through a two-year energy-monitoring programme, which is under way, to record the in-use energy performance of the building. This involves using the BMS system and energy sub-metering to provide the data for this study.

Construction process audits were carried out to monitor site impact throughout the construction process. Two main benefits of the construction process audits were found. Using a 'right first time' approach, avoiding alterations to the building, meant that a construction time of 73 weeks was achieved, against a planned 80 weeks (and the project was within budget). Furthermore, the construction audits led to recycling of 70 per cent of construction waste, avoiding landfill taxes and creating a net gain of £15,000 for the project.

DESIGN AND CONSTRUCTION SYNERGY

The 'right first time' approach involves closed systems synergy and management of the design and procurement process. The key features of this approach involve modelling and prefabrication.

At the outline design stage, the team (assisted by Bath University) created a computer model of the building, including a 'fly round' and internal views. This paid dividends: everyone on the project team knew what was involved and any adjustments could be made at a very early stage. The model was shown at board meetings, so that everyone could appreciate the nuances of the design. It was also helpful when talking to the planners.

Off-site production was key to achieving the company's goal of reducing on-site waste. So, to ensure that prefabrication of the innovative steel-frame structure was going to plan, the team commissioned a complete bay to be built off site prior to full production. They also used a full-sized wooden mock-up to show to company directors, and to assess lighting design.[38]

Energy

The energy assessment criteria are:

- sub-metering;
- predicted CO_2 emissions; and
- building envelope heat losses.

Energy consumption is approximately 100 kWh/m^2 per year. This is up to one third of that needed for a typical modern headquarters.[39]

Heat losses and unwanted solar gains were avoided through effective sun-shading and double-glazing. As part of the energy monitoring of the building, an airtightness test was carried out and infiltration was reduced further.

Monitoring of sectors of the electrical energy and resource consumption is by sub-metering through the BMS system.

Transport

Transport assessment criteria are:

- location;
- cycle facilities;
- transport plan; and
- public transport access.

The building is located 3 km outside Bath and close to a 'park and ride' public transport node. Buses carry staff and local residents to connect to the transport nodes in Bath. Cycle storage and facilities for cyclists are provided in the back of house area. Pool cars are available for office-related activities.

This is part of a broader transport plan to service the needs of the organization's core business.

Pollution

The pollution checklist criteria are:

- refrigerant control;
- leak detection and dispersion prevention;
- global warming potential assessment;
- ozone-depleting materials avoidance;
- nitrous oxide emissions minimization;
- water run-off control;
- run-off filtration; and
- thermal insulants.

The building design has included strategies to minimize pollution.

Materials

The materials assessment checklist is:

- asbestos control;
- materials storage space provision;
- element materials rating;
- façade reuse;
- structure reuse;
- use of recycled aggregates; and
- sustainable timber management.

The building structure was optimized to reduce the amount

Left. Materials included sustainable timbers, and the use of recycled aggregates in the concrete.
Right. Use of a large back of house facility allows space for recycling of materials and bicycle storage.

of concrete used in the structure; 3,000 m^3 of the concrete within the structure contains recycled aggregates. During construction a pioneering waste management system was employed to reduce construction waste, so that 75 per cent was recycled.[40]

Land use and ecology
The land use and ecology checklist is:

- brownfield sites reuse;
- regenerated sites use;
- ecology assessment checklist;
- low ecological value of land;
- change of ecological value;
- environmental management systems advice; and
- construction impact on site.

The site was originally used as a hospital, which was demolished and the site sold to Wessex Water. The new build-

ing occupies the area of the old building, so it reuses a 'brownfield' site.

The site on which the building was built was of lower ecological value than the surrounding area. The design team made positive steps by containing the building footprint and retaining the existing landscape features to improve the ecological value. Construction site impact was reduced thorough careful management.

Water
The water assessment checklist is:

- predicted consumption;
- water metering;
- leak detection; and
- sector supply shut-off.

The strategies for conserving water involve on-site harvesting of rainwater. The roof water run-off is collected in large tanks

BREEAM 98 assessment checklist for Wessex Water Regional Operations Centre, UK

Management		Pollution	
Commissioning audits		Refrigerant control	
• Monitoring by design team	✓	Leak detection and dispersion prevention	
• Monitoring of active systems by agent	✓	Global warming potential assessment	
• Pre-commissioning and Q management	✓	Ozone-depleting materials avoidance	✓
• Operational guidelines for non-experts		Nitrous oxide emissions minimization	
Construction process audits	✓	Water run-off control	
• Contractors certification – 'Considerate Contractors Scheme'	✓	Run-off, filtration	✓
• Site impact monitoring – energy, fuel, waste, pollution		Thermal insulants	✓
Energy		*Health and well-being*	
Sub-metering	✓	Maintenance of cooling towers	✓
Predicted CO_2 emissions	✓	Risk management for legionellosis	✓
Building envelope heat losses	✓	Operable windows availability	✓
Transport		Humidification control	✓
Location	✓	Air intake location	✓
Cycle facilities	✓	IAQ ventilation provision	✓
Transport plan	✓	Occupant control of glare	✓
Public transport access	✓	Electric lighting quality control	✓
Water		Provision of daylight	✓
Predicted consumption	✓	Light levels provision	✓
Water metering	✓	Lighting controls	✓
Leak detection	✓	Occupant view provision	✓
Sector supply shut-off	✓	Occupant temperature controls	✓
Materials		Thermal comfort evaluation	✓
Asbestos control	✓	Ambient noise level control	✓
Materials storage space provision	✓	*Ecology*	
Element materials rating	✓	Low ecological value of land	✓
Façade reuse	na	Change of ecological value	✓
Structure reuse	✓	EMS advice	
Use of recycle aggregates	✓	Construction impact on site	✓
Sustainable timber management	✓	*Land use*	
		Brownfield sites use	✓
		Regenerated sites reuse	na

in the courtyard for toilet-flushing. Surface rainwater run-off from roads and car parks is collected in 200,000 litre tanks at the south of the site and will be used for irrigation.[41]

Health and well-being
The health and well-being checklist is:

- maintenance of cooling towers;
- risk management for legionellosis;
- operable-windows availability;
- humidification control;
- air intake location;
- IAQ ventilation provision;
- occupant control of glare;
- electric lighting quality control;
- provision of daylight;
- light levels provision;
- lighting controls;
- occupant view provision;
- occupant temperature controls;
- thermal comfort evaluation; and
- ambient noise level control.

The quality of the internal environment appears to meet all of the above criteria. This is achieved mainly through the form and fabric of the building. The 'finger' plan design ensures a narrow plan form (i.e. less than 12 metres), which allows daylight and natural ventilation to enter the building, as well as providing views.

The aim was to use technology where necessary, with provision of user controls. Thermostats in meeting rooms were used, which allowed for a range of thermal comfort settings but did not go beyond the design criteria for energy use.[42]

Evaluation

The BREEAM assessment rating carried out by the BRE gave the design a rating of 'excellent'.

Lessons learned

Many of the lessons learned came from strategies:

The project was designed to operate at less than one-third of conventional energy consumption levels and considered environmental, social and economic factors with pioneering initiatives in the following key areas:

- energy efficiency;
- low embodied energy;
- reductions in transport;
- waste reduction and recycling;
- water recycling;
- enhanced biodiversity. [43]

Six main lessons were learned.

1   All members of the design team should commit to the sustainable agenda from the outset.
2   Adoption of industry or other targets for improved environmental performance assists with design development from the outset. For example, a target for energy consumption in use was established in the brief. This target was also matched with indoor environmental quality standards based on ECON 19: Naturally ventilated office buildings.[44]
3   Optimize passive energy use and minimize energy in use. The philosophy of allowing users responsibility for controlling the environment was adopted to enhance a sense of well-being.
4   Innovation was implemented were appropriate. Structural optimization of the primary structural systems, with a shift to precasting, reduced the amount of concrete used in the project by some 50 per cent.
5   identifying the value added by the sustainable components for life cycle benefits helped support the case for the selection of these systems. The use of open-book accounting and a cost consultant assisted with this process and facilitated the decision-making process.
6   he building process was managed to ensure sustainable construction. This was achieved through rigorous but realistic environmental management clauses within trade contracts.

Acknowledgements

Ann Bodkin and Mike Caple for assisting with data collection. Illustrations: Richard Hyde.

International Energy Agency SHC Task 28/ BCS Annex 38

SHC Task 28 / BCS Annex 38: Sustainable Solar Housing

1. Task Description

Duration: April 2000–April 2005
Objectives: The goal of this Task is to help participating countries achieve significant market penetration of sustainable solar housing by the year 2010, by providing home builders and institutional real estate investors with:

- A **Task Website** which illustrates built projects, exemplary in design, living quality, low energy demand and environmental impact.
- Documentation sets of **Exemplary Sustainable Solar Housing** as a basis for local language publications to communicate the experience from built projects and motivate planers to develop marketable designs.
- A handbook: **Marketable Sustainable Solar Housing**: with guidelines, graphs and tables derived from building monitoring, lab testing and computer modeling.
- **Demonstration Buildings** with press kits for articles and brochures in local languages. to increase the multiplication effect beyond the local region.
- **Workshops** after the Task conclusion presenting the results of the Task.

- There are experts from many countries, notable representation was from the following:
  Austria
  Australia
  Belgium
  Brazil
  Canada
  Czech Republic
  Finland
  Germany
  Italy
  Japan
  Netherlands
  New Zealand
  Norway
  Scotland
  Sweden
  Switzerland

Energy Conservation in Buildings and Community Systems

Approximately one third of primary energy is consumed in non-industrial buildings such as dwellings, offices, hospitals, and schools where it is utilised for space heating and cooling, lighting and the operation of appliances. In terms of the total energy end use, this consumption is comparable to that used in the entire transport sector. Hence energy use in buildings represents a major contributor to fossil fuel use and carbon dioxide production. Following uncertainties in energy supply and concern over the risk of global warming, many countries have now introduced target values for reducing energy consumption in buildings. Overall, these are aimed at reducing energy consumption by between 15 and 30%. To achieve such a target, international co-operation, in which research activities and knowledge can be shared, is seen as an essential activity.

In recognition of the significance of such energy use, the International Energy Agency has established an Implementing Agreement on Energy Conservation in Buildings and Community Systems (ECBCS). The function of ECBCS is to undertake research and provide an international focus for building energy efficiency. Tasks are undertaken through a series of annexes that are directed at energy saving technologies and activities that support their application in practice. Results are also used in the formulation of international and national energy conservation policies and standards.

ECBCS undertakes a diverse range of activities both through its individual annexes and through centrally organised development and information exchange. ECBCS countries are free to choose which Annexes to take part in. Activities usually take the form of a 'Task Shared' Annex in which each country commits an agreed level of effort. Occasionally an Annex may be either jointly or part jointly funded. More informal activities take place through Working Groups.

ECBCS Participating Countries: Australia - Belgium - Canada CEC - Czech Republic - Denmark - Finland - France - Germany - Greece - Israel - Italy - Japan - Netherlands - New Zealand - Norway - Poland - Portugal - Sweden - Switzerland - Turkey - UK - USA

IEA SECRETARIAT

Alan Meier
Office of Energy Efficiency, Technology, R&D
9, rue de la Federation
75739 Paris Cedex 15
France
Tel: +33 1 40 57 66 85
Email: alan.meier@iea.org

Pamela Murphy
Morse Associates, Inc
1808 Corcoran Street, NW
Washington, DC 20009 USA
Tel: +1-202-483-2393
Fax: +1-202-265-2248
E-mail: pmurphy@MorseAssociatesInc.com

Appendix 2

Further case studies available online

Additional case studies are presented online and examine the application of a number of environmental approaches to house design. The Yeang EcoHome is an examination of the use of the environmental briefing process to assist with the evolution of the design. The process involves the adoption and adaptation of the Building Research Establishment (BRE) EcoHomes environmental criteria for house design in the UK. This was adopted in the brief to establish appropriate environmental criteria. The BRE tool is also used to examine the Cairnlea project in Melbourne, Australia. This work has contributed to a discussion concerning the feasibility of generating an international standard for EcoHome design. In addition, several blueprint projects arise from the IEA Task 28 work and issues are examined concerning the application of 'solution sets' for sustainable solar housing. This includes the Peterculter House in Scotland and the Misawa House in Japan.

Additional projects demonstrate the application of the Green Globe Design and Construct tool to a range of building types. This benchmarking system provides flexibility that enables the tool to be applied to a wide range of building types, hence the inclusion of a small scale project, the Tramping Huts in New Zealand, and the Heron Island Research Station, which is a research facility linked to tourism infrastructure on Heron Island, Australia.

Links to other case studies mentioned in this book can be found at:

www.csdesign.epsa.uq.edu.au/
www.iea-shc.org/task28/
www.greenisland.net.au

Housing

Yeang EcoHome, Kuala Lumpur, Malaysia
Architects: T.R. Hamzath and Yeang Snd Bhd

Cairnlea, Melbourne, Australia
Designers: Metricon Homes, Fiona Martin

Peterculter House, UK
Architect: Gorkay Devici

Hybrid-Z Zero Energy Home, Japan
Architects: Misawa Homes Institute of Research

Prosser House, Surfers Paradise, Australia
Architects: Richard Hyde and Upendra Rajapaksha

Hotels, Resorts and Interpretation Centres

Heron Island Research Station Refurbishment, Australia
Architects: Dimitriou Architects + Interior Designers

The Crows Tramping Huts, Department of Conservation, New Zealand
Architects: Pynenburg and Collins Architects

Pittsburgh Glass Center, Pittsburgh, USA
Architects: Davis + Gannon Architects

Offices

PNC Center, Pittsburgh, USA
Architects: L.D. Astorino Companies

Reservoir Centre, Melbourne, Australia
Architects: Bzowy Architects, Dominique Hes

References

Introduction

1. Yencken, D., and Davidson, J., *Resetting the Compass: Australia's Journey towards Sustainability*, CSIRO, 2001, pp. 13–27.
2. Papanek, V., *The Green Imperative: Ecology and Ethics in Design and Architecture*, Thames and Hudson, 1995, pp. 29–48.
3. Mawhinney, M., *Sustainable Development: Understanding the Green Debates,* Blackwell Science, 2002, p. 3.
4. Ibid.
5. Wines, J., *Green Architecture*, Taschen, 2000, pp. 8–9.
6. ArchNet Digital Library http://archnet.org/library/sites/one-site.tcl?site_id=7296 (accessed 11 Jan 2005).
7. Ibid.
8. Wines, J.,*Green Architecture*, Taschen, 2000, pp. 8–9.
9. Adapted from the work of Pearson, D., *The Natural House Book*, Conran Octopus, 1989.
10. Robson, D., *Geoffrey Bawa: The Complete Works* , Thames and Hudson, 2002, p. 102.
11. Ibid., p. 199.
12. Hyams, D., *Construction Companion to Briefing*, RIBA Publications, 2001, p. 41.
13. Ibid.
14. Ibid., p. ix.
15. Wittmann, S., 'Architects' Commitment Regarding Energy Efficient/Ecological Architecture', in *Architectural Science Review*, The University of Sydney, 1998, 41: 90.
16. Ibid., p. 92.
17. Cheshire, W., *The Development and Application of a Holistic Environmental Brief*, The University of Queensland, 2000, pp. 9–23.
18. Hyams, *Construction Companion*, p. 85.
19. International Organisation of Standardisation, www.iso.ch/iso/en/iso9000-14000/iso9000/qmp.html (accessed 1 June 2004).
20. Green Building Council of Australia http://www.gbcaus.org/ (accessed 1 June 2004).
21. National Australian Built Environment Rating System (NABERS) Project, www.deh.gov.au/industry/construction/nabers/ (accessed 1 June 2004).
22. Lazarus, N., Beddington Zero (Fossil) Energy Development Construction Materials Report, *Tool Kit for Carbon Neutral Developments Part 1: BioRegional Group* www/bioregional.com (accessed 5 Jan 2005).
23. Schendler, A., and Udall, R., *LEED Is Broken: Let's Fix It*, 2005 http://grist.org/comments/soapbox/2005/10/26/leed/index1. html (accessed 11 Dec 2005).
24. Hyde, R.A., Moore R., Kavanagh, L., Watt, M., Prasad, D., and Blair, J. (2005) 'Development of a Planning and Design Tool for Assessing the Sustainability of Precincts'. *Proceedings of the ANZAScA Conference, Wellington, New Zealand.* Green Globe 21.Precinct Planning and Design Standard, www.earthcheck.org (accessed 12 Dec 2005).

Chapter 1: The environmental imperative

1. Papanek, V., *The Green Imperative: Ecology and Ethics in Design and Architecture,* Thames and Hudson, 1995.
2. Ibid., p. 17.
3. Yencken, D., and Wilkinson, D., *Resetting the Compass.* CSIRO, 2000, p. 400.
4. Ibid.
5. Yencken and Wilkinson, *Resetting the Compass*, p. 22.
6. Mawhinney, M., *Sustainable Development: Understanding the Green Debates*, Blackwell Science, 2002.
7. Brundtland, G., *Our Common Future*, World Commission on Environment and Development, Oxford University Press, 1987.
8. Cortijo, P., 'Solar Energy and Eco-design in the Tourism Sector', *UNEP Industry and Environment Journal*, April–September, 2003: 29–33.
9. Definitions of sustainable development can be found at www.ace.mmu.ac.uk/eae/english.html (accessed 6 June 2004).
10. Mawhinney, *Sustainable Development*, pp. 3–4.
11. World Business Council for Sustainable Development, www.wbcsd.ch/index.htm (accessed 3 Jan 2004).
12. Hays, P., *Main Currents in Western Environmental Thought*, University of New South Wales Press, 2002, p. 213.
13. Hamilton, C., and Dennis R., 'Impact of Microeconomic Reform on Greenhouse Gas Emissions from the Electricity Sector', in Productivity Commission, *Micro Economic Reform and the Environment*, Workshop Proceedings, AusInfo, Canberra, 2000, p 79.
14. Hamilton and Dennis, 'Impact of Microeconomic Reform', p. 87.
15. Ibid.
16. Lovins, A. 'Soft Energy Paths', in *The Schumacher Lectures*, ed. S. Kumar, Abacus, 1980, p. 46.
17. Ibid., p. 48.
18. Thomas, I., *Environmental Impact Assessment in Australia,* Federation Press, 1998, p. 51.
19. Chambers, N., Simmons, C., and Wackernagel. M., *Sharing Nature's Interest: Using Ecological Footprints as an Indicator of Sustainability,* Earthscan, 2000.
20. Ecological Footprint Calculator, www.bestfootforward.com/footprintlife.htm (accessed 1 Feb. 2005).
21. Mawhinney, *Sustainable Development,* p. 126.
22. Ibid.
23. Healthy Home Project, www.healthyhomeproject.com (accessed 1 Feb 2005).
24. Toffler, A., *Future Shock*, Random House, 1970, p. 57.
25. Lawler, G., 'Melbourne Government Policy and Procurement', *Australian Green Building Council Conference*, 2003.
26. Vale, B., and Vale R., *The New Autonomous House: Design and Planning for Sustainability*, Thames & Hudson, 2000.
27. Yencken and Wilkinson , *Resetting the Compass*, p. 248
28. Building Design Professional Environmental Design Guide, www.architecture.com.au (accessed 16 June 2004).
29. Ibid.
30. The Royal Australian Institute of Architects, *Inquiry into Sustainable Cities 2025,* Submission to the House of Representatives Standing Committee on Environment and Heritage, Australia, Dec 2003.
31. Ibid.
32. Yencken and Wilkinson, *Resetting the Compass*, p. 147.

Chapter 2: Principles, initiatives and responses

1. Collins, K., 'Forward: Greening the Future', in *Sustainable Architecture*, ed. B. Edwards, Architectural Press, 1999, p. viii.
2. Green Paper on the Urban Environment: communication from the Commission to the Council and Parliament COM(90) 218, June 1990. http://europa.eu.int/comm/off/green/index_en.htm#1990 (accessed 1 June 2004).
3. Collins, 'Forward', p. viii.
4. Edwards, B., *Sustainable Architecture*, Architectural Press, 1999, p. xiv.
5. Ibid., p. xv.

6. Department of the Environment, Transport and Regions, *Quality of Life Counts*, 1999, www.sustainabledevelopment.gov.uk/sustainable/quality99/index.htm (accessed June 16 2004).

7. Ibid.

8. Department of the Environment, *Survey of Public Attitudes to Quality of Life and to the Environment: 2001*, www.defra.gov.uk/environment/statistics/pubatt/ch2qol.htm (accessed June 16 2004).

9. www.defra.gov.uk/news/2003/030710a.htm (accessed June 16 2004).

10. Ibid.

11. SustainAbility, Definition of 'triple bottom line reporting', www.sustainability.com/philosophy/triple-bottom/tbl-intro.asp (accessed 16 June 2004).

12. See Blair, J., Prasad, D., Judd, B., Soebarto, V., Hyde, R.A., Zehner B., and Kumar, A., *Affordability and Sustainability Outcomes of 'Greenfield' Suburban Development and Master Planned Communities – A Triple Bottom Line Assessment*, Australian Housing and Urban Research Institute, University of New South Wales–University of Western Sydney Research Centre, 2003, p. 24.

13. Department of the Environment, Transport and the Regions, *Rethinking Construction:* The report of the Construction Task Force to the Deputy Prime Minister, John Prescott, on the scope for improving the quality and efficiency of UK construction (*The Egan Report*), 16 July 1988, www.dti.gov.uk/construction/rethink/report/ (accessed 13 May 2004).

14. *Accelerating Change.* A report by the Strategic Forum for Construction chaired by Sir John Egan www.strategicforum.org.uk/pdf/report_sept02.pdf (accessed 13 May 2004).

15. *Office of the Deputy Prime Minister.* Sustainable Communities, www.odpm.gov.uk/stellent/groups/odpm_communities/documents/sectionhomepage/odpm_communities_page.hcsp (accessed 13 May 2004).

16. DETR, *Rethinking Construction.*

17. Building Research Establishment. Environmental Assessment Tools, www.bre.co.uk/services/Environmental_assessment.html (accessed 13 May 2004).

18. ODPM. *Creating Sustainable Communities.* Building regulations. www.odpm.gov.uk/stellent/groups/odpm_buildreg/documents/sectionhomepage/odpm_buildreg_page.hcsp (accessed 13 May 2004).

19. Ibid. Parts L1 and L2 on thermal performance were updated in April 2002,

20. ODPM, *Creating Sustainable Communities.* Planning and Compulsory Purchase Bill, Jan 2003. Parts L1 and L2 on thermal performance were updated in April 2002, www.odpm.gov.uk/stellent/groups/odpm_control/documents/contentservertemplate/odpm_index.hcst?n=2155&l=2 located via www.odpm.gov.uk and clicked on planning, then reform of the planning system (accessed 13 May 2004).

21. Department of Trade and Industry, White Paper, *Our Energy Future: Creating a Low Carbon Economy*, Feb 2003, www.dti.gov.uk/energy/publications/whitepapers/index.shtml and www.dti.gov.uk/energy/whitepaper/index.shtml#wp (accessed 13 May 2004).

22. De Geer, B., *et al.*, *Demonstrations of Sustainability*, British Research Establishment and The Department for Enterprise, 2003, p. 8.

23. Crossley, R., *Reputations, Risk and Reward: The Business Case for Sustainability in the UK Property Sector*, The Sustainable Construction Task Group, BRC, UK, 2002, www. bre.co.uk (accessed 13 March 2004).

24. Ibid., p. 4.

25. Ibid., p. 5.

26. Ibid., p. 6.

27. HM Customs and Excise, *Climate Change Levy* www.hmce.gov.uk/business/othertaxes/ccl.htm (accessed 13 May 2004).

28. Department of Trade and Industry (DTI), *Demonstrations of Construction* www.dti.gov.uk/sectors_building.html (accessed 13 May 2004).

29. The demonstrations are vetted by peer review on a regional basis. This maintains quality within the demonstrations, and spreads knowledge on how to capture innovations and convert them first to best practice and then to standard procedure. The regional Centres of Rethinking Construction are a major dissemination route for improvement.

30. Construction Industry: Key Performance Indicators, Industry Progress Report, www.cbpp.org.uk (accessed 13 March 2004).

31. Ibid.

32. 'The F E-factor – Six Guiding Principles to Improving Sustainability in House Building', www.thehousingforum.org.uk/rc/publications/reports/HF E-Factor.pdf accessed 13 March 2004); BRE and DTI. UK Checklist. Demonstrations of Sustainability: The Rethinking Construction Demonstrations and How They Have Addressed Sustainable Construction Issues, pp. 12–13; www.constructingexcellence.org.uk/pdf/Demonstrations%20of%20Sustainability.pdf (accessed 13 March 2004, pp. 16–17 of pdf).

33. Department of Trade and Industry, *Demonstrations of Construction*, www.dti.gov.uk/sectors_building.html (accessed 13 March 2004).

34. SPeAR$_{TM}$ (Sustainable Project Appraisal Routine), Using the SPeAR$_{TM}$ Assessment tool in Sustainable Master Planning crisp.cstb.fr/view_rdworks.asp?id_rdworks=16 (accessed 14 may 2004); BREEAM for Offices products.bre.co.uk/breeam/offices.html (accessed 14 May 2004); CEEQUAL, Civil Engineering Environmental Quality Assessment Award Scheme, www.ceequal.com/ (accessed 14 May 2004); Bespoke, BREEAM products.bre.co.uk/breeam/bespoke.html (accessed 14 May 2004); BRE, *Sustainability Checklist for Developments*, The Sustainability Checklist Topics, www.sustainability-checklist.co.uk/TheChecklist/(accessed 13 March 2004).

35. Building Research Establishment, www.bre.co.uk/ (accessed 14 May 2004).

36. www.sutton.gov.uk/ (accessed 14 May 2004).

37. Environmental Management Systems, usually ISO 14000 compliant.

38. These projects have come about by Sutton Council's commitment to implementing the Eco-Management and Audit Scheme (EMAS) throughout all council groupings. The council aims to prevent, or limit, environmental accidents, and contingency procedures are in place to minimize the damage if they do happen. As part of EMAS, staff and councillors are trained in environmental issues to develop an informed sense of responsibility for the environment at all levels. In this way, we can make a significant contribution to a sustainable, healthy and a balanced environment.

39. BedZED, or Beddington Zero Energy Development, www.bedzed.org.uk/main.html (accessed 14 April 2004).

40. BedZED and Eco-Village Development, www.bioregional.com/programme_projects/ecohous_prog/bedzed/bedzed_hpg.htm (accessed 14 May 2004.)

41. www.bioregional.com/news%20page/news_stories/ZED/CNTrep2_311003.htm (accessed 16 June 2004).

42. Edwards, *Sustainable Architecture*, p. 7.

43. Ibid.

44. Bio Regional Report: 'New BedZed report shows the housing industry that sustainable buildings can give good returns', www.bioregional.com/news%20page/news_stories/ZED/CNTrep2_311003.htm (accessed 15 June 2004) .

45. Ibid.

46. Ibid.

47. Australian Greenhouse Office, www.greenhouse.gov.au/ago/index.html (accessed 16 June 2004).

48. Ibid.

49. Ibid.

50. Australian Greenhouse Office, *Tracking to the Kyoto Target: Australia's Greenhouse Emissions Trends 1990 to 2008–2012 and 2020*, p. 2.

51. Australia's National Greenhouse Gas Inventory serves the dual purpose of providing greenhouse gas emission estimates for the United Nations Framework Convention on Climate Change and tracking Australia's progress towards its Kyoto target of limiting emissions to 108 per cent of 1990 levels over the period 2008–2012. Australia produces an annual inventory of national greenhouse gas emissions since 1990. These inventories provide a baseline from which we are able to monitor and review response action and develop projections of greenhouse gas emissions. The 2001 National Greenhouse Gas Inventory, released in September 2003, provides the latest report on Australia's greenhouse gas emissions. This inventory incorporates improvements to data and methods that have been used to update emission estimates for the 1990–2000 inventories. The National Greenhouse Strategy, which was endorsed by the Commonwealth and all State and Territory govern-

ments in 1998, provides a national framework for action on climate change. The Strategy provides a broad menu of actions, some of which will be implemented by governments acting individually, some by joint intergovernmental initiatives and some through partnerships between government, various stakeholders and the community.

52. National Carbon Accounting System, (NCAS). The National Carbon Accounting System tracks emissions (sources) and removals (sinks) of greenhouse gases from Australian land-based systems. The system underpins National Greenhouse Gas Inventory reporting, and provides a basis for emissions projections to assess progress towards meeting Australia's emissions target. Key activities are:
    a. biomass – plant growth and life cycle analysis
    b. climate – surfaces and plant productivity
    c. land cover – mapping clearing and revegetation
    d. land use – mapping use and management
    e. soils – carbon measurement and modelling
    f. modelling – carbon stocks and flows
    www.greenhouse.gov.au/ago/index.html (accessed 16 June 2004).

53. Emissions for 2020 are projected to be 126 per cent of the 1990 level on an indicative basis, reflecting the impact of ongoing growth in emissions in the energy sector. This emphasizes the need to focus on lowering Australia's greenhouse emissions signature over the longer term, while maintaining a strong and internationally competitive economy. The Greenhouse Gas Abatement Program (GGAP) is a major Commonwealth government initiative to assist Australia in meeting its Kyoto Protocol target. The objective of GGAP is to reduce Australia's net greenhouse gas emissions by supporting activities that are likely to result in substantial emission reductions or substantial sink enhancement, particularly in the first commitment period under the Kyoto Protocol (2008–2012). $400 million has been allocated to the programme.

54. NCAS.

55. Australian Greenhouse Office, www.greenhouse.gov.au/household/ (accessed 5 May 2004).

56. Ibid.

57. Australian Greenhouse Office, www.greenhouse.gov.au/coolcommunities/index.html. (accessed 5 May 2004).

58. Australian Greenhouse Office, www.greenhouse.gov.au/lgmodules/index.htm (accessed 5 May 2004).

59. Australian Greenhouse Office, www.greenhouse.gov.au/community_household.html (accessed 5 May 2004).

60. Information on the energy efficiency of appliances, provided by AGO, forms an important decision-making tool.

61. USGBC, An Introduction to the US Green Building Council and the LEED$_{TM}$ Green Building Rating System, www.usgbc.org/ (accessed 23 April 2004).

62. Green Building Council of Australia, www.gbcaus.org/default.asp (accessed 16 June 2004).

63. Ibid.

64. Ibid.

65. BREEAM http://products.bre.co.uk/breeam/ (accessed 16 June 2004).

66. LEED (Leadership in Energy and Environmental Design), www.usgbc.org/leed/leed_main.asp (accessed 16 June 2004).

67. Melbourne Docklands Authority ESD Guide, www.docklands.com/docklands/about/publications/esd/index.shtml (accessed 16 June 2004).

68. GBCA Green Building Council of Australia, www.gbcaus.org/default.asp (accessed 16 June 2004).

69. Ibid.

70. Rocky Mountain Institute (2004) RMI Campus. RMI's Own Buildings Demonstrate Efficiency, www.rmi.org/sitepages/pid110.ph (accessed 23 April 2004).

71. Rocky Mountain Institute (2004), www.rmi.org/ (accessed 23 April 2004).

72. Rocky Mountain Institute (2004) RMI Campus. RMI's Own Buildings Demonstrate Efficiency, www.rmi.org/sitepages/pid110.ph (accessed 23 April 2004).

73. Hawken, P., Lovins, A., and Hunter Lovins, L., (1999) Natural Capitalism: Creating the Next Industrial Revolution, Boston: Little, Brown and Co.

74. 'Achieving a Sustainable Future: Business Opportunities, Innovation, and Governance in the 21st Century', forthcoming publication.

75. The sixth annual AIA/COTE Top Ten Green Projects initiative was developed in partnership with the US Department of Energy and Environmental Building News. The panel of jurors included Peter Bohlin, FAIA, of Bohlin Cywinski Jackson; Carol Ross Barney, FAIA, of Ross Barney + Jankowsky; Drury Crawley, AIA, US Department of Energy; Jacqueline Rose, AIA, Environmental Protection Agency; and Douglas Kelbaugh, FAIA, University of Michigan. What follows is a list of the 2003 AIA Top Ten Green Projects (in no particular order). This information was provided by the AIA. For more information, visit www.aia.org/cote/.

76. 'Achieving a Sustainable Future'.

77. Ibid.

78. In the context of these strategies, 'sustainability' always refers to 'environmental sustainability' and ESD means 'ecological sustainable development'.

79. Royal Australian Institute of Architects, *RAIA Environmental Policy –Supplemental Document, Sustainable Design Strategies for Architects*, 2001, p. 6.

80. Ibid., p 1.

81. Royal Australian Institute of Architects, *Ecologically Sustainable Development Award Checklists*, 2001, p. 6.

82. Ibid.

83. Ibid.

84. Ibid.

85. USGBC, www. usgbc.org (accessed 23 April 2004).

86. Ibid.

87. Ibid.

88. Heschong and Mahone, *Daylighting and Productivity Windows and Classrooms: A Study of Student Performance and the Indoor Environment – CEC PIER*, 2003, www.h-m-g.com/Daylighting/ (accessed 23 April 2004).

89. *Environmental Building News* (May 2001), 10 (5).

90. American College of Allergy, Asthma & Immunology, *Indoor Pollution Poses Higher Risk to Respiratory Health as People Spend More Time Indoors* [press release], 2 Nov 2000, p.12 http://allergy.mcg.edu/news/ind.html (accessed 23 April 2004).

91. Pearson, D., *The Healthy House Book*, Gaia Books,1989, p. 45.

92. US Center for Disease Control, *Forecasted State-Specific Estimates of Self-Reported Asthma Prevalence – United States, 1998,* Washington DC, USGPO, p. 1, www.cdc.gov/mmwr/preview/mmwrhtml/00055803.htm (accessed 23 April 2004).

93. *American Journal of Respiratory and Critical Care Medicine* (1998), 158: 320–34, www. usgbc.org (accessed 23 April 2004).

94. 'Trends in Asthma Morbidity and Mortality', American Lung Association, Epidemiology and Statistics Unit, Nov 1998, www. usgbc.org (accessed 23 April 2004) .

95. *Journal of Allergy and Clinical Immunology,* 1999, 103: 408–14, www. usgbc.org (accessed 23 April 2004).

96. *Environmental Building News* (May 2001), 10 (5).

97. Vale, B., and Vale, R., *Green Architecture: Design for a Sustainable Future*, Thames and Hudson, 1991, p. 161.

98. USGBC, www. usgbc.org (accessed 23 April 2004).

Chapter 3: Advancing green design

1. Yencken, D., and Wilkinson, W., *Resetting the Compass: Australia's Journey to Sustainability*, CSIRO Publishing, 2000, pp. 307–23.

2. Australian Council of Building Design Professionals, *BDP Built Environment Australia*, www.bdp.asn.au/ (accessed 30 April 2004).

3. Ibid.

4. Biophysical ecologies comprising air, land, water, flora, fauna.

5. Precautionary principle: lack of full scientific certainty shall not be used as a reason to postpone measures to prevent environmental degradation.

6. Vale, B., and Vale, R., *Green Architecture: Design for a Sustainable Future,* Thames & Hudson, 1991.

7. Healthy Home Project www.healthyhomeproject.com.html (accessed 1 June 2004).

8. Watson, S., 'Improving the Implementation of Environmental Strategies in the Design of Buildings', PhD thesis, The University of Queensland, 2005.

9. Pedrini, A., and Hyde, R. A., 2001, 'A Database Energy Tool for Design-Phase Assessment of Offices Buildings', *Proceedings of PLEA 2001*, Florianapolis, Brazil, paper PLO1-50.

10. Watson, 'Improving the Implementation'.
11. Wittmann, S., 1998, 'Architects' Commitment Regarding Energy-efficient/Ecological Architecture', *Architectural Science Review*, 41 (2): 89–92.
12. Royal Australian Institute of Architects, 2003, *Practice Note: The Design Brief. AN 10.03.100 July*, 1998, RAIA (1996-) Advisory Notes [cd rom v2] Melbourne: RAIA, p. 1.
13. Wittmann, 'Architects' Commitment', p. 90.
14. Watson, 'Improving the Implementation'.
15. Watson, S., Cheshire W., and Hyde, R.A, 'Development of a Holistic Environmental Brief for use as a Design Phase Building Environmental Assessment Tool', *Proceedings of the ANZAScA Conference*, The University of Sydney, Nov 2000, pp. 189–96.
16. Royal Institute of British Architects, *Plan of Work for Design Team Operation*, RIBA Publications, 1973.
17. American Institute of Architects, *Understanding the Design Process*, 1999, American Institute of Architects.
18. Broadbent, G., and Ward, A., *Design Methods in Architecture*, Lund Humphries, 1968.
19. Schon, D., *The Reflective Practitioner: How Professionals Think in Action*, Arena, 1995.
20. Larsson, N., 2000. 'Moving Towards a Green Building Design Process', *Sustainable Design 2000 Proceedings*, 22–25 Oct 2000, The Netherlands, pp. 141–3.
21. Wittmann, 'Architects' Commitment',
22. International Energy Agency (IEA) SHC Task 28, 'Solar Sustainable Housing', Task Force from the International Energy Agency, 1999, www.iea-shc.org/task28/index.html (accessed 1 June 2004).
23. Australian Building Energy Council (ABEC), case studies of energy-efficient buildings, www.netspeed.com.au/abeccs/buxton/buxton.htm (accessed 1 June 2004).
24. *Your Home: Good Residential Design Guide*, Australian Greenhouse Office. www.greenhouse.gov.au/yourhome/technical/fs00.htm (accessed 1 June 2004).
25. ABEC case studies.
26. Healthy Home Project.
27. See the Environmental Brief structure, www.csdesign.epsa.uq.edu.au/index2.php?dir=145 (accessed 1 June 2004).
28. Wittmann, 'Architects' Commitment', p. 92.
29. ISO9000, Quality Management Principles, www.iso.ch/iso/en/iso9000-14000/iso9000/qmp.html (accessed 1 June 2004).
30. ISO14000, Environmental management model, www.iso.ch/iso/en/prods-services/otherpubs/iso14000/index.html (accessed 1 June 2004).
31. Baldwin, R., 'Results of IEA-ECBCS annex 31 Work on Environmental Assessment of Buildings and Related Tools', *Sustainable Design 2000 Proceedings*, 22–25 Oct 2000, The Netherlands, p. 218.
32. www.uni-weimar.de/ANNEX31 (accessed 1 June 2004).
33. Baldwin, 'Results of IEA-ECBCS', p. 218.
34. Watson, 'Improving the Implementation'.
35. Todd, J., 'Comparative Assessment of GBC2000 and LEED: Lessons Learned for International and National Systems', *Sustainable Design 2000 Proceedings*, 22–25 Oct 2000, The Netherlands, pp. 210–12.
36. Lavery, G. 'Environmental Considered Design, the Changing Paradigm', unpublished PhD thesis, The University of Queensland, 1999.
37. Balcomb, B., 'MCDM-23: A Multi Criteria Decision Making Tool for Buildings', *Sustainable Design 2000 Proceedings*, 22–25 Oct 2000, The Netherlands, p. 219.
38. Williamson, T., 'A Critical Review Of Home Energy Rating in Australia', *Proceedings of the 34th Conference of ANZAScA*, University of Adelaide, 1–3 Dec 2000, pp. 101–10.
39. Nibel, S., 'ESCALE, Assessment Method of Buildings Environmental Performance', *Sustainable Design 2000 Proceedings*, 22–25 Oct 2000, The Netherlands, pp. 699–701
40. Larsson, N., 2000, 'Moving Towards a Green Building Design Process', *Sustainable Design 2000 Proceedings*, 22–25 Oct 2000, The Netherlands, p. 141.
41. Hyde, R.A., *A Prototype Environmental Work and Home Infrastructure Building for Warm Climates: A Study of environmental Efficiency and Effectiveness*, Australian Research Council SPIRT Grant, 1999.
42. Larsson, 'Moving Towards', p. 142.
43. Addis, B., 'How Should Engineers Help Deliver Sustainable Construction?', *Sustainable Design 2000 Proceedings*, 22–25 Oct 2000, The Netherlands, pp. 411–13.

44. Ibid.
45. www.rmi.org/sitepages/pid199.php (accessed 7 Dec 2004).
46. IEA Task Report Number: IEA28-STD-TR, Fraunhofer ISE, Freiburg I.B (forthcoming).
47. www.healthyhomeproject.com (accessed 7 Dec 2004).
48. The INTEGER Millennium House, Watford, UK, www.integerproject.co.uk/watford.html (accessed 12 Jan 2005).
49. www.greenhouse.gov.au/yourhome/technical/fs70.htm (accessed 7 Dec 2004).
50. Wines, J., *Green Architecture*, Taschen, 2000, pp. 8–9.
51. Ibid.
52. See the following for further IT potentials: The INTEGER Millennium House, Watford, UK. www.integerproject.co.uk/watford.html (accessed 12 Jan 2005).

Chapter 4: The environmental briefing system

1. Watson, S., Cheshire W., and Hyde, R.A., 'Development of a Holistic Environmental Brief for use as a Design Phase Building Environmental Assessment Tool', in *Proceedings of the ANZAScA Conference*, the University of Sydney, Nov 2000, pp. 189–96.
2. Royal Australian Institute of Architects (RAIA), 'The Design Brief', Clause AN10.03.100 *Practice Notes*, 1998, p. 2.
3. Watson, S, 'Improving the Implementation of Environmental Strategies in the Design of Buildings', PhD thesis, The University of Queensland, 2004.
4. Watson *et al.*, 'Development', p. 4.
5. Preiser, W.E., 'Built Environment Evaluation: Conceptual Basis. Benefits and Uses', in *Directions in Person–Environment Research and Practice*, J. L. Nasar and W. F. E. Preiser, Ashgate, 1999, pp. 84–5.
6. Hillier, B., Musgrove, J., and Sullivan, P., 'Knowledge and Design', in 'Environmental Design: Research and Practice 2', *Proceedings of the EDRA 3/AR 8*

Conference, ed. W. J. Mitchell, University of California, Los Angeles, 1972, pp. 29-3-1 to 14.
7. Cheshire, W., 'The Development and Application of a Holistic Environmental Brief', unpublished BArch thesis, The University of Queensland, 2000, p. 9.
8. Psychometric chart. Source: DA Sketch Pack.
9. Watson, 'Improving the Implementation'.
10. RAIA, 'Design Brief', p. 1.
11. Ibid.

Chapter 5: Benchmarking systems

1. Green Globe 21 information, www.greenglobe21.com/ (accessed 13 Aug 2004).
2. International Standards Organization, www.iso.org/iso/en/ISOOnline.frontpage (accessed 13 Aug 2004).
3. Agenda 21 is a comprehensive plan of action to be taken globally, nationally and locally by organizations of the United Nations system, governments, and major groups in every area in which human activity impacts on the environment. www.un.org/esa/sustdev/documents/agenda21/index.htm (accessed 13 Aug 2004).
4. www.wttc.org/2004tsa/PDF/World.pdf (accessed 19 Sept 2004).
5. GDP: gross domestic product.
6. WTTC *Travel and Tourism's Economic Impact*. World Travel and Tourism Council, 1999.
7. Ibid.
8. www.world-tourism.org/market_research/facts/menu.html (accessed 19 Sept 2004).
9. BTR, *Travel by Australians 1998,* Bureau of Tourism Research, Canberra, 1999; BTR, *International Visitors in Australia 1998,* Bureau of Tourism Research, Canberra, 1999; BTR, *Tourism's Economic Contribution 1996–7,* Bureau of Tourism Research, Canberra, 1999.
10. BTR, *BTR Occasional paper Number 29, Tourism Expenditure by International Visitors in Regional Australia, 1998,* Bureau of Tourism Research, Canberra (draft only, May 2000).

11. Volker, R., Hyde, R. A., and Prasad, D., *Benchmarking of Efficiency in Construction, Operation and Maintenance of Buildings for Remote Tourist Resorts,* Collaborative Research Centre for Sustainable Tourism, 1999.

12. GBC Building Assessment Tool http://greenbuilding.ca/gbc98cnf/sponsors/gbtool.htm (accessed 13 Aug 2004.)

13. Ibid.

14. Global Green Standards ISO 14000 and Sustainable Development, *International Institute for Sustainable Development,* Canada, 1996.

15. Rogers, S., *Green Globe – Beyond ISO 14000 for the Travel and Tourism Sector,* 2002. Principal Consultant, Avteq Consulting Services, Australia, email: Mail@Avteq.Com.Au.

16. Ibid.

17. Ibid.

18. Earth Check$_{TM}$, www.earthcheck.org (accessed 5 Jan 2006).

19. Hyde, R.A., *et al., The Green Globe Design and Construct Handbook,* Green Globe Asia Pacific, 2004, p. 80.

20. Green Globe 21, www.greenglobe21.com (accessed 17 Aug 2004).

21. GBC '98, 'Benefits to Industry ' in *2002 Process Overview,* 2002, www.iisbe.org/iisbe/gbc2k2/gbc2k2-start.htm (accessed 19 Aug 2004).

22. Larsson, N., *Review of GBTool and Analysis of GBC 2002 Case-Study Projects,* 2002, p. 2. www.iisbe.org/iisbe/gbc2k2/gbc2k2-start.htm (accessed 19 Aug 2004).

23. Larsson, N., *Green Building: An Overview,* 2002, p. 1, *www.*iisbe.org/iisbe /gbc2k2/gbc2k2-start.htm (accessed 19 Aug 2004).

24. Ibid.

25. Ibid., p. 3.

26. Ibid., p. 11.

27. Ibid., p. 5.

28. Ibid.

29. Ibid., p. 7.

30. Ibid.

31. Ibid., p. 2.

32. www.iisbe.org/iisbe/gbc2k2/gbc2k2-start.htm (accessed 18 Aug 2004).

33. Larsson, *Green Building*, p. 4.

34. GBC *The Performance Assessment Process for 2002*, www.iisbe.org/ iisbe/gbc2k2/gbc2k2-start.htm (accessed 18 Aug 2004).

35. *C-2000 Program Requirements*, ed. N. Larsson, Natural Resources Canada; Ottawa, Oct 1993, updated April 1996.

36. *Incremental Costs in the C-2000 and CBIP Programs,* N. Larsson and J. Clark, March 2000, to be issued in a forthcoming issue of *Building Research and Information*.

37. Larsson, *Green Building,* p. 9.

Chapter 6: Rating systems

1. Bernstone, R., 'Rating the Rating Systems', *Building Australia*, Oct 2003, p. 24.

2. Government Construction Client's Panel, 2000, *Achieving Sustainability in Construction Procurement*, Office of Government Commerce (UK), June 2000.

3. Ibid.

4. NatHERs:
www.nathers.com/ (accessed 1 Dec 2004);
BASIX:
www.planning.nsw.gov.au/settingthedirection/basix.html (accessed 1 Dec 2004);
FirstRate:
www.seav.vic.gov.au/buildings/firstrate/index.asp (accessed 1 Dec 2004);
ABGR:
www.abgr.com.au/new/default.asp (accessed 1 Dec 2004);
NABERS:
www.deh.gov.au/industry/construction/nabers/ (accessed 1 Dec 2004).

5. www.housingcorp.gov.uk/resources/sustain.htm (accessed 4 Aug 2004).

6. Telephone conversation between David Clark and Alan Yates on 17 Nov 2004.

7. BRE, *Design and Procurement Assessment Checklist,* 2002.

8. http://projects.bre.co.uk/envbuild/index.html (accessed 9 Aug 2004).

9. Ibid.

10. Ibid.
11. Fedrizzi, R., 2003, *Getting Your Hands On Green Dollars,* address to Inaugural Green Building Conference, Sydney, Australia, 14–15 Oct 2003.
12. Howard, N., *Green Building Ratings: What Why & How,* Inaugural Green Building Conference, Sydney, Australia, 14–15 Oct 2003.
13. *The Costs and Financial Benefits of Green Buildings,* A Report to California's Sustainable Building Task Force, Oct 2003.
14. Huston Eubank, Rocky Mountain Institute, *Australian Financial Review*, 14 Aug 2003.
15. Green Building Council of Australia, www.gbcaus.org/ (accessed 4 Aug 2004).
16. Peter James, who has had experience working with rating schemes, in an Environmental Design Guide Note; he presents a user perspective of Green Star and reports that there are a number of projects that have applied for certification. One issue concerns the cost of carrying out a rating. There are two main costs: that incurred by the Accredited Green Star Professional, A$6,500 to A$15,000, and that incurred for the additional documentation to comply with the Green Star requirements, namely from A$30,000 to about A$70,000. These figures depend on the size and complexity of the project. See James, P., 'Green Star – A Users Perspective', forthcoming in BDP Environmental Design Guide Note 63, 2004, www.architecture.com.au/ (accessed 1 Dec 2004).

Chapter 7: Blueprinting

1. Microsoft, *Microsoft Word Dictionary.*
2. International Energy Agency. *IEA Solar Heating and Cooling Programme.* www.iea-shc.org/ (accessed 1 April 2004).
3. Ibid.
4. Ibid.
5. Ibid
6. Passive House Institute.: www.passivhaus-institut.de/ (access 1 April 2004).
7. Ibid.
8. Microsoft, *Word Dictionary.*
9. See Part 1.
10. Wheeler, J., 'One million sustainable homes,' *Industry and Environment*, UNEP(2003), 26 (2–3): 26–7.
11. Edwards, B., and Turrent, D., *Sustainable Housing Principles and Practice*, E & FN Spon, 2000, p. 24.
12. Environmental Protection Agency Queensland, *The Healthy Home Project,* www.healthyhomeproject.com (accessed 1 April. 2004).
13. Sustainable Energy Authority, Victoria, *Cost Benefit Analysis of New Housing Energy Performance Regulations – Executive Summary*, 2003, p. 3. www.seav.vic.gov.au/buildings/5starhousing/ (accessed 1 Feb 2004).
14. Ibid., p.36.
15. Nevin, R., and Watson, G. (1998) Evidence of Rational Market Valuations for Home Energy Efficiency, *The Appraisal Journal* (October), 66 (4): 401–9.
16. Rapoport, A., *House Form and Culture*, Prentice-Hall, 1969.
17. Nolan, W.L., and Hufnagel, J.A., 'A Closer Look: Blueprint 2000', *Better Homes and Gardens* (Nov 1999), 77(11): 218, 220, 222, 224, 226, 228, 230, 232, 234, 236, 123, 174.
18. Ibid.
19. Australian Greenhouse Office, *Your Home,* updated 28 Jan 2003, www.greenhouse.gov.au/yourhome/ (accessed 1 April 2004).
20. Discussions with Professor Roger Fay.
21. Australian Greenhouse Office, p. 11.
22. Australian Greenhouse Office, p. 12.
23. Australian Greenhouse Office, p. 23.
24. Australian Greenhouse Office, p. 26
25. Sustainable Energy Authority, Victoria.
26. Purdey, B. (Managing Director, KODO), *Comments.* Available email: bpurdey@kodointernational.com (accessed Feb 2004).
27. Australian Greenhouse Office, p. 31.
28. British Broadcasting Corporation, *BBC Lifestyle Property Homes,* www.bbc.net.uk/homes/property/selling/adding_value.shtml (accessed 1 April 2004).
29. Heschong, L., *Thermal Delight in Architecture*, MIT Press, 1979.

30. World Business Council for Sustainable Development, *Ecoefficiency: Overview.* www.wbcsd.org/templates/TemplateWBCSD4/layout.asp ?MenuID=1 (accessed 1 April 2004).

31. World Business Council for Sustainable Development, *Ecoefficiency.*

32. Australian Greenhouse Office, p. 37.

33. World Business Council for Sustainable Development, *Ecoefficiency.*

Chapter 8: Transforming industry, reducing environmental impact and addressing the myths

1. Cooperative Research Centre for Sustainable Tourism Pty Ltd, www.crctourism.com.au/CRCServer/default.aspx (accessed 16 June 2004).

2. Green Globe 21 Design and Construct Standard, www.greenglobe21.com/Documents%5CGeneral%5CDe signPhaseStandard.pdf (accessed 16 June 2004).

3. Robson, D., *Geoffrey Bawa: The Complete Works,* Thames and Hudson, 2002, p. 200.

4. Benchmarking is a process named from surveying where it means establishing a position or elevation. In environmental assessment a benchmark is a value ascribed to a particular indicator measure. Benchmarking is a process of comparing building performance to agreed values.

5. Kats, G., *Green Building Costs and Financial Benefits, 2003,* p. iv, www.cap-e.com/spotlight/index.cfm?Page=1&NewsID=25770 (accessed 16 June 2004).

6. Ibid.

7. Hyde, R. A, Hanson, V., and Edmonds, I., 'The Use Of Light Pipes for Deep Plan Office Buildings: A Case Study of Ken Yeang's Bioclimatic Skyscraper Proposal for KLCC, Malaysia, *Proceedings of the Experts Meeting,* Dept of Building, NUS Singapore, 2002;

8. Hanson, V., Edmonds, I., and Hyde, R. A., 'The Use of Light Pipes for Deep Plan Office Buildings: A Case Study Of Ken Yeang's Bioclimatic Skyscraper Proposal for KLCC, Malaysia Conference', *Proceedings from ANZAScA,* Wellington, NZ, 2001.

9. Law, J., 'Bioclimatic Highrise', unpublished MPhil thesis, University of Queensland, 2005.

10. Chandri, S., 'The Environmental Justification For Green Buildings', presentation, *Green Globe Training Course,* Coollangatta, 2004.

11. Ibid.

12. Kats, *Green Building Costs,* p. viii.

13. Ibid.

14. Chandri, 'Environmental Justification'.

15. Kats, *Green Building Costs,* p viii.

16. Ibid.

17. Watson, S., *Improving the Implementation of Environmental Strategies in the Design of Buildings,* unpublished PhD thesis, The University of Queensland.

18. Howard, N., *Green Building Ratings – What, Why & How,* presentation to the Inaugural Green Building Conference, Sydney, 14–15 Oct 2003.

Case Studies

Housing

1. The triple bottom line reporting is used to try to balance environmental, social and economic factors.

2. Bioregional, *Beddington Zero Energy Development,* www.bioregional.com, www.zedfactroy.com (accessed 29 Sept 2003).

3. Ibid.

4. Zold, A., and Szokolay, S.V., Thermal Insulation, *Plea Note* 2, Department of Architecture, The University of Queensland, 1997, p. 96.

5. Ibid.

6. Edwards, B., 'BedZED – Beddington Zero-fossil Energy Development,' in *Green Buildings Pay,* 2nd edn, EF&N Spons, 2002, p. 169.

7. BRESCU General Information Report, 89. *BedZED – Beddington Zero Energy Development, Sutton,* Energy Efficient Best Practice in Housing initiative, p. 11, www.est.org.uk/bestpractice (accessed 29 Sept 2003).

8. Edwards. p. 169.

9.   BRESCU, p. 31.
10. Ibid.
11. Ibid.
12. Ibid.
13. This is an independent non-profitmaking organization.
14. Lawson, B., *Building Materials, Energy and the Environment*, RAIA, 1996.
15. BRESCU, p. 20.
16. Edwards, p. 173.
17. BRESCU, pp. 18–19.
18. Lazarsu, N., *Construction Materials Report. Toolkit for Carbon Neutral Developments – Part 1, BioRegional Group*, 2003, p. 50.
19. BRESCU, p.32.
20. Sartogo, F., *Integration of Renewable Energies in a Historical City Center,* Yearbook 1994, James & James, 1995.
21. Edwards, B., and Turret, D., *Sustainable Housing, Principles and Practice*, EF&N Spon, 2000, p. 24.
22. Susheel Rao *et al.*, *EcoHomes: The Environmental Rating of Homes*, BRE, 2000, p. 18.
23. Eek, H., *Houses Without Heating Systems*, EFEM. Goteborg.
24. *Australian Good Residential Design Guide,* www.greenhouse.gov.au/yourhome/ (accessed 1 April 2004).
25. Eek, H., and Feist, W., Göteborg International Environmental Prize 2003 for the Passive House Concept, Expression of Thanks, www.passivhaus-institute/de (access 1 April 2004).
26. Ibid.

Hotels, resorts and interpretation centres

1.   www.sydneyolympicpark.nsw.gov.au
2.   Ibid.
3.   Average temperatures are in degrees Celsius. Rainfall amounts are in millimetres; 25 millimetres is approximately equal to 1 inch. A rainy day is considered to be when rainfall exceeds 0.2 mm.
4.   www.greenglobe.org
5.   Copy of draft obtained – Operational EMP Draft#6, June 1999.
6.   Energy Manager, 1999.
7.   *The Hotel Engineer*, 1999–2000, 5 (1).
8.   Accor media release.
9.   Ibid.
10. Design and Construction Environmental Initiatives, Sept 1999.
11. Accor media release
12. Hotel booklet – *Our Reason for being...*
13. *Green Hotelier*, 2000.
14. Accor media release.
15. www.wwf.org.au/contents/news_events.htm
16. Novotel fact sheet.
17. This is extracted from the article 'Setting the Stage for the Sydney 2000 Games', www.sydneyolympicpark.nsw.gov.au/images/default/the-place/rhs_bubblebtm.gif
18. Ibid.
19. www.industry.gov.au/content/itrinternet/cmscontent; *Conservation Action 2001 – Working with Communities*, Department of Conservation, New Zealand, July 2001; *Discover New Zealand's Natural Heritage (folded card)*, Department of Conservation, New Zealand; *Introducing the Department of Conservation (brochure)*, Department of Conservation, New Zealand; *Restoring the Dawn Chorus 2001–2004*, Department of Conservation, New Zealand.
20. Hill, K., 'Introduction', in *Architecture Bali*, P. Goad, Berkeley Books, 2000, p. 7.
21. Green Globe 21. www.greenglobe.org/ (accessed 5 Jan 2006).
22. The term 'business-as-usual' is used for buildings designed with no or minimal environmental measures.
23. Queensland Tourism, 1999, *Lark Quarry; Preserving and Presenting the Trackways*, p. 3.
24. Econnect, 2001, *Lark Quarry Heritage Trails Network Project, Communication Plan (revised)*.
25. Queensland Tourism,, p .81.
26. Wilrath, H., unpublished solar logic report.
27. Wilrath, p. 4.
28. www.skydome.com.au (accessed 14 Jan 2004).
29. Wilrath, p. 3.
30. Wilrath, p. 5.
31. Hybrid toilet system.: www.goughplastic.com.au (accessed 12 May 2006).

32. Lawson, B., *Building Materials, Energy and the Environment,* Royal Australian Institute of Architects, 1996.

Offices

1. Mick Pearce, discussions as design manager.
2. Calculation of the R value for American buildings is based on the imperial system of measurement and will be different for countries adopting the metric system.
3. A Smart Growth Funding area is a designated area promoting local development.
4. McKee, B., 'The Green Machine', *Architecture,* Feb 2001.
5. Encarta® *World English Dictionary* © 1999 Microsoft Corporation. All rights reserved. Developed for Microsoft by Bloomsbury Publishing PLC. CFC deduction in HVAC&R equipment required (heating, ventilation, air conditioning and refrigeration).
6. Credits are given for the percentage diverted to from landfill.
7. Credits are given for the percentage of local regional material.
8. See ASHRAE 62-2001, Appendix H, for a complete compilation of the Ventilation Rate Procedure.
9. MacCormac, Richard, quoted by Jane Darke, 'The Primary Generator and the Design Process', in *Developments in Design Methodology*, ed. N. Cross, John Wiley and Sons, 1984, pp.175–8.
10. SEDA tool is now the Australian Green Building Rating Scheme.
11. Australian Green Building Rating Scheme: 'Building managers, owners and tenants can self assess the greenhouse performance of their base building, whole building or tenancy at no cost using the Australian Building Greenhouse Performance Rating Calculator. Using 12 months of energy consumption (from bills) and some other details such as the number of people, number of computers, net lettable area and the hours of occupancy, a star rating that indicates the greenhouse performance of your office building can be obtained', www.abgr.com.au/ (accessed 19 June 2004).
12. Queensland Government, Department of Public Works, *William McCormack Place*, unpublished report for the Facilities Management Awards 2003, p. 11.
13. GBTool, www.buildingsgroup.nrcan.gc.ca/projects/gbc_e.html (accessed 19 June 2004).
14. Hyde, R.A, Watson, S., and Cheshire, W., 1999, *The Environmental Briefing System,* www.csdesign.epsa.uq.edu.au (accesses 19 June 2004).
15. GBTool.
16. Queensland Government, Department of Public Works, p. 1.
17. Australian Building Green Rating System. www.abgr.com.au (accessed 19 June 2004).
18. Queensland Government, Department of Public Works.
19. QSG: Queensland State Government.
20. Queensland Government, Department of Public Works, p. 8.
21. Built Environment Research Unit, Queensland Government, A *Planning Brief for an Energy Efficient Office*, 2002, p. 1.
22. Queensland Government, *Cairns Office Building Base Building Brief*, 2000, p. 61.
23. Ibid., p. 3.
24. Ibid., p. 7.
25. Ibid., p. 11.
26. Ibid., p.12.
27. Ibid.
28. Bennetts Associates, Wessex Water Operations Centre, unpublished report, Bennetts Associates Architects, p. 2.
29. Hawkes, D., 'Flow of Ideas: Bennetts Architects in Bath', *Architecture Today* (Nov 2000), 113: 60.
30. Hawkes, 'Flow of Ideas', p. 61.
31. Mace Ltd, unpublished report.
32. Site area divided by building area.
33. Department of Trade and Industry, Construction Best Practice Report, CB192, p. 1, www.cbpp.org.uk (accessed 12 Aug 2003.04).
34. From design notes by Ann Bodkin.
35. CABE's On-Line Digital Library, www.cbpp.org.uk. (accessed 28 Aug 2004).
36. Operational Health and Safety.

37. Building Research Establishment, *Rethinking
    Construction: The Movement for Innovation*,
    Sustainability Working Group Report, 2004.
38. Department of Trade and Industry, p. 1.
39. Department of Trade and Industry, p. 2.
40. Mace, p. 3.
41. Department of Trade and Industry, p. 2
42. Ding, M., Wessex Water Information Text, 19 June 2003,
    Bennetts Associates, p. 2.
43. www.bennettsassociates.com/ (accessed 28 Aug 2004).
44. Ding, M., p. 1.

Glossary

AGO	Australian Greenhouse Office
AIA	American Institute of Architects
BEA	Building Environmental Assessment
CCTV	Close circuit television
CFC and HFC	Chlorofluorocarbons or hydrochlorofluorocarbons.
EMS	Environmental Management System
EPA	Environmental Protection Agency
ESD	Ecological Sustainable Development
EU Law	European Union Law
FMA	Facilities Management Association
GBC	Green Building Challenge
GB Tool	Green Building Challenge Tool
Green Globe	International benchmarking system for the tourism industry
HVAC	Heating, ventilation and air conditioning
IAQ	Indoor air quality
IT	Information technology
Lux	One lux is equal to one lumen per square metre

OTTV	Overall Thermal Transfer Value
PV	Photovoltaic Systems
QSG	Queensland Stage Government
RAIA	Royal Australian Institute of Architects
RMI	Rocky Mountain Institute
R-value	A measure of the thermal resistance of a material, calculated from the thermal conductivity (k) of the material and its thickness (SI units are Km^2/W). Some countries use non SI units, the conversion between the two is $1\ ft^2 \cdot {}^\circ F \cdot h/Btu \approx 0.1761\ K \cdot m^2/W$, or $1\ K \cdot m^2/W \approx 5.67446\ ft^2 \cdot {}^\circ F \cdot h/Btu$
SEDA	Sustainable Energy Development Authority, New South Wales
U-value	A more user friendly measure of the thermal conductance of a material, the reciprocal of the R value
VOC	Volatile Organic Compounds

Index